Practice*Planner*

Arthur E. Jongsma, Jr., Series Editor

Helping therapists help their clients...

Treatment Planners cover all the necessary elements for developing formal treatment plans, including detailed problem definitions, long-term goals, short-term objectives, therapeutic interventions, and DSM-IV™ diagnoses.

- ☐ The Complete Adult Psychotherapy Treatment Planner, Fourth Edition.................0-471-76346-2 / $49.95
- ☐ The Child Psychotherapy Treatment Planner, Fourth Edition.............................0-471-78535-0 / $49.95
- ☐ The Adolescent Psychotherapy Treatment Planner, Fourth Edition ....0-471-78539-3 / $49.95
- ☐ The Addiction Treatment Planner, Third Edition..0-471-72544-7 / $49.95
- ☐ The Couples Psychotherapy Treatment Planner ....0-471-24711-1 / $49.95
- ☐ The Group Therapy Treatment Planner, Second Edition....................................0-471-66791-9 / $49.95
- ☐ The Family Therapy Treatment Planner ....0-471-34768-X / $49.95
- ☐ The Older Adult Psychotherapy Treatment Planner ....0-471-29574-4 / $49.95
- ☐ The Employee Assistance (EAP) Treatment Planner ....0-471-24709-X / $49.95
- ☐ The Gay and Lesbian Psychotherapy Treatment Planner ....0-471-35080-X / $49.95
- ☐ The Crisis Counseling and Traumatic Events Treatment Planner ....0-471-39587-0 / $49.95
- ☐ The Social Work and Human Services Treatment Planner ....0-471-37741-4 / $49.95
- ☐ The Continuum of Care Treatment Planner ....0-471-19568-5 / $49.95
- ☐ The Behavioral Medicine Treatment Planner ....0-471-31923-6 / $49.95
- ☐ The Mental Retardation and Developmental Disability Treatment Planner ....0-471-38253-1 / $49.95
- ☐ The Special Education Treatment Planner..0-471-38872-6 / $49.95
- ☐ The Severe and Persistent Mental Illness Treatment Planner............................0-471-35945-9 / $49.95
- ☐ The Personality Disorders Treatment Planner ....0-471-39403-3 / $49.95
- ☐ The Rehabilitation Psychology Treatment Planner ....0-471-35178-4 / $49.95
- ☐ The Pastoral Counseling Treatment Planner ....0-471-25416-9 / $49.95
- ☐ The Juvenile Justice and Residential Care Treatment Planner ....0-471-43320-9 / $49.95
- ☐ The School Counseling and School Social Work Treatment Planner....................0-471-08496-4 / $49.95
- ☐ The Psychopharmacology Treatment Planner ....0-471-43322-5 / $49.95
- ☐ The Probation and Parole Treatment Planner ....0-471-20244-4 / $49.95
- ☐ The Suicide and Homicide Risk Assessment and Prevention Treatment Planner ...0-471-46631-X / $49.95
- ☐ The Speech-Language Pathology Treatment Planner...0-471-27504-2 / $49.95
- ☐ The College Student Counseling Treatment Planner ....0-471-46708-1 / $49.95
- ☐ The Parenting Skills Treatment Planner ....0-471-48183-1 / $49.95
- ☐ The Early Childhood Education Intervention Treatment Planner ....0-471-65962-2 / $49.95
- ☐ The Co-Occurring Disorders Treatment Planner ....0-471-73081-5 / $49.95
- ☐ The Sexual Abuse Victim and Sexual Offender Treatment Planner ....0-471-21979-7 / $49.95
- ☐ The Complete Women's Psychotherapy Treatment Planner ....0-470-03983-3 / $49.95

The **Complete Treatment and Homework Planners** series of books combines our bestselling *Treatment Planners* and *Homework Planners* into one easy-to-use, all-in-one resource for mental health professionals treating clients suffering from the most commonly diagnosed disorders.

- ☐ The Complete Depression Treatment and Homework Planner..........................0-471-64515-X / $39.95
- ☐ The Complete Anxiety Treatment and Homework Planner ....0-471-64548-6 / $39.95

Over 500,000 Practice*Planners* sold ...

WILEY

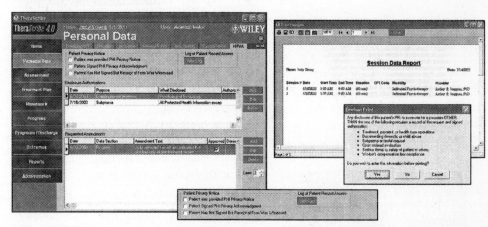

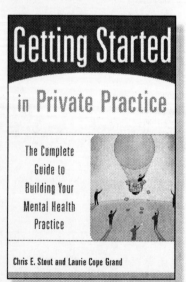

The Adolescent Psychotherapy Progress Notes Planner,
Third Edition

PRACTICE*PLANNERS*® SERIES

Treatment Planners

The Complete Adult Psychotherapy Treatment Planner, Fourth Edition
The Child Psychotherapy Treatment Planner, Fourth Edition
The Adolescent Psychotherapy Treatment Planner, Fourth Edition
The Addiction Treatment Planner, Third Edition
The Continuum of Care Treatment Planner
The Couples Psychotherapy Treatment Planner
The Employee Assistance Treatment Planner
The Pastoral Counseling Treatment Planner
The Older Adult Psychotherapy Treatment Planner
The Behavioral Medicine Treatment Planner
The Group Therapy Treatment Planner, Second Edition
The Gay and Lesbian Psychotherapy Treatment Planner
The Family Therapy Treatment Planner
The Severe and Persistent Mental Illness Treatment Planner
The Mental Retardation and Developmental Disability Treatment Planner
The Social Work and Human Services Treatment Planner
The Crisis Counseling and Traumatic Events Treatment Planner
The Personality Disorders Treatment Planner
The Rehabilitation Psychology Treatment Planner
The Special Education Treatment Planner
The Juvenile Justice and Residential Care Treatment Planner
The School Counseling and School Social Work Treatment Planner
The Sexual Abuse Victim and Sexual Offender Treatment Planner
The Probation and Parole Treatment Planner
The Psychopharmacology Treatment Planner
The Speech-Language Pathology Treatment Planner
The Suicide and Homicide Risk Assessment & Prevention Treatment Planner
The College Student Counseling Treatment Planner
The Parenting Skills Treatment Planner
The Early Childhood Education Intervention Treatment Planner
The Co-Occurring Disorders Treatment Planner
The Complete Women's Psychotherapy Treatment Planner

Progress Notes Planners

The Child Psychotherapy Progress Notes Planner, Third Edition
The Adolescent Psychotherapy Progress Notes Planner, Third Edition
The Adult Psychotherapy Progress Notes Planner, Third Edition
The Addiction Progress Notes Planner, Second Edition
The Severe and Persistent Mental Illness Progress Notes Planner
The Couples Psychotherapy Progress Notes Planner
The Family Therapy Progress Notes Planner

Homework Planners

Brief Therapy Homework Planner
Brief Couples Therapy Homework Planner
Brief Employee Assistance Homework Planner
Brief Family Therapy Homework Planner
Grief Counseling Homework Planner
Group Therapy Homework Planner
Divorce Counseling Homework Planner
School Counseling and School Social Work Homework Planner
Child Therapy Activity and Homework Planner
Addiction Treatment Homework Planner, Third Edition
Adolescent Psychotherapy Homework Planner II
Adolescent Psychotherapy Homework Planner, Second Edition
Adult Psychotherapy Homework Planner, Second Edition
Child Psychotherapy Homework Planner, Second Edition
Parenting Skills Homework Planner

Client Education Handout Planners

Adult Client Education Handout Planner
Child and Adolescent Client Education Handout Planner
Couples and Family Client Education Handout Planner

Complete Planners

The Complete Depression Treatment and Homework Planner
The Complete Anxiety Treatment and Homework Planner

PracticePlanners®

Arthur E. Jongsma, Jr., Series Editor

The Adolescent Psychotherapy Progress Notes Planner, Third Edition

Arthur E. Jongsma, Jr.

L. Mark Peterson

William P. McInnis

David J. Berghuis

WILEY

JOHN WILEY & SONS, INC.

To the memory of Rick Smeenge, adolescent social worker and wonderful friend, who taught me what it means to dance the soft shoe. I miss you, Rick.

—A.E.J.

To my children, Katy and Mike. You make your mother and me proud.

—D.J.B.

To Breanne, Kelsey, and Andrew for all the love you bring in my life.

—W.P.M.

To Harold Kunze, in gratitude for forty years of close friendship.

—L.M.P.

CONTENTS

PRACTICE*PLANNERS*® SERIES PREFACE

Accountability is an important dimension of the practice of psychotherapy. Treatment programs, public agencies, clinics, and practitioners must justify and document their treatment plans to outside review entities in order to be reimbursed for services. The books and software in the Practice*Planners*® series are designed to help practitioners fulfill these documentation requirements efficiently and professionally.

The Practice*Planners*® series includes a wide array of treatment planning books including not only the original *Complete Adult Psychotherapy Treatment Planner, Child Psychotherapy Treatment Planner,* and *Adolescent Psychotherapy Treatment Planner,* all now in their fourth editions, but also *Treatment Planners* targeted to a wide range of specialty areas of practice, including:

- Addictions
- Behavioral medicine
- College students
- Co-occurring disorders
- Couples therapy
- Crisis counseling
- Early childhood education
- Employee assistance
- Family therapy
- Gays and lesbians
- Group therapy
- Juvenile justice and residential care
- Mental retardation and developmental disability
- Neuropsychology
- Older adults
- Parenting skills
- Pastoral counseling
- Personality disorders
- Probation and parole
- Psychopharmacology
- School counseling
- Severe and persistent mental illness
- Sexual abuse victims and offenders
- Special education
- Suicide and homicide risk assessment

In addition, there are three branches of companion books that can be used in conjunction with the *Treatment Planners* or on their own:

- *Progress Notes Planners* provide a menu of progress statements that elaborate on the client's symptom presentation and the provider's therapeutic intervention. Each *Progress Notes Planner* statement is directly integrated with the behavioral definitions and therapeutic interventions from its companion *Treatment Planner.*

- *Homework Planners* include homework assignments designed around each presenting problem (such as anxiety, depression, chemical dependence, anger management, eating disorders, or panic disorder) that is the focus of a chapter in its corresponding *Treatment Planner.*

- *Client Education Handout Planners* provide brochures and handouts to help educate and inform clients on presenting problems and mental health issues, as well as life skills techniques. The handouts are included on CD-ROMs for easy printing from your computer and are ideal for use in waiting rooms, at presentations, as newsletters, or as information for clients struggling with mental illness issues. The topics covered by these handouts correspond to the presenting problems in the *Treatment Planners.*

The series also includes:

- **Thera*Scribe*®**, the #1 selling treatment planning and clinical record-keeping software system for mental health professionals. Thera*Scribe*® allows the user to import the data from any of the *Treatment Planner, Progress Notes Planner,* or *Homework Planner* books into the software's expandable database to simply point and click to create a detailed, organized, individualized, and customized treatment plan along with optional integrated progress notes and homework assignments.

Adjunctive books, such as *The Psychotherapy Documentation Primer* and *The Clinical Documentation Sourcebook,* contain forms and resources to aid the clinician in mental health practice management.

The goal of our series is to provide practitioners with the resources they need in order to provide high-quality care in the era of accountability. To put it simply: We seek to help you spend more time on patients and less time on paperwork.

ARTHUR E. JONGSMA, JR.
Grand Rapids, Michigan

ACKNOWLEDGMENTS

The original authors are deeply indebted to David J. Berghuis, who again managed the update of this third edition of *The Adolescent Progress Notes Planner*. He is responsible for adding the new material for the chapters in which Evidence-Based Treatment content was added to *The Adolescent Psychotherapy Treatment Planner, Fourth Edition*. Thank you, Dave, for your fine work.

A.E.J.

PROGRESS NOTES INTRODUCTION

ABOUT PRACTICE*PLANNERS*® PROGRESS NOTES

Progress notes are not only the primary source for documenting the therapeutic process, but also one of the main factors in determining the client's eligibility for reimbursable treatment. The purpose of the *Progress Notes Planners* series is to assist the practitioner in easily and quickly constructing progress notes that are thoroughly unified with the client's treatment plan.

Each *Progress Notes Planner:*

- Saves you hours of time-consuming paperwork.
- Offers the freedom to develop customized progress notes.
- Features over 1,000 prewritten progress notes summarizing patient presentation and treatment delivered.
- Provides an array of treatment approaches that correspond with the behavioral problems and *Diagnostic and Statistic Manual of Mental Disorders,* Fourth Edition (*DSM-IV ™*) diagnostic categories in the corresponding companion *Treatment Planner.*
- Offers sample progress notes that conform to the requirements of most third-party payors and accrediting agencies, including the Joint Commission on Accreditation of Healthcare Organizations (JCAHO), the Council on Accreditation (COA), the Commission on Accreditation of Rehabilitation Facilities (CARF), and the National Committee for Quality Assurance (NCQA).

HOW TO USE THIS PROGRESS NOTES PLANNER

This *Progress Notes Planner* provides a menu of sentences that can be selected for constructing progress notes based on the behavioral definitions (or client's symptom presentation) and therapeutic interventions from its companion *Treatment Planner.* All *Progress Notes* must be tied to the patient's treatment plan—session notes should elaborate on the problems, symptoms, and interventions contained in the plan.

Each chapter title in this book is a reflection of the client's potential presenting problem. The first section of the chapter, "Client Presentation," provides a detailed menu of statements that may describe how that presenting problem manifested itself in behavioral signs and symptoms. The numbers in parentheses within the Client Presentation section correspond to the numbers of the Behavioral Definitions from the corresponding *Treatment Planner.*

The second section of each chapter, "Interventions Implemented," provides a menu of statements related to the action that was taken within the session to assist the client in making progress. The numbering of the items in the Interventions Implemented section follows exactly the numbering of Therapeutic Intervention items in the corresponding *Treatment Planner.*

All item lists begin with a few keywords. These words are meant to convey the theme or content of the sentences that are contained in that listing. The clinician may peruse the list of keywords to find content that matches the client's presentation and the clinician's intervention.

It is expected that the clinician will modify the prewritten statements contained in this book to fit the exact circumstances of the client's presentation and treatment. To maintain complete client records, in addition to progress note statements that may be selected and individualized from this book, the clinician should enter in the client's record the date, time, and length of a session; those present within the session; the provider; provider's credentials; and a signature.

A FINAL NOTE ABOUT PROGRESS NOTES AND HIPAA

Federal regulations under the Health Insurance Portability and Accountability Act (HIPAA) govern the privacy of a client's psychotherapy notes as well as other protected health information (PHI). PHI and psychotherapy notes must be kept secure, and the client must sign a specific authorization to release this confidential information to anyone beyond the client's therapist or treatment team. Further, psychotherapy notes receive other special treatment under HIPAA; for example, they may not be altered after they are initially drafted. Instead, the clinician must create and file formal amendments to the notes if he or she wishes to expand, delete, or otherwise change them. Our Thera*Scribe*™ software provides functionality to help clinicians maintain the proper rules concerning handling PHI, by giving the ability to lock progress notes once they are created, to acknowledge patient consent for release of PHI, and to track amendments to psychotherapy notes over time.

Does the information contained in this book, when entered into a client's record as a progress note, qualify as a "psychotherapy note" and therefore merit confidential protection under HIPAA regulations? If the progress note that is created by selecting sentences from the database contained in this book is kept in a location separate from the client's PHI data, then the note could qualify as psychotherapy note data, which are more protected than general PHI. However, because the sentences contained in this book convey generic information regarding the client's progress, the clinician may decide to keep the notes mixed in with the client's PHI and not consider them psychotherapy note data. In short, how you treat the information (separate from or integrated with PHI) can determine if this Progress Notes Planner's data are psychotherapy note information. If you modify or edit these generic sentences to reflect more personal information about the client or if you add sentences that contain more confidential information, the argument for keeping these notes separate from PHI and treating them as psychotherapy notes becomes stronger. For some therapists, our sentences alone reflect enough personal information to qualify as psychotherapy notes, and they will keep these notes separate from the client's PHI and require specific authorization from the client to share them with a clearly identified recipient for a clearly identified purpose.

ACADEMIC UNDERACHIEVEMENT

CLIENT PRESENTATION

1. Academic Underachievement (1)*

A. The client's teachers and parents reported a history of academic performance that is below the expected level given the client's measured intelligence or performance on standardized achievement tests.

B. The client verbally admitted that his/her current academic performance is below his/her expected level of functioning.

C. The client has started to assume more responsibility for completing his/her school and homework assignments.

D. The client has taken active steps (e.g., studying at routine times, seeking outside tutor, consulting with teacher before or after class) to improve his/her academic performance.

E. The client's academic performance has improved to his/her level of capability.

2. Incomplete Homework Assignments (2)

A. The client has consistently failed to complete his/her classroom or homework assignments in a timely manner.

B. The client has refused to comply with parents' and teachers' requests to complete classroom or homework assignments.

C. The client expressed a renewed desire to complete his/her classroom and homework assignments on a regular basis.

D. The client has recently completed his/her classroom and homework assignments on a consistent basis.

E. The client's regular completion of classroom and homework assignments has resulted in higher grades.

3. Disorganization (3)

A. Parents and teachers described a history of the client being disorganized in the classroom.

B. The client has often lost or misplaced books, school papers, or important things necessary for tasks or activities at school.

C. The client has started to take steps (e.g., using planner or agenda to record school/homework assignments, consulting with teachers before or after school, scheduling routine study times) to become more organized at school.

D. The client's increased organization abilities have contributed to his/her improved academic performance.

---

*The numbers in parentheses correlate to the number of the Behavioral Definition statement in the companion chapter with the same title in *The Adolescent Psychotherapy Treatment Planner,* Fourth Edition (Jongsma, Peterson, McInnis, and Bruce) by John Wiley & Sons, 2006.

4. Poor Study Skills (3)

A. The parents and teachers reported that the client has historically displayed poor study skills.

B. The client acknowledged that his/her lowered academic performance is primarily due to his/her lack of studying.

C. The client has recently spent little time studying.

D. The client reported a recent increase in studying time.

E. The client's increased time spent in studying has been a significant contributing factor to his/her improved academic performance.

5. Procrastination (4)

A. The client has repeatedly procrastinated or postponed doing his/her classroom or homework assignments in favor of engaging in social, leisure, or recreational activities.

B. The client has continued to procrastinate doing his/her classroom or homework assignments.

C. The client agreed to postpone social, leisure, or recreational activities until he/she has completed his/her homework assignments.

D. The client has demonstrated greater self-discipline by completing homework assignments before engaging in social, leisure, or recreational activities.

E. The client has achieved and maintained a healthy balance between accomplishing academic goals and meeting his/her social and emotional needs.

6. Family History of Academic Problems (5)

A. The client and parents described a family history of academic problems and failures.

B. The client's parents have demonstrated little interest or involvement in the client's school-work or activities.

C. The client expressed a desire for his/her parents to show greater interest or involvement in his/her schoolwork or activities.

D. The parents verbalized a willingness to show greater interest and become more involved in the client's schoolwork or activities.

E. The parents have sustained an active interest and involvement in the client's schoolwork and implemented several effective interventions to help the client achieve his/her academic goals.

7. Depression (6)

A. The client's feelings of depression, as manifested by his/her apathy, listlessness, and lack of motivation, have contributed to and resulted from his/her low academic performance.

B. The client appeared visibly depressed when discussing his/her lowered academic performance.

C. The client expressed feelings of happiness and joy about his/her improved academic performance.

D. The client's academic performance has increased since his/her depression has lifted.

8. Low Self-Esteem (6)

A. The client's low self-esteem, feelings of insecurity, and lack of confidence have contributed to and resulted from his/her lowered academic performance.

B. The client displayed a lack of confidence and expressed strong self-doubts about being able to improve his/her academic performance.

C. The client verbally acknowledged his/her tendency to give up easily and withdraw in the classroom when feeling insecure and unsure of himself/herself.

D. The client verbalized positive self-descriptive statements about his/her academic performance.

E. The client has consistently expressed confidence in his/her ability to achieve academic goals.

9. Disruptive/Attention-Seeking Behavior (7)

A. The client has frequently disrupted the classroom with his/her negative attention-seeking behavior instead of focusing on his/her schoolwork.

B. The parents have received reports from teachers that the client has continued to disrupt the classroom with his/her negative attention-seeking behavior.

C. The client acknowledged that he/she tends to engage in disruptive behavior when he/she begins to feel insecure or become frustrated with his/her schoolwork.

D. The client has started to show greater self-control in the classroom and inhibit the impulse to act out in order to draw attention to himself/herself.

E. The client has demonstrated a significant decrease in his/her disruptive and negative attention-seeking behavior.

10. Low Frustration Tolerance (7)

A. The client has developed a low frustration tolerance, as manifested by his/her persistent pattern of giving up easily when encountering difficult or challenging academic tasks.

B. The client's frustration tolerance with his/her schoolwork has remained very low.

C. The client has started to show improved frustration tolerance and has not given up as easily or as often on his/her classroom or homework assignments.

D. The client has demonstrated good frustration tolerance and consistently completed his/her classroom/homework assignments without giving up.

11. Test-Taking Anxiety (8)

A. The client described a history of becoming highly anxious before or during tests.

B. The client's heightened anxiety during tests has interfered with his/her academic performance.

C. The client shared that his/her test-taking anxiety is related to fear of failure and of being met with disapproval or criticism by significant others.

D. The client has begun to take steps (e.g., using deep breathing, making positive self-statements, challenging irrational thoughts) to reduce his/her anxiety and feel more relaxed during the taking of tests.

E. The client reported a significant decrease in the level of anxiety while taking tests.

12. Excessive Parental Pressure (9)

A. The client has viewed his/her parents as placing excessive or unrealistic pressure on him/her to achieve academic success.

B. The parents acknowledged that they have placed excessive or unrealistic pressure on the client to achieve academic success.

C. The parents denied placing excessive or unrealistic pressure on the client to achieve; instead, they attributed the client's lowered academic performance to his/her lack of motivation and effort.

D. The client reported that the parents have decreased the amount of pressure that they have placed on him/her to achieve academic success.

E. The parents have established realistic expectations of the client's level of capabilities.

13. Excessive Criticism (9)

A. The client described the parents as being overly critical of his/her academic performance.

B. The client expressed feelings of sadness and inadequacy about critical remarks that his/her parents have made in regard to his/her academic performance.

C. The client acknowledged that he/she deliberately refuses to do school assignments when he/she perceives the parents as being overly critical.

D. The parents acknowledged that they have been overly critical of the client's academic performance.

E. The parents have significantly reduced the frequency of their critical remarks about the client's academic performance.

14. Environmental Stress (10)

A. The client's academic performance has markedly declined since experiencing stressors within his/her personal and/or family life.

B. The client's academic performance has decreased since his/her family moved and he/she had to change schools.

C. The client has not been able to invest as much time or energy into his/her schoolwork because of having to deal with environmental stressors.

D. The client has begun to manage his/her stress more effectively so that he/she has more time and energy to devote to schoolwork.

E. The client's academic performance has increased since resolving or finding effective ways to cope with the environmental stressor(s).

15. Loss or Separation (10)

A. The client's academic performance has decreased significantly since experiencing the separation or loss.

B. The client verbalized feelings of sadness, hurt, and disappointment about past separation(s) or loss(es).

C. The client has taken active steps (e.g., socializing regularly with peers, studying with peers, participating in extracurricular activities) to build a positive support network at school to help him/her cope with the past separation(s) or loss(es).

D. The client's academic interest and performance have increased substantially since working through his/her grief issues.

INTERVENTIONS IMPLEMENTED

1. Refer for Psychoeducational Testing (1)*

A. The client received a psychoeducational evaluation to rule out the presence of a possible learning disability that may be contributing to his/her academic underachievement.

B. The client received a psychoeducational evaluation to determine whether he/she is eligible to receive special education services.

C. As noted, the client was cooperative during the psychoeducational testing and appeared motivated to do his/her best.

D. The client was uncooperative during the psychoeducational testing and did not appear to put forth good effort; he/she was urged to provide a better effort.

E. The client's resistance during the psychoeducational testing was interpreted to be due to his/her feelings of insecurity and opposition to possibly receiving special education services.

2. Refer for Psychological Testing for ADHD/Emotional Factors (2)

A. The client received a psychological evaluation to help determine whether he/she has ADHD, which may be contributing to his/her low academic performance.

B. The client received psychological testing to help determine whether emotional factors are contributing to his/her low academic performance.

C. The client was uncooperative and resistant during the evaluation process; he/she was urged to provide a better effort.

D. It was noted that the client approached the psychological testing in an honest, straightforward manner and was cooperative with the examiner.

E. Feedback was provided to the client, his/her family, and school officials regarding the psychological evaluation.

3. Obtain Psychosocial History (3)

A. A psychosocial assessment was completed to gather pertinent information about the client's past academic performance, developmental milestones, and family history of educational achievements and failures.

B. The client and parents were positively reinforced for being cooperative in providing information about the client's early developmental history, school performance, and family background.

C. A review of the client's background revealed a history of developmental delays and low academic performance.

*The numbers in parentheses correlate to the number of the Therapeutic Intervention statement in the companion chapter with the same title in *The Adolescent Psychotherapy Treatment Planner,* Fourth Edition (Jongsma, Peterson, McInnis, and Bruce) by John Wiley & Sons, 2006.

D. The psychosocial assessment revealed a family history of academic underachievement and failures.

E. The psychosocial assessment revealed a history of strong expectations being placed on family members to achieve academic success.

F. The psychosocial assessment revealed a healthy family history regarding academic success.

4. Refer for Hearing/Vision/Medical Examination (4)

A. The client was referred for a hearing and vision examination to rule out possible hearing or visual problems that may be interfering with his/her school performance.

B. The client was referred for a medical evaluation to rule out possible health problems that may be interfering with his/her school performance.

C. The hearing examination results revealed the presence of hearing problems that are interfering with the client's academic performance.

D. The vision examination revealed the presence of visual problems that are interfering with the client's school performance.

E. The medical examination revealed the presence of health problems that are interfering with the client's school performance.

F. The client and his/her parents have not followed through on a hearing, vision, or medical examination and were redirected to do so.

5. Attend Individual Educational Planning Committee (IEPC) Meeting (5)

A. The client's IEPC meeting was held with parents, teachers, and school officials to determine the client's eligibility for special education services, to design educational interventions, and to establish educational goals.

B. The recommendation was made at the IEPC meeting that the client receive special education services to address his/her learning problems.

C. At the IEPC meeting, it was determined that the client is not in need of special education services because he/she does not meet the criteria for a learning disability.

D. The IEPC meeting was helpful in identifying specific educational goals.

E. The IEPC meeting was helpful in designing several educational interventions for the client.

6. Move to Appropriate Classroom (6)

A. Based on the IEPC goals and recommendations, the client was moved to an appropriate classroom setting to maximize his/her learning.

B. Based on the IEPC goals and recommendations, the client has been provided with additional services, including changing to a more appropriate classroom for some academic areas.

C. Based on the IEPC goals and recommendations, no changes in classroom setting were identified.

7. Consult about Teaching Intervention Strategies (7)

A. A consultation was held with the client, parents, and school officials about designing effective teaching programs or intervention strategies that build on the client's strengths and compensate for his/her weaknesses.

B. The client, parents, and teachers identified several learning or personality strengths that the client can utilize to improve his/her academic performance; these were summarized.

C. The consultation meeting with client, parents, and school officials identified the client's weaknesses and intervention strategies that he/she can utilize to overcome his/her problems.

8. Refer for Private Tutoring (8)

A. The recommendation was given to the parents to seek private tutoring for the client after school to boost his/her skills in the area of his/her academic weakness.

B. The client and parents were provided with positive feedback for being agreeable to seeking private tutoring after school.

C. The client and parents were opposed to the idea of seeking private tutoring; they were urged to recognize this need.

D. The client and parents reported that the private tutoring has helped to improve the client's academic performance.

E. The client and parents reported that the private tutoring has not led to the desired improvements in the area of the client's academic weakness.

9. Refer to Private Learning Center (9)

A. The client was referred to a private learning center for extra tutoring in the areas of academic weakness and assistance in improving his/her study and test-taking skills.

B. The client reported that the extra tutoring and support provided by the private learning center have helped improve his/her performance in the areas of his/her academic weakness.

C. The client reported that his/her performance in the areas of academic weakness has not improved since attending the private learning center.

D. The client reported that his/her study and test-taking skills have improved since attending the private learning center.

E. The client's study skills and test performance have not improved since attending the private learning center.

F. The client and parents were opposed to the idea of seeking a private learning center for extra tutoring and were encouraged to reconsider this resource.

10. Identify Academic Goals (10)

A. The client and parents were assisted in identifying specific academic goals in today's therapy session.

B. The client's history of academic failure was noted to contribute to his/her resistance to formulating goals for successful achievement.

C. It was reflected that the family history of underachievement and academic disinterest has contributed to the client's reluctance to establish academic goals.

11. Teach Study Skills (11)

A. The client was assisted in identifying good locations to study.

B. The client was instructed to remove noise sources and clear away as many distractions as possible when studying.

C. The client was instructed to outline or underline important details when studying or reviewing for tests.

D. The client was encouraged to use a tape recorder to help him/her study for tests and review important facts.

E. The client was instructed to take breaks in studying when he/she becomes distracted and has trouble staying focused.

12. Utilize Peer Tutor (12)

A. The recommendation was given to parents and teachers that the client be assigned a peer tutor to improve his/her study skills and address areas of academic weakness.

B. The client verbalized a desire and willingness to work with a peer tutor to improve his/her study skills and academic performance; he/she was positively reinforced for this willingness.

C. The client expressed opposition to the idea of working with a peer tutor to improve his/her study skills and academic performance, and this was processed.

D. The client reported that the peer tutoring has helped to improve his/her study skills and academic performance; the benefits of this were reviewed.

E. The client reported that the peer tutoring has not helped to improve his/her study skills and academic performance, and this was problem-solved.

13. Teach Test-Taking Strategies (13)

A. The client was provided with a list of effective test-taking strategies to improve his/her academic performance.

B. The client was encouraged to review classroom material regularly and study for tests over an extended period of time.

C. The client was instructed to read the instructions twice before responding to questions on a test.

D. The client was taught about the need to recheck his/her work to correct any careless mistakes or improve an answer.

14. Train in Anxiety-Reducing Techniques (14)

A. The client was taught guided imagery and relaxation techniques to help decrease the level of his/her anxiety and frustration in the taking of tests.

B. The client was encouraged to utilize positive self-talk as a means to decrease anxiety and reduce frustration in the taking of tests.

C. The client was taught cognitive restructuring techniques to decrease his/her anxiety and frustration associated with test taking.

D. The client reported that the use of positive coping mechanisms (e.g., relaxation techniques, positive self-talk, cognitive restructuring) has helped to decrease his/her level of anxiety and frustration during test taking, and positive feedback was provided in this area.

E. The client reported experiencing little to no reduction in the level of his/her anxiety or frustration through the use of relaxation techniques, positive self-talk, and cognitive restructuring and was provided with remedial assistance in this area.

15. Maintain Communication between Home and School (15)

A. The parents and teachers were encouraged to maintain regular communication with each other via phone calls or written notes regarding the client's academic progress.

B. The client's teachers were asked to send home daily or weekly progress notes informing the parents of the client's academic progress.

C. The client was informed of his/her responsibility to bring home daily or weekly progress notes from school, allowing for regular communication between parents and teachers.

D. The parents identified the consequences of the client's failure to bring home a daily or weekly progress note from school, and this was reinforced to the client.

E. It was noted that the increased communication between teachers and parents via phone calls or regular progress notes has been a significant contributing factor to the client's improved academic performance.

16. Assign Self-Monitoring Checklists (16)

A. The client was encouraged to utilize self-monitoring checklists to increase completion of school assignments and improve academic performance.

B. The client reported that use of the self-monitoring checklists has helped him/her to become more organized and complete school assignments on time; positive feedback was provided.

C. The client has failed to consistently use the self-monitoring checklists and as a result has continued to have trouble completing his/her school/homework assignments; brainstorming techniques were used to problem-solve.

D. The client's teachers were consulted about the use of self-monitoring checklists in the classroom to help him/her complete school/homework assignments on a regular, consistent basis.

E. Parents and teachers were instructed to utilize a reward system in conjunction with the self-monitoring checklists to increase the client's completion of school/homework assignments and improve his/her academic performance.

17. Use Assignment Planner or Calendar (17)

A. The client was strongly encouraged to use a planner or calendar to record school/homework assignments and plan ahead for long-term assignments.

B. It was noted that the client's regular use of a planning calendar has helped him/her complete classroom and homework assignments on a regular, consistent basis.

C. The client has failed to use the assigned planning calendar consistently and has continued to struggle to complete school/homework assignments.

D. The client reported that the use of the assigned planning calendar has helped him/her plan ahead for long-term assignments.

E. The client's ADHD symptoms have contributed to his/her failure to use a planner or calendar on a regular basis; solution-focused techniques were used to problem-solve this failure.

18. Assign "Break It Down into Small Steps" Program (18)

A. The client and parents were instructed to utilize the "Break It Down into Small Steps" program in the *Adolescent Psychotherapy Homework Planner,* 2nd ed. (Jongsma, Peterson, and McInnis) to help client complete projects or long-term assignments on time.

B. The client and parents were encouraged to utilize the reward system outlined in the "Break It Down into Small Steps" program to reinforce the client for completing each identified step and the final project on time.

C. The client and parents were assisted in identifying a list of rewards and negative consequences for either successfully completing or failing to complete each step of the long-term project.

D. The client reported that the "Break It Down into Small Steps" program has helped to end his/her pattern of procrastinating or waiting until the last minute to begin working on a large or long-term project; the benefits of this success were reviewed.

E. The client has failed to utilize the "Break It Down into Small Steps" program in the *Adolescent Psychotherapy Homework Planner,* 2nd ed. (Jongsma, Peterson, and McInnis) as recommended and subsequently has failed to complete his/her large or long-term projects on time.

19. Develop Study and Recreation Schedule (19)

A. The client and parents were assisted in developing a routine schedule to help the client achieve a healthy balance between completing homework assignments and engaging in recreational activities or socializing with peers.

B. The client has followed the agreed-upon schedule and has been able to successfully complete homework assignments and engage in recreational or social activities.

C. The client has failed to consistently complete his/her homework assignments because he/she has not followed the agreed-upon schedule.

20. Encourage Positive Reinforcement (20)

A. The parents and teachers were encouraged to provide frequent positive reinforcement to maintain the client's interest and motivation in completing his/her school/homework assignments.

B. The parents and teachers were challenged to look for opportunities to praise the client for being responsible or successful at school instead of focusing on times when the client failed to behave responsibly or achieve success.

C. The contributing factors or underlying dynamics that prevent the parents from offering praise and positive reinforcement on a consistent basis were explored.

21. Instruct Parents to Record Responsible Behaviors (21)

A. The parents were instructed to observe and record three to five responsible behaviors by the client between therapy sessions that pertain to his/her schoolwork.

B. The parents were encouraged to reinforce the client for engaging in responsible behavior.

C. The client was strongly encouraged to continue to be responsible for completing schoolwork in order to build self-esteem, earn parents' approval, and receive affirmation from others.

D. The parents' recognition and reinforcement of the client's responsible behaviors have been noted to help to ease family tensions and to increase the client's willingness to complete schoolwork.

22. Identify Rewards to Maintain Motivation (22)

A. The client was asked to develop a list of possible rewards or positive reinforcers that would increase his/her motivation to achieve academic success.

B. The client was directed to sign a written contract specifying the positive reinforcers that are contingent on his/her achieving specific academic goals.

23. Explore/Resolve Family Conflicts (23)

A. A family therapy session was held to explore the dynamics that contribute to the client's lowered academic performance.

B. The family members identified stressors that have had a negative impact on the family.

C. The family members were asked to brainstorm possible solutions to the conflicts that exist within the family and interfere with the client's academic performance.

D. Marital stressors were identified and assessed to reduce stress for the client.

E. The family members have now resolved the differences between themselves over how to address the client's learning problems.

24. Conduct Individual Therapy Sessions (24)

A. Individual therapy sessions were conducted to help the client work through and resolve painful emotions, core conflicts, or stressors that impede academic performance.

B. The client has resolved his/her painful emotions, core conflicts, and stressors that impede academic performance; positive feedback was provided in this area.

C. The client has not sought individual therapy to resolve his/her painful emotions, core conflicts, and stressors that impede academic performance, and he/she was redirected to do so.

25. Encourage Parents' Interest in Client's Homework (25)

A. The parents were encouraged to maintain regular involvement in the client's homework (e.g., attend school functions, review planners or calendars to see if the client is staying caught up with the schoolwork).

B. The parents were reinforced for implementing a more regular involvement in the client's homework schedule.

C. The parents have not increased their involvement in the client's homework activity, and their resistance was processed.

26. Design and Implement Reward System (26)

A. A reward system was developed to help the parents reinforce the client's responsible behaviors, completion of school assignments, and academic success.

B. The parents were assisted in implementing the reward system to reinforce responsible behaviors, completion of school assignments, and academic success.

C. Contingency contracts were built into the reward system in order to reinforce the client's responsible behaviors, completion of school assignments, and academic success.

27. Direct Parents to Record Responsible Behavior (27)

A. The parents were instructed to observe and record three to five responsible behaviors by the client between therapy sessions that pertain to his/her schoolwork.

B. The parents were encouraged to reinforce the client for engaging in responsible behavior.

C. The client was strongly encouraged to continue to be responsible for completing schoolwork in order to build self-esteem, earn parents' approval, and receive affirmation from others.

D. The parents' recognition and reinforcement of the client's responsible behaviors have been noted to help to ease family tension and increase the client's willingness to complete schoolwork.

28. Explore Unrealistic Parental Expectations (28)

A. A family therapy session was held to explore whether the parents have developed unrealistic expectations or are placing excessive pressure on the client to perform.

B. Discussion was held with client and parents to identify more realistic expectations about the client's academic performance.

C. The parents were confronted and challenged about placing excessive pressure on the client to achieve academic success.

D. The client was seen individually to allow him/her to express thoughts and feelings about excessive pressure placed on him/her by parents.

E. A family therapy session was held to provide the client with an opportunity to express anger, frustration, and hurt about parents' placing excessive pressure on him/her.

29. Urge Parents to Set Firm Limits for Homework Refusal (29)

A. The parents were strongly encouraged to set firm, consistent limits and to utilize natural, logical consequences for the client's refusal to do his/her homework.

B. The parents were assisted in identifying a list of consequences for the client's refusal to do homework.

C. The parents reported that the client has responded positively to their limits or consequences and has begun to complete his/her homework assignments on a regular, consistent basis; the benefits of this were reinforced.

D. The client has refused to comply with his/her parents' request to complete homework assignments, even though the parents have begun to set firm limits; the parents were urged to "stay the course."

30. Assess Parent's Overprotectiveness (30)

A. A family therapy session was conducted to explore whether a parent's overprotectiveness of the client contributes to his/her academic underachievement.

B. The parents were helped to see how a pattern of overprotectiveness contributes to the client's academic underachievement.

C. The client and parents were helped to recognize the secondary gain that is achieved through a parent's pattern of overindulging the client.

31. Challenge Parents Not to Overprotect Client (31)

A. The parents were challenged not to protect the client from the natural consequences of his/her academic performance (e.g., loss of credits, detention, delayed graduation, inability to take driver's training, higher cost of car insurance) and instead were encouraged to allow the client to learn from his/her mistakes or failures.

B. The parents were supported as they reported that they have allowed the client to experience the natural consequences of his/her poor academic performance.

C. The parents acknowledged that they have protected the client from experiencing the consequences of his/her academic performance because they didn't want him/her to fail or repeat a grade; the long-term effects of this pattern were reviewed.

D. The parents were instructed to follow through with firm, consistent limits and not become locked into unhealthy power struggles or arguments with the client over his/her homework each night.

E. The client and parents were taught effective communication and assertiveness skills to learn how to express feelings in a controlled fashion and to avoid becoming locked into unhealthy arguments over homework.

F. The parents were instructed to read *Negotiating Parent/Adolescent Conflict* (Robin and Foster) to help resolve conflict and issues related to schoolwork more effectively with their son/daughter.

32. Consult School Officials to Improve On-Task Behavior (32)

A. The therapist consulted with school officials about ways to improve the client's on-task behavior.

B. The recommendation was made that the client sit toward the front of the class or near positive peer role models to help him/her stay focused and on task.

C. The teachers were encouraged to call on the client often during the class to maintain the client's interest and attention.

D. The teachers were instructed to provide frequent feedback to the client to maintain interest and motivation to complete his/her school assignments.

E. The recommendation was given to teachers to break the client's larger assignments into a series of smaller tasks.

33. Reinforce Successful School Experiences (33)

A. The parents and teachers were encouraged to reinforce the client's successful school experiences.

B. The client was given the homework assignment of making one positive statement about school each day.

C. All positive statements by client about school were noted and reinforced.

34. Place Client in Charge of Task at School (34)

A. The teachers were encouraged to place the client in charge of a task at school to demonstrate confidence in his/her ability to behave responsibly.

B. The client and teachers identified a list of tasks for which the client could assume responsibility at school; this was reviewed and processed.

C. The client was noted to display an increase in confidence and motivation to achieve academic success after being placed in charge of a task or responsibility at school.

D. The client failed to follow through in performing the agreed-on task or responsibility at school, and the reason for this failure was processed.

35. Record Positive Statements about School (35)

A. The client was assigned the task of making one positive statement daily about school and either recording the statement in a journal or writing it on a sticky note to place in his/her bedroom or kitchen.

B. The client was compliant with the homework assignment to record at least one positive statement daily about his/her school experiences.

C. The client did not cooperate with the homework assignment to record at least one positive statement daily about his/her school experiences.

D. After reviewing the positive statements about school recorded in the journal, the client was encouraged to engage in similar positive behaviors that would help make school a more rewarding or satisfying experience.

36. Teach Self-Control Strategies (36)

A. The client was taught deep breathing and relaxation techniques to inhibit the impulse to act out or engage in negative attention-seeking behaviors when encountering frustration with his/her schoolwork.

B. The client was encouraged to utilize positive self-talk when encountering frustration with his/her schoolwork instead of acting out or engaging in negative attention-seeking behaviors.

C. The client was taught mediational, self-control strategies (e.g., "stop, think, listen, and act") to inhibit the impulse to act out or engage in negative attention-seeking behaviors when encountering frustration with schoolwork.

37. Explore Past Periods of Academic Success (37)

A. The client was asked to explore periods of time when he/she completed schoolwork regularly and achieved academic success.

B. The client was encouraged to use strategies or organizational skills similar to those that he/she used in the past to achieve academic success, and he/she was accepted for the insight.

C. The client shared the realization that involvement in extracurricular or positive peer group activities increased his/her motivation to achieve academic success and was accepted for the insight.

D. The session revealed that the client was more disciplined in his/her study habits when he/she received strong family support and affiliated with positive peer groups.

E. The client recognized that he/she achieved greater academic success in the past when he/she scheduled routine times to complete homework, and he/she was supported for this realization.

38. Examine Past Successful Coping Strategies (38)

A. The client was assisted in exploring other coping strategies that he/she used to solve other problems.

B. The client was encouraged to use similar coping strategies that he/she used successfully in the past to overcome current problems associated with learning.

C. The session revealed that the client overcame past learning problems when he/she sought extra assistance from teachers, parents, or peers.

D. The client was encouraged as he/she recognized that he/she was more successful in completing school assignments in the past when he/she used a planning calendar to record homework assignments and long-term projects.

E. The client denied having any past successful coping strategies and was offered tentative examples of such.

39. Identify Positive Role Models (39)

A. The client was assisted in identifying three to five role models and listing several reasons why he/she thought the role model was successful in achieving goals.

B. The client identified his/her personal goals and was encouraged to begin to take steps to accomplish goals by employing strategies similar to those that his/her positive role models have used to achieve their goals or success.

C. The client was noted to recognize that many of his/her positive role models achieved success, in part, by attending school regularly and achieving academic goals.

D. The client denied awareness of positive role models and was provided with tentative examples.

40. Identify Resource People within School (40)

A. The client was assisted in developing a list of resource people within the school to whom he/she can turn for support, assistance, or instruction when encountering difficulty or frustration with learning.

B. After identifying a list of school resource people, the client was given the directive to seek support at least once from one of these individuals before the next therapy session.

C. The client reported that the extra assistance that he/she received from other individuals in the school helped him/her to overcome difficulty and learn new concepts or skills.

ADOPTION

CLIENT PRESENTATION

1. Questions about Bioparents (1)*

A. The client presented with numerous questions about his/her bioparents that he/she would like immediate answers to.

B. There is an air of expectation and hope to the client's mood and affect regarding learning about bioparents.

C. The client verbalized being very unsure about exploring his/her biological family of origin.

D. Although the client has raised questions about his/her biological parents, there has been no genuine interest in actively seeking answers.

2. Identity Confusion (2)

A. The parents reported that the client often makes comments regarding his/her identity related to the adoption.

B. The client described confusing thoughts and feelings regarding the adoption and his/her identity.

C. The client has many uncertainties regarding his/her biological family and why the adoption occurred.

D. As the client has reported less confusion about his/her identity linked to the adoption, he/she feels more stable in his/her identity as a member of his/her adoptive family.

3. Not Feeling a Part of the Family (3)

A. The parents reported that the client has recently expressed that he/she does not feel like he/she fits into the family.

B. The client verbalized feeling different and not like other family members.

C. The client indicated that being adopted makes him/her feel like he/she is not a part of this family.

D. The client reported a change in his/her feeling toward now being a part of the family.

4. Search for Bioparents (4)

A. The client's manner was one of concern, caution, and putting others before self as he/she discussed searching for biological parents.

B. The client expressed concern about upsetting or hurting the adoptive parents if he/she pursues searching for bioparents.

C. Despite approval given by adoptive parents to search for biological parents, the client seemed concerned about what he/she might discover and how that information will affect him/her.

*The numbers in parentheses correlate to the number of the Behavioral Definition statement in the companion chapter with the same title in *The Adolescent Psychotherapy Treatment Planner,* Fourth Edition (Jongsma, Peterson, McInnis, and Bruce) by John Wiley & Sons, 2006.

D. The client has worked through his/her concerns regarding searching for bioparents and is now more comfortable with moving ahead.

5. Shift in Peer Group (5)

A. The parents noted a recent major shift in the client's peer group, dress, and interests.
B. The parents labeled the new peer group and dress as negative and contrary to the family's standards.
C. The client explained his/her change in dress, peers, and interests as something he/she needed to do to define himself/herself.
D. The client has modified his/her changes in peers and dress as he/she has started to deal with the adoption issue.

6. Excessive Clingy and Helpless Behavior (6)

A. The parents indicated that the client has always been very clingy and has a pattern of helpless behavior.
B. The client expressed that he/she feels most comfortable when he/she is close to parents.
C. The parents reported being frustrated with the client's helpless behavior now that he/she is getting older.
D. The client refused to talk with the therapist without the parents being there and then allowed them to do all the talking.
E. There has been a marked decrease in the client's clinginess and helplessness since he/she started working on his/her adoption issues.

7. Testing Limits (7)

A. The parents reported that the client has been acting out dramatically and consistently testing their limit setting.
B. The client indicated he/she has recently been in constant trouble for lying, stealing, or breaking rules.
C. The client has experienced difficulty at school for failing grades, truancy, and verbal abuse of authority figures.
D. The client's extreme testing of limits (e.g., stealing, substance abuse, sexual promiscuity) seemed to be directly connected to his/her issues about being adopted.
E. The client's testing of limits has decreased as he/she acknowledged and has started to work on his/her adoption issues.

8. Rude/Rebellious (7)

A. The client presented in a rude and rebellious manner.
B. The client clearly stated that he/she doesn't care what others think about him/her.
C. The parents and teachers reported a marked increase in the client's rude and rebellious attitude since he/she entered the teens, and it is beyond what is normal for these years.
D. The client's rebellious attitude and rudeness have begun to settle down since he/she started to openly share his/her feelings and thoughts about being adopted.

9. Adoptive Parents' Fear (8)

A. The adoptive parents verbalized fear related to the client wanting to search for and meet with his/her bioparents.

B. The adoptive parents presented strong, specific justifications regarding the negative impact of the client meeting his/her bioparents.

C. The adoptive parents raised numerous questions about adoptive children meeting their bioparents.

D. The adoptive parents have reached a reasonable level of comfort with the client meeting his/her bioparents.

10. Adoption of Special-Needs Children (9)

A. The parents have recently adopted a special-needs child/sibset.

B. The parents expressed feeling overwhelmed by the demands of the children.

C. The parents asked for support and resources to assist them in coping with the special needs of the adopted child/children.

D. The parents have gradually and slowly adjusted to and become accepting of the special-needs child/children.

11. Frustration with Child Development and Achievement Level (10)

A. The parents expressed frustration with the adopted child's level of achievement and development.

B. The parents expressed unrealistic expectations of where they felt the child should be in terms of his/her development.

C. The parents expressed disappointment about the child's achievement level and stated that they expected much more from him/her.

D. The parents have worked to adjust their expectations of the child to more realistic levels.

INTERVENTIONS IMPLEMENTED

1. Establish Trust-Based Relationship (1)*

A. Initial trust level was established with the client through use of unconditional positive regard.

B. Warm acceptance and active listening techniques were utilized to establish the basis for a nurturing relationship.

C. The client has formed a trust-based relationship and has begun to express his/her thoughts and feelings regarding his/her adoption; positive feedback was provided.

D. Despite the use of active listening, warm acceptance, and unconditional positive regard, the client remains resistant to trust and does not share his/her thoughts and feelings.

---

*The numbers in parentheses correlate to the number of the Therapeutic Intervention statement in the companion chapter with the same title in *The Adolescent Psychotherapy Treatment Planner,* Fourth Edition (Jongsma, Peterson, McInnis, and Bruce) by John Wiley & Sons, 2006.

2. Solicit Family Therapy Participation (2)

A. The family was asked to make a firm commitment to being an active part of the client's psychotherapy treatment in both attendance and participation.

B. The value to the client of having his/her family involved was presented to the family to reinforce their decision to participate in counseling.

C. The family were confronted about their hesitancy to become involved in the client's treatment and their belief that it was all his/her issue.

D. The family's commitment to the counseling process was highlighted, as it is evident in their consistent attendance and constructive participation.

3. Expand Knowledge of Family (3)

A. A family genogram that included biofamily was created, along with a list of questions members had regarding adopted and bioparents.

B. The process of raising questions about biological or adopted family was normalized, and fears regarding the child's knowing certain information were addressed by asking parents, "Who would you be protecting?"

C. Unanswered questions about family history were explored and assigned to appropriate members for follow-up and reporting back to family.

4. List Losses Related to Adoption (4)

A. The client was requested to list the losses he/she has experienced in life.

B. The list of losses was processed, and connections were made between specific losses and being adopted.

C. The loss of biological parents and a sense of extended family identity were noted to be the strongest issues cited by the client.

5. Support Grieving Process (5)

A. The stages of the grieving process were explained to the client to support him/her in understanding and working through the grief process.

B. Identified losses were processed, and the client's expressed feelings connected to each were supported with empathic responses.

C. Positive feedback was provided as client has processed the losses surrounding his/her adoption and has become more accepting of his/her current identity within the adoptive family.

D. The client continues to hold onto the hurt, sad, and angry feelings related to being abandoned by bioparents; he/she was urged to work to let go of the hurt.

6. Assign Reading on Adoption Grief (6)

A. The client was directed to read information regarding the losses associated with being adopted.

B. The client was asked to read *Common Threads of Teenage Grief* (Tyson) and select five ideas to process.

C. Key ideas the client selected about grieving were processed, and the client's questions were answered.

D. The client has not read information on the losses associated with being adopted and was redirected to do so.

7. Identify Feelings of Abandonment/Rejection (7)

A. The client was assisted in identifying and expressing feelings of rejection and abandonment connected with his/her adoption.

B. The client's feelings of abandonment and rejection were recognized and confirmed as normal and to be expected.

C. The client has successfully worked through the feelings of rejection and abandonment and has come to see bioparents as possibly having his/her best interest at heart when they released him/her for adoption; he/she was supported for these changes.

8. Assign Reading on Release Decisions (8)

A. The client was directed to read information regarding decisions bioparents make to put a child up for adoption.

B. The client was asked to read *Why Didn't She Keep Me?* (Burlingham-Brown) to assist him/her in resolving key feelings of rejection, abandonment, and guilt/shame.

C. The client's readings have helped him/her move toward resolving the feelings of rejection, abandonment, and guilt/shame he/she has regarding his/her adoption.

D. The client was assisted and supported in working through the guilt/shame, abandonment, and rejection he/she experienced connected to his/her adoption.

E. The client has successfully worked through the feelings of rejection and abandonment and has come to see bioparents as possibly having his/her best interest at heart when they released him/her for adoption; he/she was supported for these changes.

F. The client has not read the information on why bioparents make decisions for adoption and was redirected to do so.

9. Assign Reading on Being Adopted (9)

A. The client was directed to read information about being an adopted child.

B. The client was asked to read *How It Feels to Be Adopted* (Krementz) and make a list of key concepts gathered from the reading.

C. The feelings the client identifies with from the adoption book were processed.

D. The client has successfully worked through the feelings of rejection and abandonment and has come to see bioparents as possibly having his/her best interest at heart when they released him/her for adoption.

E. The client has not read the information on being an adopted child and was redirected to do so.

10. Identify Irrational Adoption Beliefs (10)

A. The client was assisted in identifying a list of beliefs that he/she has about adoption.

B. Irrational thoughts and beliefs were separated from client's general belief list and then replaced with new, healthy, rational beliefs.

C. The client reported that the new, reality-based beliefs have helped to reduce his/her feelings of guilt, shame, anger, and sadness; the benefits of the new beliefs were highlighted.

11. Refer to Support Group (11)

A. Options for possible support groups were explored with the family and the client.

B. The parents and the client were given information on the various support groups and asked to make a commitment to attend one.

C. The family questioned their need for support outside of therapy and were noncommittal about trying even one meeting; they were urged to reconsider this need.

D. The client and his/her parents were provided with positive reinforcement for attending a support group; they have reported that it has been beneficial to them.

12. Assign "Three Ways to Change Yourself" Exercise (12)

A. The client was assisted in exploring what aspects of himself/herself he/she would like to change.

B. The client was assisted in developing an action plan to achieve the changes that he/she would like to make.

C. The client was asked to complete the "Three Ways to Change Yourself" exercise from the *Adolescent Psychotherapy Homework Planner,* 2nd ed. (Jongsma, Peterson, and McInnis) to help him/her learn to express needs and desires.

D. The "Three Ways to Change Yourself" exercise was used as a means of assisting the client in developing the skill to express his/her needs and desires.

E. The client has not completed assignments regarding setting goals for changing himself/herself, and reasons for this failure were reviewed and problem-solved.

13. Assign *SEALS & PLUS* Exercise (13)

A. The client was asked to complete a *SEALS & PLUS* (Korb-Khara, Azok, and Leutenberg) exercise directed at assisting him/her in developing self-knowledge, acceptance, and confidence.

B. The client reported that the assigned self-awareness exercise was helpful in building confidence.

C. The client has not followed through on completing the self-awareness exercise and was redirected to do so.

14. Teach Concept of True/False Self (14)

A. The concept of a true and false self was taught to the client, and he/she was directed to read more about this concept in *The Journal of the Adopted Self* (Lifton).

B. The pros and cons of a false or hidden self were explored with the client, and the disadvantages were verbally reinforced.

C. Using the approach of unconditional positive regard, the value of being genuine and real was discussed with the client.

15. Assign "Who Am I?" Exercise (15)

A. The client was asked to keep a daily journal of "Who am I?" and to share his/her entries with the therapist.

B. "Who am I?" journal entries were reviewed, and positive identifications were verbally acknowledged and reinforced.

C. The client's negative journal entries were confronted in a warm, firm, realistic manner.

D. The client's self-descriptive journal entries have been noted to be more positive.

16. Assign Parents to Read Books on Adoption (16)

A. The parents were directed to read books on adoption to advance their knowledge and understanding of adopted teens.

B. The parents were encouraged to read *The Whole Life Adoption Book* (Schouler) or *Making Sense of Adoption* (Melina) to advance their knowledge and understanding of adopted teens.

C. The parents were taught various aspects of teen development with a special focus on adoptive teens to increase their knowledge and understanding of their teen.

D. The parents rebuffed attempts to be taught more about teens because they felt their knowledge was adequate.

E. The parents' belief that developmental issues are the same for adopted and nonadopted teenagers was confronted and restructured to a more healthy, realistic view.

F. The parents have not read the assigned books on adoption and were redirected to do so.

17. Teach about the Search for Identity (17)

A. The parents were taught specifically about the search for identity that is a primary focus of teenagers and how this issue is even more crucial to adopted teens.

B. Actions that the parents could take to promote the client's independent identity were probed, and several of the actions were chosen to be implemented.

C. The parents had difficulty accepting the importance of a teen developing an independent identity, which they viewed as a sign they were failing as parents; they were provided with a healthier outlook on this issue.

18. Discuss Adoptive Parents' Fear of Bioparent Search (18)

A. The adoptive parents were asked to discuss their fears and concerns about the adopted teen looking for bioparents and their own openness to meeting the bioparents.

B. Adoptive parents' rights regarding the search were clarified and affirmed, and all their questions were answered.

C. The parents were empowered to make a difficult decision regarding the search: to either support, curtail, or postpone it.

D. The parents were not able to tolerate the idea of the client's search and quickly vetoed the process; the long-term effects of this decision were underscored.

E. The adoptive parents were encouraged, as they have given their support to the adopted client for a search for his/her bioparents.

19. Clarify Parents' Support for Client Searching (19)

A. Support commitments were elicited verbally from the parents in family session along with a commitment from the client to keep the parents up-to-date on all progress.

B. In family session, both the parents and the client were asked to agree in principle to support the search for bioparents and to keep all informed, but they would not specifically verbally state it.

C. The parents were not able to tolerate the idea of the client's search and quickly vetoed the process; they were urged to consider this at a later time.

20. Clarify Parents' Rejection of Client Searching (20)

A. A family session was conducted that focused on the client's desire to search for bioparents and the parents' position on the issue.

B. Clear statement of approval or disapproval of client's search for bioparents was sought from adoptive parents, along with a rationale for their decision.

C. The client's right to search for his/her own bioparents at the age of 18 was clarified and confirmed with both parents.

D. The client has decided not to pursue a meeting with his/her bioparents, and this was accepted.

21. Affirm Parents' Right of Refusal (21)

A. The adoptive parents' decision to deny the search was affirmed, and the client's feelings about their decision were processed.

B. The client appears to be accepting parents' decision to deny the search, having worked through his/her feelings of anger, disappointment, and hurt; his/her opinions about these decisions were processed.

C. The parents' right to deny the search was again affirmed, although the client does not accept this and remains very angry.

22. Locate Expert (22)

A. A meeting was arranged between the client and a willing adult who was adopted as a child and who searched for bioparents.

B. The meeting with the adopted adult was very beneficial, providing the client with many useful insights.

23. Prepare Client for Search (23)

A. The client was prepared to begin the search for bioparents by responding to probing questions, by having hopes and fears affirmed, and by having all other concerns addressed.

B. A list of questions the client would like answered was developed in case the search process resulted in a meeting being scheduled with bioparents.

24. Assign Reading about Search (24)

A. The parents and the client were directed to read literature about the process of searching for bioparents.

B. The parents and the client were asked to read *Searching for a Past* (Schooler) to advance their knowledge of the process and to answer questions they have concerning it.

C. The parents were given information about the search process, and questions they had were answered.

D. The parents and client have not read literature regarding the search process for bioparents and were redirected to do so.

25. Review or Create Life Book (25)

A. The client's life book was reviewed as a preparatory step toward beginning his/her search.

B. The client was assisted in developing a life book to be shared with new biological relatives and others that he/she will meet in the search process.

26. Contact Adoption Agency (26)

A. The client was directed to contact the agency through which his/her adoption occurred and schedule an appointment with its search specialist.

B. The client scheduled and followed through with his/her first appointment with an adoption agency search specialist; the outcome of the appointment was processed.

C. The client has the agency's name and number but remains hesitant to make an appointment, and this was normalized and accepted.

D. Issues of fear about taking the first step in the bioparent search were processed and resolved, leading to the client calling and scheduling an appointment with the agency.

27. Review Search Information (27)

A. The information gathered from the agency was reviewed, and the client's feelings about the information were identified, expressed, and supported.

B. Information gathered as part of the search was processed and feelings of upset and hurt over the information were supported and processed.

28. Process Reaching a Dead End (28)

A. The client was assisted and supported in working through the reality of reaching a dead end regarding contact with bioparents.

B. Dreams regarding contact with bioparents were explored and verbalized to assist the client in resolving the disappointment of reaching a dead end.

29. Reinforce Client-Parent Communication (29)

A. Both the client and the parents were asked individually and in family session to confirm that information regarding the search was being communicated between them as agreed upon.

B. The client's failure to keep the parents informed of the progress of the search was addressed, and a renewed agreement was made as well as a plan for how this information exchange would occur.

30. Decide on Reunion with Bioparents (30)

A. The client was helped in identifying and weighing the pros and cons of pursuing a reunion with bioparents.

B. With the support of the parents and therapist, the client was able to reach a decision to pursue reunion.

C. Despite support from the parents, search worker, and therapist, the client remains ambivalent to the point of being unable to reach a decision whether to pursue reunion.

D. The client has decided not to pursue a meeting with his/her bioparents, and this was accepted as a reasonable decision.

31. **Prepare Client for Reunion with Bioparents (31)**

A. Preparation for the scheduled reunion with bioparents consisted of helping the client examine his/her expectations to make them as realistic as possible and giving the message to let the relationship build slowly.

B. The client's unrealistic expectations regarding the upcoming reunion with bioparents were processed and adjusted to increase likelihood of a successful meeting.

C. The message was seeded with the client to let the new relationship build slowly and naturally.

32. **Practice Reunion Meeting (32)**

A. The client role-played a bioparent reunion and afterward processed the experience, identifying how this experience decreased his/her anxiety.

B. The client's level of anxiety seemed to dissipate as the role-playing of a scheduled meeting with the bioparents was processed.

C. The client remains very anxious and threatened by the scheduled meeting with the bioparents, and therefore the meeting was postponed to a later date.

33. **Hold Family Meeting with Bioparents (33)**

A. A meeting was arranged with the client and the bioparents to facilitate the expression of feelings surrounding this event and to explore with each the next steps they see.

B. It was noted that the client's meeting with the bioparents was successful and rewarding in that significant information was shared between them and feelings of love and concern were affirmed.

C. The client's meeting with the bioparents was difficult, disappointing, and tense, with little information shared and no support verbalized; support and comfort were provided.

34. **Process Contact with Bioparents (34)**

A. The client was asked to process his/her reunion experience and verbalize next step(s) he/she foresees happening.

B. It was interpreted to the client that he/she was very pleased with the first reunion meeting with the bioparents and plans to meet with them in the near future.

C. The client was satisfied with the meeting with the bioparents but does not feel a need to meet with them again, and he/she was accepted for this decision.

35. **Explore Future Relationship with Bioparents (35)**

A. A plan was created with the client that mapped out a possible path for a new relationship with bioparents based on the tactic of taking things slowly.

B. The client's desire to push the relationship with bioparents was addressed, with possible negative effects being emphasized.

C. The client was noted to have no plans for a further relationship with bioparents beyond this reunion.

36. **Update Adoptive Parents on Reunion (36)**

A. The parents were given an update on the reunion meeting with bioparents by the client, who also shared the next possible steps for building a relationship with the bioparents.

B. New possible family configurations were presented to adoptive parents and the client to help them in moving in the direction of a new family system.

C. The adoptive parents were encouraged for being affirming and supportive of the client's continuing to build a relationship with the bioparents.

D. The adoptive parents were resistive to any further relationship building between the client and his/her bioparents, and the long-term effects of this resistance were processed.

ANGER MANAGEMENT

CLIENT PRESENTATION

1. Angry Outbursts (1)*

A. The client has exhibited frequent angry outbursts that are out of proportion to the degree of the precipitating event.

B. The client appeared angry, hostile, and irritable during today's therapy session.

C. The client has recently exhibited several angry outbursts at home and school.

D. The client has started to show greater control of his/her anger and does not react as quickly or intensely when angry or frustrated.

E. The client reported a significant reduction in the frequency and intensity of his/her angry outbursts.

2. Verbally Abusive Language (2)

A. The client has a history of yelling, swearing, or becoming verbally abusive when his/her needs go unmet or when asked to do something that he/she does not want to do.

B. The client began to yell and swear during today's therapy session.

C. The frequency and intensity of the client's screaming, cursing, and use of verbally abusive language have decreased to a mild degree.

D. The client has begun to express his/her feelings of anger in a controlled fashion.

E. The client has consistently demonstrated good control of his/her anger and not yelled or become verbally abusive toward others.

3. Physical Aggression/Violence (3)

A. The client described a history of engaging in acts of physical aggression or violence.

B. The client has recently been physically aggressive or violent.

C. The client has gradually started to develop greater control of his/her anger and has not become involved in as many fights in the recent past.

D. The client has recently exercised good self-control and has not engaged in any physically aggressive or violent behaviors.

4. Verbal Threats/Intimidation (4)

A. The client has a history of threatening or intimidating others to meet his/her own needs.

B. The client became verbally threatening during today's therapy session.

C. The client has continued to threaten or intimidate others at home, at school, and in the community.

D. The client reported a mild reduction in the frequency and intensity of his/her verbal threats and acts of intimidation.

*The numbers in parentheses correlate to the number of the Behavioral Definition statement in the companion chapter with the same title in *The Adolescent Psychotherapy Treatment Planner*, Fourth Edition (Jongsma, Peterson, McInnis, and Bruce) by John Wiley & Sons, 2006.

E. The client has recently displayed good anger control and reported that he/she has not threatened or intimidated others.

5. Destructive Behaviors (5)

A. The client described a persistent pattern of becoming destructive or throwing objects when angry or frustrated.

B. The client described incidents in which he/she has been destructive of property.

C. The client has started to control the impulse to destroy or throw objects when angry.

D. The client reported that he/she has not thrown any objects or been destructive of property in the recent past.

6. Blaming/Projecting (6)

A. The client has a history of projecting the blame for his/her angry outbursts or aggressive behaviors onto other people or outside circumstances.

B. The client did not accept responsibility for his/her recent angry outbursts or aggressive behaviors.

C. The client has begun to accept greater responsibility for his/her anger control problems and blames others less often for his/her angry outbursts or aggressive behaviors.

D. The client verbalized an acceptance of responsibility for the poor control of his/her anger or aggressive impulses.

E. The client expressed guilt about his/her anger control problems and apologized to significant others for his/her loss of control of anger.

7. Passive-Aggressive Behavior (7)

A. The parents and teachers described a persistent pattern of the client engaging in passive-aggressive behaviors (e.g., forgetting, pretending not to listen, dawdling, procrastinating).

B. The client verbally acknowledged that he/she often deliberately annoys or frustrates others through his/her passive-aggressive behaviors.

C. The client has started to verbalize his/her anger directly toward others instead of channeling his/her angry or hostile feelings through passive-aggressive behaviors.

D. The client expressed his/her feelings of anger in a direct, controlled, and respectful manner.

E. The client has recently demonstrated a significant reduction in the frequency of his/her passive-aggressive behaviors.

8. Oppositional/Rebellious Behavior (7)

A. The client's anger is frequently channeled into his/her oppositional and rebellious behaviors.

B. The client appeared highly oppositional during today's therapy session and seemed to argue just for the sake of arguing.

C. The client has recently been defiant of the rules and regulations established by authority figures at home, at school, and in the community.

D. The client has exhibited mild improvements in his/her willingness to comply with the rules and regulations at home, at school, and in the community.

E. The client reports that recently he/she has been cooperative and compliant with the rules at home, at school, and in the community.

9. Poor Peer Relationships (8)

A. The client's anger control problems have been a significant contributing factor to his/her strained interpersonal relationships with peers.

B. The client has often projected the blame for his/her interpersonal problems onto peers and refused to acknowledge how his/her anger control problems contribute to the conflict.

C. The client is beginning to recognize how his/her anger control problems interfere with his/her ability to establish and maintain peer friendships.

D. The client reported that his/her effective anger control has led to improved relations with his/her peers.

10. Lack of Empathy (8)

A. The client displayed little empathy or concern for how his/her angry outbursts or aggressive behaviors impact others.

B. The client has demonstrated a willingness to use intimidation or force to meet his/her needs at the expense of others.

C. The client verbalized an awareness of how his/her rebellious, aggressive, or destructive behaviors negatively affect others.

D. The client verbalized empathy and concern for others in today's therapy session.

E. The client has made progress in consistently demonstrating empathy and sensitivity to the thoughts, feelings, and needs of others.

11. Feelings of Depression and Anxiety (9)

A. The client's anger control problems have often masked a deeper feeling of depression and/or anxiety.

B. The client expressed feelings of depression and anxiety about the struggles to control his/her angry or hostile feelings.

C. The client verbally recognized that he/she often reacts with anger and aggression when he/she begins to feel depressed or anxious.

D. The client expressed feelings of happiness and contentment about his/her ability to control his/her anger more effectively.

E. The client has taken active steps (e.g., expressing feelings of sadness to supportive individuals, facing anxiety-producing situations, socializing with positive peer groups) to reduce his/her feelings of depression and anxiety.

12. Low Self-Esteem (9)

A. The client's angry outbursts and aggressive behaviors have often masked deeper feelings of low self-esteem, insecurity, and inadequacy.

B. The client's persistent anger control problems have resulted in him/her developing a negative self-image and feelings of low self-esteem.

C. The client verbally recognized that his/her angry outbursts and aggressive behaviors are often associated with feelings of inadequacy and insecurity.

D. The client expressed positive self-statements in today's therapy session about his/her improved ability to control his/her anger.

E. The client has taken active steps to improve his/her self-esteem and build a positive self-image.

INTERVENTIONS IMPLEMENTED

1. Assess Anger Dynamics (1)*

A. The client was assessed for various stimuli that have triggered his/her anger.

B. The client was helped to identify situations, people, and thoughts that have triggered his/her anger.

C. The client was assisted in identifying the thoughts, feelings, and actions that have characterized his/her anger responses.

2. Refer for Physical Examination (2)

A. The client was referred to a physician for a complete physical examination to rule out organic contributors (e.g., brain damage, tumor, elevated testosterone levels) to his/her anger.

B. The client has complied with the physical examination, and the results were shared with him/her.

C. The physical examination has identified organic contributors to poor anger control, and treatment was suggested.

D. The physical examination has not identified any organic contributors to poor anger control, and this was reflected to the client.

E. The client has not complied with the physical examination to assess organic contributors, and he/she was redirected to do so.

3. Refer/Conduct Psychological Testing (3)

A. A psychological evaluation was conducted to determine whether ADHD or emotional factors are contributing to the client's anger control problems.

B. The client was reinforced as he/she approached the psychological testing in an honest, straightforward manner and was cooperative with any requests presented to him/her.

C. The client was uncooperative and resistant to engage during the evaluation process and was encouraged to comply with the testing.

D. The client was resistive during the psychological testing and refused to consider the possibility of having ADHD or any serious emotional problems; support and redirection were provided.

E. Feedback was provided to the client and parents regarding the results of the psychological testing.

---

*The numbers in parentheses correlate to the number of the Therapeutic Intervention statement in the companion chapter with the same title in *The Adolescent Psychotherapy Treatment Planner*, Fourth Edition (Jongsma, Peterson, McInnis, and Bruce) by John Wiley & Sons, 2006.

4. Refer/Conduct Substance Abuse Evaluation (4)

A. The client was referred for a substance abuse evaluation to assess the extent of his/her drug/alcohol usage and determine the need for treatment.

B. The findings from the substance abuse evaluation revealed the presence of a substance abuse problem and the need for treatment.

C. The findings from the substance abuse evaluation revealed the presence of a substance abuse problem that appears to be contributing to the client's anger control problems.

D. The evaluation findings did not reveal the presence of a substance abuse problem or the need for treatment in this area.

5. Consult with Criminal Justice Officials (5)

A. A consultation was held with criminal justice officials about the need for appropriate consequences for the client's destructive or aggressive behaviors.

B. The client has been required to make restitution and/or perform community service for his/her destructive or aggressive behaviors.

C. The client was placed on probation for his/her destructive or aggressive behaviors and instructed to comply with all the rules pertaining to his/her probation.

D. The client was placed in an intensive surveillance treatment program as a consequence of his/her destructive or aggressive behaviors.

6. Place in Alternative Setting (6)

A. A consultation was held with parents, school officials, and criminal justice officials about placing the client in an alternative secure setting because of his/her destructive or aggressive behaviors.

B. Recommendation was made that the client be placed in a juvenile detention facility as a consequence of his/her destructive or aggressive behaviors.

C. Recommendation was made that the client be placed in a foster home to help prevent future occurrences of his/her destructive or aggressive behaviors.

D. Recommendation was made that the client be placed in a residential program to provide external structure and supervision for the client.

E. It is recommended that the client be placed in an inpatient or residential substance abuse program to address his/her substance abuse problems.

7. Reinforce Natural Consequences (7)

A. The parents were encouraged and challenged not to protect the client from the natural or legal consequences of his/her destructive or aggressive behaviors.

B. The parents were supported as they agreed to contact the police or appropriate criminal justice officials if the client engages in any serious destructive or aggressive behaviors in the future.

C. The parents followed through and contacted the police or probation officer after the client engaged in the destructive or aggressive behaviors; they were provided with emotional support for this difficult decision.

D. The parents failed to contact the police and/or criminal justice officials after the client engaged in some serious destructive or aggressive behaviors; the reasons for this lapse were reviewed.

E. The parents acknowledged that they often failed to follow through with setting limits because of their desire to avoid conflict and tension, and they were reminded of the long-term effects of this pattern.

8. Refer for Medication Evaluation (8)

A. The client was referred for a medication evaluation to help stabilize his/her mood and improve anger control.

B. The client and parents were supported as they agreed to follow through with a medication evaluation by a physician.

C. It was noted that the client was strongly opposed to being placed on medication to help stabilize his/her mood and improve anger control.

D. The client reported that the medication has helped to stabilize his/her mood and decrease the frequency and intensity of his/her angry outbursts, and he/she was supported for this improvement.

E. The client reported that the medication has not helped to stabilize his/her moods or decrease the frequency or intensity of his/her angry outbursts, and he/she was referred back to the prescribing clinician.

9. Monitor Medication Compliance/Effectiveness (9)

A. The issues of medication compliance and effectiveness were addressed with the parents and the client.

B. The client's resistance to taking medication was processed and addressed.

C. Information related to the client's medication compliance and its effectiveness was communicated to his/her physician.

D. The client's responsible compliance with medications was verbally reinforced.

E. The client reported that the use of the psychotropic medication has been effective in reducing his/her experience of anger.

10. Use Parent Management Training (10)

A. Parent Management Training was used, as developed in *Living with Children* (Patterson).

B. The parents were taught that parent-child behavioral interactions can encourage or discourage positive or negative behavior.

C. The parents were taught that changing key elements of parent-child interactions can be used to promote positive change.

D. The parents were provided with specific examples of how prompting and reinforcing positive behaviors can be used to promote positive change.

E. The parents were provided with positive feedback for the use of Parent Management Training approaches.

F. The parents have not used the Parent Management Training approach and were redirected to do so.

11. Teach Parents to Define Aspects of Situation (11)

A. The parents were taught how to specifically define and identify their child's problem behaviors.

B. The parents were taught how to identify their reactions to their child's behavior, and whether the reaction encourages or discourages the behavior.

C. The parents were taught to generate alternatives to their child's problem behavior.

D. Positive feedback was provided to the parents for their skill at specifically defining and identifying problem behaviors, reactions, outcomes, and alternatives.

E. Parents were provided with remedial feedback as they struggled to correctly identify their child's problem behaviors and their own reactions, responses, and alternatives.

12. Teach Consistent Parenting (12)

A. The parents were taught to implement key parenting practices on a consistent basis.

B. The parents were taught about establishing realistic, age-appropriate rules for their child's acceptable and unacceptable behavior.

C. The parents were taught about prompting positive behavior and use of positive reinforcement.

D. The parents were taught about clear, direct instruction as well as time out and other loss-of-privilege techniques for their child's problem behaviors.

E. The parents were taught about negotiation and renegotiation with adolescents.

F. The parents were provided with positive feedback, as they have been able to develop consistent parenting practices.

G. The parents have not developed consistent parenting practices, and they were redirected to do so.

13. Assign Home Exercises to Implement Parenting Techniques (13)

A. The parents were assigned home exercises in which they implement parenting techniques and record results of the implementation exercises.

B. The parents were assigned "Clear Rules, Positive Reinforcement, Appropriate Consequences" in the *Adolescent Psychotherapy Homework Planner*, 2nd ed. (Jongsma, Peterson, and McInnis).

C. The parents' implementation of homework exercises was reviewed within the session.

D. Corrective feedback was used to help develop improved, appropriate, and consistent use of skills.

E. The parents have not completed the assigned homework, and they were redirected to do so.

14. Assign Parent Training Manuals (14)

A. The parents were directed to read parent training manuals.

B. The parents were directed to read *Parenting Through Change* (Forgatch).

C. The parents were directed to watch videotapes demonstrating the techniques used in parent training sessions.

D. The parents' study of pertinent parent training media was reviewed and processed.

E. The parents have not reviewed the assigned parent training media, and they were redirected to do so.

15. Refer-Conduct to Anger Management Group (15)

A. The client was referred to an anger management group to improve his/her anger control and interpersonal skills.

B. The client was given the directive to self-disclose at least one time during the group therapy session.

C. The client was encouraged to demonstrate empathy and concern for the thoughts, feelings, and needs of others during the group therapy sessions.

16. Document Persons/Situations That Evoke Anger (16)

A. The client was instructed to keep a daily journal in which he/she documents persons and situations that evoke strong feelings of anger.

B. The client was directed to complete the "Anger Journal" exercise in the *Adult Psychotherapy Homework Planner,* 2nd ed. (Jongsma).

C. The client was noted to have made productive use of the journal to document persons or situations that evoke strong feelings of anger.

D. The client failed to comply with the homework assignment to use a journal to document persons and situations that evoke strong feelings of anger, and he/she was redirected to do so.

E. After processing the client's feelings of anger that were expressed in the journal, the client was able to identify constructive ways to resolve conflict or overcome his/her problems.

17. List Triggers and Causes of Anger (17)

A. The client was instructed to develop a thorough list of all triggers and causes of anger.

B. The client was assisted in developing a list of individual(s) whom he/she has experienced strong feelings of anger toward in the past.

C. The client was able to identify and list several situations or events that have produced strong feelings of anger, and these were processed in the session.

D. The client had difficulty identifying the triggers and causes of his/her anger and was provided with tentative examples.

18. Identify Role Models for Anger Expression (18)

A. The client was assisted in identifying ways that key life figures (e.g., father, mother, teachers) have expressed angry feelings.

B. The client was assisted in identifying how the manner in which key life figures have expressed anger positively or negatively influences the way he/she handles anger.

C. The client was reinforced for his/her insight into anger role models.

D. The client did not display much insight into anger role models, and he/she was provided with tentative feedback in this area.

19. Identify Consequences of Anger (19)

A. The client was asked to list ways in which anger has negatively impacted his/her daily life.

B. The client was supported as he/she listed several ways in which anger has negatively impacted his/her daily life.

C. The client was provided with tentative examples of how anger negatively impacts an individual (e.g., injuries to others or self, legal conflicts, loss of respect from self and others, destruction of property, health problems).

20. Reconceptualize Anger (20)

A. The client was assisted in reconceptualizing anger as involving different components that go through predictable phases.

B. The client was taught about the different components of anger, including cognitive, physiological, affective, and behavioral components.

C. The client was taught how to better distinguish between relaxation and tension.

D. The client was taught about the predictable phases of anger: demanding expectations that are not met, which lead to increased arousal and anger, which lead to acting out.

E. The client displayed a clear understanding of the ways to conceptualize anger, and he/she was provided with positive reinforcement.

F. The client has struggled to understand the ways to conceptualize anger, and he/she was provided with remedial feedback in this area.

21. Identify Positive Consequences of Anger Management (21)

A. The client was asked to identify the positive consequences he/she has experienced in managing his/her anger.

B. The client was assisted in identifying positive consequences of managing anger (e.g., respect from others and self, cooperation from others, improved physical health).

C. The client was encouraged to learn new ways to conceptualize and manage anger.

22. Train in Relaxation or Guided Imagery (22)

A. The client was trained in the use of progressive relaxation or guided imagery techniques to help calm himself/herself and decrease the intensity of angry feelings.

B. The client reported a positive response to the use of the progressive relaxation or guided imagery techniques taught to help control anger.

C. The client appeared uncomfortable and unable to relax when being instructed in the use of progressive relaxation and guided imagery techniques.

23. Assign Use of Calming Techniques (23)

A. The client was assigned to implement calming techniques in his/her daily life when facing anger trigger situations.

B. The client related situations in which he/she has appropriately used calming techniques when facing anger trigger situations; this progress was reinforced.

C. The client describes situations in which he/she has not used calming techniques, and these failures were reviewed and redirected.

24. Explore Self-Talk (24)

A. The client's self-talk that mediates his/her angry feelings was explored.

B. The client was assessed for self-talk such as demanding expectations, reflected in "should," "must," or "have to" statements.

C. The client was assisted in identifying and challenging his/her biases and in generating alternative self-talk that corrects for the biases.

D. The client was taught how to use correcting self-talk to facilitate a more flexible and temperate response to frustration.

25. Assign Self-Talk Homework (25)

A. The client was assigned a homework exercise in which he/she identifies angry self-talk and generates alternatives that help moderate angry reactions.

B. The client's use of self-talk alternatives was reviewed within the session.

C. The client was reinforced for his/her success in changing angry self-talk to more moderate alternatives.

D. The client was provided with corrective feedback to help improve his/her use of alternative self-talk to moderate his/her angry reactions.

26. Assign Thought-Stopping Technique (26)

A. The client was directed to implement a "thought-stopping" technique on a daily basis between sessions.

B. The client was assigned "Making Use of the Thought-Stopping Technique" in the *Adult Psychotherapy Homework Planner,* 2nd ed. (Jongsma).

C. The client's use of the thought-stopping technique was reviewed.

D. The client was provided with positive feedback for his/her helpful use of the thought-stopping technique.

E. The client was provided with corrective feedback to help improve his/her use of the thought-stopping technique.

27. Teach Assertive Communication (27)

A. The client was taught about assertive communication through instruction, modeling, and role-playing.

B. The client was referred to an assertiveness training class.

C. The client displayed increased assertiveness, and he/she was provided with positive feedback in this area.

D. The client has not increased his/her level of assertiveness, and he/she was provided with additional feedback in this area.

28. Assign Practice of Skills (28)

A. The client was assigned to practice assertion, problem-solving, and conflict resolution skills.

B. Positive reinforcement was used to reinforce the client's use of coping skills.

C. The client has not regularly practiced his/her coping skills, and he/she was redirected to do so.

29. Conduct Conjoint Session for Assertiveness (29)

A. The client was asked to invite his/her significant other for a conjoint session.

B. The client and his/her significant other were seen together to help implement assertiveness, problem-solving, and conflict resolution skills.

C. The client was reinforced for his/her increased use of assertiveness, problem-solving, and conflict resolution skills with his/her significant other.

D. The client's significant other was urged to assist the client in his/her use of assertiveness, problem-solving, and conflict resolution skills.

E. The client has not regularly used assertiveness, problem-solving, and conflict resolution skills with his/her significant other, and he/she was assisted in identifying barriers to this success.

30. Teach Conflict Resolution Skills (30)

A. The client was taught conflict resolution skills through modeling, role-playing, and behavioral rehearsal.

B. The client was taught about empathy and active listening.

C. The client was taught about "I messages," respectful communication, assertiveness without aggression, and compromise.

D. The client was reinforced for his/her clear understanding of the conflict resolution skills.

E. The client displayed a poor understanding of the conflict resolution skills and was provided with remedial feedback.

31. Construct Strategy for Managing Anger (31)

A. The client was assisted in constructing a strategy for managing his/her anger.

B. The client was encouraged to combine somatic, cognitive, communication, problem-solving, and conflict resolution skills relevant to his/her needs.

C. The client was reinforced for his/her comprehensive anger management strategy.

D. The client was redirected to develop a more comprehensive anger management strategy.

32. Select Challenging Situations for Managing Anger (32)

A. The client was provided with situations in which he/she may be increasingly challenged to apply his/her new strategies for managing anger.

B. The client was asked to identify his/her likely upcoming challenging situations for managing anger.

C. The client was urged to use his/her strategies for managing anger in successively more difficult situations.

33. Monitor/Decrease Outbursts (33)

A. The client's reports of angry outbursts were monitored, with the goal of decreasing their frequency, intensity, and duration.

B. The client was urged to use his/her new anger management skills to decrease the frequency, intensity, and duration of his/her anger outbursts.

C. The client was assigned "Alternatives to Destructive Anger" in the *Adult Psychotherapy Homework Planner,* 2nd ed. (Jongsma).

D. The client's progress in decreasing his/her angry outbursts was reviewed.

E. The client was reinforced for his/her success at decreasing the frequency, intensity, and duration of his/her anger outbursts.

F. The client has not decreased the frequency, intensity, or duration of his/her anger outbursts, and corrective feedback was provided.

34. Encourage Disclosure (34)

A. The client was encouraged to discuss his/her anger management goals with trusted persons who are likely to support his/her change.

B. The client was assisted in identifying individuals who are likely to support his/her change.

C. The client has reviewed his/her anger management goals with trusted persons, and their response was processed.

D. The client has not discussed his/her anger management goals, and he/she was redirected to do so.

35. Differentiate between Lapse and Relapse (35)

A. A discussion was held with the client regarding the distinction between a lapse and a relapse.

B. A lapse was associated with an initial and reversible return of angry outbursts.

C. A relapse was associated with the decision to return to the old pattern of anger.

D. The client was provided with support and encouragement as he/she displayed an understanding of the difference between a lapse and a relapse.

E. The client struggled to understand the difference between a lapse and a relapse, and he/she was provided with remedial feedback in this area.

36. Discuss Management of Lapse Risk Situations (36)

A. The client was assisted in identifying future situations or circumstances in which lapses could occur.

B. The session focused on rehearsing the management of future situations or circumstances in which lapses could occur.

C. The client was reinforced for his/her appropriate use of lapse management skills.

D. The client was redirected in regard to his/her poor use of lapse management skills.

37. Encourage Routine Use of Strategies (37)

A. The client was instructed to routinely use the strategies that he/she has learned in therapy (e.g., calming, adaptive self-talk, assertion, conflict resolution).

B. The client was urged to find ways to build his/her new strategies into his/her life as much as possible.

C. The client was reinforced as he/she reported ways in which he/she has incorporated coping strategies into his/her life and routine.

D. The client was redirected about ways to incorporate his/her new strategies into his/her routine and life.

38. Develop a Coping Card (38)

A. The client was provided with a coping card on which specific coping strategies were listed.

B. The client was assisted in developing his/her coping card in order to list his/her helpful coping strategies.

C. The client was encouraged to use his/her coping card when struggling with anger-producing situations.

39. Schedule Maintenance Sessions (39)

A. Maintenance sessions were proposed to help the client maintain therapeutic gains and adjust to life without anger outbursts.

B. The client was reinforced for agreeing to the scheduling of maintenance sessions.

C. The client refused to schedule maintenance sessions, and this was processed.

40. Assign Reading Material (40)

A. The client was assigned to read material that educates him/her about anger and its management.

B. The client was directed to read *Overcoming Situational and General Anger: Client Manual* (Deffenbacher and McKay).

C. The client was directed to read *The Angry Child* (Murphy).

D. The client was directed to read *The Anger Control Workbook* (McKay).

E. The client has read the assigned material on anger management, and key concepts were reviewed.

F. The client has not read the assigned material on anger management and was redirected to do so.

ANXIETY

CLIENT PRESENTATION

1. Excessive Worry (1)*
A. The client presented for the session upset and worried about recent events.
B. The client was upset and worried to the point that he/she could not be easily settled down by the therapist.
C. The client was able to work on the core issues that have caused him/her to be upset.
D. The client reported that he/she has been significantly less worried and less preoccupied with anxieties in the recent past.

2. Fearful/Urgent (1)
A. The client revealed a strong sense of urgency and sought any possible reassurance for his/her fears.
B. The urgency surrounding the client's fear is overwhelming.
C. The client's sense of urgency is not diminished by reassurance from the therapist.
D. The sense of urgency that surrounds the client's fears is no longer existent, and he/she no longer presses for reassurance.

3. Restless/Tense (2)
A. The client was restless and tense, making it difficult for him/her to sit in session or to complete thoughts or activities.
B. The client is becoming less tense and is now able to respond to questions attentively.
C. The client is more relaxed and able to focus throughout the session, even when addressing issues that cause him/her anxiety.

4. Autonomic Hyperactivity Symptoms (3)
A. The client presented as being very anxious and experiencing a rapid heartbeat and shortness of breath.
B. The client has been plagued by nausea and diarrhea brought on by his/her anxiety, as all physical reasons have been medically ruled out.
C. The client complained of having a dry mouth and frequently feeling dizzy.
D. The client indicated that he/she has not experienced symptoms of a rapid heartbeat or shortness of breath since he/she started to talk about what makes him/her anxious.

5. Hypervigilant (4)
A. The client presented in a tense, on-edge manner.
B. The client's level of tension and anxiety was so high that he/she was unable to concentrate on anything and was irritable.

*The numbers in parentheses correlate to the number of the Behavioral Definition statement in the companion chapter with the same title in *The Adolescent Psychotherapy Treatment Planner,* Fourth Edition (Jongsma, Peterson, McInnis, and Bruce) by John Wiley & Sons, 2006.

C. The client reported sleep disturbance related to anxious worry.

D. The client's anxiety has diminished, and he/she is significantly more relaxed.

6. Specific Fear/Phobia (5)

A. The client presented as being anxious over the specific stimulus situation to the point of being able to function only on a limited basis.

B. The client reported that the phobic anxiety gradually increased to the point that it now interferes with his/her daily life and family's life as well.

C. The client indicated that he/she has no idea why the phobic fear has come to dominate his/her daily existence.

D. The client's daily ability to function has increased steadily as he/she has begun to face the phobic fear.

7. Parental Causes for Anxiety (6)

A. The client complained of being worried and anxious about the constant arguing of his/her parents.

B. The parents reported that they restrict the client's freedom and physical activity to protect him/her from the dangers present today.

C. It was observed that the parents' use of excessive guilt and threats of abandonment caused worry and anxiety in the client.

D. The client indicated that he/she now feels less anxious, as the parents have stopped arguing so often.

E. The parents' relaxing their restrictions and control has reduced the client's level of worry and anxiety.

INTERVENTIONS IMPLEMENTED

1. Establish Trust/Express Anxieties (1)*

A. An initial trust level was established with the client through the use of unconditional positive regard.

B. Warm acceptance and active listening techniques were utilized to establish the basis for a trusting relationship with the client.

C. Due to the level of acceptance, the client has formed a trust-based relationship and has started to express his/her anxious feelings.

D. Despite the use of active listening, warm acceptance, and unconditional positive regard, the client remains hesitant to trust and share his/her anxious feelings.

2. Assess Nature of Anxiety Symptoms (2)

A. The client was asked about the frequency, intensity, duration, and history of his/her anxiety symptoms, fear, and avoidance.

---

*The numbers in parentheses correlate to the number of the Therapeutic Intervention statement in the companion chapter with the same title in *The Adolescent Psychotherapy Treatment Planner,* Fourth Edition (Jongsma, Peterson, McInnis, and Bruce) by John Wiley & Sons, 2006.

B. *The Anxiety Disorder's Interview Schedule for Children—Parent Version* or *Child Version* (Silverman and Nelles) was used to assess the client's anxiety symptoms.

C. "Finding and Losing your Anxiety" from the *Adolescent Psychotherapy Homework Planner,* 2nd ed. (Jongsma, Peterson, and McInnis) was used to help assess the client's level of anxiety symptoms.

D. The assessment of the client's anxiety symptoms indicated that his/her symptoms are extreme and severely interfere with his/her life.

E. The assessment of the client's anxiety symptoms indicates that these symptoms are moderate and occasionally interfere with his/her daily functioning.

F. The results of the assessment of the client's anxiety symptoms indicate that these symptoms are mild and rarely interfere with his/her daily functioning.

G. The results of the assessment of the client's anxiety symptoms were reviewed with the client.

3. Administer Patient-Report Measure (3)

A. A patient-report measure was used to further assess the depth and breadth of the client's anxiety responses.

B. *The Penn State Worry Questionnaire* (Meyer, Miller, Metzger, and Borkevec) was used to assess the depth and breadth of the client's anxiety responses.

C. The patient-report measure indicated that the client's anxiety is extreme and severely interferes with his/her life.

D. The patient-report measure indicated that the client's anxiety is moderate and occasionally interferes with his/her life.

E. The patient-report measure indicated that the client's anxiety is mild and rarely interferes with his/her life.

F. The client declined to complete the patient-report measure, and the focus of treatment was changed to this resistance.

4. Refer for Medication Consultation (4)

A. The value of a medication consultation was discussed with the parents and the client.

B. A medication consultation was scheduled, and the client followed through.

C. The therapist and psychiatrist conferred regarding the recommendation for a medication evaluation.

D. The client and the parents were resistant to the use of medication and have not followed through with the referral to a physician for an evaluation; additional prompts were provided.

5. Monitor Medication Compliance/Effectiveness (5)

A. The issues of medication compliance and effectiveness were addressed with the parents and the client.

B. The client's resistance to taking medication was processed and addressed.

C. Information related to the client's medication compliance and its effectiveness was communicated to his/her psychiatrist.

D. The client's responsible compliance with medications was verbally reinforced.

E. The client reported that the use of the psychotropic medication has been effective in reducing his/her experience of anxiety.

6. Discuss Anxiety Cycle (6)

A. The client was taught how anxious fears are maintained by a cycle of unwarranted fear and avoidance that precludes positive, corrective experiences with the feared object or situation.

B. The client was taught how treatment breaks the anxiety cycle by encouraging positive, corrective experiences.

C. The client was taught information from *Helping Your Anxious Child* (Rapee, Spence, Cobham, and Wignall).

D. The client was reinforced as he/she displayed a better understanding of the anxiety cycle of unwarranted fear and avoidance, and of how treatment breaks the cycle.

E. The client displayed a poor understanding of the anxiety cycle and was provided with remedial feedback in this area.

7. Discuss Target of Treatment (7)

A. A discussion was held about how treatment targets worry, anxiety symptoms, and avoidance to help the client manage worry effectively.

B. The reduction of overarousal and unnecessary avoidance were emphasized as treatment targets.

C. The client displayed a clear understanding of the target of treatment, and he/she was provided with positive feedback in this area.

D. The client struggled to understand the target of treatment and was provided with specific examples in this area.

8. Assign Reading on Anxiety (8)

A. The client was assigned to read psychoeducational chapters of books or treatment manuals on anxiety.

B. The client was assigned information from *Helping Your Anxious Child* (Rapee, Spence, Cobham, and Wignall).

C. The client has read the assigned information on anxiety, and key points were reviewed.

D. The client has not read the assigned information on anxiety, and he/she was redirected to do so.

9. Teach Relaxation Skills (9)

A. The client was taught relaxation skills.

B. The client was taught progressive muscle relaxation, guided imagery, and slow diaphragmatic breathing.

C. The client was taught how to better discriminate between relaxation and tension.

D. The client was taught how to apply relaxation skills to his/her daily life.

E. The client was provided with feedback about his/her use of relaxation skills.

10. Assign Relaxation Homework (10)

A. The client was assigned to do homework exercises in which he/she practices relaxation on a daily basis.

B. The client has regularly used relaxation exercises, and the helpful benefits of these exercises were reviewed.

C. The client has not regularly used relaxation exercises, and he/she was provided with corrective feedback in this area.

D. The client has used some relaxation exercises but does not find these to be helpful; he/she was assisted in brainstorming how to modify these exercises to be more helpful.

11. Assign Reading on Relaxation and Calming Strategies (11)

A. The client was assigned to read about progressive muscle relaxation and other calming strategies in relevant books and treatment manuals.

B. The client was directed to read about muscle relaxation and other calming strategies in *New Directions in Progressive Relaxation Training* (Bernstein and Borkovec).

C. The client has read the assigned information on progressive muscle relaxation, and key points were reviewed.

D. The client has not read the assigned information on progressive muscle relaxation, and he/she was redirected to do so.

12. Use Biofeedback Techniques (12)

A. Biofeedback techniques were used to facilitate the client's success in learning relaxation skills.

B. The client was provided with consistent feedback about his/her physiological responses to relaxation skill training.

C. The client was reinforced for his/her increase in relaxation skills through biofeedback training.

D. The client has not increased his/her success at learning skills through biofeedback techniques, and remedial instruction was provided.

13. Discuss Estimation Errors (13)

A. In today's session, examples were discussed of how unrealistic worry typically overestimates the probability of threats.

B. It was noted that unrealistic worry often underestimates the client's ability to manage realistic demands.

C. The client was assisted in identifying specific examples of how his/her unrealistic worry involves estimation errors.

D. The client was reinforced for his/her insightful identification of unrealistic worry and inappropriate estimation.

E. The client has struggled to identify estimation errors in regard to his/her unrealistic worry, and he/she was provided with tentative examples in this area.

14. Challenge Fears (14)

A. The client was assisted in challenging his/her fear or worry by examining the actual probability of the negative expectation occurring, the real consequences of it occurring, the ability to manage the likely outcome, the worst possible outcome, and his/her ability to accept it.

B. Techniques described in *Helping Your Anxious Child* (Rapee, Spence, Cobham, and Wignall) were used to help the client challenge his/her fears and worries.

C. The client was reinforced for his/her regular use of challenging thoughts regarding his/her fear or worry, and he/she was provided with positive feedback in this area.

D. The client has not regularly challenged his/her fears and worries, and he/she was redirected to do so.

15. Develop Insight into Worry as Avoidance (15)

A. The client was assisted in gaining insight into how worry is a form of avoidance of a fear problem and how it creates chronic tension.

B. The client was reinforced for his/her insightful understanding of how his/her worry creates avoidance and tension.

C. The client struggled to understand the nature of worry as a form of avoidance, and he/she was provided with remedial information in this area.

16. Identify Distorted Thoughts (16)

A. The client was assisted in identifying the distorted schemas and related automatic thoughts that mediate anxiety responses.

B. The client was taught the role of distorted thinking in precipitating emotional responses.

C. The client was reinforced as he/she verbalized an understanding of the cognitive beliefs and messages that mediate his/her anxiety responses.

D. The client was assisted in replacing distorted messages with positive, realistic cognitions.

E. The client failed to identify his/her distorted thoughts and cognitions and was provided with tentative examples in this area.

17. Assign Exercises on Self-Talk (17)

A. The client was assigned homework exercises in which he/she identifies fearful self-talk and creates reality-based alternatives.

B. "Bad Thoughts Lead to Depressed Feelings" from the *Adolescent Psychotherapy Homework Planner*, 2nd ed. (Jongsma, Peterson, and McInnis) was assigned to help the client identify fearful self-talk.

C. The client's replacement of fearful self-talk with reality-based alternatives was critiqued.

D. The client was reinforced for his/her successes at replacing fearful self-talk with reality-based alternatives.

E. The client was provided with corrective feedback for his/her failure to replace fearful self-talk with reality-based alternatives.

F. The client has not completed his/her assigned homework regarding fearful self-talk, and he/she was redirected to do so.

18. Teach Thought Stopping (18)

A. The client was taught thought-stopping techniques that involve thinking of a stop sign and replacing negative thoughts with a pleasant scene.

B. "Making Use of the Thought-Stopping Technique" from the *Adult Psychotherapy Homework Planner,* 2nd ed. (Jongsma) was assigned to help teach the client techniques for stopping thoughts that lead to fears or worries.

C. The client's implementation of the thought-stopping technique was monitored, and his/her success with this technique was reinforced.

D. The client reported that the thought-stopping technique has been beneficial in reducing his/her preoccupation with anxiety-producing cognitions; he/she was encouraged to continue this technique.

E. The client has failed to use the thought-stopping techniques, and his/her attempts to use these techniques were reviewed and problem-solved.

19. Read about Cognitive Restructuring of Fears (19)

A. The client was assigned to read about cognitive restructuring of fears or worries in books or treatment manuals.

B. *Helping Your Anxious Child* (Rapee, Spence, Cobham, and Wignall) was assigned to the client to help teach him/her about cognitive restructuring.

C. Key components of cognitive restructuring were reviewed.

D. The client and parents have not done the assigned reading on cognitive restructuring, and they were redirected to do so.

20. Assign Reading on Worry Exposure (20)

A. The client was assigned to read about worry exposure in relevant books or treatment manuals.

B. The client was assigned *Mastery of Your Anxiety and Worry—Client Guide* (Zinbarg, Craske, Barlow, and O'Leary) to learn about worry exposure.

C. Key concepts related to worry exposure were reviewed and processed within the session.

D. The client has not done the reading on worry exposure, and he/she was redirected to do so.

21. Construct Anxiety Stimulus Hierarchy (21)

A. The client was assisted in constructing a hierarchy of anxiety-producing situations associated with two or three spheres of worry.

B. It was difficult for the client to develop a hierarchy of stimulus situations, as the causes of his/her anxiety remain quite vague; he/she was assisted in completing the hierarchy.

C. The client was successful at creating a focused hierarchy of specific stimulus situations that provoke anxiety in a gradually increasing manner; this hierarchy was reviewed.

22. Select Initial Exposures (22)

A. Initial exposures were selected from the hierarchy of anxiety-producing situations, with a bias toward likelihood of being successful.

B. A plan was developed with the client for managing the symptoms that may occur during the initial exposure.

C. The client was assisted in rehearsing the plan for managing the exposure-related symptoms within his/her imagination.

D. Positive feedback was provided for the client's helpful use of symptom management techniques.

E. The client was redirected for ways to improve his/her symptom management techniques.

23. Assign Imagination Exercises (23)

A. The client was asked to vividly imagine worst-case consequences of worries, holding them in mind until the anxiety associated with them weakened.

B. The client was asked to imagine consequences of his/her worries as described in *Mastery of Your Anxiety and Worry—Therapist Guide* (Craske, Barlow, and O'Leary).

C. The client was supported, as he/she has maintained a focus on the worst-case consequences of his/her worry until the anxiety weakened.

D. The client was assisted in generating reality-based alternatives to the worst-case scenarios, and these were processed within the session.

24. Assign Homework on Situational Exposures (24)

A. The client was assigned homework exercises to perform worry exposures and record his/her experience.

B. The client was assigned situational exposure homework from *Mastery of Your Anxiety and Worry—Client Guide* (Zinbarg, Craske, Barlow, and O'Leary).

C. The client was assigned situational exposure homework from *Phobic and Anxiety Disorders in Children and Adolescents* (Ollendick and March).

D. The client was assigned "Gradually Facing a Phobic Fear" from the *Adolescent Psychotherapy Homework Planner,* 2nd ed. (Jongsma, Peterson, and McInnis).

E. The client's use of worry exposure techniques was reviewed and reinforced.

F. The client has struggled in his/her implementation of worry exposure techniques, and he/she was provided with corrective feedback.

G. The client has not attempted to use the worry exposure techniques, and he/she was redirected to do so.

25. Develop List of Key Concepts (25)

A. The client was asked to develop a list of key concepts that trigger fear or worry.

B. The client's list of conflicts was processed toward resolution.

C. Problem-solving skills and assertiveness techniques were used to help the client resolve his/her key conflicts.

D. Techniques of acceptance and cognitive restructuring were used to help the client reduce the emotional disregulation that occurs from his/her key conflicts.

E. It was noted that the client has significantly decreased his/her fear and worry by resolving some of his/her key conflicts.

F. The client continues to have significant conflicts despite the use of problem-solving, assertiveness, acceptance, and cognitive restructuring skills; he/she was provided with remedial feedback in this area.

26. Assign Problem-Solving Exercise (23)

A. The client was assigned a homework exercise in which he/she problem-solves a current problem.

B. The client was assigned to solve a problem as described in *Helping Your Anxious Child* (Rapee, Spence, Cobham, and Wignall).

C. The client was provided with feedback about his/her use of the problem-solving assignment.

27. Encourage Increased Activities (27)

A. The client was encouraged to strengthen his/her new nonavoidant approach by using distraction from anxious thoughts through increased activities.

B. The client was encouraged to use social and academic activities to help distract him/her from anxious thoughts.

C. The client was encouraged to use his/her own list of potentially rewarding experiences as a distraction from his/her anxious thoughts.

D. The client was reinforced for his/her use of distraction from anxious thoughts.

E. The client has not regularly used distraction techniques for his/her anxious thoughts, he/she was redirected to do so.

28. Differentiate between Lapse and Relapse (28)

A. A discussion was held with the client regarding the distinction between a lapse and a relapse.

B. A lapse was associated with an initial and reversible return of symptoms, fear, or urges to avoid.

C. A relapse was associated with the decision to return to fearful and avoidant patterns.

D. The client was provided with support and encouragement, as he/she displayed an understanding of the difference between a lapse and a relapse.

E. The client struggled to understand the difference between a lapse and a relapse, and he/she was provided with remedial feedback in this area.

29. Discuss Management of Lapse Risk Situations (29)

A. The client was assisted in identifying future situations or circumstances in which lapses could occur.

B. The session focused on rehearsing the management of future situations or circumstances in which lapses could occur.

C. The client was reinforced for his/her appropriate use of lapse management skills.

D. The client was redirected in regard to his/her poor use of lapse management skills.

30. Encourage Routine Use of Strategies (30)

A. The client was instructed to routinely use the strategies that he/she has learned in therapy (e.g., cognitive restructuring, exposure).

B. The client was urged to find ways to build his/her new strategies into his/her life as much as possible.

C. The client was reinforced as he/she reported ways in which he/she has incorporated coping strategies into his/her life and routine.

D. The client was redirected about ways to incorporate his/her new strategies into his/her routine and life.

31. Develop a Coping Card (31)

A. The client was provided with a coping card on which specific coping strategies were listed.

B. The client was assisted in developing his/her coping card on which to list his/her helpful coping strategies.

C. The client was encouraged to use his/her coping card when struggling with anxiety-producing situations.

32. Involve Parents in Treatment (32)

A. A discussion was held with the client about the extent to which his/her parents should be involved in treatment.

B. The parents were encouraged to participate in selective activities of the client's treatment.

33. Frame Family as an Expert Team (33)

A. The family was emphasized as an expert team for assisting the client in his/her recovery.

B. The parents were taught skills for effectively responding to the client's fears and anxieties with calm and reassurance.

C. The client's parents were encouraged to reward the client's treatment successes.

D. The parents were urged to use calm persistence in prompting coping skills when needed.

E. The family has provided support and redirection to the client; this success was reinforced.

F. The client's family has not provided much support or reassurance to the client, and the family was redirected in this area.

34. Teach Modeling of Nonavoidance Skills (34)

A. The parents were taught to use the same nonavoidance skills that the client is learning in order to approach and manage their own fears and worries.

B. The client's parents were encouraged to use problem-solving skills and communication when approaching their own problem areas.

C. The parents were taught techniques described in *Keys to Parenting Your Anxious Child* (Manassis).

D. The parents were reinforced for their consistent use of nonavoidant skills.

E. The parents have not regularly used nonavoidant skills in facing their own fears and worries, and they were redirected to do so.

35. Explore Anxiety-Related Developmental Themes (35)

A. The client's experience of loss, abandonment, and other anxiety-related developmental themes was explored.

B. The effect that the client's historical experiences have on his/her current fears and worries was emphasized.

C. The client was assisted in processing his/her history of loss, abandonment, and other anxiety-related developmental themes.

ATTENTION-DEFICIT/HYPERACTIVITY DISORDER (ADHD)

CLIENT PRESENTATION

1. Short Attention Span (1)*

A. The parents and teachers reported that the client displays a short attention span and has difficulty staying focused for extended periods of time.

B. The client had trouble staying focused in today's therapy session and often switched from one topic to another.

C. The client remained focused and was able to discuss pertinent topics for a sufficient length of time.

D. The client's attention span has improved in structured settings where he/she receives supervision and greater individualized attention.

E. The parents and teachers reported that the client has consistently demonstrated good attention and concentration at home and school.

2. Distractibility (2)

A. The parents and teachers reported that the client is easily distracted by extraneous stimuli and his/her own internal thoughts.

B. The client appeared highly distractible during today's therapy session and often had to be redirected to the topic being discussed.

C. The client often has to be redirected to task at home or school because of his/her distractibility.

D. The client appeared less distractible and more focused during today's therapy session.

E. The client appeared less distractible and more focused at home and school.

3. Poor Listening Skills (3)

A. The client has often given others the impression at home and school that he/she is not listening to what is being said.

B. The client did not appear to be listening well to the topics being discussed in today's therapy session.

C. The client listened well during today's therapy session.

D. The client has recently demonstrated improved listening skills at home and school.

4. No Follow Through on Instructions (4)

A. The parents and teachers reported that the client does not consistently follow through on instructions.

---

*The numbers in parentheses correlate to the number of the Behavioral Definition statement in the companion chapter with the same title in *The Adolescent Psychotherapy Treatment Planner,* Fourth Edition (Jongsma, Peterson, McInnis, and Bruce) by John Wiley & Sons, 2006.

B. The client's repeated failure to follow through on instructions has interfered with his/her ability to complete school assignments, chores, and job responsibilities in a timely manner.

C. The client has generally been able to follow single or simple instructions but has had trouble following through on multiple, complex instructions.

D. The client has begun to demonstrate improvement in his/her ability to follow through on instructions.

E. The client has recently followed through on instructions from parents and teachers on a consistent basis.

5. Incomplete Classroom/Homework Assignments (4)

A. The client has consistently failed to complete his/her classroom and homework assignments in a timely manner.

B. The client has often rushed through his/her classroom work and does not fully complete his/her assignments.

C. The client has recently demonstrated mild improvement in his/her ability to complete classroom and homework assignments.

D. The client has consistently completed his/her classroom and homework assignments.

6. Unfinished Chores (4)

A. The client often failed to comply with parents' requests to complete his/her chores at home.

B. The parents reported that the client often gets sidetracked and does not complete his/her chores.

C. The client has demonstrated mild improvement in his/her ability to finish chores or household responsibilities.

D. The client has been responsible in completing his/her chores on a consistent basis.

7. Poor Organizational Skills (5)

A. The client has displayed poor organizational skills and often loses or misplaces important things necessary for tasks or activities at home and school.

B. The client has a tendency to become more disorganized and impulsive in his/her responding in unstructured settings where there is a great deal of external stimulation.

C. The client has recently taken active steps (e.g., utilizing planner, consulting with teachers about homework, performing homework and chores at routine times) to become more organized at home and school.

D. The client has demonstrated good organizational skills at home and school on a regular basis.

8. Hyperactivity (6)

A. The parents and teachers described the client as being a highly energetic and hyperactive individual.

B. The client presented with a high energy level and had difficulty sitting still for extended periods of time.

C. The client has trouble channeling his/her high energy into constructive or sustained, purposeful activities.

D. The parents and teachers reported a decrease in the client's level of hyperactivity.

E. The client has consistently channeled his/her energy into constructive and purposeful activities.

9. Impulsivity (7)

A. The client presents as a highly impulsive individual who seeks immediate gratification of his/her needs and often fails to consider the consequences of his/her actions.

B. The client has considerable difficulty inhibiting his/her impulses and tends to react to what is going on in his/her immediate environment.

C. The client has begun to take steps toward improving his/her impulse control and to delay the need for immediate gratification.

D. The client has recently displayed good impulse control, as evidenced by an improved ability to stop and think about the possible consequences of his/her actions before reacting.

10. Disruptive/Attention-Seeking Behavior (8)

A. The parents and teachers described a history of the client frequently disrupting the classroom with his/her silly, immature, and negative attention-seeking behavior.

B. The client has often disrupted the classroom by blurting out remarks at inappropriate times.

C. The client has started to exercise greater self-control and recently has not disrupted the classroom as much.

D. The client has demonstrated a significant reduction in the frequency of his/her disruptive or negative attention-seeking behavior at home and school.

11. Angry Outbursts/Aggressive Behavior (8)

A. The client reported a history of losing control of his/her anger and exhibiting frequent angry outbursts or aggressive behaviors.

B. The client appeared angry and hostile during today's therapy session.

C. The client reported incidents of becoming easily angered over trivial matters.

D. The client has begun to take steps to control his/her anger and aggressive impulses.

E. The client has recently demonstrated good control of his/her anger and has not exhibited any major outbursts or aggressive behavior.

12. Careless/Potentially Dangerous Behavior (9)

A. The client described a history of engaging in careless or potentially dangerous behavior in which he/she shows little regard for the welfare or safety of self and others.

B. The client's impulsivity has contributed to his/her propensity for engaging in careless, risky, or dangerous activity.

C. The client verbally recognized a need to stop and think about the possible consequences of his/her actions for self and others before engaging in risky or potentially dangerous behavior.

D. The client has not engaged in any recent careless or potentially dangerous behaviors.

13. Blaming/Projecting (10)

A. The client has often resisted accepting responsibility for the consequences of his/her actions and has frequently projected the blame for his/her poor decisions or problems onto other people or outside circumstances.

B. The client appeared defensive and made excuses or blamed others for his/her poor decisions and behavior.

C. The client has slowly begun to accept greater responsibility for his/her actions and has less often placed the blame for his/her wrongdoing on other people.

D. The client admitted to his/her wrongdoing and verbalized an acceptance of responsibility for his/her actions.

14. Low Self-Esteem (11)

A. The client expressed feelings of low self-esteem and inadequacy as a consequence of his/her poor decisions and impulsive actions.

B. The client's defensiveness and unwillingness to accept responsibility for the consequences of his/her actions have reflected deeper feelings of low self-esteem, inadequacy, and insecurity.

C. The client verbalized an awareness of how his/her feelings of inadequacy contribute to an increase in disruptive and impulsive behavior.

D. The client verbalized positive self-descriptive statements during today's therapy session.

E. The client has taken active steps to improve his/her self-esteem and develop a positive self-image.

15. Poor Social Skills (11)

A. The client historically has had difficulty establishing and maintaining lasting peer friendships because of his/her poor social skills and impulsivity.

B. The client frequently becomes entangled in interpersonal disputes because of his/her failure to pick up on important social cues or interpersonal nuances.

C. The client's interpersonal relationships are strained by his/her intrusive behaviors.

D. The client has begun to take steps (e.g., listening better, complimenting others, allowing others to go first) to improve his/her social skills.

E. The client has recently demonstrated good social skills and related well to siblings, peers, and adults on a consistent basis.

INTERVENTIONS IMPLEMENTED

1. Obtain Psychological Testing (1)*

A. A psychological evaluation was conducted to determine whether the client has ADHD or whether emotional factors are contributing to his/her impulsive or maladaptive behaviors.

B. The client was uncooperative during the evaluation and did not appear to put forth good effort; he/she was encouraged to comply with the testing.

C. The client was cooperative during the psychoeducational evaluation and appeared motivated to do his/her best.

D. The examiner provided feedback on the evaluation results to the client, parents, or school officials and discussed appropriate interventions.

---

*The numbers in parentheses correlate to the number of the Therapeutic Intervention statement in the companion chapter with the same title in *The Adolescent Psychotherapy Treatment Planner,* Fourth Edition (Jongsma, Peterson, McInnis, and Bruce) by John Wiley & Sons, 2006.

E. The evaluation results supported the diagnosis of ADHD.

F. The evaluation revealed the presence of underlying emotional problems that contribute to the client's problems with inattentiveness, distractibility, and impulsivity.

G. The evaluation process did not reveal the presence of any learning disability, emotional problems, or ADHD that have contributed to the client's problems with attention, distractibility, or impulsivity.

2. Refer for Medication Evaluation (2)

A. The client was referred for a medication evaluation to improve his/her attention span, concentration, and impulse control.

B. The client was referred for a medication evaluation to help stabilize his/her moods.

C. Positive feedback was provided to the client and parents as they agreed to follow through with a medication evaluation.

D. The client was strongly opposed to being placed on medication to help improve his/her attention span and impulse control; his/her feelings were acknowledged.

3. Monitor Medication Compliance and Effectiveness (3)

A. The client reported that the medication has helped to improve his/her attention, concentration, and impulse control without any side effects, and the benefits of this were reviewed.

B. The client reported little to no improvement while taking the medication and was redirected to his/her physician.

C. The client has not complied with taking his/her medication on a regular basis and was redirected to do so.

D. The client and parents were encouraged to report the side effects of the medication to the prescribing physician or psychiatrist.

4. Educate Family about ADHD (4)

A. The client's parents and siblings were educated about the symptoms of ADHD.

B. The therapy session helped the client's parents and siblings gain a greater understanding and appreciation of the symptoms of ADHD.

C. The family members were given the opportunity to express their thoughts and feelings about having a child or sibling with ADHD.

5. Assign Parents to Read ADHD Information (5)

A. The parents were assigned to read information to increase their knowledge about symptoms of ADHD.

B. The client's parents were directed to read *Taking Charge of ADHD* (Barkley).

C. The parents were directed to read *ADHD and Teens* (Alexander-Roberts).

D. The client's parents were directed to read *Teenagers with ADD* (Zeigler-Dendy).

E. The parents have read the information about ADHD, and key points were processed.

F. The client's parents have not read the information about ADHD and were redirected to do so.

6. Assign Reading on ADHD (6)

A. The client was instructed to read information about ADHD and adolescence.

B. The client was instructed to read *ADHD—A Teenager's Guide* (Crist) to increase his/her knowledge and understanding of ADHD.

C. The client was instructed to read *Adolescence and ADD* (Quinn) to increase his/her knowledge about ADHD and ways to manage symptoms.

D. The client identified several helpful strategies that he/she learned from readings assigned from *ADHD—A Teenager's Guide* to help improve attention span, academic performance, social skills, and impulse control.

E. The client has not read the helpful information on ADHD and teenagers, and he/she was redirected to do so.

7. Implement Organizational System (7)

A. The parents were assisted in developing an organizational system to increase the client's on-task behavior and completion of school assignments, chores, or work responsibilities.

B. The parents were encouraged to communicate regularly with the teachers through the use of notebooks or planning agendas to help the client complete his/her school or homework on a regular, consistent basis.

C. The client and parents were encouraged to use a calendar or chart to help remind the client of when he/she was expected to complete chores or household responsibilities.

D. The client and parents were instructed to ask the teacher for a course syllabus and use a calendar to help plan large or long-term projects by breaking them into smaller steps.

E. The client and parents were encouraged to purchase a binder notebook to help the client keep track of his/her school or homework assignments.

F. The client and his/her parents have not implemented an organizational system to increase the client's on-task behavior, and they were redirected to do so.

8. Develop Routine Schedule (8)

A. The client and parents were assisted in developing a routine schedule to increase the completion of school/homework assignments.

B. The client and parents were assisted in developing a list of chores for the client and identified times and dates when the chores are expected to be completed.

C. A reward system was designed to reinforce the completion of school, household, or work-related responsibilities.

D. The client, parents, and therapist signed a contingency contract specifying the consequences for the client's success or failure in completing school assignments or household responsibilities.

E. The client and parents have not developed a routine schedule to increase the completion of school/homework assignments and were redirected to do so.

9. Increase Communication between Home and School (9)

A. The parents and teachers were encouraged to maintain regular communication with each other via phone calls or written notes regarding the client's academic, behavioral, emotional, and social progress.

B. Consultation was held with the teachers about sending home daily or weekly progress notes informing the parents of the client's academic, behavioral, and social progress.

C. The client was informed of his/her responsibility to bring home daily or weekly progress notes to allow regular communication between parents and teachers.

D. The parents identified the consequences for the client of failure to bring home the daily or weekly progress notes from school and were provided with support.

E. The parents and teachers have not maintained regular contact and communication regarding the client's progress and were redirected to establish this communication.

10. Teach Effective Study Skills (10)

A. The client was assisted in identifying a list of good locations for studying.

B. The client was instructed to remove noise sources and clear away as many distractions as possible when studying.

C. The client was instructed to outline or underline important details when studying or reviewing for tests.

D. The client was encouraged to use a tape recorder to help him/her study for tests and review important facts.

E. The client was instructed to take breaks from studying when he/she becomes distracted and starts to have trouble staying focused.

11. Read about Study Skills (11)

A. The client was directed to read information about study skills to improve his/her organizational and study skills.

B. The client was instructed to read *13 Steps to Better Grades* (Silverman) to improve his/her organizational and study skills.

C. After reading *13 Steps to Better Grades,* the client was able to identify several positive study skills that will help him/her remain organized in the classroom; these were reviewed and summarized.

D. The client has not read the information about study skills and was redirected to do so.

12. Consult with Teachers (12)

A. Consultation was held with the client's teachers to implement strategies to improve school performance.

B. The client was assigned a seat near the teacher or in a low-distraction work area to help him/her remain on task.

C. The client, teacher, and therapist agreed to the use of a prearranged signal to redirect the client to task when his/her attention begins to wander.

D. The client's schedule was modified to allow for breaks between tasks or difficult assignments to help maintain attention and concentration.

E. The teachers were encouraged to obtain and provide frequent feedback to help maintain the client's attention, interest, and motivation.

F. The client was directed to arrange for a listening buddy.

13. Use "Getting It Done" Program (13)

A. The parents and teachers were encouraged to utilize a school contract and reward system to reinforce completion of the client's assignments.

B. The parents and teachers were given the "Getting It Done" program from the *Adolescent Psychotherapy Homework Planner,* 2nd ed. (Jongsma, Peterson, and McInnis) to help client complete his/her school and homework assignments regularly.

C. The parents and teachers were encouraged to utilize the school contract and reward system outlined in the "Getting It Done" program to reinforce the regular completion of school assignments.

D. The parents and teachers have used the school contract and reward system to reinforce the client's regular completion of school assignments, and the benefits of this program were reviewed.

E. The parents and teachers have not used the school contract and reward system to reinforce the client's regular completion of school assignments and were redirected to do so.

14. Teach Test-Taking Strategies (14)

A. The client and therapist reviewed a list of effective test-taking strategies to improve his/her academic performance.

B. The client was encouraged to review classroom material regularly and study for tests over an extended period of time.

C. The client was instructed to read the directions twice before responding to the questions on a test.

D. The client was taught to recheck his/her work to correct any careless mistakes or to improve an answer.

15. Teach Self-Control Strategies (15)

A. The client was taught mediational and self-control strategies (e.g., relaxation techniques, "stop, think, listen, and act") to help delay the need for immediate gratification and inhibit impulses.

B. The client was encouraged to utilize active-listening skills to delay the impulse to act out or react without considering the consequences of his/her actions.

C. The client was asked to identify the benefits of delaying his/her need for immediate gratification in favor of longer-term gains.

D. The client was assisted in developing an action plan to achieve longer-term goals.

16. Focus on Delay of Gratification (16)

A. The therapy session focused on helping the parents increase the structure in the home to help the client delay his/her needs for immediate gratification in order to achieve longer-term goals.

B. The parents were supported as they established the rule that the client is not permitted to engage in social, recreational, or leisure activities until completing his/her chores or homework.

C. The parents were supported as they identified consequences for the client's failure to complete responsibilities; client verbalized recognition of these consequences.

D. The client and parents were encouraged as they designed a schedule of dates and times when the client is expected to complete chores and homework.

17. Use Parent Management Training (17)

A. Parent Management Training was used, as developed in *Living with Children* (Patterson).

B. The parents were taught how parent-child behavioral interactions can encourage or discourage positive or negative behavior.

C. The parents were taught how changing key elements of parent-child interactions can promote positive change.

D. The parents were provided with specific examples of how prompting and reinforcing positive behaviors can promote positive change.

E. The parents were directed to review information from *Parenting the Strong-Willed Child* (Forehand and Long) and *Living with Children* (Patterson).

F. The parents were provided with positive feedback for the use of Parent Management Training approaches.

G. The parents have not used the Parent Management Training approach and were redirected to do so.

18. Teach Parents to Define Aspects of Situation (18)

A. The parents were taught how to specifically define and identify their child's problem behaviors.

B. The parents were taught how to identify their reactions to their child's behavior, and whether the reaction encourages or discourages the behavior.

C. The parents were taught to generate alternatives to their child's problem behavior.

D. Positive feedback was provided to the parents for their skill at specifically defining and identifying problem behaviors, reactions, outcomes, and alternatives.

E. Parents were provided with remedial feedback as they struggled to correctly identify their child's problem behaviors and their own reactions, responses, and alternatives.

19. Teach Consistent Parenting (19)

A. The parents were taught how to implement key parenting practices on a consistent basis.

B. The parents were taught about establishing realistic, age-appropriate rules for their child's acceptable and unacceptable behavior.

C. The parents were taught about prompting positive behavior and using positive reinforcement.

D. The parents were taught about clear, direct instruction as well as time out and other loss-of-privilege techniques for reducing their child's problem behaviors.

E. The parents were taught about negotiation and renegotiation with adolescents.

F. The parents were provided with positive feedback, as they have been able to develop consistent parenting practices.

G. The parents have not developed consistent parenting practices, and they were redirected to do so.

20. Assign Home Exercises to Implement Parenting Techniques (20)

A. The parents were assigned home exercises in which they implement parenting techniques and record results of the implementation exercises.

B. The parents were assigned "Clear Rules, Positive Reinforcement, Appropriate Consequences" in the *Adolescent Psychotherapy Homework Planner*, 2nd ed. (Jongsma, Peterson, and McInnis).

C. The parents' implementation of homework exercises was reviewed within the session.

D. Corrective feedback was used to help develop improved, appropriate, and consistent use of skills.

E. The parents have not completed the assigned homework and were redirected to do so.

21. Assign Parent Training Manuals (21)

A. The parents were directed to read parent training manuals.

B. The parents were directed to read *Parenting through Change* (Forgatch).

C. The parents were directed to watch videotapes demonstrating the techniques used in parent training sessions.

D. The parents' study of pertinent parent training media was reviewed and processed.

E. The parents have not reviewed the assigned parent training media and were redirected to do so.

22. Build Communication Skills (22)

A. Instruction, modeling, and role-playing techniques were used to help build the client's general social and communication skills.

B. The client was assisted in practicing general social and communication skills.

C. The client was reinforced for his/her increase in social and communication skills.

D. The client was redirected in areas in which he/she continues to struggle with communication and social skills.

23. Assign Books/Manuals on Building Social Skills (23)

A. The client was assigned to read about general social and/or communication skills in books or treatment manuals on building social skills.

B. The client was assigned to read *Your Perfect Right* (Alberti and Emmons).

C. The client was assigned to read *Conversationally Speaking* (Garner).

D. The client was assigned the "Social Skills Exercise" in the *Adolescent Psychotherapy Homework Planner,* 2nd ed. (Jongsma, Peterson, and McInnis).

E. Key points from the client's reading material were reviewed and processed.

F. The client has not read the assigned information on social and communication skills, and he/she was redirected to do so.

24. Teach Problem-Solving Skills (24)

A. The client was taught effective problem-solving skills (i.e., identify the problem, brainstorm alternate solutions, select an option, implement a course of action, and evaluate) in the therapy session.

B. The client was encouraged to use effective problem-solving strategies to solve or overcome a problem or stressor that he/she is currently facing.

C. The client was given a directive to use problem-solving strategies at home or school on at least three occasions before the next therapy session.

25. Assign "Stop, Think, and Act" Technique (25)

A. The client and parents were given the "Stop, Think, and Act" assignment from the *Adolescent Psychotherapy Homework Planner,* 2nd ed. (Jongsma, Peterson, and McInnis) to increase the client's ability to delay impulses and solve problems more effectively.

B. The client reported that he/she was able to successfully resolve a problem by following the problem-solving steps outlined in the "Stop, Think, and Act" assignment; feedback about the helpful techniques was provided.

26. Assign Parents to Read about Resolving Conflict (26)

A. The client's parents were directed to read information about resolving conflict with adolescents.

B. The parents were instructed to read *Negotiating Parent/Adolescent Conflict* (Robin and Foster) to help resolve conflict more effectively.

C. The parents verbalized that the book *Negotiating Parent/Adolescent Conflict* was helpful in identifying constructive ways to resolve conflict; the benefits of these techniques were reviewed.

D. The client's parents have not read the information about resolving conflict with adolescents and were redirected to do so.

27. Confront Behavior (27)

A. The client was firmly and consistently confronted with the fact that his/her impulsive behavior negatively affects himself/herself and others.

B. The client was asked to list the negative consequences of his/her impulsive behavior for both self and others.

C. Role-reversal techniques were used to help the client realize how his/her impulsive behavior negatively impacted others.

28. Teach Acceptance of Responsibility (28)

A. The client was consistently confronted and challenged to cease blaming others for his/her impulsive behavior and accept greater responsibility for his/her actions.

B. The client was asked to list how his/her poor decisions and impulsive actions resulted in negative consequences for himself/herself and others.

C. The client was assisted in identifying more effective ways to resolve conflict and/or meet his/her needs instead of acting out in an impulsive manner.

D. The client was instructed to apologize to others for the negative consequences of his/her impulsive actions.

E. The client has not taken responsibility for his/her actions and was redirected to do so.

29. Identify Trigger Events to Impulsivity (29)

A. The therapy session explored the stressful events or contributing factors that frequently lead to an increase in the client's hyperactivity, impulsivity, and distractibility.

B. The client was supported as he/she identified the stressful events or other factors that have contributed to an increase in his/her hyperactivity, impulsivity, and distractibility.

C. Role-playing and modeling techniques were used to teach appropriate ways to manage stress or resolve conflict more effectively.

D. The "Stop, Listen, Think, and Act" technique, relaxation techniques, and positive self-talk were taught to the client in order to help him/her manage stress more effectively.

E. The client and parents were assisted in identifying more effective coping strategies to manage stress or meet important needs instead of responding impulsively to a situation.

F. The client was unable to identify trigger events for impulsivity and was offered some examples in this area.

30. Explore Future Stressors or Roadblocks (30)

A. The client was helped to explore possible stressors, roadblocks, or hurdles that might cause impulsive and acting out behavior to increase in the future.

B. The client was supported as he/she identified successful coping strategies that could be used in the future when facing similar stressful events, roadblocks, or hurdles.

C. Guided imagery techniques were employed to help the client visualize how he/she can cope with potential problems or stressors in the future.

D. The client was encouraged to consult and/or enlist the support of family members or significant others when facing problems or stressors in the future.

31. Review Periods of Good Impulse Control (31)

A. The client was helped to identify periods when he/she demonstrated good impulse control in the past and engaged in significantly fewer impulsive behaviors.

B. The client was encouraged to use coping strategies similar to those used successfully in the past to control his/her impulses.

C. The therapy session revealed that the client exercised greater self-control and was better behaved during periods when he/she received strong family support and affiliated with positive peer groups.

32. Urge Parents to Reinforce Positive Behaviors (32)

A. The parents were instructed to observe and record three to five positive behaviors by the client between therapy sessions.

B. The parents were encouraged to reinforce the client for engaging in positive behaviors.

C. The client was strongly encouraged to continue to engage in positive behaviors to build self-esteem, gain parents' approval, and receive affirmation from others.

33. Encourage One-on-One Time with Parents (33)

A. The client and parents acknowledged that there have been many negative interactions between them in the recent past and were directed to the need to spend one-on-one time together to provide an opportunity for positive experiences.

B. The client and parents were instructed to spend 10 to 15 minutes of daily one-on-one time together to increase the frequency of positive interactions and improve the lines of communication.

C. The client and parents have spent 10 to 15 minutes of daily one-on-one time together, and the benefits of this were reviewed and processed.

D. The client and parents have not spent one-on-one time together and were redirected to do so.

34. Refer to ADHD Parental Support Group (34)

A. The parents were referred to an ADHD support group to increase their understanding and knowledge of ADHD symptoms.

B. The parents were asked how their participation in the ADHD support group has increased their understanding and knowledge of ADHD.

C. The parents reported that they have learned new strategies for dealing with the client's impulsive behavior through attending the ADHD support group.

35. Identify Strengths or Interests (35)

A. The client was given a homework assignment to identify 5 to 10 strengths or interests.
B. The client was assigned to complete the exercise "Show Your Strengths" in the *Adolescent Psychotherapy Homework Planner,* 2nd ed. (Jongsma, Peterson, and McInnis).
C. The client's interests or strengths were reviewed and he/she was encouraged to utilize strengths or interests to establish friendships.
D. The client has not completed the assignment to identify 5 to 10 strengths or interests and was redirected to do so.

36. Assign Demonstrations of Empathy and Kindness (36)

A. The client was given the homework assignment of performing three altruistic or caring acts before the next therapy session to increase his/her empathy and sensitivity to the thoughts, feelings, and needs of others.
B. The client was encouraged to volunteer in a community service organization or fund-raising activity to demonstrate empathy and concern for others.
C. Feedback was provided for the client as he/she described altruistic acts and demonstrations of empathy and kindness.
D. The client was unable to identify any demonstrations of empathy and kindness toward others and was redirected to complete these tasks.

37. Clarify Effects of High Energy Level (37)

A. The client was given a homework assignment to identify the positive and negative aspects of his/her high energy level.
B. The client completed his/her assigned homework and identified the positive and negative aspects of his/her high energy level.
C. The client was encouraged to channel his/her energy into healthy physical outlets and positive social activities.

38. Use Art Therapy Technique (38)

A. The client was instructed to draw a picture reflecting his/her feelings about what it is like to have ADHD.
B. The client was instructed to draw a series of pictures reflecting the positive and negative aspects of ADHD.
C. After completing the drawing of what it is like to have ADHD, the client was asked to identify the positive changes he/she would like to make in his/her life.
D. After completing the drawing of what it is like to have ADHD, the client was asked to identify constructive ways to channel his/her energy.

AUTISM/PERVASIVE DEVELOPMENTAL DISORDER

CLIENT PRESENTATION

1. Aloof/Unresponsive (1)*
A. The client presented in an aloof, unresponsive manner.
B. The client showed virtually no interest in the counseling process or in even small interactions with the therapist.
C. All attempts to connect with the client were met with no discernable response.
D. The client has begun to respond in small ways to the therapist's interaction attempts.

2. Detached/Uninterested (1)
A. The client presented in a detached manner with no interest in others outside of self.
B. The parents reported a history of pervasive uninterest in other people.
C. The client has started to acknowledge others on a somewhat consistent basis.
D. The client has shown more interest in relating with the therapist in sessions.

3. Social Connectedness (2)
A. The client has little or no interest in social relationships.
B. The parents indicate that from an early age the client has not shown interest in friendships or other social connections.
C. With encouragement, the client has started to interact on a limited basis with a selected peer.
D. The client has started to show somewhat more interest in connecting with the therapist, family members, and selected peers.

4. Nonverbal/Rigid (3)
A. The client's general manner is rigid and nonverbal.
B. The parents indicate that the client rarely verbalizes unless he/she is disturbed or upset.
C. The client has started to talk at intervals with the therapist in sessions.
D. Both with the parents and with the therapist, the client has begun to verbalize on a regular basis on his/her own initiative.

5. Lack of Social/Emotional Spontaneity (3)
A. The client exhibits virtually no spontaneity, in either mood or behavior.
B. When others show emotions, the client remains unchanged.
C. The client at times has shown glimmers of spontaneity.

---

*The numbers in parentheses correlate to the number of the Behavioral Definition statement in the companion chapter with the same title in *The Adolescent Psychotherapy Treatment Planner,* Fourth Edition (Jongsma, Peterson, McInnis, and Bruce) by John Wiley & Sons, 2006.

6. Language Deficits (4)

A. The parents reported significant delays in the client's language development.

B. The client has developed only a few words and is far below developmental language expectations.

C. The client engages in very limited verbalizations with the therapist during sessions.

D. There has been a slight but significant increase in the client's skill in and use of language with others.

7. Conversation Deficits (5)

A. The parents reported significant delays in the client's language development.

B. The parents reported that the client has never demonstrated conversational skills with family members.

C. The parents reported that the client has given brief responses to their inquiries on occasion.

D. The parents report a slight increase in instances of the client initiating a conversation and consistent single-word responses to their initiatives.

8. Speech and Language Oddities (6)

A. The client presented with a variety of speech oddities such as echolalia and pronominal reversal.

B. Metaphorical language was used as the primary speech pattern throughout the therapy session.

C. The client echoed every sound and word he/she heard while with the therapist.

D. The parents indicated that the client's language oddities have increased and intensified as he/she has grown older.

E. The parents reported that all their efforts and those of professionals to interrupt and advance the client's speech patterns have been frustrating and nonproductive.

F. The speech oddities of the client have decreased as he/she has started to communicate with others in a didactic manner.

9. Inflexible/Repetitive Behavior (7)

A. The behavioral patterns of the client are entirely inflexible and repetitive.

B. The parents report that the client becomes upset if his/her behavioral routine is changed or interrupted.

C. The client has started to decrease his/her repetitive behaviors and seems more open to trying some different activities.

10. Preoccupied/Focused (8)

A. The client appears to be preoccupied nearly all the time and focused on narrowly selected objects or areas of interest.

B. It is nearly impossible to intrude on the client's preoccupation or break his/her focus.

C. The client has started to allow others to interrupt his/her preoccupation and focus.

D. The client is now less focused and preoccupied on any one thing and is open to new outside stimulants.

11. Impaired Intellectual/Cognitive Functioning (9)

A. There appears to be marked impairment in the client's intellectual and cognitive functioning.

B. The parents indicate that it is difficult to follow and understand the client's thought process.

C. The client's thinking appears unaffected by the thinking and feedback of others.

D. The client has begun to show some positive adjustments in his/her cognitive functioning.

12. Intellectual Variability (9)

A. The client showed severe deficits in language-related intellectual abilities but significant advances in other, very focused, areas such as numerical recall.

B. The client's drawing and memory abilities are superior, whereas language skills are severely limited.

C. The client shows extreme variability in intellectual skills.

13. Resistant to Change (10)

A. The client is resistant to outside stimulation and attempts to engage him/her.

B. The parents and teachers report that the client is very resistant to any changes in his/her daily schedule, routine, or behaviors.

C. The client has started to tolerate small changes in his/her routine without becoming resistant.

D. The client is now trying new things with the therapist without any show of resistance.

14. Flat Affect (11)

A. There is a continual flatness to the client's affect.

B. The parents report that the client shows more than flat affect only on rare occasions.

C. The client has begun to show more affect in interacting with the therapist.

D. The client's range of affect has slowly started to expand.

15. Self-Abuse (12)

A. The client has exhibited a pattern of self-abusive behavior such as head banging and hitting self.

B. The parents report that the client becomes self-abusive when he/she is frustrated in any way.

C. The client has decreased the frequency of his/her episodes of self-abuse.

INTERVENTIONS IMPLEMENTED

1. Assess Cognitive/Intellectual Functioning (1)*

A. An intellectual and cognitive assessment was conducted on the client to determine his/her strengths and weaknesses.

*The numbers in parentheses correlate to the number of the Therapeutic Inervention statement in the companion chapter with the same title in *The Adolescent Psychotherapy Treatment Planner,* Fourth Edition (Jongsma, Peterson, McInnis, and Bruce) by John Wiley & Sons, 2006.

B. The client was uncooperative and resistive in the assessment process and was encouraged to be more open to the evaluation.

C. With the parents' assistance, the client was moderately cooperative with the assessor.

D. Feedback was provided to the parents and the client regarding the results of the intellectual and cognitive assessments.

2. Refer for Speech/Language Evaluation (2)

A. The client was referred for a speech and language evaluation.

B. The client was praised for his/her cooperation throughout the entire speech and language evaluation process.

C. Due to client resistance, the speech and language evaluation could not be completed.

D. With urging from the parents and the therapist, the client followed through with the speech and language evaluation with only minimal resistance.

E. The results from the speech and language evaluation were shared with the client and his/her parents.

3. Refer for Neurological/Neuropsychological Evaluation (3)

A. The client was referred for neuropsychological testing to rule out organic factors.

B. With parent encouragement, the client followed through with and completed the neurological evaluation.

C. Neuropsychological testing could not be completed because the client was not cooperative.

D. The parents were helped to see the need for neuropsychological testing.

E. The results of the neurological evaluation or neuropsychological testing were reviewed with the client and his/her parents.

4. Refer for Psychiatric Evaluation (4)

A. The client was referred for a psychiatric evaluation.

B. With the parents' assistance, the client followed through with and completed the psychiatric evaluation.

C. A psychiatric evaluation could not be completed as the client was uncooperative and nonverbal.

D. The parents were supported as they made a verbal commitment to follow through on the recommendations of the psychiatric evaluation.

E. The client has not been psychiatrically evaluated, and his/her parents were redirected in this area.

5. Complete an IEPC (5)

A. The parents were asked to request an IEPC for the client to become eligible to receive special education services.

B. The IEPC meeting was attended by the parents, teachers, therapist, and other interested professionals.

C. Goals and interventions for the client's educational program were revised by the IEPC to enhance the success of the client in the school setting.

6. Design Effective Teaching Program (6)

A. The parents, teachers, and school officials were consulted for their input in designing an effective teaching program for the client.

B. Specific educational/behavioral interventions and assignments were identified that would build on the client's strengths and compensate for his/her weaknesses.

C. The parents and teacher assisted the therapist in designing and implementing an effective teaching program with the client.

D. The designed teaching plan was monitored for its effectiveness in building the client's strengths.

E. The client's parents, teachers, and school officials have not implemented the effective teaching program for the client and were redirected to do so.

7. Explore Need for Alternative Placement (7)

A. The parents, school officials, and mental health professionals were consulted regarding the client's need for an alternative placement outside the home.

B. Placement options were explored with the parents and the client.

C. Measures short of alternative placement that were recommended by mental health professionals were implemented by the parents.

D. An alternative placement was located for the client and a plan for him/her to move into it was developed.

8. Refer for Speech/Language Therapy (8)

A. The client was referred to a speech and language pathologist.

B. The parents and the client have followed through on the referral and have been regularly attending speech therapy sessions.

C. The client has been cooperative in speech and language therapy, and those skills are noted to be improving.

D. Speech therapy has been deemed ineffective, as the client remains uncooperative and resistant.

9. Build Trust (9)

A. Frequent attention, unconditional positive regard, and consistent eye contact were used to build a level of trust with the client.

B. An initial level of trust has been established with the client as he/she has increased verbalization with the therapist.

C. Despite use of warm acceptance, frequent attention, and unconditional positive regard, the client remains detached and rarely communicates directly with the therapist.

10. Increase Initiation of Verbalizations (10)

A. Praise and positive reinforcement were frequently used to attempt to increase the client's initiation of verbalization.

B. The use of praise and positive reinforcement has been successful in increasing the client's acknowledgment of and responsiveness to other's verbalizations.

C. Despite frequent praise and positive reinforcement, the client initiates verbalizations with others only on rare occasions.

11. Support Parental Language Development Efforts (11)

A. Encouragement, support, and reinforcement were given to the parents in their efforts to foster the client's language development.

B. Various modeling methods were demonstrated to the parents to aid them in their work in fostering the client's language development.

C. The parents' efforts in fostering language development in the client have produced noticeable gains; the benefits of these gains were reviewed.

D. Gains in language development were encouraged and reinforced with the client and the parents.

E. The parents have not used the demonstrated methods to foster the client's language development and were redirected to do so.

12. Facilitate Language Development (12)

A. The speech therapist assisted in designing and implementing a response-shaping program for the client that incorporates positive reinforcement principles.

B. The parents were trained in the response-shaping program and are implementing it with the client in their daily family life.

C. The client has cooperated with the response-shaping program and its positive reinforcement principle, and this has resulted in significant gains in his/her language skills and a decrease in speech and language peculiarities.

D. The client has minimally embraced the response-shaping program, and this has resulted in only small gains in his/her language development; he/she was encouraged to increase his/her involvement in the program.

13. Teach Behavior Management Techniques (13)

A. Behavioral management techniques were taught to the parents to assist them in handling the client's difficult behaviors.

B. Plans were developed with the parents for implementing behavioral management techniques in their day-to-day parenting of the client.

C. Role-playing and behavioral rehearsal techniques were used with the parents to give them the opportunity to practice new skills.

D. The parents were verbally reinforced for their consistent use of behavioral techniques.

E. Behavioral management techniques were reinforced and evaluated for their effectiveness with the client.

F. The parents have not used the behavior management techniques on a consistent basis and were redirected to do so.

14. Design Token Economy (14)

A. The parents were assisted in designing a token economy and planning how to implement and administrate it.

B. The token economy was monitored for its effectiveness and to make any necessary adjustments.

C. The parents' effective, consistent implementation and administration of the token economy were reinforced with praise and encouragement.

D. The client's embracing of the token economy was noted to produce improvement in his/her social skills, anger management, impulse control, and language development.

E. The client has resisted cooperating with the token economy system and was redirected to do so.

15. Create Parental Reward System (15)

A. A reward system was developed to assist the client in improving his/her social skills and anger control.

B. The parents were asked to make a verbal commitment to implementing and administering a reward system.

C. Rewards have had mixed results on the client's social skills and anger control.

16. Stop Self-Abuse with Aversive Techniques (16)

A. Aversive therapy techniques were used with the client to decrease self-abusive and self-stimulating behavior.

B. The parents were trained in the proper use of aversive techniques and encouraged to implement them in their daily parenting.

C. Role-play was used with the parents to give them the opportunity to practice aversive techniques.

D. Self-abusive behaviors have decreased due to the use of aversive techniques.

17. Stop Self-Abuse with Positive Reinforcement (17)

A. The parents were assisted in developing positive reinforcement interventions to manage self-abusive behaviors.

B. The interventions developed by the parents to terminate the client's self-abuse were implemented and monitored for their effectiveness.

C. New interventions of positive reinforcement and response cost have reduced the client's self-abuse behaviors.

D. The parents' effective interventions on self-abusive behavior were affirmed and reinforced.

E. The parents have not used positive reinforcement on a regular basis and were redirected to do so.

18. Educate Family on Developmental Disabilities (18)

A. The parents and family members were educated on the maturation process in individuals with autism and pervasive development disorders.

B. Challenges in the maturation process for the client were identified and processed with the parents and family members.

C. Unrealistic maturation expectations of parents and family members were confronted and addressed.

D. Realistic hope and encouragement were reinforced with respect to the client's maturation and development.

19. Refer to Autism Society of America (19)

A. The parents were directed and encouraged to join the Autism Society of America to expand their knowledge of the disorder and to gain support and encouragement.

B. The parents have received helpful interaction and gained support and encouragement from their contact with the Autism Society of America.

C. The parents remain hesitant and noncommittal in seeking out support services; support was provided to the parents regarding investigating these services.

20. Refer to Support Group (20)

A. The parents' opinions and feelings about support groups were explored.

B. The parents were referred to and encouraged to attend a support group for families of an individual with a developmental disability.

C. Attentive listening was used as the parents described having attended an autism/developmental disability support group and indicated that they found the experience positive and helpful.

D. Despite encouragement, the parents have continued to be resistive to any involvement in an autism/developmental disability support group.

21. Use Respite Care (21)

A. Options for respite care were given and explained to the parents.

B. Advantages to using respite care were identified, and the parents were encouraged to use this resource regularly.

C. Resistance by the parents to respite care was confronted and resolved.

D. The parents were asked to develop a regular schedule for respite care.

22. Encourage Self-Care Skills (22)

A. Various ways to teach and develop self-care skills were processed with the parents.

B. The parents were reinforced for committing to actively working with the client on a daily basis to teach and develop his/her self-care skills.

C. The parents' work with the client has produced significant gains in the client's hygiene and other self-care skills, and they were encouraged to continue.

D. The parents have not regularly taught the client self-care skills and were redirected to do so.

23. Monitor Self-Care Progress (23)

A. The client's progress in developing self-care skills was monitored, and frequent feedback was provided to reinforce his/her progress.

B. Positive feedback on the client's achievement in self-care skills was verbally acknowledged by the client.

C. The parents were encouraged to keep working toward and reinforcing the client's progress in the area of self-care skills.

D. The client's resistance toward developing self-care skills has decreased, and he/she was encouraged for his/her daily hygiene improvement.

24. Assist in Developing Self-Help Skills (24)

A. Operant conditioning principles were used to assist the client in developing self-help skills.

B. Response-shaping techniques were used to assist the client in learning skills for independent living (e.g., dressing self, making bed, making a sandwich, improving personal hygiene).

C. Operant conditioning and response-shaping techniques have been useful in teaching the client to learn skills for independent living.

D. Despite the use of operant conditioning and response-shaping techniques, the client has not learned self-help skills.

25. Assess Family's Emotional Reaction to the Disorder (25)

A. A family therapy session was conducted to provide the parents and siblings with the opportunity to share their feelings pertaining to the client's pervasive developmental disorder.

B. Family members were assisted in working through their feelings about the client's pervasive developmental disorder.

26. Build Trust and Mutual Dependence (26)

A. A task was assigned to the client and the parents to foster trust and mutual dependence.

B. The parents and client were assisted in identifying activities they could do at home to build trust and mutual dependence.

C. It was noted that a level of trust is building between the parents and the client as they continue to follow through on engaging in activities together regularly.

D. The client's parents have not followed through on participating in a structured task with the client and were redirected to do so.

27. Encourage Structured Family Interaction (27)

A. The family was encouraged to include structured work and playtimes with the client in their daily routine.

B. Positive feedback was provided as the parents developed and implemented structured work and playtimes with the client.

C. Structured playtimes and work times have improved the client's social initiation and interest in others; the continued use of these techniques was emphasized.

D. The family has not used structured interaction times with the client and was redirected to do so.

28. Involve Detached Parent (28)

A. Ways to involve the detached parent in interaction with the client were explored with the detached parent.

B. The detached parent was asked to spend _____ minutes (fill in number) daily with the client in social or physical interaction.

C. Despite efforts to increase his/her involvement, the detached parent has become only slightly more involved.

D. The detached parent was reminded of the importance of his/her involvement in the client's growth and development.

29. Redirect Preoccupation (29)

A. The client's preoccupation with objects and restricted areas of interest was redirected to more productive and socially involved activities.

B. The client's willingness and cooperation in trying new activities were affirmed and positively reinforced.

C. The client has accepted redirection and become actively engaged in several productive activities.

D. The client was reminded and redirected when he/she started becoming preoccupied again with objects.

30. Use Applied Behavior Analysis to Alter Maladaptive Behavior (30)

A. Applied behavior analysis concepts were used in the home, school, or residential setting to alter maladaptive behaviors.

B. Target behaviors were defined and operationally identified.

C. Antecedents and consequences were identified for specific behaviors.

D. The client's responses to reinforcement interventions were observed and recorded.

E. Data were analyzed to assess behavior modification treatment effectiveness.

31. Increase Social Contacts (31)

A. Consultation was held with the client's parents and teachers about increasing the frequency of his/her social contacts with his/her peers.

B. Specific opportunities for increased social contact were reviewed with the client's parents and teachers (e.g., working with a student aide in class, attending Sunday school, participating in Special Olympics).

C. The client and his/her parents and teachers have been consulted and agreed to increase social contacts between the client and his/her peers; a schedule for these contacts was established.

D. The client's parents and teachers have been unwilling to increase social contacts between the client and his/her peers and were provided with additional encouragement in this area.

32. Refer to Camp (32)

A. The client was referred to a summer camp to promote independence and to foster social contacts.

B. The client's camp experience was processed, and the client's accomplishments in making social contacts were acknowledged and reinforced.

33. Refer for Vocational Training (33)

A. The client was referred to a vocational training program to develop basic job skills.

B. The client was cooperative in following through with his/her vocational training interview, and this was reflected to him/her.

C. The positive aspects of a job training program were explored and reinforced with the client and the parents.

34. Facilitate Family Review of Vocational Training (34)

A. The family was assisted in arranging interviews with school-based vocational programs.

B. The family followed through with the scheduled interviews, and these were reviewed.

C. The family was assisted in processing the possible program for the client and reached a consensus on which program they felt was the best for him/her.

35. Enhance Independent Living Skills (35)

A. The client was referred to a life skills program to acquire the skills to live independently.

B. The client has started to attend a life skills program to learn things necessary for independent activities of daily living (IADL).

C. The client has become actively involved in a life skills program and is developing the skills to live independently.

36. Address Family Resistance to Client Emancipation (36)

A. The parents were asked to make a list of concerns they have about the client living independently.

B. The parents' list of concerns about the client's emancipation was processed, and feelings concerning independence were identified and expressed.

C. The parents' concerns have been addressed, and the parents are starting to feel comfortable about the client living independently.

D. Concerns about the client's living independently were explored and processed; however, the parents remain fearful and resistant to such a move.

37. Develop Step Plan toward Independence (37)

A. The parents were assisted in developing a step program that will move the client toward living and working independently.

B. As the time approaches for a step program to be implemented that would make the client more independent, the parents have become less anxious about him/her living independently.

38. Implement Step Plan for Independence (38)

A. The parents are being guided and encouraged in implementing a plan for the client's independent living.

B. The parents' follow-through plan for client's independence was monitored.

C. Encouragement was given to the client and the parents as they moved through the stages of progress toward independent living.

D. Parental resistance to working out the step plan for client independence was confronted and addressed.

39. Assess Independent Living Possibilities (39)

A. The family was assisted in exploring all the possible options of independent living arrangements.

B. Each independent living arrangement was visited and assessed for suitability to the client's needs and level of functioning.

C. The family was assisted in reaching a decision on the choice of independent living arrangements for the client.

BLENDED FAMILY

CLIENT PRESENTATION

1. Angry/Hostile (1)*
A. Anger and hostility have dominated the client's manner since the parents have blended their two families.
B. The client was extremely angry and hostile about having to be a part of the new blended family.
C. The client's level of anger and hostility has started to diminish as he/she has accepted being a part of the new blended family.
D. The client has dropped his/her anger and hostility and has become a cooperative member of the blended family.

2. Frustrated/Tense (1)
A. There was a deep sense of frustration and tension present in the client as he/she talked of the blended family situation.
B. The client reported being frustrated and tense about feeling pushed into a new blended family.
C. The client's level of tension has subsided as he/she is feeling more comfortable with the idea of being a part of a stepfamily.

3. Resistant toward Stepparent (2)
A. The client presented in a defiant manner toward the stepparent.
B. In a defiant way, the client reported that he/she will have no part of the new stepparent.
C. The client threatened to make it difficult for the new stepparent.
D. The client has dropped some of his/her resistance and seems to be warming a little to the new stepparent.

4. Defiant of Stepparent (2)
A. The client showed a pattern of making alliances and causing conflicts in an attempt to have a degree of control over the new stepparent.
B. The client reported no interest in taking direction or accepting limits from the stepparent.
C. Gradually, the client has begun to give up his/her rebellion toward the stepparent and to accept some direction from him/her.

5. Stepsibling Conflict (3)
A. The siblings have engaged in ongoing conflict with one another.
B. The two sibling groups stated clearly their dislike of and resentment toward one another.

*The numbers in parentheses correlate to the number of the Behavioral Definition statement in the companion chapter with the same title in *The Adolescent Psychotherapy Treatment Planner,* Fourth Edition (Jongsma, Peterson, McInnis, and Bruce) by John Wiley & Sons, 2006.

C. The parents indicated their frustration with the siblings' apparent attempt to sabotage their efforts to form a new family group.

D. The two sibling groups have stopped their open conflicts and started to tolerate and show basic respect for each other.

6. Defiance of Stepparent (4)

A. The client presented a negativistic, defiant attitude toward the stepparent.

B. The client seemed very closed and extremely resistant to the new stepparent.

C. The limited disclosures by the client reflected strong resistance to joining the new blended family.

D. The client has started to warm to and be a little more open to the idea of being a member of the new blended family.

7. Threats of Moving to Other Parent's House (5)

A. The parents reported feeling like hostages to siblings' threats to move to the other parents' homes whenever the children were crossed or told no.

B. The siblings presented as being ambivalent and manipulative regarding where they would like to live and why.

C. The siblings indicated that they have changed their minds several times regarding where they want to reside and are presently still undecided.

D. The siblings have decreased their threats of going to the other parents' homes and have started to join the new family unit.

8. Ex-Spouse Interference (6)

A. Both spouses reported frequent incidents of interference in their new family by their ex-spouses.

B. Ex-spouse interference has caused ongoing conflict and upheaval in the new family unit.

C. Efforts to keep ex-spouses out of the new family's business have been unsuccessful and sabotaged by the siblings.

D. Efforts to keep ex-spouses out of the daily life of the new family have started to be effective, and the new family has started to solidify and become connected.

9. Parental Anxiety (7)

A. The client's parents presented with anxiety about the blending of their two families.

B. The parents seemed unsure about how to respond to issues being raised by the new blended family.

C. The parents looked for reassurance and some sense of security about how best to respond to blended family issues.

D. Parental anxiety has decreased as both parties have become more comfortable with working toward forming a new blended family.

10. Lack of Responsibility Definitions (8)

A. The family presented as very chaotic, lacking clear boundaries, rules, and responsibility definitions for members.

B. The parents reported that they have struggled in their attempts to establish clear definitions of expectations for responsibility for family members.

C. Siblings indicated that they are not clear about their roles, responsibilities, or expectations in their new family.

D. The family has begun to develop and institute clear areas of responsibility for all members, which has also reduced the chaos and confusion for all.

11. Internal Loyalty Conflicts (9)

A. The client demonstrated ambivalence and uncertainty about whether to attach himself/herself to the stepparent.

B. The client verbalized loyalty toward the biological, noncustodial parent.

C. The client reported fearing hurting the feelings of the biological, noncustodial parent if he/she made an attachment to the stepparent.

D. Internal conflicts have been resolved, and a sense of loyalty and belonging is beginning to develop between the client and stepparent.

INTERVENTIONS IMPLEMENTED

1. Build Trust and Express Feelings (1)*

A. Warm acceptance and active listening techniques were utilized to establish the basis for a trust relationship with the client.

B. The client seems to have formed a trust-based relationship with the therapist and has started to share his/her feelings.

C. Despite the use of active listening, warm acceptance, and unconditional positive regard, the client and family appear to be hesitant to trust the therapist and share their feelings and conflicts.

2. Address Family and Marital Issues (2)

A. Family sessions were conducted that focused on addressing and facilitating relationship building and joining rituals.

B. Each family member was asked to make a list of his/her recent losses to share with other members in a family session.

C. The parents were educated in the dynamics of stepfamilies and how they work.

D. Conflict negotiation skills were taught to family members and practiced in role-play situations particular to stepfamilies.

E. It was identified that family members have gained information and understanding about stepfamilies, learning to use negotiation skills and building relationships with each other.

F. Despite attempts to address family and marital issues, conflicts continue to occur on a frequent basis.

---

* The numbers in parentheses correlate to the number of the Therapeutic Intervention statement in the companion chapter with the same title in *The Adolescent Psychotherapy Treatment Planner,* Fourth Edition (Jongsma, Peterson, McInnis, and Bruce) by John Wiley & Sons, 2006.

3. Assign Cooperative Family Drawing (3)

A. Each family member took part in interpreting and listening to others' interpretations of a drawing that was made through the cooperative effort of all family members.

B. All family members were willing to take part in making the family drawing but were resistant to interpreting it.

C. The family drawing exercise revealed that the family members have a very difficult time cooperating with each other, as there was resistance to the exercise and bickering within the family during the exercise.

4. List Expectations for New Family (4)

A. Each family member was asked to list his/her expectations for the new family.

B. Each family member's list or expectations regarding the future of the blended family was shared and processed in family session, with common realistic expectations being affirmed and reinforced.

C. Unrealistic expectations of family members were gently confronted and reframed into more realistic and attainable expectations.

5. Remind Family That Instant Love Is a Myth (5)

A. The family was reminded of the myth of "instant love" between new members.

B. Family members' expectations of instant love and connections between blended family members were confronted with the reality that time is necessary for relationships to grow.

C. All the family members have become more realistic regarding the time necessary for meaningful relationships to develop between them, and this was noted to be a healthy response.

D. Although the family members have been reminded that instant love is a myth, they continue to expect an immediate harmonious relationship.

6. Reinforce Kindness and Respect (6)

A. The family was reminded that new members need not love or like each other but that they need to treat each other with kindness and respect.

B. Family members were confronted when they failed to treat each other with kindness and respect.

C. The parents were taught ways to model respect and kindness for all members and to confront and give consequences for disrespectful interactions.

D. It was noted that there is a discernable growth of respect and consideration between new family members that is being positively reinforced by the parents.

7. List Losses and Changes (7)

A. Each sibling was asked to make a list of all the losses and changes he/she had experienced in the last year.

B. Each sibling's list of losses was shared with other family members, and similarities between each list were identified.

C. Reviewing each sibling's list of losses enhanced the degree of understanding and the feeling of similarity between the siblings.

8. Read Changing Families (8)

A. The family was asked to read *Changing Families* (Fassler, Lash, and Ives) to identify and reinforce the recent changes each of them has experienced in family life.

B. The family members struggled to identify the losses and changes that each of them had experienced even after reading *Changing Families.*

C. The family was reminded that change is an opportunity to grow and thrive, not just survive.

D. After reading *Changing Families,* the family members have a better understanding of the difficult process they have gone through recently in forming the blended family.

E. The family members have not read *Changing Families* and were redirected to do so.

9. Play Games to Promote Self-Understanding (9)

A. The family was directed to play either The Ungame (Ungame Company) or The Thinking, Feeling, and Doing Game (Gardner) to increase members' awareness of self and their feelings.

B. Expressions of self-awareness and identification of feelings were reinforced in family sessions.

C. The family members were very uncomfortable during the playing of therapeutic games together, and most of them had significant difficulty in identifying and expressing feelings; additional encouragement was provided.

10. Educate Family Regarding Feelings (10)

A. The family was taught the basic concepts regarding identifying, labeling, and appropriately expressing their feelings.

B. Through the use of role-playing and modeling, each family member was assisted in identifying, labeling, and expressing his/her feelings in family sessions.

C. Family members were prompted when they ignored or skipped over their feelings in dealing with family issues.

11. Practice Identifying and Expressing Feelings (11)

A. Various feelings exercises were used with the family to help expand their ability to identify and express feelings.

B. Positive affirmation was given to family members when they identified and expressed their feelings appropriately.

C. Each family member was confronted and reminded when he/she was not identifying and expressing his/her feelings.

12. Read Books on Blended Families (12)

A. It was suggested to the parents and the teen that they read material to expand their knowledge of step families and their development.

B. The parents and teens were asked to read all or sections of *Stepfamily Realities* (Newman) and *Stepfamilies Stepping Ahead* (Burt) to expand their knowledge of stepfamily dynamics.

C. The parents and teens were encouraged to talk with other stepfamilies and to gather knowledge of their experience, past and present.

D. Parents and teens were asked to make a list of questions they had about stepfamilies and to process the list with the therapist.

E. Reading books on blended families and talking to other people who have experienced successful blending of families has helped members gather information and develop understanding of the blending process.

F. The parents and teen have not read the assigned books on blended families and were redirected to do so.

13. Refer to Stepfamily Association (13)

A. The parents were referred to the Stepfamily Association of America in order to gather information on the process of blending families.

B. Information gathered from the Stepfamily Association of America was processed and incorporated into a more realistic view of the reality of stepfamilies.

C. The reality of stepfamilies not being inferior to regular families, just different, was introduced along with the new information the parents received from Stepfamily Association of America.

D. The parents have not followed through on obtaining further information from the Stepfamily Association of America and were again encouraged to do so.

14. Read *How to Win as a Stepfamily* (14)

A. The parents were asked to read *How to Win as a Stepfamily* (Visher and Visher).

B. Key concepts from the parents' reading of *How to Win as a Stepfamily* were identified and reinforced.

C. Several ideas learned from reading *How to Win as a Stepfamily* were implemented by the parents in their present situations.

D. The parents have not completed the assignment to read the book *How to Win as a Stepfamily* and were encouraged to do so.

15. Build Negotiating Skills (15)

A. The family members were taught essential negotiating skills.

B. Role-play was utilized to give family members the opportunity to practice new skills in negotiating conflicts.

C. Family members tried out their new negotiation skills in a family session on a present family conflict.

D. The family struggled to maintain negotiating skills in the family sessions, and they often reverted to arguing and attacking each other.

16. Assign "Negotiating a Peace Treaty" Exercise (16)

A. The siblings were asked to specify their conflicts and suggest solutions.

B. The siblings were asked to complete and process the "Negotiating a Peace Treaty" exercise from the *Adolescent Psychotherapy Homework Planner,* 2nd ed. (Jongsma, Peterson, and McInnis).

C. Through the use of the "Negotiating a Peace Treaty" exercise, the clients were assisted in identifying their conflicts and exploring a variety of solutions.

D. The siblings were asked to select, commit to, and implement one of the solutions they identified in the negotiation exercise.

E. The siblings' completion of the negotiation exercise revealed how far they are from having any common ground, and this was reflected to them.

17. Use Humor to Decrease Tension (17)

A. Humor was injected into sessions when it was appropriate to decrease tension and to model balance and perspective.

B. Family members were directed to each tell one joke daily to other family members.

C. Positive feedback was given to family members who created appropriate humor during a session.

D. It was reflected to the family members that they have extreme difficulty being light and humorous toward each other, as tension levels are high and teasing is reacted to angrily.

18. Use "Cloning the Perfect Sibling" Exercise (18)

A. A family sibling session was held in which each child was asked to list and verbalize an appreciation of each sibling's unique traits and abilities.

B. Siblings were asked to complete the "Cloning the Perfect Sibling" exercise from the *Adolescent Psychotherapy Homework Planner,* 2nd ed. (Jongsma, Peterson, and McInnis).

C. In processing the cloning exercise, siblings were assisted in identifying and affirming the positive aspects of individual differences.

D. Siblings continued to argue and bicker with each other, complaining about unique traits and characteristics despite the use of the cloning exercise.

19. Normalize Conflict as a Stage (19)

A. A brief solution-focused intervention was utilized with the family to normalize conflict as a stage.

B. Family members were assisted in identifying the next stage after conflict and determining how they might begin to move in that direction.

C. The intervention of normalizing the conflict as a stage has, according to family reports, reduced the frequency of conflicts.

D. The family was unwilling to embrace any reframing or normalizing interventions.

20. Read *Stone Soup* (20)

A. *Stone Soup* (Brown) was read and processed with family.

B. After reading *Stone Soup,* the family members were asked to list all the possible positive things that come about when people cooperate and share.

21. Read *The Sneetches* (21)

A. *The Sneetches* (Seuss) was read and discussed with family.

B. The folly of perceiving people as top dog/low dog and insider/outsider was seeded with family members.

C. Family members were asked to list each way they felt better than or superior to new members.

22. Emphasize Primary Parenting Role for Biological Parent (22)

A. The parents were educated in the positive aspects of each biological parent taking the main role with the children.

B. The parents were assisted in developing ways to redirect the parenting of the stepchildren.

C. The parents were asked to refrain from all negative references to ex-spouses.

D. Incidents of a parent making negative references to ex-spouses were confronted and processed.

23. Refer to Parenting Group (23)

A. The parents were referred to a parenting group designed for stepparents.

B. The parents were assisted in implementing new concepts that were learned from the parenting group.

C. The parents were confronted on their poor attendance at the stepparenting group.

24. Institute Family Meeting (24)

A. The parents were assisted in developing a process for and scheduling a weekly family meeting.

B. Family meetings were monitored and the parents were assisted in solving conflictual issues.

C. The parents were given positive verbal support and encouragement for their follow-through on implementing weekly family meetings.

D. The parents have not followed through on implementing regularly scheduled meetings, and a commitment for this scheduling was obtained from them.

25. Develop Family Rituals (25)

A. The positive aspects of family rituals were taught to the parents.

B. The parents were asked to develop a list of possible rituals for their new family unit.

C. The parents were assisted in selecting family rituals and developing a plan for their implementation.

D. Family rituals were monitored for their implementation and effectiveness.

E. Verbal affirmation and encouragement were given to the parents for their effort to implement and enforce new family rituals.

26. Select Past Family Rituals (26)

A. Members were asked to make a list of rituals that were followed in their previous family.

B. Rituals from previous families were discussed, and key rituals were chosen to implement in the new family.

C. Plans were developed to implement the chosen rituals from previous families.

D. Family members were assisted in establishing the new rituals and making the necessary adjustments to increase their effectiveness.

27. Create Birthday Rituals (27)

A. The family was given the assignment of creating new birthday rituals for the new family.

B. The parents were asked to implement the new birthday rituals at the first opportunity.

C. The value of birthday rituals was reinforced with the parents.

D. A new birthday ritual has been implemented, and the family members have responded very favorably to this recognition of their special status.

E. New birthday rituals have not been developed by the family, and they were redirected to complete this task.

28. Teach Patterns of Family Interactions (28)

A. The parents were taught key aspects and patterns of family interaction.

B. Past family interaction patterns were explored and identified, with a special focus on those involving triangulation.

C. The parents were assisted in blocking patterns of triangulation that are occurring within the family.

D. The episodes of triangulation within the family have diminished significantly.

E. The parents have not identified patterns of triangulation within the family and were provided with tentative examples of how this occurs.

29. Refer for Marital Therapy (29)

A. The parents were referred to a skills-based marital therapy program.

B. Gains made in marital therapy were affirmed and reinforced with the parents.

C. The parents were asked to identify the gains they achieved in the skills-based therapy program and how they would improve parenting.

D. The parents have not obtained marital therapy and were urged again to do so.

30. Identify Individual Parental Needs (30)

A. The parents were assisted in exploring and identifying their individual needs within the relationship and family.

B. The needs of each partner were recognized and affirmed, and plans were developed for meeting these needs on a consistent basis.

C. The parents were confronted when they failed to take care of their individual needs and did not follow through on the plans developed to do this.

D. The importance of meeting individual needs in a relationship was reinforced with the parents.

31. Process Sharing of Affection (31)

A. The ways the parents show affection to each other were explored with them in a conjoint session.

B. The negative aspects of blatant displays of parental physical affection were processed with them.

C. The parents were assisted in developing appropriate ways to show affection to each other when in the presence of their children.

D. Blatant displays of affection between the parents were confronted, and they were reminded of the negative impact these displays could have on their children.

32. Plan One-on-One Time (32)

A. The parents were encouraged to build time into their schedules for one-on-one contact with each child and stepchild.

B. The parents were reminded of the importance of taking the time to build parent-child relationships.

C. The parents have not developed one-on-one contact with each child and stepchild and were encouraged to coordinate this.

33. Recommend Initiatives Camp (33)

A. The family was asked to attend an initiatives weekend to build the trust, cooperation, and conflict-resolution skills of each family member.

B. The initiatives experience was processed with the family, with each member identifying the positive gains they received from the weekend.

C. The family was assisted in identifying how they could continue to use and expand the gains from the weekend.

34. Coordinate "Cost-Benefit Analysis" Exercise (34)

A. The family was asked to complete the "Cost-Benefit Analysis" exercise (in *Ten Days to Self-Esteem* by Burns) to evaluate a plus-and-minus system of becoming a blended family.

B. The "Cost-Benefit Analysis" exercise was processed, with the positives of joining the family being emphasized.

C. Family members' resistance to working together and accepting one another was confronted using the positive items identified in the "Cost-Benefit Analysis."

35. Emphasize That Relationships Build Slowly (35)

A. The necessity of allowing relationships to build slowly was emphasized to the family in family sessions.

B. Ways to build trust in relationships were explored with the parents to help them slowly build relationships with stepchildren.

C. The parents' exhibiting patience in allowing relationships to build was verbally reinforced.

36. Draw Family Genogram (36)

A. A genogram was developed with the family that contained all members and showed how they are connected.

B. From the genogram, the family was asked to identify the ways in which they see themselves being connected.

C. Constructing the family genogram revealed that some family members are virtually unconnected to other family members, and ways to reverse this fact were discussed.

37. Complete Coat-of-Arms Exercise (37)

A. The family was asked to create a coat of arms for their new family by drawing a collage on posterboard.

B. The experience of creating the coat of arms was processed with the family, with both old and new identities being acknowledged and reinforced.

C. The parents were asked to display the coat of arms in their new home.

CHEMICAL DEPENDENCE

CLIENT PRESENTATION

1. Substance Use (1)*

A. The client reported using a mood-altering substance frequently throughout a month and regularly using until intoxicated or high.

B. The client indicated that on at least two occasions, he/she was caught high or drunk.

C. The client, friends, family, and others have confronted him/her or expressed concern about his/her substance use.

D. The client has stopped all substance use and now is starting to admit to himself/herself that it was a problem.

2. Caught/Observed High or Intoxicated (2)

A. The parents indicated that they have observed the client visibly intoxicated on numerous occasions in recent months.

B. School officials have caught the client being high on two or more occasions in recent months.

C. The client reported that parents and school officials have caught him/her both high and intoxicated on at least two occasions in recent months.

D. The client reported that he/she has not been high or intoxicated in months, and this self-report has been corroborated by authority figures.

3. Peer Group Changes (3)

A. The client described changing his/her peer group to one that was "cooler and more fun."

B. The client reported losing positive friends due to his/her recent issues with the law and other authority figures.

C. The client indicated that he/she was upset that the parents and old friends were labeling his/her new friends as "druggies and losers."

D. The client has dropped his/her substance-using friends and reestablished his/her connection with a more positive peer group.

4. Possession of Alcohol/Drug Paraphernalia (4)

A. The client has been caught with drug paraphernalia both at home and at school.

B. The client reported being recently caught by parents with alcohol in his/her bedroom.

C. The client indicated that he/she has disposed of all his/her drug paraphernalia.

D. The client reported that he/she no longer keeps an alcohol stash at home, in his/her car, or at school.

*The numbers in parentheses correlate to the number of the Behavioral Definition statement in the companion chapter with the same title in *The Adolescent Psychotherapy Treatment Planner,* Fourth Edition (Jongsma, Peterson, McInnis, and Bruce) by John Wiley & Sons, 2006.

5. Behavioral Changes (5)

A. The client reported that he/she has been avoiding formerly close friends and keeping a distance from family members.

B. The client indicated that he/she has been sleeping a lot lately and seems to always feel tired.

C. The parents reported that the client has shown a loss of interest in most activities and has had a low energy level.

D. The client reported that he/she used to be outgoing and socially active but now prefers to spend most of his/her time alone because others bother him/her.

E. The parents reported a significant drop in the client's grades in past months.

F. The client has gradually returned to more positive social interaction and academic success since stopping all substance use.

6. Physical Withdrawal Symptoms (6)

A. The client has experienced shaking, nausea, sweating, and headaches when withdrawing from alcohol.

B. The client reported that his/her withdrawal symptoms of sweating, anxiety, and insomnia have gradually subsided and are now minimal.

C. The client indicated that he/she is no longer experiencing withdrawal symptoms and is remaining alcohol free.

7. Continued Substance Use Despite Negative Consequences (7)

A. Despite legal and family problems, the client has continued to use alcohol and illicit drugs.

B. The client reported losing several longtime friendships because he/she liked to party too much, but this has not deterred his/her substance abuse.

C. The client has experienced financial, school, family, and legal problems, all directly related to his/her alcohol and/or drug use, but none of these consequences has stopped him/her from using.

D. The client has started to acknowledge that his/her negative consequences are directly due to his/her substance use.

8. Denial (7)

A. The client reported that he/she has not had any major problems due to his/her use of substances.

B. The client indicated that his/her difficulties at school (e.g., skipping classes, falling grades) were due to boredom and denied that they were related to substance use.

C. The client believes that the parents and others are not aware of his/her substance use.

D. The client's level of denial has begun to decrease, and he/she has acknowledged more of his/her alcohol/drug use and its effect on his/her life.

9. Mood Swings (8)

A. The client reported rapid, sudden mood swings.

B. The client indicated that others have told him/her they do not know what to expect given how quickly his/her mood can change.

C. The parents reported that the client can suddenly become defensive, angry, and withdrawn.

D. The client's mood swings have been less frequent and less severe since he/she stopped use of all substances.

10. School Issues (9)

A. There has been a reported, unexplainable drop in the client's grades.

B. The client reported skipping school and being tardy and absent on a regular basis.

C. The client has been expelled from school for being high and drunk on several occasions.

D. All school issues have subsided or improved since the client stopped all substance use.

11. Low Self-Esteem (10)

A. The client reported feeling like a total loser and inadequate in most areas.

B. The client indicated he/she rarely looks at or makes eye contact with others when speaking to them.

C. The client described himself/herself in totally negative terms.

D. The client has begun to make eye contact and verbalize positive things about himself/herself.

E. The client has started to connect his/her low self-esteem to his/her substance abuse.

F. The client's self-image has improved as abstinence from substance abuse continues.

12. Negative/Hostile (11)

A. The client presented in a negative, hostile manner.

B. The client's views of life, others, and the world have been very negative and hostile.

C. The client has virtually nothing good to say about anything or anyone.

D. The client has started to have positive, as well as negative, things to say about life, others, and the world.

13. Stealing Alcohol (12)

A. The client has been caught stealing alcohol on several occasions.

B. The parents reported that they have caught the client stealing alcohol from them on numerous occasions.

C. The client confessed to stealing alcohol from wherever and whomever he/she could.

14. Legal Conflicts (13)

A. The client has been caught stealing alcohol from stores and friends' parents' homes.

B. The client reported illegal drug and alcohol consumption that dated back to his/her early teens.

C. The client reported that he/she is currently on probation for driving under the influence of liquor (DUIL) and minor in possession (MIP) charges.

D. There seemed to be present with the client a consistent disregard for laws, rules, and authority figures.

E. The client's behavior and talk have started to reflect some respect for the law and a willingness to consistently obey laws.

15. Family History of Substance Abuse (14)

A. The client reported a positive history of chemical dependence in the immediate and extended family.

B. The client stated that his/her family has always believed you can't have fun without alcohol.

C. The family indicated that they think all kids go through a phase of experimenting a little with alcohol and drugs.

D. The client and family have become more open and honest about the substance abuse problems within the family.

INTERVENTIONS IMPLEMENTED

1. Gather Drug/Alcohol History (1)*

A. The client was asked to describe his/her alcohol/drug use in terms of the amount and pattern of use, symptoms of abuse, and negative life consequences that have resulted from chemical dependence.

B. The client openly discussed his/her substance abuse history and was reinforced as he/she gave complete data regarding its nature and extent.

C. It was reflected to the client that he/she was minimizing his/her substance abuse and was not giving reliable data regarding the nature and extent of his/her chemical dependence problem.

D. As therapy has progressed, the client has become more open in acknowledging the extent and seriousness of his/her substance abuse problem.

2. Administer Objective Substance Abuse Assessment (2)

A. The client was administered an objective test of drug and/or alcohol abuse.

B. The Adolescent Substance Abuse Subtle Screening Inventory (SASSI-A2) was administered to the client.

C. The Alcohol Severity Index test was administered to the client.

D. The Michigan Alcohol Screening Test (MAST) was administered to the client.

E. The results of the objective substance abuse assessment, which indicated a significant substance abuse problem, were processed with the client.

F. The results of the objective substance abuse assessment indicated that the client's problem with chemical dependence is relatively minor, and this feedback was given to the client.

3. Refer for Physical Examination (3)

A. The client was referred for a thorough physical examination to seek any negative medical effects of his/her chemical dependence.

B. The client has followed through with obtaining a physical examination and was told that his/her chemical dependence has produced negative medical consequences; these results were processed.

---

*The numbers in parentheses correlate to the number of the Therapeutic Intervention statement in the companion chapter with the same title in *The Adolescent Psychotherapy Treatment Planner,* Fourth Edition (Jongsma, Peterson, McInnis, and Bruce) by John Wiley & Sons, 2006.

C. The client has obtained a physical examination from a physician and has been told that there are no significant medical effects of his/her chemical dependence; these results were processed.

D. The client has not followed through with obtaining a physical examination and was again directed to do so.

4. Arrange Evaluation for Psychotropic Medications (4)

A. Arrangements were made for the client to have a physician's evaluation for the purpose of considering psychotropic medication to alleviate chemical dependence.

B. The client has followed through with seeing a physician for an evaluation of the need for psychotropic medication to control the chemical dependence.

C. The client has not cooperated with the referral to a physician for a medication evaluation and was encouraged to do so.

5. Monitor Medication Compliance (5)

A. The client reported that he/she has taken the prescribed medication consistently and that it has helped to control his/her chemical dependence; this was relayed to the prescribing clinician.

B. The client reported that he/she has not taken the prescribed medication consistently and was encouraged to do so.

C. The client reported taking the prescribed medication and stated that he/she has not noted any beneficial effect from it; this was reflected to the prescribing clinician.

D. The client was evaluated but was not prescribed any psychotropic medication by the physician.

6. List Negative Consequences (6)

A. The client was asked to make a list of the ways that substance abuse has negatively impacted his/her life.

B. The client was assigned "Taking Your First Step" in the *Adolescent Psychotherapy Homework Planner,* 2nd ed. (Jongsma, Peterson, and McInnis).

C. It was reflected that the client was minimizing the negative impact of substance abuse on his/her life.

D. The client openly acknowledged the negative consequences of drug/alcohol abuse on his/her life; he/she was supported during these disclosures.

7. Obtain Feedback from Significant Others (7)

A. The client was assigned to ask two or three people who were close to him/her to write a letter about how chemical dependence has had a negative impact on the client's life.

B. Letters received from friends about the negative impact of chemical dependence on the client's life were processed to reinforce and identify the negative impact of the chemical dependence.

C. The client was reminded that much of the negative impact is not seen by the user and that this helps to keep the usage going.

D. The client has not asked others to write a letter about how his/her chemical dependence has had a negative effect on the client's life and was redirected to do so.

8. Complete First-Step Paper (8)

A. The client was asked to write an Alcoholics Anonymous (AA) first-step paper and present it to the therapist or group.

B. The client completed the AA first-step paper, presented it to the therapist/group, and received their feedback.

C. The client was confronted on his/her failure to complete the AA first-step paper.

D. The client marginally completed his/her AA first-step paper after numerous reminders from the therapist.

E. The client's AA first-step paper was completed but was noted to show significant denial of his/her powerlessness over substance use.

F. The client completed the AA first-step paper; review of the first-step paper shows an open, honest appraisal of the seriousness of his/her substance abuse.

9. Reinforce Breakdown of Denial (9)

A. The client was reinforced for any statement that reflected acceptance of his/her chemical dependence and acknowledgment of the destructive consequences that it has had on his/her life.

B. The client was noted to have decreased his/her level of denial as evidenced by fewer statements that minimize the amount of his/her alcohol/drug abuse and its negative impact on his/her life.

10. Assign Learning Opportunities (10)

A. The client was asked to attend didactic lectures related to chemical dependence and the process of recovery.

B. The client was directed to films, reading, and other media to learn about the process of recovery.

C. The client was asked to identify in writing several key points attained from each presentation.

D. Key points about the recovery process that were noted by the client were processed in individual sessions.

E. The client has become more open in acknowledging and accepting his/her chemical dependence; this openness was noted and reinforced.

F. The client has not sought out helpful learning material and was redirected to do so.

11. Require Meeting with Group Member (11)

A. The client was directed to meet with experienced AA/NA members to elicit from them specific things they did that helped them stay sober, after which he/she would process findings with the therapist.

B. The client was assigned to read "Welcome to Recovery" in the *Adolescent Psychotherapy Homework Planner,* 2nd ed. (Jongsma, Peterson, and McInnis).

C. Information gathered from the experienced AA/NA members by the client was processed, and key ideas were developed for use in the client's own recovery.

D. The client has not followed through with making contact with an AA member and was redirected to do so.

12. Develop Abstinence Contract (12)

A. The client was asked to sign an abstinence contract in which he/she promises to avoid any and all contact with his/her drug of choice.

B. The client has signed the abstinence contract, and the emotional impact of this action was processed.

C. Although the client states that he/she would like to give up involvement with his/her drug of choice, he/she refused to sign an abstinence contract; he/she was confronted with this inconsistency.

D. The client indicated that he/she feels afraid of what his/her life will be like when there will be no contact with his/her drug of choice; these fears were normalized.

13. Refer to 12-Step Group (13)

A. The different types of AA or Narcotics Anonymous (NA) support meetings were explained to the client.

B. The client was directed to attend an NA or Young People's AA meeting and report on the experience to the therapist.

C. The AA support group experience was processed, with benefits and possible liabilities being identified and affirmed.

D. The client was asked to make a commitment to attend an AA support group on a regular basis.

E. The client has not followed through with the recommendation to attend an AA support group.

14. Assess Intellectual, Personality, and Cognitive Functioning (14)

A. The client's intellectual, personality, and cognitive functioning were assessed by means of psychological testing.

B. The client's intellectual, personality, and cognitive functioning were assessed by means of a clinical interview.

C. The results of the psychological assessment were given to the client, and the factors that may contribute to his/her chemical dependence were highlighted.

15. Facilitate Understanding of Risk Factors (15)

A. The client was assisted in understanding how his/her genetic, personality, social, family, and childhood factors can lead to chemical dependence.

B. The client was taught how his/her risk factors may create a relapse.

C. The client was reinforced as he/she displayed an understanding of his/her risk factors for relapse.

D. The client struggled to understand the risk factors for his/her relapse and was provided with remedial information in this area.

16. List Positive Sobriety Effects (16)

A. The client was asked to make a list of positive effects that maintaining sobriety could have on his/her life.

B. The client has produced a list of positive sobriety effects, and this list was processed and reinforced.

C. The client was assisted in making a list of positive sobriety effects, and this list was processed and reinforced.

D. The client has not followed through with making a list of positive sobriety effects and was redirected to do so.

17. Review Negative Peer Influence (17)

A. A review of the client's negative peers was performed, and the influence of these people on his/her substance abuse patterns was identified.

B. The client accepted the interpretation that maintaining contact with substance-abusing friends would reduce the probability of successful recovery from his/her chemical dependence.

C. A plan was developed to help the client initiate contact with sober people who could exert a positive influence on his/her own recovery.

D. The client has begun to reach out socially to sober individuals in order to develop a social network that has a more positive influence on his/her recovery; he/she was reinforced for this progress.

E. The client has not attempted to reach out socially to sober individuals in order to develop a social network that has a more positive influence on his/her recovery and was reminded about this important facet of his/her recovery.

18. Plan Social and Recreational Activities (18)

A. A list of social and recreational activities that are free from association with substance abuse was developed.

B. The client was verbally reinforced as he/she agreed to begin involvement in new recreational and social activities that will replace substance abuse–related activities.

C. The client has begun to make changes in his/her social and/or recreational activities and reports feeling good about these changes; the benefits of this progress were reviewed.

D. The client was very resistive to any changes in social and recreational activities that have previously been a strong part of his/her life; he/she was encouraged to begin with small changes in this area.

19. Plan Project Completion (19)

A. The client was assisted in developing a list of household- or work-related projects that could be accomplished in order to build his/her self-esteem, now that sobriety affords time and energy for such constructive activity.

B. The client has begun to involve himself/herself in constructive projects that have affirmed his/her self-esteem; the benefits of this technique were reviewed.

C. The client has not followed through with using his/her time constructively to accomplish household- or work-related projects and was redirected to do so.

20. Evaluate Living Situation (20)

A. The client's current living situation was reviewed as to whether it fosters a pattern of chemical dependence.

B. The client was supported as he/she agreed that his/her current living situation does encourage continuing substance abuse.

C. The client could not see any reason why his/her current living situation would have a negative effect on his/her chemical dependence recovery; he/she was provided with tentative examples in this area.

21. Identify Sobriety's Positive Family Effects (21)

A. The client was assisted in identifying the positive changes that will occur within family relationships as a result of his/her chemical dependence recovery.

B. The client reported that his/her family is enjoying a reduction in stress and increased cooperation since his/her chemical dependence recovery began; his/her reaction to these changes was processed.

C. The client was unable to identify any positive changes that have or could occur within family relationships as a result of his/her chemical dependence recovery, and he/she was provided with tentative examples in this area.

22. Reinforce Making Amends (22)

A. The negative effects that the client's substance abuse has had on family, friends, and work relationships were identified.

B. A plan for making amends to those who have been negatively affected by the client's substance abuse was developed.

C. The client's implementation of his/her plan to make amends to those who have been hurt by his/her substance abuse was reviewed.

D. The client reported feeling good about the fact that he/she has begun to make amends to others who have been hurt by his/her substance abuse; this progress was reinforced.

E. The client has not followed through on making amends to others who have been negatively affected by his/her pattern of substance abuse and was reminded to do so.

23. Obtain Commitment Regarding Making Amends (23)

A. The client was asked to make a verbal commitment to make amends to key individuals.

B. The client was urged to make further amends while working through Steps Eight and Nine of a 12-step program.

C. The client was supported as he/she made a verbal commitment to make initial amends now and to make further amends as he/she works through Steps Eight and Nine of the 12-step program.

D. The client declined to commit to making amends and was redirected to review the need to make this commitment.

24. Use Family Therapy to Strengthen Attachment and Support (24)

A. Family therapy was used toward the goal of strengthening family-client attachment.

B. Family therapy was used to develop greater family support of the client's recovery goals.

C. Family therapy has been successful in developing greater attachment between the family members and the client, and in developing family support of recovery goals.

D. The client's need for support was emphasized to the family.

E. The family commitment to family therapy was noted to be quite tenuous, as are their attachment to and support of the client.

25. Enroll Client in Drug Screening Voucher Program (25)

A. The client was enrolled in a drug screening program that provides him/her with vouchers, with increasing monetary value for each urine screen that is passed.

B. The client has been regularly passing urine screens, with the motivation to increase his/her monetary vouchers.

C. The client has not passed the urine screens, and his/her monetary vouchers have been discontinued.

D. The voucher program for passing drug screening has helped the client to successfully refrain from substance use.

E. Despite the use of the drug screen voucher program, the client continues to use substances.

26. Explore Schema and Self-Talk (26)

A. The client's schema and self-talk that weaken his/her resolve to remain abstinent were explored.

B. The biases that the client entertains regarding his/her schema and self-talk were challenged.

C. The client was assisted in generating more realistic self-talk to correct for his/her biases and build resilience.

D. The client was provided with positive feedback for his/her replacement of self-talk and biases.

E. The client struggled to identify his/her self-talk and biases that weaken his/her resolve to remain abstinent and was provided with tentative examples in this area.

27. Rehearse Replacement of Negative Self-Talk (27)

A. The client was assisted in identifying situations in which his/her negative self-talk occurs.

B. The client was assisted in generating empowering alternatives to his/her negative self-talk.

C. The client's success in rehearsing the response to negative self-talk was reviewed and reinforced.

28. Teach about "Coping Package" (28)

A. The client was taught a variety of techniques to help manage urges to use chemical substances.

B. The client was taught calming strategies, such as relaxation and breathing techniques.

C. The client was taught cognitive techniques, such as thought stopping, positive self-talk, and attention-focusing skills (e.g., distraction from urges, staying focused, behavioral goals of abstinence).

D. The client has used his/her coping package techniques to help reduce his/her urges to use chemical substances; this progress was reinforced.

E. The client has not used the coping package for managing urges to use chemical substances, and he/she was redirected to do so.

29. Develop Hierarchy of Urge-Producing Cues (29)

A. The client was directed to construct a hierarchy of urge-producing cues to use substances.

B. The client was assisted in developing a hierarchy of urge-producing cues to use substances.

C. The client was helped to identify a variety of cues that prompt his/her use of substances.

30. Practice Response to Urge-Producing Cues (30)

A. The client was assisted in selecting urge-producing cues with which to practice, with a bias toward cues that are likely to result in a successful experience.

B. Behavioral techniques were used to help the client cognitively restructure his/her urge-producing cues.

C. The exercise "Gradually Facing Your Phobic Fear" from the *Adolescent Psychotherapy Homework Planner,* 2nd ed. (Jongsma, Peterson, and McInnis) was assigned to the client.

D. The client's use of cognitive restructuring strategies was reviewed and processed.

31. Assess Stress Management Skills (31)

A. The client's current level of skill in managing everyday stressors was assessed.

B. The client was assessed in regard to his/her ability to meet role demands for work, social, and family expectations.

C. Behavioral and cognitive restructuring techniques were used to help build social and communication skills to manage everyday challenges.

D. The client was provided with positive feedback regarding his/her ability to manage common everyday stressors.

E. The client continues to struggle with common everyday stressors and was provided with remedial feedback in this area.

32. Assign Social and Communication Information (32)

A. The client was assigned to read about social skills.

B. The client was assigned to read about communication skills.

C. The client was assigned to read *Your Perfect Right* (Alberti and Emmons).

D. The client was assigned to read *Conversationally Speaking* (Garner).

E. Exercises from the *Adolescent Psychotherapy Homework Planner,* 2nd ed. (Jongsma, Peterson, and McInnis) were assigned to the client (e.g., "Social Skills Exercise," "Greeting Peers," "Reach Out and Call," "Show Your Strengths").

F. The client has read the assigned information about social and communication skills, and key points were reviewed.

G. The client has not read the assigned information on social and communication skills and was redirected to do so.

33. Differentiate between Lapse and Relapse (33)

A. A discussion was held with the client regarding the distinction between a lapse and a relapse.

B. A lapse was associated with an initial and reversible return of symptoms or urges to use substances.

C. A relapse was associated with the decision to return to regular use of substances.

D. The client was provided with support and encouragement as he/she displayed an understanding of the difference between a lapse and a relapse.

E. The client struggled to understand the difference between a lapse and a relapse, and he/she was provided with remedial feedback in this area.

34. Discuss Management of Lapse Risk Situations (34)

A. The client was assisted in identifying future situations or circumstances in which lapses could occur.

B. The exercise "Keeping Straight" from the *Adolescent Psychotherapy Homework Planner,* 2nd ed. (Jongsma, Peterson, and McInnis) was assigned to the client to help manage lapse situations.

C. The session focused on rehearsing the management of future situations or circumstances in which lapses could occur.

D. The client was reinforced for his/her appropriate use of lapse management skills.

E. The client was redirected in regard to his/her poor use of lapse management skills.

35. Encourage Routine Use of Strategies (35)

A. The client was instructed to routinely use the strategies that he/she has learned in therapy (e.g., cognitive restructuring, exposure).

B. The client was urged to find ways to build his/her new strategies into his/her life as much as possible.

C. The client was reinforced as he/she reported ways in which he/she has incorporated coping strategies into his/her life and routine.

D. The client was redirected about ways to incorporate his/her new strategies into his/her routine and life.

36. Recommend Relapse Prevention Workbooks (36)

A. The client was referred to relapse prevention workbooks.

B. The client was referred to books such as *Staying Sober: A Guide to Relapse Prevention* (Gorski and Miller) and *The Staying Sober Workbook* (Gorski) as material that would help develop strategies for constructively dealing with trigger situations.

C. The client has obtained the recommended reading material on relapse prevention and stated that he/she has found the material helpful.

D. The client has used the recommended reading material to identify potential relapse triggers and to help him/her develop strategies for constructively dealing with each trigger.

E. The client has not followed through on obtaining the recommended reading material and was redirected to do so.

37. Develop Aftercare Plan (37)

A. The client was assisted in developing an aftercare plan that will support the maintenance of long-term sobriety.

B. The client has listed several components to an aftercare plan that will support his/her sobriety, such as family activities, counseling, self-help support groups, and sponsors; feedback about his/her list was provided.

C. The client has not followed through on developing an aftercare plan and was redirected to do so.

CONDUCT DISORDER/DELINQUENCY

CLIENT PRESENTATION

1. Failure to Comply (1)*

A. The client has demonstrated a persistent failure to comply with the rules or expectations at home, at school, and in the community.

B. The client voiced his/her opposition to the rules at home and school.

C. The client has started to comply with the rules and expectations at home, at school, and in the community.

D. The client verbalized his/her willingness to comply with the rules and expectations at home, at school, and in the community.

E. The client has consistently complied with the rules and expectations at home, at school, and in the community.

2. Aggressive/Destructive Behaviors (2)

A. The client described a series of incidents where he/she became aggressive or destructive when upset or frustrated.

B. The client projected the blame for his/her aggressive/destructive behaviors onto other people.

C. The client has begun to take steps to control his/her hostile/aggressive impulses.

D. The client has recently demonstrated good self-control and has not engaged in any aggressive or destructive behaviors.

3. Angry/Hostile (2)

A. The client appeared angry, hostile, and irritable during today's session.

B. The client reported incidents of becoming easily angered over trivial matters.

C. The client has recently exhibited frequent angry outbursts at home and school.

D. The client has recently exhibited mild improvements in his/her anger control.

E. The client has demonstrated good control of his/her anger and has not exhibited any major loss-of-control episodes.

4. Stealing (3)

A. The client has a history of stealing and/or breaking and entering illegally into others' places of residence or businesses.

B. The client has recently engaged in stealing or illegal breaking and entering.

C. The client has stolen from others in his/her home.

D. The client has stolen from others in the school setting.

---

*The numbers in parentheses correlate to the number of the Behavioral Definition statement in the companion chapter with the same title in *The Adolescent Psychotherapy Treatment Planner,* Fourth Edition (Jongsma, Peterson, McInnis, and Bruce) by John Wiley & Sons, 2006.

E. The client has not engaged in any stealing or illegal breaking and entering in the recent past.

F. The client has ceased stealing or illegally breaking and entering into places of residence or businesses.

5. Legal Conflicts (3)

A. The parents reported an extensive history of the client engaging in illegal antisocial behaviors.

B. The client has continued to break laws and has failed to learn from his/her past mistakes or experiences.

C. The client has often minimized the seriousness of his/her offenses against other people or the law.

D. The client verbalized an awareness that his/her antisocial behavior has produced negative or undesirable consequences for himself/herself and others.

E. The client and parents reported a reduction in the frequency and severity of illegal behaviors.

6. School Behavior Problems (4)

A. A review of the client's history revealed numerous acting out and rebellious behaviors in the school setting.

B. The client has often disrupted the classroom with his/her silly, immature, or negative attention-seeking behaviors.

C. The client has missed a significant amount of time from school due to truancy.

D. The client has had frequent conflicts with authority figures in the school setting.

E. The client has started to exercise greater self-control in the classroom setting.

F. The client has recently demonstrated a significant reduction in the frequency of his/her acting out or rebellious behaviors at school.

7. Authority Conflicts (5)

A. The client displayed a negativistic attitude and was highly argumentative during today's therapy session.

B. The client has often tested the limits and challenged authority figures at home, at school, and in the community.

C. The client has often talked back to authority figures in a disrespectful manner when reprimanded.

D. The client has recently been more cooperative with authority figures.

E. The client has been cooperative and respectful toward authority figures on a consistent basis.

8. Thrill Seeking (6)

A. The client historically has presented as a highly impulsive individual who seeks immediate gratification of his/her needs and often fails to consider the consequences of his/her actions.

B. The client has engaged in impulsive/thrill-seeking behaviors in order to achieve a sense of excitement and fun.

C. The client has begun to take steps toward improving his/her impulse control and delaying the need for immediate gratification.

D. The client has recently demonstrated good impulse control and has not engaged in any serious acting out or antisocial behaviors.

E. The client has ceased engaging in acting out or thrill-seeking behaviors because of his/her improved ability to stop and think about the possible consequences of his/her actions.

9. Lying/Conning (7)

A. The client described a pattern of lying, conning, and manipulating others to meet his/her needs and avoid facing the consequences of his/her actions.

B. The client appeared to be lying in the therapy session about his/her misbehaviors or irresponsible actions.

C. The client was honest in the therapy session and admitted to his/her wrongdoing or irresponsibility.

D. The parents reported that the client has been more honest and accepting of their decisions at home.

10. Blaming/Projecting (8)

A. The client was unwilling to accept responsibility for his/her poor decisions and behaviors, instead blaming others for his/her decisions and actions.

B. The client has begun to accept greater responsibility for his/her actions and placed the blame less often for his/her wrongdoings onto other people.

C. The client admitted to his/her wrongdoings and verbalized an acceptance of responsibility for his/her actions.

11. Lack of Remorse/Guilt (9)

A. The client expressed little or no remorse for his/her irresponsible, acting out, or aggressive behaviors.

B. The client expressed remorse for his/her actions, but apparently only because he/she had been caught and suffered the consequences of his/her actions.

C. The client appeared to express genuine remorse or guilt for his/her misbehavior.

12. Insensitivity/Lack of Empathy (10)

A. The client displayed little concern or empathy for the thoughts, feelings, and needs of other people.

B. The client has often demonstrated a willingness to ride roughshod over the rights of others to meet his/her needs.

C. The client verbalized an understanding of how his/her actions negatively impacted others.

D. The client has demonstrated empathy and sensitivity to the thoughts, feelings, and needs of other people.

13. Sexual Promiscuity (11)

A. The client reported a history of having multiple sexual partners where there has been little or no emotional attachment.

B. The client displayed little awareness or concern for the possible consequences (e.g., unwanted pregnancy, contracting sexually transmitted diseases) of his/her irresponsible or promiscuous behavior.

C. The client verbalized an awareness of the negative consequences or potential dangers associated with his/her sexually promiscuous behavior.

D. The client has demonstrated good control over his/her sexual impulses and has not engaged in any risky or irresponsible sexual behavior.

14. Use of Mood-Altering Substances (12)

A. The client reported frequently using mood-altering substances until intoxicated or high.

B. The client indicated that on at least two occasions he/she was caught high or drunk.

C. The client's friends, family, and others have confronted him/her or expressed concern about his/her substance use.

D. The client has ceased all substance use and has admitted that it was a problem.

15. Gang Involvement (13)

A. The client has been identified as a gang member.

B. The client reports participation in gang membership and associated activities.

C. The client has identified the need to break away from the gang setting.

D. The client has discontinued affiliation with the gang.

INTERVENTIONS IMPLEMENTED

1. Assess Anger Dynamics (1)*

A. The client was assessed for various stimuli that have triggered his/her anger.

B. The client was helped to identify situations, people, and thoughts that have triggered his/her anger.

C. The client was assisted in identifying the thoughts, feelings, and actions that have characterized his/her anger responses.

2. Refer for Physical Examination (2)

A. The client was referred to a physician for a complete physical examination to rule out organic contributors (e.g., brain damage, tumor, elevated testosterone levels) to his/her anger.

B. The client has complied with the physical examination, and the results were shared with him/her.

C. The physical examination has identified organic contributors to poor anger control, and treatment was suggested.

D. The physical examination has not identified any organic contributors to poor anger control, and this was reflected to the client.

---

*The numbers in parentheses correlate to the number of the Therapeutic Intervention statement in the companion chapter with the same title in *The Adolescent Psychotherapy Treatment Planner*, Fourth Edition (Jongsma, Peterson, McInnis, and Bruce) by John Wiley & Sons, 2006.

E. The client has not complied with the physical examination to assess organic contributors, and he/she was redirected to do so.

3. Provide Psychological Testing (3)

A. A psychological evaluation was conducted to determine whether ADHD or emotional factors are contributing to the client's impulsivity and acting out behaviors.

B. The client was uncooperative and resistant to engaging in the evaluation process.

C. The client approached the psychological testing in an honest, straightforward manner and was cooperative with any requests.

D. Feedback from the psychological testing was given to the client, parents, school officials, or criminal justice officials and appropriate interventions were discussed.

4. Refer for Substance Abuse Evaluation (4)

A. The client was referred for a substance abuse evaluation to assess the extent of his/her drug/alcohol usage and determine the need for treatment.

B. The findings from the substance abuse evaluation revealed the presence of a substance abuse problem and the need for treatment.

C. The evaluation findings did not reveal the presence of a substance abuse problem or the need for treatment in this area.

5. Consult with Criminal Justice Officials (5)

A. A consultation was held with criminal justice officials about the need for appropriate consequences for the client's antisocial behavior.

B. The client was placed on probation for his/her antisocial behaviors and instructed to comply with all the rules pertaining to his/her probation.

C. The client was encouraged as he/she agreed to make restitution and/or perform community service for his/her past antisocial behavior.

D. The client was placed in an intensive surveillance treatment program as a consequence of his/her antisocial behavior.

6. Review Alternative Placement (6)

A. Consultation was held with parents, school officials, and criminal justice officials about placing the client in an alternative setting because of his/her antisocial behavior.

B. It is recommended that the client be placed in a juvenile detention facility as a consequence of his/her antisocial behavior.

C. It is recommended that the client be placed in a foster home to help prevent recurrences of antisocial behavior.

D. The recommendation was made that the client be placed in a residential program to provide external structure and supervision for the client.

E. The recommendation was made that the client be placed in an inpatient substance abuse program.

7. Reinforce Legal Consequences (7)

A. The parents were encouraged and challenged not to protect the client from the legal consequences of his/her actions.

B. The parents agreed to contact the police or appropriate criminal justice officials if the client engages in any future antisocial behavior; they were reinforced for this decision.

C. The parents followed through and contacted the police or probation officer after the client engaged in antisocial behavior; they were supported for this decision.

D. The parents failed to contact the police and/or criminal justice officials after the client engaged in antisocial behavior, and the reasons for this were processed.

8. Medication Evaluation Referral (8)

A. The client was referred for a medication evaluation to improve his/her impulse control and stabilize moods.

B. The client and parents agreed to follow through with a medication evaluation.

C. The client was strongly opposed to being placed on medication to help improve his/her impulse control and stabilize moods.

D. The client's response to the medication was discussed.

E. The client reported that medication has helped to improve impulse control and stabilize moods.

F. The client reports little or no improvement from the medication.

G. The client has not complied with taking his/her medication on a regular basis and was encouraged to do so.

9. Build Therapeutic Trust (9)

A. An attempt was made to build trust with the client in therapy sessions through consistent eye contact, active listening, unconditional positive regard, and warm acceptance.

B. The client's concerns were listened to closely, and his/her feelings were reflected in a non-judgmental manner.

C. Thoughts and feelings expressed by the client during the therapy session were supported empathetically.

D. The client's mistrustfulness has contributed to his/her reluctance to share underlying thoughts and feelings during the therapy sessions; he/she was reminded to share these thoughts as he/she is able.

10. Confront Antisocial Behavior (10)

A. The client was firmly and consistently confronted with how his/her antisocial behaviors negatively affect himself/herself and others.

B. The client was assigned to read "My Behavior and Its Full Impact" from the *Adolescent Psychotherapy Homework Planner,* 2nd ed. (Jongsma, Peterson, and McInnis).

C. The client was directed to complete the "Patterns of Stealing" exercise from the *Adolescent Psychotherapy Homework Planner,* 2nd ed. (Jongsma, Peterson, and McInnis).

D. The client was asked to list the negative consequences of his/her antisocial behavior and negativistic attitude.

E. Role-reversal techniques were used in the therapy session to help the client realize how his/her antisocial behavior negatively impacts others.

F. The client was asked to write a letter of apology to the victim(s) of his/her antisocial behavior.

11. Teach Acceptance of Responsibility (11)

A. The client was consistently confronted and challenged to cease blaming others for his/her misbehavior and accept greater responsibility for his/her actions.

B. The client was asked to list how his/her poor decisions and irresponsible behavior resulted in negative consequences for himself/herself and others.

C. The client was praised as he/she identified ways to resolve conflict and/or meet his/her needs that were more effective than acting out or behaving in an irresponsible manner.

D. The client was instructed to verbally acknowledge his/her wrongdoing and apologize to others.

12. Explore Blaming (12)

A. The underlying factors contributing to the client's pattern of blaming others for his/her misbehavior were explored.

B. The client was challenged to accept the consequences of his/her actions instead of arguing and blaming others.

C. The client identified how the pattern of blaming others is associated with underlying feelings of low self-esteem, inadequacy, and insecurity, and this was processed.

D. The client has modeled other family members' patterns of blaming others.

E. The parents identified natural, logical consequences (e.g., grounding, removing privileges, taking away desired objects) that can be used if the client is caught in a lie, and they were supported for this.

13. Reconceptualize Anger (13)

A. The client was assisted in reconceptualizing anger as involving different components that go through predictable phases.

B. The client was taught about the different components of anger, including cognitive, physiological, affective, and behavioral components.

C. The client was taught how to better discriminate between relaxation and tension.

D. The client was taught about the predictable phases of anger, including demanding expectations that are not met, which lead to increased arousal and anger, which lead to acting out.

E. The client displayed a clear understanding of the ways to conceptualize anger, and he/she was provided with positive reinforcement.

F. The client has struggled to understand the ways to conceptualize anger, and he/she was provided with remedial feedback in this area.

14. Identify Positive Consequences of Anger Management (14)

A. The client was asked to identify the positive consequences he/she has experienced in managing his/her anger.

B. The client was assisted in identifying positive consequences of managing anger (e.g., respect from others and self, cooperation from others, improved physical health).

C. The client was asked to agree to learn new ways to conceptualize and manage anger.

15. Teach Calming and Coping Strategies (15)

A. The client was assigned to read about calming and coping strategies in books or treatment manuals.

B. The client was assisted in learning specific calming and coping strategies.

C. The client has read the information about calming and coping strategies, and key points were reviewed.

D. The client was assisted in developing specific ways that he/she can implement calming and coping strategies.

E. The client has not read the information about calming and coping strategies, and he/she was redirected to do so.

16. Explore Self-Talk (16)

A. The client's self-talk that mediates his/her angry feelings was explored.

B. The client was assessed for self-talk such as demanding expectations, reflected in "should," "must," or "have to" statements.

C. The client was assisted in identifying and challenging his/her biases and in generating alternative self-talk that corrects for the biases.

D. The client was taught how to use correcting self-talk to facilitate a more flexible and temperate response to frustration.

17. Assign Thought-Stopping Technique (17)

A. The client was directed to implement a thought-stopping technique on a daily basis between sessions.

B. The client was assigned to read "Making Use of the Thought-Stopping Technique" in the *Adult Psychotherapy Homework Planner,* 2nd ed. (Jongsma).

C. The client's use of the thought-stopping technique was reviewed.

D. The client was provided with positive feedback for his/her successful use of the thought-stopping technique.

E. The client was provided with corrective feedback to help improve his/her use of the thought-stopping technique.

18. Teach Assertive Communication (18)

A. The client was taught about assertive communication through instruction, modeling, and role-playing.

B. The client was referred to an assertiveness training class.

C. The client displayed increased assertiveness and was provided with positive feedback in this area.

D. The client has not increased his/her level of assertiveness and was provided with additional feedback in this area.

19. Teach Conflict Resolution Skills (19)

A. The client was taught conflict resolution skills through modeling, role-playing, and behavioral rehearsal.

B. The client was taught about empathy and active listening.

C. The client was taught about "I messages," respectful communication, assertiveness without aggression, and compromise.

D. The client was reinforced for his/her clear understanding of the conflict resolution skills.

E. The client displayed a poor understanding of the conflict resolution skills and was provided with remedial feedback.

20. Construct Strategy for Managing Anger (20)

A. The client was assisted in constructing a client-tailored strategy for managing his/her anger.

B. The client was encouraged to combine somatic, cognitive, communication, problem-solving, and conflict resolution skills relevant to his/her needs.

C. The client was reinforced for his/her comprehensive anger management strategy.

D. The client was redirected to develop a more comprehensive anger management strategy.

21. Select Challenging Situations for Managing Anger (21)

A. The client was provided with situations in which he/she may be increasingly challenged to apply his/her new strategies for managing anger.

B. The client was asked to identify his/her likely upcoming challenging situations for managing anger.

C. The client was urged to use his/her strategies for managing anger in successively more difficult situations.

22. Assign Anger Control Homework (22)

A. The client was assigned homework exercises to help him/her practice newly learned calming, assertion, conflict resolution, or cognitive restructuring skills.

B. The client was assigned the "Anger Control" exercise from the *Adolescent Psychotherapy Homework Planner,* 2nd ed. (Jongsma, Peterson, and McInnis).

C. The client has practiced the anger management skills, and his/her experience was reviewed and processed with the goal of consolidation of such skills.

D. The client has not regularly practiced anger control skills and was redirected to do so.

23. Monitor/Decrease Outbursts (23)

A. The client's reports of angry outbursts were monitored with the goal of decreasing their frequency, intensity, and duration.

B. The client was urged to use his/her new anger management skills to decrease the frequency, intensity, and duration of his/her anger outbursts.

C. The client was assigned to read "Alternatives to Destructive Anger" in the *Adult Psychotherapy Homework Planner,* 2nd ed. (Jongsma).

D. The client's progress in decreasing his/her angry outbursts was reviewed.

E. The client was reinforced for his/her success at decreasing the frequency, intensity, and duration of his/her anger outbursts.

F. The client has not decreased the frequency, intensity, or duration of his/her anger outbursts, and corrective feedback was provided.

24. Encourage Disclosure (24)

A. The client was encouraged to discuss his/her anger management goals with trusted persons who are likely to support his/her change.

B. The client was assisted in identifying individuals who are likely to support his/her change.

C. The client has reviewed his/her anger management goals with trusted persons, and their response was processed.

D. The client has not discussed his/her anger management goals and was redirected to do so.

25. Use Parent Management Training (25)

A. Parent Management Training was used, as developed in *Living with Children* (Patterson).

B. The parents were directed to read *Parenting the Strong-Willed Child* (Forehand and Long).

C. The parents were taught how parent-child behavioral interactions can encourage or discourage positive or negative behavior.

D. The parents were taught how changing key elements of parent-child interactions can promote positive change.

E. The parents were provided with specific examples, such as how prompting and reinforcing positive behaviors can be used to promote positive change.

F. The parents were provided with positive feedback for the use of Parent Management Training approaches.

G. The parents have not used the Parent Management Training approach and were redirected to do so.

26. Teach Parents to Define Aspects of Situation (26)

A. The parents were taught how to specifically define and identify problem behaviors.

B. The parents were taught how to specifically identify their reactions to the behavior and determine whether the reaction encourages or discourages the behavior.

C. The parents were taught to generate alternatives to the problem behavior.

D. Positive feedback was provided to the parents for their skill at specifically defining and identifying problem behaviors, reactions, outcomes, and alternatives.

E. Parents were provided with remedial feedback as they struggled to correctly identify problem behaviors, reactions, responses, and alternatives.

27. Teach Consistent Parenting (27)

A. The parents were taught how to implement key parenting practices on a consistent basis.

B. The parents were taught about establishing realistic, age-appropriate roles for acceptable and unacceptable behavior.

C. The parents were taught about prompting positive behavior and using positive reinforcement.

D. The parents were taught about clear, direct instruction as well as time out and other loss-of-privilege techniques for problem behavior.

E. The parents were provided with positive feedback, as they have been able to develop consistent parenting practices.

F. The parents have not developed consistent parenting practices, and they were redirected to do so.

28. Assign Home Exercises to Implement Parenting Techniques (28)

A. The parents were assigned home exercises in which they implement parenting techniques and record the results of the implementation exercises.

B. The parents were assigned to read "Clear Rules, Positive Reinforcement, Appropriate Consequences" in the *Adolescent Psychotherapy Homework Planner,* 2nd ed. (Jongsma, Peterson, and McInnis).

C. The parents' implementation of homework exercises was reviewed within the session.

D. Corrective feedback was used to help develop improved, appropriate, and consistent use of skills.

E. The parents have not completed the assigned homework and were redirected to do so.

29. Assign Parent Training Manuals (29)

A. The parents were directed to read parent training manuals.

B. The parents were directed to read *Parenting Through Change* (Forgatch).

C. The parents were directed to watch videotapes demonstrating the techniques used in parent training sessions.

D. The parents' study of pertinent media was reviewed and processed.

E. The parents have not reviewed the assigned pertinent media and were redirected to do so.

30. Develop Reward System/Contingency Contract (30)

A. The client and parents were assisted in compiling a list of rewards to reinforce desired, positive behavior by the client.

B. A reward system was designed to reinforce positive behavior and deter impulsive or aggressive acts.

C. The client signed a contingency contract prepared to specify the consequences for his/her impulsive/acting out behavior.

31. Expose Family Abuse History (31)

A. The client's family background was explored for a history of neglect or physical or sexual abuse.

B. The client's parents were confronted and challenged to cease physically abusive or overly punitive methods of discipline.

C. An apology from the parents to the client for abusive behaviors and overly harsh methods of discipline was coordinated.

D. The abuse was reported to the appropriate agency.

E. A recommendation was made about which family members should be removed from the home and seek treatment.

F. Necessary steps were identified to minimize the risk of abuse occurring in the future.

G. The nonabusive parent verbalized a commitment to protect the client and siblings from physical abuse in the future; the importance of this role was emphasized.

32. Explore Feelings about Neglect or Abuse (32)

A. The client was given the opportunity in session to express his/her feelings about past neglect, abuse, separation, or abandonment.

B. The client shared the extent of contact with the absent or uninvolved parent in the past and was encouraged to discuss possible reasons for the lack of involvement.

C. The client was instructed to use a journal to record his/her thoughts and feelings about past neglect, abuse, separation, or abandonment.

D. The empty-chair technique was employed to facilitate expression of feelings surrounding past neglect or abuse.

E. The client was instructed to write a letter to the absent parent to express and work through feelings about abandonment or lack of contact.

F. The empty-chair technique was utilized to help the client express his/her feelings toward the absent parent.

G. The client has been reluctant to explore feelings about neglect and abuse and was urged to process these feelings as he/she feels capable of doing so.

33. Teach Empathy (33)

A. Role-playing and role-reversal techniques were used to increase the client's sensitivity to how antisocial behaviors affect others.

B. The client was able to verbally recognize how his/her antisocial behaviors affect others through use of role-playing and role-reversal techniques.

34. Assign Altruistic Acts (34)

A. The client was given the homework assignment of performing three altruistic or benevolent acts before the next therapy session to increase his/her empathy and sensitivity to the thoughts, feelings, and needs of others.

B. A recommendation was made that the client perform community service as part of probation to increase empathy and concern for the welfare of others.

C. The client's failure to comply with the homework assignment that he/she perform altruistic or benevolent acts was noted to reflect his/her lack of empathy and concern for the welfare of others.

35. Assign Empathy Homework (35)

A. The client was assigned homework to increase his/her empathy and sensitivity toward the thoughts, feelings, and needs of others.

B. The client was assigned the "Headed in the Right Direction" exercise from the *Adolescent Psychotherapy Homework Planner,* 2nd ed. (Jongsma, Peterson, and McInnis) as homework to help increase his/her empathy and sensitivity toward the thoughts, feelings, and needs of others.

C. After completing the "Headed in the Right Direction" exercise, the client was able to identify three ways in which he/she could demonstrate caring behavior toward others.

D. The client has not completed the homework assignment regarding increasing empathy and sensitivity, and he/she was redirected to do so.

36. Assign Household Tasks (36)

A. The client and parents were assisted in developing a list of responsible behaviors that the client could perform at home.

B. The parents placed the client in charge of tasks at home to demonstrate confidence in his/her ability to act responsibly; the results of this risk were reviewed.

37. Refer for Vocational Training (37)

A. The client was referred for a vocational assessment.

B. The recommendation was made that the client receive vocational training to develop basic job skills that will hopefully lead to steady employment.

C. The client has not participated in vocational training and was redirected to do so.

38. Encourage Seeking of Employment (38)

A. The client was challenged to find employment instead of obtaining money or material goods through illegal activities.

B. The client was praised and reinforced for securing employment.

C. The client explored the factors that contribute to his/her reluctance to obtain employment, and these were processed.

39. Provide Sex Education (39)

A. The client was provided with sex education in an attempt to eliminate his/her pattern of engaging in sexually promiscuous behaviors.

B. The client identified the risks involved with his/her irresponsible or promiscuous sexual behaviors and was encouraged to give weight to these.

C. The client was assisted in exploring the factors contributing to his/her sexually irresponsible or promiscuous behaviors.

D. The client was helped to identify more effective ways to meet his/her needs instead of through sexually acting out.

E. The client's irrational thoughts that underlie his/her sexually promiscuous behaviors were explored and processed.

40. Assess Marital Conflicts (40)

A. The therapist assessed the marital dyad for possible conflict and/or triangulation that places the focus on the client's acting out behaviors and away from marital problems.

B. The parents recognized that their marital problems are creating stress for the client and agreed to seek marital counseling.

C. The parents refused to follow through with a recommendation to pursue marital counseling and were urged to reconsider this.

DEPRESSION

CLIENT PRESENTATION

1. Sad, Depressed Moods (1)*

A. The parents and teachers reported that the client has appeared sad and depressed for a significant length of time.

B. The client appeared visibly sad during today's therapy session and reported that he/she feels depressed most of the time.

C. The frequency and intensity of the client's depressed moods are gradually beginning to diminish.

D. The client expressed happiness and joy about recent life events.

E. The client's depression has lifted, and his/her moods are much more elevated.

2. Flat, Constricted Affect (1)

A. The parents and teachers reported that the client's affect often appears flat and constricted at home and school.

B. The client's affect appeared flat and constricted, and he/she reports that he/she does not feel any emotion.

C. The client appeared more animated in his/her affective presentation and showed a wider range of emotions.

D. The client has consistently appeared more animated in his/her emotional presentation since the onset of treatment.

3. Preoccupation with Death (2)

A. The parents and teachers reported that the client displays a strong preoccupation with the subject of death.

B. The client displayed a preoccupation with the subject of death during today's therapy session and reported that death is on his/her mind often.

C. The client's preoccupation with the subject of death is gradually beginning to decrease.

D. The client did not talk about the subject of death in today's therapy session.

E. The client's preoccupation with the subject of death has ceased, and he/she has demonstrated a renewed interest in life.

4. Suicidal Thoughts/Actions (3)

A. The client reported experiencing suicidal thoughts on a number of occasions.

B. The client made a recent suicide attempt.

C. The client has made suicidal gestures in the past as a cry for help.

D. The client denied that suicidal thoughts or urges are a problem any longer.

---

*The numbers in parentheses correlate to the number of the Behavioral Definition statement in the companion chapter with the same title in *The Adolescent Psychotherapy Treatment Planner,* Fourth Edition (Jongsma, Peterson, McInnis, and Bruce) by John Wiley & Sons, 2006.

5. Moody Irritability (4)

A. The client has displayed a pervasive irritability at home and school.

B. The client's angry, irritable moods often mask deeper feelings of depression.

C. The client appeared moody and irritable during today's therapy session.

D. The frequency and intensity of the client's irritable moods have started to diminish.

E. The client's moods have stabilized, and he/she has demonstrated significantly fewer irritable moods.

6. Isolation from Family and Peers (5)

A. The client has become significantly more isolated and withdrawn from family members and peers since the onset of his/her depression.

B. The client appeared withdrawn in today's therapy session.

C. The client's social isolation has started to diminish, and he/she is beginning to interact more often with family members and peers.

D. The client was much more talkative and spontaneous in today's therapy session.

E. The client has become much more outgoing and has interacted with his/her family members and peers on a regular, consistent basis.

7. Academic Performance Decline (6)

A. The client has experienced a decline in his/her academic performance since the onset of his/her depression.

B. The client appeared visibly depressed when discussing his/her lowered academic performance.

C. The client's academic performance has improved since his/her depression has lifted.

D. The client expressed feelings of happiness and joy about his/her improved academic performance.

8. Lack of Interest (7)

A. The client reported experiencing little interest or enjoyment in activities that used to bring him/her pleasure in the past.

B. The parents and teachers reported that the client has shown little interest or enjoyment in activities at home and school.

C. The client's depression has started to decrease, and he/she has shown signs of interest in previously enjoyed activities.

D. The client reported that he/she was recently able to experience joy or happiness in several activities.

E. The client has developed a renewed interest in and zest for life.

9. Lack of Communication about Painful Emotions (8)

A. The client has often suppressed and/or avoided talking about his/her painful emotions or experiences with others.

B. The client avoided talking about any painful emotions or topics during today's therapy session.

C. The client's avoidance of or refusal to talk about his/her painful emotions or experiences has been a significant contributing factor to his/her depression.

D. The client has started to talk about his/her painful emotions or experiences.

E. The client's willingness to talk about his/her painful emotions or experiences has helped to lift his/her depression.

10. Substance Abuse (9)

A. The client's substance abuse has masked deeper feelings of depression.

B. The client acknowledged that he/she has often turned to illegal drugs or alcohol to elevate his/her mood and block out any painful emotions.

C. The client reported that he/she has experienced an increase in feelings of depression since he/she ceased using drugs or alcohol.

D. The client's moods have stabilized since he/she ceased abusing drugs and alcohol.

E. The client reported that he/she is able to enjoy many activities without drugs or alcohol.

11. Low Energy, Listlessness, and Apathy (10)

A. The client's depression has been manifested, in part, by his/her low energy level, fatigue, listlessness, and apathy.

B. The client appeared tired, listless, and apathetic during today's therapy session.

C. The client reported a recent mild increase in his/her level of energy.

D. The client reported experiencing a return to his/her normal level of energy.

12. Lack of Eye Contact (11)

A. The parents and teachers reported that the client displays very little eye contact during his/her social interactions with others.

B. The client displayed poor eye contact during today's therapy session and acknowledged this to be a common practice.

C. The client has demonstrated satisfactory eye contact with individuals with whom he/she feels comfortable but poor eye contact with unfamiliar people.

D. The client maintained good eye contact during today's therapy session and stated that he/she is increasing eye contact with others as well.

E. The parents and teachers reported that the client consistently maintains good eye contact.

13. Low Self-Esteem (12)

A. The client has been troubled by strong feelings of low self-esteem, inadequacy, and insecurity.

B. The client verbalized negative and disparaging remarks about himself/herself.

C. The client's low self-esteem, lack of confidence, and feelings of insecurity are significant concomitant aspects of his/her depression.

D. The client verbalized several positive self-descriptive statements during today's therapy session.

E. The client has taken active steps to improve his/her self-esteem (e.g., reaching out to others, challenging self with new activities).

14. Appetite Disturbance (13)

A. The client reported experiencing a loss of appetite during his/her depressive episodes.

B. The client has lost a significant amount of weight since becoming depressed.

C. The client reports that he/she has often turned to food to feel better during periods of depression.

D. The client reported a significant weight gain since the onset of his/her depression.

E. The client's appetite has returned to a normal level since his/her feelings of depression have decreased.

15. Sleep Disturbance (14)

A. The client reported having difficulty falling asleep and/or experiencing early morning awakenings since he/she became depressed.

B. The client reported sleeping more than usual during his/her bout of depression.

C. The client reported sleeping well recently.

D. The client's sleep has returned to a normal level.

16. Poor Concentration and Indecisiveness (15)

A. The client reported to having difficulty concentrating and making decisions since feeling depressed.

B. The client had trouble concentrating and staying focused during today's therapy session.

C. The client's low self-esteem, lack of confidence, and feelings of insecurity have contributed to his/her difficulty in making decisions.

D. The client reported being able to concentrate and stay focused for longer periods of time now that he/she has ceased feeling depressed.

E. The client's ability to make some constructive decisions has helped to decrease his/her feelings of depression.

17. Feelings of Hopelessness/Helplessness (16)

A. The client has developed a pessimistic outlook on the future and is troubled by feelings of hopelessness and helplessness.

B. The client expressed feelings of helplessness and voiced little hope that his/her life will improve in the future.

C. The client expressed confidence about his/her ability to overcome problems or stress and improve his/her life in the future.

D. The client has experienced a renewed sense of hope and feelings of empowerment.

18. Feelings of Guilt (16)

A. The client expressed strong feelings of guilt about his/her past actions.

B. The client's strong feelings of irrational guilt are a significant contributing factor to his/her depression and inability to move ahead with life.

C. The client made productive use of today's therapy session by exploring his/her feelings of guilt about past actions.

D. The client denied being troubled by any significant feelings of guilt.

E. The client has successfully worked through and resolved his/her feelings of guilt about his/her past actions.

19. Unresolved Grief Issues (17)

A. The client's unresolved feelings of grief have been a significant contributing factor to his/her episode of depression.

B. The client expressed strong feelings of sadness and grief about past separations or losses.

C. The client was guarded and reluctant to talk about his/her past losses or separations.

D. The client's depression has begun to lift as he/she works through his/her feelings of grief about past losses or separations.

E. The client has experienced a significant increase in the frequency and duration of his/her happy or contented mood since working through the issues of grief.

INTERVENTIONS IMPLEMENTED

1. Assess Mood Episodes (1)*

A. An assessment was conducted of the client's current and past mood episodes, including the features, frequency, intensity, and duration of the mood episodes.

B. The *Inventory to Diagnose Depression* (Zimmerman, Coryell, Corenthal, and Wilson) was used to assess the client's current and past mood episodes.

C. The results of the mood episode assessment reflected severe mood concerns, and this was presented to the client.

D. The results of the mood episode assessment reflected moderate mood concerns, and this was presented to the client.

E. The results of the mood episode assessment reflected mild mood concerns, and this was presented to the client.

2. Identify Depression Causes (2)

A. The client was asked to verbally identify the source of his/her depressed mood.

B. Active-listening skills were used as the client listed several factors that he/she believes contribute to his/her feelings of hopelessness and sadness.

C. The client struggled to identify significant causes for his/her depression and was provided with tentative examples in this area.

3. Clarify Depressed Feelings (3)

A. The client was encouraged to share his/her feelings of depression in order to clarify them and gain insight into their causes.

B. The client was supported as he/she has continued to share his/her feelings of depression and identified causes for them.

---

*The numbers in parentheses correlate to the number of the Therapeutic Intervention statement in the companion chapter with the same title in *The Adolescent Psychotherapy Treatment Planner,* Fourth Edition (Jongsma, Peterson, McInnis, and Bruce) by John Wiley & Sons, 2006.

C. Distorted cognitive messages were noted to contribute to the client's feelings of depression.

D. The client demonstrated sad affect and tearfulness when describing his/her feelings.

4. Administer Psychological Tests for Depression (4)

A. Psychological testing was arranged to objectively assess the client's depression and suicide risk.

B. The Beck Depression Inventory–2 was used to assess the client's depression and suicide risk.

C. The Beck Hopelessness Scale was used to assess the client's depression and suicide risk.

D. The results of the testing indicated severe concerns related to the client's depression and suicide risk, and this was reflected to the client.

E. The results of the testing indicated moderate concerns related to the client's depression and suicide risk, and this was reflected to the client

F. The results of the testing indicated mild concerns related to the client's depression and suicide risk, and this was reflected to the client.

5. Explore History of Suicide (5)

A. The client's history of suicide urges was explored.

B. The client's current state of suicide urges was explored.

C. The client was noted to have experienced many previous urges regarding suicide.

D. The client has not had many significant urges related to suicide, and this was reflected to him/her.

6. Explore Suicide Potential (6)

A. The client's experience of suicidal urges and his/her history of suicidal behavior were explored.

B. It was noted that the client has stated that he/she does experience suicidal urges but feels that they are clearly under his/her control and that there is no risk of engagement in suicidal behavior.

C. The client identified suicidal urges as being present but contracted to contact others if the urges became strong.

D. Because the client's suicidal urges were assessed to be very serious, immediate referral to a more intensive, supervised level of care was made.

E. Due to the client's suicidal urges and his/her unwillingness to voluntarily admit himself/herself to a more intensive, supervised level of care, involuntary commitment procedures were begun.

7. Arrange for Hospitalization (7)

A. Because the client was judged to be uncontrollably harmful to himself/herself, arrangements were made for psychiatric hospitalization.

B. The client cooperated voluntarily with admission to a psychiatric hospital.

C. The client refused to cooperate voluntarily with admission to a psychiatric facility, and therefore commitment procedures were initiated.

8. Refer to Physician (8)

A. The client was referred to a physician for a physical examination to rule out organic causes for depression.

B. A referral to a physician was made for the purpose of evaluating the client for a prescription for psychotropic medication.

C. The client has followed through on a referral to a physician and has been assessed for a prescription of psychotropic medication.

D. The client has been prescribed antidepressant medication.

E. The client has refused the prescription of psychotropic medication prescribed by the physician.

9. Monitor Medication (9)

A. The client's response to his/her psychotropic medications was discussed, and he/she reported that the medication has helped decrease his/her symptoms of depression and stabilize his/her mood.

B. The client's psychotropic medications were reviewed, and he/she indicated there were no improvements since starting to take the medication.

C. The client's compliance with his/her medication regimen was reviewed, and he/she was noted to be quite regular in his/her medication usage.

D. The client was noted to have been noncompliant in taking his/her medication.

E. The client was encouraged to report side effects of the medication to the prescribing physician.

F. Contact will be made with the prescribing physician regarding the need for adjustment in the client's psychotropic medication prescription.

10. Identify Depressogenic Schemata (10)

A. The client was assisted in developing an awareness of his/her automatic thoughts that reflect depressogenic schemata.

B. The client was assisted in developing an awareness of his/her distorted cognitive messages that reinforce hopelessness and helplessness.

C. The client was helped to identify several cognitive messages that occur on a regular basis and feed feelings of depression.

D. The client recalled several incidents of engaging in negative self-talk that precipitated feelings of helplessness, hopelessness, and depression; these were processed.

11. Assign Automatic Thought Journal (11)

A. The client was assigned to keep a daily journal of automatic thoughts associated with depressed feelings.

B. "Bad Thoughts Lead to Depressed Feelings" from the *Adolescent Psychotherapy Homework Planner,* 2nd ed. (Jongsma, Peterson, and McInnis) was used to help identify automatic thoughts associated with depressive feelings.

C. "Daily Record of Dysfunctional Thoughts" from *Cognitive Therapy of Depression* (Beck, Rush, Shaw, and Emery) was used to identify automatic thoughts associated with depressive feelings.

D. The Socratic method was used to challenge the client's dysfunctional thoughts and to replace them with positive, reality-based thoughts. ·

E. The client was reinforced for instances of successful replacement of negative thoughts with more realistic, positive thinking.

12. Conduct Behavioral Experiments (12)

A. The client was encouraged to do "behavioral experiments" in which depressive automatic thoughts are treated as hypotheses/predictions and are tested against reality-based alternative hypotheses.

B. The client's automatic depressive thoughts were tested against the client's past, present, and/or future experiences.

C. The client was assisted in processing the outcome of his/her behavioral experiences.

D. The client was encouraged by his/her experience of the more reality-based hypotheses/predictions; this progress was reinforced.

E. The client continues to focus on depressive automatic thoughts and was redirected toward the behavioral evidence of the more reality-based alternative hypotheses.

13. Reinforce Positive Self-Talk (13)

A. The client was reinforced for any successful replacement of distorted negative thinking with positive, reality-based cognitive messages.

B. It was noted that the client has been engaging in positive, reality-based thinking that has enhanced his/her self-confidence and increased adaptive action.

C. The client was assigned to complete the "Positive Self-Talk" assignment from the *Adult Psychotherapy Homework Planner*, 2nd ed. (Jongsma).

14. Develop Coping Strategies (14)

A. The client was assisted in developing coping strategies for feelings of depression.

B. The client was assisted in identifying specific coping strategies, such as more physical exercise, less internal focus, increased social involvement, more assertiveness, greater need sharing, and more anger expression.

C. The client was reinforced for his/her success in developing positive coping strategies.

D. The client was redirected for his/her lack of development or use of coping strategies.

15. Engage in Behavioral Activation (15)

A. The client was engaged in "behavioral activation" by scheduling activities that have a high likelihood for pleasure and mastery.

B. The client was directed to complete tasks from the "Identify and Schedule Pleasant Events" assignment from the *Adult Psychotherapy Homework Planner*, 2nd ed. (Jongsma).

C. Rehearsal, role-playing, role reversal, and other techniques were used to engage the client in behavioral activation.

D. The client was reinforced for his/her successes in scheduling activities that have a high likelihood for pleasure and mastery.

E. The client has not engaged in pleasurable activities and was redirected to do so.

16. Employ Self-Reliance Training (16)

A. Self-reliance training was used to help the client assume increased responsibility for routine activities (e.g., cleaning, cooking, shopping).

B. The client was urged to take responsibility for routine activities in order to overcome depression symptoms.

C. The client was reinforced for his/her increased self-reliance.

D. The client has not assumed increased responsibility for routine activities, and his/her struggles in this area were redirected.

17. Assess the Interpersonal Inventory (17)

A. The client was asked to develop an "interpersonal inventory" of important past and present relationships.

B. The client's interpersonal inventory was assessed for potentially depressive themes (e.g., grief, interpersonal disputes, role transitions, interpersonal deficits).

C. The client's interpersonal inventory was found to have significant depressive themes, and this was reflected to the client.

D. The client's interpersonal inventory was found to have minimal depressive themes, and this was reflected to the client.

18. Explore Unresolved Grief (18)

A. The client's history of losses that have triggered feelings of grief was explored.

B. The client was assisted in identifying losses that have contributed to feelings of grief that have not been resolved.

C. The client's unresolved feelings of grief are noted to be contributing to current feelings of depression and were provided a special focus.

19. Teach Conflict Resolution Skills (19)

A. The client was taught conflict resolution skills such as practicing empathy, active listening, respectful communication, assertiveness, and compromise.

B. Using role-playing, modeling, and behavioral rehearsal, the client was taught implementation of conflict resolution skills.

C. The client reported implementation of conflict resolution skills in his/her daily life and was reinforced for this utilization.

D. The client reported that resolving interpersonal conflicts has contributed to a lifting of his/her depression; the benefits of this progress were emphasized.

E. The client has not used the conflict resolution skills that he/she has been taught and was provided with specific examples of when to use these skills.

20. Decrease Effect of Interpersonal Problems (20)

A. The client was assisted in resolving interpersonal problems through the use of reassurance and support.

B. The "Applying Problem-Solving to Interpersonal Conflict" assignment from the *Adult Psychotherapy Homework Planner*, 2nd ed. (Jongsma) was used to help resolve interpersonal problems.

C. The client was helped to clarify cognitive and affective triggers that ignite conflicts.

D. The client was taught active problem-solving techniques to help him/her resolve interpersonal problems.

E. It was reflected to the client that he/she has significantly reduced his/her interpersonal problems.

F. The client continues to have significant interpersonal problems, and he/she was provided with remedial assistance in this area.

21. Address Interpersonal Conflict (21)

A. A conjoint session was held to assist the client in resolving interpersonal conflicts with his/her partner.

B. The client reported that the conjoint sessions have been helpful in resolving interpersonal conflicts with his/her partner and that this has contributed to a lifting of his/her depression.

C. It was reflected that ongoing conflicts with a partner have fostered feelings of depression and hopelessness.

22. Reinforce Physical Exercise (22)

A. A plan for routine physical exercise was developed with the client, and a rationale for including this in his/her daily routine was made.

B. The client and therapist agreed to make a commitment to implement daily exercise as a depression reduction technique.

C. The client has performed routine daily exercise, and he/she reports that it has been beneficial; these benefits were reinforced.

D. The client has not followed through on maintaining a routine of physical exercise and was redirected to do so.

23. Recommend *Exercising Your Way to Better Mental Health* (23)

A. The client was encouraged to read *Exercising Your Way to Better Mental Health* (Leith) to introduce him/her to the concept of combating stress, depression, and anxiety with exercise.

B. The client has followed through with reading the recommended book on exercise and mental health and reported that it was beneficial; key points were reviewed.

C. The client has implemented a regular exercise regimen as a depression reduction technique and reported successful results; he/she was verbally reinforced for this progress.

D. The client has not followed through with reading the recommended material on the effect of exercise on mental health and was encouraged to do so.

24. Build Relapse Prevention Skills (24)

A. The client was assisted in building relapse prevention skills through the identification of early warning signs of relapse.

B. The client was directed to consistently review skills learned during therapy.

C. The client was assisted in developing an ongoing plan for managing his/her routine challenges.

25. Teach Assertiveness (25)

A. Role-playing, modeling, and behavioral rehearsal were used to train the client in assertiveness.

B. The client was referred to an assertiveness training group for intense education in acquiring assertiveness skills.

C. The client reported that as a result of the training he/she has become more assertive in expressing his/her needs, desires, and expectations.

D. The client continues to have difficulties in being assertive, as lack of confidence, low self-esteem, and social withdrawal inhibit him/her; remedial education was provided in this area.

26. Recommend Depression Self-Help Books (26)

A. Several self-help books on the topic of coping with depression were recommended to the client.

B. The client was directed to read *The Feeling Good Handbook* (Burns).

C. The client has followed through with reading self-help books on depression and reported key ideas that were processed.

D. The client reported that reading the assigned self-help books on depression has been beneficial and identified several coping techniques that he/she has implemented as a result of the reading.

E. The client has not followed through with reading the self-help books that were recommended and was encouraged to do so.

27. Assess Understanding of Self-Defeating Behaviors (27)

A. The client was assessed for his/her level of self-understanding of self-defeating behaviors.

B. The client was asked to explain his/her understanding of how self-defeating behaviors are linked to depression.

C. The client was asked to apply his/her understanding of self-defeating behaviors to his/her own experience of depression.

D. The client was reinforced for his/her clear understanding of the issues related to self-defeating behaviors and depression.

E. The client struggled to understand the connection between self-defeating behaviors and depression, and he/she was provided with remedial feedback in this area.

28. Identify Unmet Emotional Needs (28)

A. The client was assisted in identifying his/her unmet emotional needs.

B. The client's acting out behaviors were interpreted as avoidance of the real conflict involving his/her unmet needs.

C. Depression symptoms were noted to be a common reflection of the client's unmet needs and avoidance of the real conflict in his/her life.

D. The client was reinforced as he/she displayed a clear understanding of how his/her unmet emotional needs contribute to depression and acting out behavior.

29. Teach Connection between Surface Behavior and Inner Feelings (29)

A. The client was taught about the connection between angry, irritable behaviors (on the surface) and feelings of hurt or sadness (as inner feelings).

B. The client was given the "Surface Behavior/Inner Feelings" exercise from the *Adolescent Psychotherapy Homework Planner,* 2nd ed. (Jongsma, Peterson, and McInnis) to show the connection between his/her angry, irritable, acting out behaviors and feelings of hurt or sadness.

C. The client successfully completed the "Surface Behavior/Inner Feelings" homework and was assisted in identifying how his/her angry, irritable behaviors are connected to underlying feelings of hurt and sadness.

D. The client successfully completed the homework assignment and reported that he/she was able to share feelings of hurt and sadness with other trusted individuals; the benefits of this closeness were reviewed.

E. The client did not complete the "Surface Behavior/Inner Feelings" homework and was asked again to do it.

30. Explore Emotional Pain from Past (30)

A. Today's therapy session explored the emotional pain from the client's past that contributes to his/her feelings of hopelessness and low self-esteem.

B. The client was given empathy and support in expressing his/her painful emotions about the past experiences that have contributed to current feelings of hopelessness and low self-esteem.

C. The client was encouraged to utilize positive self-talk as a means to offset his/her pattern of negative thinking and overcome feelings of hopelessness.

D. Guided imagery techniques were utilized to help the client visualize a brighter future.

E. The client consistently denied any emotional pain from the past and was provided with tentative examples of areas where he/she may have experienced emotional pain.

31. Encourage Sharing of Anger (31)

A. The client was encouraged to share his/her feelings of anger regarding pain inflicted on him/her in childhood.

B. The client was assisted in recognizing that his/her feelings of anger from childhood problems are contributing to his/her current depressed state.

C. The client was reinforced for his/her identification and expression of angry feelings.

D. It was reflected to the client that he/she seems to be minimizing, blocking, or avoiding his/her feelings of anger.

32. Identify Unmet Emotional Needs and Plans to Satisfy Needs (32)

A. The client was assisted in identifying his/her unmet emotional needs.

B. The client was assisted in identifying specific ways in which his/her unmet emotional needs could be met.

C. The client was assigned the "Unmet Emotional Needs—Identification and Satisfaction" exercise from the *Adolescent Psychotherapy Homework Planner,* 2nd ed. (Jongsma, Peterson, and McInnis) to help identify his/her unmet emotional needs and specific ways to meet those needs in the future.

D. The client completed the "Unmet Emotional Needs—Identification and Satisfaction" exercise and was helped to identify his/her unmet emotional needs and several effective ways to meet them.

E. The client failed to complete the exercise and was again asked to work on it.

33. Address Family Conflict (33)

A. A family therapy session was held to facilitate a discussion of the conflict that exists in the family.

B. Today's family therapy session was helpful in identifying the core areas of conflict that contribute to the client's depression.

C. The family members were asked to brainstorm possible ways to resolve the conflictual issues affecting the family.

D. The family members were able to agree on solutions to the problem(s) that is (are) contributing to the client's depression and were encouraged to implement the solutions.

E. The client and family members were unable to reach an agreement on how to resolve the conflict that is contributing to the client's depression, despite guidance from the therapist.

34. Encourage Expression of Emotional Needs (34)

A. The client was given the opportunity to respectfully express his/her emotional needs to family members and significant others.

B. The family members were encouraged for responding with empathy and support to the client's expression of his/her needs.

C. The client and family members were helped to identify ways to meet the client's emotional needs.

D. The client was given a specific task to perform with the family members or significant others to meet his/her emotional needs.

E. Although the client was provided with the opportunity to respectfully express his/her emotional needs to family members, he/she declined to provide significant information in this area.

35. Encourage Academic Effort (35)

A. The client was helped to establish academic goals to help lift his/her depression and improve self-esteem.

B. The client and parents were assisted in developing a routine schedule of study times to mobilize the client and help him/her achieve academic success.

C. A reward system was designed to reinforce the client to achieve his/her academic goals.

D. The client and parents were encouraged to maintain regular communication with the teachers via phone calls or progress notes to help him/her stay organized and achieve academic goals.

E. The client and parents were encouraged to work with a tutor to improve the client's academic performance.

F. The client reported that tutoring has helped to improve his/her academic performance, and he/she was directed to continue use of the tutor.

G. The client reported little or no improvement in his/her academic performance while working with a tutor but was urged to continue.

36. Monitor Sleep Patterns (36)

A. Today's therapy session explored the factors that interfere with the client's ability to sleep restfully through the night.

B. The client was trained in the use of guided imagery and relaxation techniques to help induce calm before attempting to sleep.

C. The client was asked to track his/her sleep patterns to determine whether he/she should be referred for a medication evaluation.

D. The client was instructed to monitor his/her sleep patterns to help determine whether the medication needs to be changed or the dosage adjusted.

E. The client was administered electromyographic (EMG) biofeedback to reinforce a successful relaxation response to help him/her sleep restfully at night.

37. Assess Substance Abuse (37)

A. A diagnostic interview was conducted to determine whether the client is using alcohol or drugs as a means of coping with depressive feelings.

B. The client was referred for a substance abuse evaluation to assess the extent of his/her drug or alcohol use and determine the need for treatment.

C. The client appeared to be cooperative when asked questions about his/her past alcohol or drug usage.

D. The client was resistant to discussing his/her past alcohol or drug usage and was encouraged to be open in this area.

38. Refer for Substance Abuse Treatment (39)

A. The findings from the substance abuse evaluation revealed the presence of a substance abuse problem, and therefore the client was referred for chemical dependence treatment.

B. The client expressed a willingness to seek treatment for his/her substance abuse problem and was referred for this treatment.

C. The client expressed resistance to receiving the substance abuse treatment for which he/she is being referred.

D. The findings from the substance abuse evaluation did not reveal the presence of a substance abuse problem or the need for treatment in this area.

39. Assess, Confront, and Treat Sexual Acting Out (39)

A. The client was assessed for the factors contributing to his/her pattern of irresponsible or sexually promiscuous behavior.

B. The client was confronted and taught about the potential dangers or risks involved with his/her irresponsible sexual acting out behavior.

C. The client shared the realization that he/she has tried to overcome depression and meet his/her dependency needs through sexually promiscuous behavior, and he/she was assisted in listing other ways to meet these needs.

D. Today's therapy session explored the client's irrational or unrealistic beliefs that underlie his/her sexually promiscuous behavior.

E. The client had difficulty identifying the factors contributing to his/her sexually promiscuous behavior and was provided with tentative feedback in this area.

40. Assess Unresolved Grief Issues (40)

A. Today's therapy session explored whether unresolved grief and loss issues are contributing to the client's depression.

B. The client was given the opportunity to express his/her feelings about past separations or losses.

C. The client was instructed to write a letter to the deceased or absent person to help him/her express feelings about past separations or losses.

D. The client was instructed to use a journal to record his/her daily thoughts and feelings about past grief issues.

E. The empty-chair technique was employed to facilitate expression of feelings surrounding past separations or losses.

F. The client was instructed to draw pictures reflecting his/her feelings about past losses and how they have affected his/her life.

DIVORCE REACTION

CLIENT PRESENTATION

1. Reduced Contact with a Parent (1)*

A. The client has had infrequent or no contact with one of his/her parents since the separation or divorce.

B. The client was guarded and reluctant to talk about the infrequency or loss of contact with one of his/her parents.

C. The client expressed feelings of sadness, hurt, and disappointment about the infrequency or loss of contact with one of his/her parents.

D. The client verbalized strong feelings of anger about the limited contact with one of his/her parents.

E. The client has worked through many of his/her emotions surrounding the infrequency or loss of contact with one of his/her parents.

2. Intense Emotional Outbursts/Sudden Shifts in Mood (2)

A. The client has exhibited frequent, intense emotional outbursts and sudden shifts in mood since the separation or divorce.

B. The client acknowledged that he/she has difficulty controlling his/her emotions when discussing topics related to the separation or divorce.

C. The client exhibited a wide range of emotions when discussing the separation or divorce.

D. The client's moods have begun to stabilize as he/she works through his/her feelings about the separation or divorce.

3. Substance Abuse (3)

A. The client has engaged in a significant amount of substance abuse since his/her parents' separation or divorce.

B. The client acknowledged that he/she has often turned to alcohol or drug abuse to block out the emotional pain related to his/her parents' separation or divorce.

C. The client verbalized an awareness of the negative consequences or potential dangers associated with his/her substance abuse.

D. Instead of turning to drug or alcohol abuse, the client has started to develop more adaptive coping mechanisms to help him/her deal with the stress and emotional pain surrounding the separation or divorce.

E. The client stated that he/she has terminated his/her substance abuse.

4. Feelings of Grief and Sadness (4)

A. The client has experienced strong feelings of grief and sadness since his/her parents' separation or divorce.

B. The client was visibly sad when talking about his/her parents' separation or divorce.

*The numbers in parentheses correlate to the number of the Behavioral Definition statement in the companion chapter with the same title in *The Adolescent Psychotherapy Treatment Planner,* Fourth Edition (Jongsma, Peterson, McInnis, and Bruce) by John Wiley & Sons, 2006.

C. The client has begun to work through his/her feelings of grief and sadness about the separation or divorce.

D. The client's affect appeared more happy and/or contented in today's therapy session.

E. The client reported a significant recent reduction in the frequency and severity of his/her depressed mood.

5. Low Self-Esteem (4)

A. The client's self-esteem has decreased significantly since his/her parents' separation or divorce.

B. The client verbalized feelings of low self-esteem, inadequacy, and insecurity.

C. The client has begun to take steps to improve his/her self-esteem and develop a positive self-image.

D. The client expressed positive self-descriptive statements during today's therapy session.

E. The client has developed a healthy self-image after working through many of his/her feelings surrounding his/her parents' separation or divorce.

6. Social Withdrawal (4)

A. The client has become significantly more withdrawn and isolated since his/her parents' separation or divorce.

B. The client appeared very quiet and withdrawn during today's therapy session and initiated few conversations.

C. The client has gradually started to socialize more often with his/her peers.

D. The client was more communicative and outgoing during today's therapy session.

7. Feelings of Guilt/Self-Blame (5)

A. The client expressed feelings of guilt about having in some way caused his/her parents' divorce.

B. The client has continued to hold onto the unreasonable belief that he/she behaved in some manner that either caused his/her parents' divorce or failed to prevent it from occurring.

C. The client has started to work through his/her feelings of guilt about his/her parents' separation or divorce.

D. The parent(s) verbalized that the client is not responsible for the separation or divorce.

E. The client has successfully worked through his/her feelings of guilt and no longer blames himself/herself for the parents' separation or divorce.

8. Oppositional, Acting-Out, and Aggressive Behaviors (6)

A. The client has exhibited a significant increase in the frequency and severity of his/her oppositional, acting out, and aggressive behaviors since his/her parents' separation or divorce.

B. The client appeared angry and irritable when discussing the separation or divorce.

C. The frequency of the client's oppositional, acting out, and aggressive behaviors has gradually started to diminish.

D. The client has recently demonstrated good self-control and has not engaged in a significant amount of oppositional, acting out, or aggressive behaviors.

E. The client has successfully worked through many of his/her feelings surrounding the separation or divorce and has demonstrated a significant reduction in the frequency and severity of his/her oppositional, acting out, and aggressive behaviors.

9. Decline in School Performance (7)

A. The client's school performance has declined markedly since his/her parents' separation or divorce.

B. The client verbalized that he/she has experienced a loss of interest or motivation to achieve academic success since the separation or divorce.

C. The client has experienced a renewed interest in his/her schoolwork and has begun to take steps to improve his/her academic performance.

D. The client reported completing his/her school or homework assignments on a regular basis.

10. Sexually Promiscuous Behavior (8)

A. The client described a pattern of engaging in sexually promiscuous or seductive behavior since his/her parents' separation or divorce.

B. The client acknowledged that he/she has engaged in sexually promiscuous or seductive behavior to compensate for the loss of security or support within the family system.

C. The client verbalized an awareness of the negative consequences and potential dangers associated with his/her sexually promiscuous behavior.

D. The client has demonstrated good control over his/her sexual impulses and has not engaged in any risky or irresponsible sexual behavior.

11. Pseudomaturity (9)

A. The client has responded to his/her parents' separation or divorce by displaying an air of pseudomaturity.

B. The client presented with a facade of pseudomaturity and coolly denied being troubled by any painful emotions about his/her parents' separation or divorce.

C. The client has responded to the separation or divorce by often assuming parental roles or responsibilities.

D. The client verbalized an awareness that his/her willingness to take on many parental roles or responsibilities has prevented him/her from meeting his/her own emotional or social needs.

E. The client has achieved a healthy balance between fulfilling his/her school or household responsibilities and meeting his/her social and emotional needs.

12. Psychosomatic Ailments (10)

A. The client has demonstrated a significant increase in psychosomatic complaints since his/her parents' separation or divorce.

B. The client complained of not feeling well when the issue of his/her parents' separation or divorce was being discussed.

C. The client was resistant to the interpretation that his/her psychosomatic complaints are related to his/her underlying painful emotions about the separation or divorce.

D. The client verbalized an understanding of the connection between his/her psychosomatic complaints and anticipated separations, stress, or frustration related to the parents' marital conflict.

E. The client has demonstrated a significant reduction in the frequency of his/her psychosomatic complaints.

13. Loss of Contact with Positive Support Network (11)

A. The client has experienced a loss of contact with his/her previous support network due to his/her geographic move.

B. The client expressed feelings of sadness about having to move after his/her parents' separation or divorce because it resulted in a loss of contact with his/her previous support network.

C. The client expressed feelings of anger about having to move after his/her parents' separation or divorce.

D. The client has taken active steps to build a positive support network since moving to a new geographic area.

E. The client reported establishing a strong, supportive social network outside of his/her immediate family.

INTERVENTIONS IMPLEMENTED

1. Build Therapeutic Trust (1)*

A. The objective of today's therapy session was to establish trust with the client so that he/she can begin to express and work through his/her feelings related to the parents' separation or divorce.

B. Attempts were made to build the level of trust with the client through consistent eye contact, active listening, unconditional positive regard, and warm acceptance.

C. The therapy session was helpful in building a level of trust with the client.

D. The therapy session was not successful in establishing trust with the client, as he/she remained guarded in sharing his/her feelings about the separation or divorce.

2. Explore and Encourage Expression of Feelings (2)

A. Today's therapy session explored the client's feelings associated with his/her parents' separation or divorce.

B. The client was given encouragement and support in expressing and clarifying his/her feelings associated with the separation or divorce.

C. Client-centered therapy principles were utilized to assist the client in expressing his/her thoughts and feelings about the parents' separation or divorce.

D. The client made productive use of today's therapy session and was assisted in expressing a variety of emotions related to his/her parents' separation or divorce.

E. The client remained guarded in sharing his/her feelings regarding the separation or divorce, despite receiving encouragement and support.

*The numbers in parentheses correlate to the number of the Therapeutic Intervention statement in the companion chapter with the same title in *The Adolescent Psychotherapy Treatment Planner,* Fourth Edition (Jongsma, Peterson, McInnis, and Bruce) by John Wiley & Sons, 2006.

3. Utilize the Empty-Chair Technique (3)

A. The empty-chair technique was used to help the client express the mixed emotions that he/she feels toward both parents about the separation or divorce.

B. The empty-chair technique was helpful in allowing the client to identify and express the emotions that he/she feels toward both parents about the separation or divorce.

C. The client appeared uncomfortable with the use of the empty-chair technique and was reluctant to share the emotions that he/she feels toward both parents about the separation or divorce.

D. The empty-chair technique was useful in allowing the client to express his/her thoughts and feelings about the custodial and noncustodial parent.

4. Assign Keeping a Journal (4)

A. The client was instructed to keep a journal in which he/she records experiences or situations that evoke strong emotions pertaining to the separation or divorce.

B. Active listening techniques were used as the client shared entries from his/her journal that reflected his/her thoughts and feelings about the separation or divorce.

C. The use of the journal has proven to be helpful in allowing the client to express and work through his/her feelings about the separation or divorce.

D. The client has failed to keep a journal reflecting his/her thoughts and feelings about the separation or divorce and was redirected to do so.

5. Develop a Time Line (5)

A. The client developed a time line on which he/she recorded significant developments that have positively or negatively impacted his/her family life, both before and after the separation or divorce, and this was reviewed in the session.

B. The use of the time line was helpful in allowing the client to express his/her thoughts and feelings about the impact of the separation or divorce on his/her life.

C. The use of the time line exercise was not helpful in facilitating a discussion about the impact of the parents' separation or divorce on the client's life.

D. Active-listening skills were used as the client identified a number of positive and negative changes that have occurred within the family system since the parents' separation or divorce.

E. The client used the time line to express his/her ambivalent feelings about the divorce and the subsequent changes within the family system; he/she was supported as these feelings were discussed.

F. The client did not develop a time line and was redirected to do so.

6. Develop a List of Questions (6)

A. The client was assisted in developing a list of questions about the parents' separation or divorce.

B. The client first identified the questions that he/she has about the separation or divorce and then was assisted in exploring possible answers for each question.

C. The client carefully considered whether he/she wanted to ask the parent(s) specific questions about the separation or divorce; the pros and cons of this choice were reviewed.

D. The client was encouraged to ask each parent specific questions about the separation or divorce to help him/her gain a greater understanding of the factors contributing to the separation or divorce.

E. The client decided not to ask specific questions to each parent about the separation or divorce because of the possible negative responses that he/she might receive, and this was accepted.

7. Facilitate Expression of Feelings (7)

A. A family therapy session was held to allow the client and his/her siblings to express feelings and ask questions about the separation or divorce in the presence of the parents.

B. The custodial parent was provided with positive feedback for being supportive in allowing the client and siblings to express their feelings and ask questions about the separation or divorce.

C. The noncustodial parent was provided with positive feedback for being supportive in allowing the client and siblings to express their feelings and ask questions about the separation or divorce.

D. The custodial parent was redirected when he/she became defensive when the client and siblings began expressing their feelings and asking questions about the separation or divorce.

E. The noncustodial parent was redirected when he/she became defensive when the client and siblings began expressing their feelings and asking questions about the separation or divorce.

8. Provide Opportunities at Home to Express Feelings (8)

A. The parent(s) were encouraged to provide opportunities at home to allow the client and siblings to express their feelings and ask questions about the separation or divorce and subsequent changes in the family system.

B. The parent(s) were encouraged to hold family meetings at home to allow the client and siblings an opportunity to express their feelings and ask questions about the separation or divorce and subsequent changes in the family system.

C. The family members were helped to identify healthy and unhealthy ways to express their feelings about the separation or divorce and subsequent changes in the family system.

D. The parent(s) were encouraged to explore the client's feelings about the separation or divorce and subsequent changes in the family system when he/she becomes more withdrawn or demonstrates an increase in emotional outbursts.

E. The client and siblings were asked to identify the specific positive changes that they would like to see happen in the family.

F. The client's parents have not allowed the client to regularly express his/her feelings (in a respectful manner) and were redirected to do so.

9. Explore Guilt and Self-Blame (9)

A. Today's therapy session explored and identified the factors contributing to the client's feelings of guilt and self-blame about the parents' separation or divorce.

B. The client indicated that he/she believes his/her rebellious behavior may have contributed to his/her parents' separation, and he/she was helped to understand that his/her negative behavior did not cause his/her parents' separation.

C. Today's therapy session did not reveal any specific events that have contributed to the client's feelings of guilt and self-blame about the parents' separation, and he/she denied being troubled by these types of feelings.

D. The client has continued to hold on to feelings of guilt that his/her negative behaviors caused his/her parents' separation and was provided with additional assurance that he/she is not responsible.

10. Dissuade Client from Attempts to Reunite Parents (10)

A. The client was gently confronted with the fact that he/she does not have the power or control to bring his/her parents back together.

B. The client was confronted regarding his/her belief that his/her negative behavior can help bring his/her parents back together.

C. The client has acknowledged that he/she does not have the power to decide whether his/her parents will remain together or divorced.

11. Affirm Client as Not Being Responsible for Separation/Divorce (11)

A. The custodial parent strongly affirmed that the client and siblings were not responsible for the separation or divorce, and the therapist emphasized this concept.

B. The noncustodial parent strongly affirmed that the client and siblings were not responsible for the separation or divorce, and the therapist emphasized this concept.

C. The parent(s) were supported for verbalizing responsibility for the separation or divorce.

D. The client and siblings responded positively to the parents' affirmation that they are not responsible for the separation or divorce, and the meaning of this affirmation was elaborated.

E. The client has continued to be troubled by feelings of guilt about his/her parents' divorce despite the parents' statements that he/she is not responsible, and this was normalized.

12. Confront Blaming by Parents (12)

A. The custodial parent was challenged and confronted about making statements that place the blame or responsibility for the separation or divorce on the client or siblings.

B. The noncustodial parent was challenged and confronted about making statements that place the blame or responsibility for the separation or divorce on the client or siblings.

C. The custodial parent was reinforced for a verbalized commitment to cease making statements that place the blame or responsibility for the separation or divorce on the client or siblings.

D. The noncustodial parent was reinforced for a verbalized commitment to cease making statements that place the blame or responsibility for the separation or divorce on the client or siblings.

E. The parent(s) have continued to make statements that place the blame or responsibility for the separation or divorce on the client or siblings despite challenges to cease making such remarks.

13. List Positive and Negative Aspects of Divorce (13)

A. The client was given a homework assignment to list both the positive and negative aspects of his/her parents' divorce.

B. The client was reassured of the normalcy of feeling a variety of emotions while processing both the positive and negative aspects of his/her parents' divorce.

C. The client was supported as he/she expressed his/her emotions about the negative aspects of his/her parents' divorce but was unable to identify any positive aspects.

D. The client's failure to complete the homework assignment of listing both the positive and negative aspects of his/her parents' divorce appeared to be due to his/her desire to avoid dealing with any painful emotions, and this was reflected to him/her.

14. Encourage Parents to Spend Time with Client (14)

A. The parent(s) were given the directive to spend 10 to 15 minutes of one-on-one time with the client and siblings on a regular or daily basis, in order to identify the client's needs.

B. It was noted that the one-on-one time spent with the parent(s) has helped the client to decrease his/her feelings of depression.

C. The client and parents reported that the one-on-one time spent together has helped to improve his/her anger control, and they were encouraged to continue this one-on-one time.

D. The client and parents reported that they have spent little time together because of their busy schedules, and a specific time to be together was identified.

E. The client and parents were strongly challenged to spend time together in order to help the client adjust to his/her parents' divorce.

15. Develop Understanding of Unmet Needs and Help Satisfy Them (15)

A. The client was assigned homework to list unmet needs and identify the steps that he/she can take to meet those needs.

B. The client was assigned the "Unmet Emotional Needs—Identification and Satisfaction" exercise from the *Adolescent Psychotherapy Homework Planner,* 2nd ed. (Jongsma, Peterson, and McInnis) to help him/her identify unmet needs and the steps that he/she can take to meet those needs.

C. The client completed the "Unmet Emotional Needs—Identification and Satisfaction" exercise, and it was noted that he/she has begun to take steps to meet his/her unmet needs.

D. The client failed to complete the homework assignment and was asked again to work on it before the next therapy session.

16. Reinforce Healthy Coping with Divorce (16)

A. The therapy session focused on empowering the client's ability to cope with his/her parents' divorce.

B. The client was asked to identify a list of behaviors or signs that would indicate he/she has made a healthy adjustment to the parents' divorce.

C. The client was reinforced for the positive steps that he/she has taken to adjust to his/her parents' divorce.

D. The client remains pessimistic and resistant to the idea that he/she can make a healthy adjustment to the divorce, but was encouraged to keep this possibility open.

17. Connect Painful Emotions to Angry Outbursts (17)

A. The session was helpful in identifying how the client's underlying, painful emotions about his/her parents' divorce are related to an increase in the frequency of his/her angry outbursts or aggressive behaviors.

B. The client was helped to verbalize an understanding of how his/her aggressive behaviors are connected to underlying feelings of sadness, hurt, or disappointment about his/her parents' divorce.

C. Role-playing and modeling techniques were used to demonstrate appropriate ways for the client to express his/her underlying painful emotions.

D. The client was asked to list ways to express his/her painful emotions about the divorce that would be more appropriate than reacting impulsively with anger or aggression.

E. The client denied any connection between painful emotions and angry outbursts and was encouraged to reconsider this connection.

18. Teach Appropriate versus Inappropriate Anger Expressions (18)

A. The client was helped to identify appropriate and inappropriate ways to express or control his/her anger about the parents' separation, divorce, or changes in family.

B. The client was taught mediational and self-control strategies (e.g., relaxation, "stop, listen, think, and act") to help express anger through appropriate verbalizations and healthy physical outlets.

C. The client was encouraged to utilize active listening skills to delay the impulse or urge to react with anger or physical aggression when upset about his/her parents' separation, divorce, or changes in family.

D. The client identified healthy physical outlets for his/her strong feelings of anger and aggressive impulses, and positive feedback was provided.

E. Despite being taught appropriate anger expression, the client continues to use inappropriate means to express his/her anger about the changes in the family structure and dynamics.

19. Teach Relaxation or Guided Imagery Techniques (19)

A. The client was taught relaxation and guided imagery techniques to help control his/her anger.

B. The client reported a positive response to the use of the relaxation or guided imagery technique to help control anger.

C. The client has failed to consistently use the relaxation or guided imagery technique and, as a result, has continued to display anger control problems; he/she was redirected to the use of these techniques.

20. Reinforce Parents in Setting Consistent Limits (20)

A. The parents were strongly encouraged to set firm, consistent limits for the client's acting out, oppositional, or aggressive behaviors and not to allow guilt feelings about the divorce to interfere with the need to impose consequences for such behaviors.

B. The parent(s) acknowledged the failure to follow through with firm, consistent limits for the client's acting out, oppositional, or aggressive behavior because of guilty feelings about the divorce; brainstorming techniques were used to develop ways to implement consistent limits.

C. The parents reported that they have begun to set firm, consistent limits and were encouraged for not allowing their guilt feelings to interfere with the need to impose consequences.

D. The parents reported that the client has demonstrated improvements in his/her behavior since they began to set firm, consistent limits for his/her acting out, oppositional, or aggressive behavior, and the benefits of these limits were reviewed.

21. Encourage Parents to Establish Clear Rules (21)

A. The parents were helped to establish clearly defined rules and boundaries for the client.

B. The client and parents were helped to identify natural, logical consequences for the client's acting out, oppositional, or aggressive behaviors.

C. The client was asked to repeat the rules to demonstrate an understanding of the expectations of him/her.

D. The client verbally disagreed with the rules and expectations identified by the parents, but the right of the parents to set these rules was affirmed.

22. Assist Parents in Developing Homework Routine (22)

A. The parents were assisted in establishing a new routine to help the client complete his/her school or homework assignments.

B. The client and parent(s) were helped to develop a routine schedule of times to increase the completion of homework assignments.

C. The parents were strongly encouraged to maintain regular communication with the teachers or school officials via phone calls or written notes regarding the client's academic progress.

D. A consultation was held with the teachers about sending home daily or weekly progress notes informing the parents of how well the client has been doing at completing his/her school or homework assignments.

E. The parents have not developed a routine to help the client complete his/her school assignments and were redirected to do so.

23. Develop Reward System to Improve Academic Performance (23)

A. The client and parents were assisted in identifying a list of rewards to reinforce the client for completing his/her school or homework assignments on a regular basis.

B. A reward system was designed to reinforce the client for completing his/her school or homework assignment.

C. The client and parents were directed to sign a contingency contract specifying the consequences for his/her failure to complete school or homework assignments.

D. The client and parents verbally agreed to the terms of the reward system and/or contingency contract developed to improve academic performance.

E. The client and parents have not used the reward system to improve academic performance and were redirected to do so.

24. Explore Relationship of Physical Complaints to Emotional Conflicts (24)

A. Today's therapy session focused on the relationship between the client's somatic complaints and underlying emotional conflicts associated with the parents' divorce.

B. Today's therapy session attempted to refocus the discussion away from the client's physical complaints and onto the underlying emotional conflicts and the expression of feelings associated with the parents' divorce.

C. Today's therapy session explored the secondary gain that is achieved by the client's somatic complaints.

D. Positive feedback was provided as the client verbally acknowledged that his/her somatic physical complaints are associated with the stress and conflict surrounding his/her parents' divorce.

E. The client verbalized an understanding of how his/her somatic complaints are related to unfulfilled dependency needs and was assisted in developing these concepts.

25.   Encourage Limit Setting by Noncustodial Parent (25)

A. The noncustodial parent was strongly encouraged to set firm, consistent limits for the client's misbehavior and to refrain from overindulging the client's desires during visits.

B. The noncustodial parent was helped to identify logical, natural consequences for the client's misbehavior.

C. The noncustodial parent verbally acknowledged how his/her pattern of overindulgence contributes to the client's immaturity and resistance to take on responsibilities and was urged to develop alternative behaviors.

D. The noncustodial parent acknowledged his/her reluctance to set limits for the client's misbehavior because of his/her feelings of guilt and desire to avoid conflict during visits and was assisted in developing alternative behaviors.

E. The noncustodial parent reported that the frequency of the client's misbehavior has decreased since he/she began setting firm, consistent limits on the client's acting out, and the benefits of this pattern of interacting was emphasized.

26.   Emphasize Assignment of Responsibilities by Noncustodial Parent (26)

A. The noncustodial parent was given the directive to assign chore(s) to the client and siblings during their visits.

B. The noncustodial parent was encouraged to schedule times for the client and siblings to complete their homework.

C. The noncustodial parent acknowledged that he/she is reluctant to assign chores or require the children to complete homework because of the desire to avoid upsetting the client or siblings or creating potential conflict, and the long-term negative consequences of this pattern were emphasized.

D. The noncustodial parent was helped to develop a reward system to reinforce the client and siblings for completing chores and homework during visits.

E. The noncustodial parent was helped to identify consequences for the failure of his/her children to complete chores or homework.

27.   Teach Enmeshed Parent(s) to Set Limits (27)

A. The enmeshed or overly protective parent was helped to see how his/her failure to set limits reinforces the client's immature or irresponsible behavior.

B. The enmeshed or overly protective parent was helped to identify natural, logical consequences for the client's immature or irresponsible behavior.

C. The parent(s) were encouraged to offer frequent praise and positive reinforcement for the client's responsible behavior.

D. A reward system was designed to reinforce the client for behaving in a responsible manner.

28. Identify Age-Appropriate Ways to Meet Needs (28)

A. The client and parent(s) were helped to identify age-appropriate ways for the client to meet his/her needs for affiliation, acceptance, and approval.

B. The client was given the homework assignment to engage in a specific, age-appropriate behavior three to five times before the next therapy session.

C. Role-playing and modeling techniques were utilized to demonstrate age-appropriate ways to gain affiliation, acceptance, and approval from others.

D. The client was taught effective communication skills to help meet his/her needs for affiliation, acceptance, and approval.

E. Although the client has been taught age-appropriate ways to meet his/her needs, he/she often fails to use these techniques; he/she was redirected to increase his/her use of these healthy, helpful techniques.

29. Urge Parents to Stop Criticizing Ex-Spouse (29)

A. The parent was challenged and confronted about making hostile or overly critical remarks about the other parent in the presence of the client and siblings.

B. The client's parent(s) verbally recognized that hostile or overly critical remarks about the other parent are upsetting to the client and siblings, and positive feedback was provided.

30. Teach Parents to Avoid Placing Client in Middle (30)

A. The parent(s) were challenged to cease the pattern of placing the client in the middle role by soliciting information about the other parent or sending messages through the client to the other parent about adult matters.

B. The parent(s) verbalized an awareness that placing the client in the middle role is upsetting to him/her, and assistance was provided in developing alternative roles.

31. Confront Playing One Parent against the Other (31)

A. The client was challenged and confronted about playing one parent against the other to meet his/her needs, obtain material goods, or avoid responsibility.

B. Today's therapy session explored the reasons for the client's attempt to play one parent against the other.

C. The parent(s) were encouraged to deal directly with the client and set limits on his/her manipulative behaviors.

D. The client was helped to identify ways to meet his/her needs or obtain material goods that are more constructive than manipulating the parent(s).

E. The client acknowledged that his/her pattern of playing one parent against the other is aimed at trying to bring the parents back together, and he/she was disabused of this notion.

32. Encourage Noncustodial Parent to Maintain Visitation (32)

A. The noncustodial parent was challenged and encouraged to maintain regular visitation and involvement in the client's life.

B. The client asserted his/her wish in today's family therapy session for the noncustodial parent to maintain regular visitation and involvement in his/her life.

C. Today's therapy session explored the factors contributing to the noncustodial parent's failure to maintain regular visitation and involvement in the client's life.

D. The noncustodial parent was supported as he/she verbally recognized that the lack of regular visitation has exacerbated the client's adjustment problems to the divorce.

E. The family therapy session focused on developing a regular visitation schedule between the noncustodial parent and the client.

33. Assign Disengaged Parent to Increase Time with Client (33)

A. The disengaged parent was given a directive to spend more quality time with the client and siblings.

B. The disengaged parent was given a homework assignment of performing a specific task with the client.

C. The client and disengaged parent were assisted in developing a list of tasks or activities that they would like to do together.

D. The client reported that the increased time spent with the previously disengaged parent has helped the two of them establish a closer relationship, and the benefits of this involvement were reviewed.

E. The client was supported as he/she reported that his/her relationship with the disengaged parent remains distant because the two have spent little time together.

34. Utilize Art Therapy Techniques (34)

A. The client was instructed to draw pictures reflecting his/her feelings about the parents' divorce, family move, or change in schools.

B. The client's drawings were interpreted as reflecting his/her feelings of anger, sadness, and hurt about the parents' divorce.

C. The client's drawings were interpreted as reflecting feelings of anger, sadness, and loneliness about the family move and/or change in school.

D. After completing his/her drawings, the client was helped to verbalize his/her feelings about the parents' divorce, family move, or change in schools.

35. Utilize Music Therapy Techniques (35)

A. The client shared a song that reflected his/her feelings about the parents' separation or divorce, and this was processed.

B. The client shared a song that led to a discussion of how the song reflects his/her feelings about the parents' separation or divorce and what he/she can do to cope with the changes in his/her life.

36. Encourage Participation in Positive Peer Group Activities (36)

A. The client was strongly encouraged to participate in school, extracurricular, or positive peer group activities to offset the loss of time spent with his/her parents.

B. The client developed a list of school, extracurricular, or positive peer group activities that will help him/her cope with the parents' divorce and establish meaningful friendships, and these were reviewed.

C. The client reported that the participation in school, extracurricular, or positive peer group activities has helped him/her cope with the parents' divorce and feel less depressed or lonely, and he/she was encouraged to continue.

D. The client has continued to struggle with his/her parents' divorce, but as yet has not taken many steps to become involved in school, extracurricular, or positive peer group activities; he/she was redirected to be more socially involved.

37. Refer to Group Therapy (37)

A. The client was referred for group therapy to help him/her share and work through his/her feelings about the divorce with other adolescents who are going through a similar experience.

B. The client was given the directive to self-disclose at least once during the group therapy session about his/her parents' divorce.

C. The client's involvement in group therapy has helped him/her realize that he/she is not alone in going through the divorce process.

D. The client's active participation in group therapy sessions has helped him/her share and work through many of his/her emotions pertaining to the parents' divorce.

E. The client has not made productive use of the group therapy sessions and has been reluctant to share his/her feelings about the divorce.

38. Identify Supportive Adults (38)

A. The client was assisted in developing a list of supportive adults outside of the family to whom he/she can turn for support and guidance in coping with the divorce.

B. The client was given the homework assignment to seek guidance and support from at least one adult outside of the family before the next therapy session.

C. The client reported that he/she has talked with other significant adults outside of the family who have been helpful in offering support and guidance, and the results were summarized.

D. The client was reinforced as he/she has taken active steps to develop a network of significant adults outside of the family system to whom he/she can turn for guidance and support when needed.

E. The client has failed to follow through with the recommendation to make contact with significant adults outside of the family because of his/her mistrust and expectation of experiencing further disappointment, but he/she was encouraged to seek out at least one adult.

39. Provide Sex Education (39)

A. The client was provided with sex education in an attempt to eliminate his/her pattern of engaging in sexually promiscuous behavior.

B. The client was helped to identify the risks involved in his/her sexually promiscuous or seductive behavior.

C. The client responded favorably to the sex education provided by asking several pertinent questions and openly sharing his/her past sexual experiences.

D. The client displayed an attitude of cool indifference when discussing the potential risks involved in his/her sexually promiscuous or seductive behavior.

40. Explore Reasons for Sexually Promiscuous Behaviors (40)

A. The client's sexual history was gathered to help gain insight into the factors contributing to the emergence of his/her sexually promiscuous behavior.

B. The client's irrational beliefs about his/her sexually promiscuous behavior were challenged.

C. Psychoanalytic therapy approaches were used to explore the etiology of the client's sexually promiscuous behavior.

D. Client-centered therapy approaches were employed to help the client discover ways to meet his/her unmet needs that are more effective than sexually promiscuous behaviors.

E. A brief solution-focused therapy approach was utilized to help the client identify ways to cope with stress that are more effective than sexually promiscuous behaviors.

41. Arrange for Substance Abuse Evaluation/Treatment (41)

A. The client was referred for a substance abuse evaluation to determine whether he/she has developed a substance abuse problem in response to his/her parents' divorce.

B. The findings from the substance abuse evaluation revealed the presence of a substance abuse problem and the need for treatment.

C. The chemical dependence evaluation did not reveal the presence of a substance abuse problem or the need for treatment in this area.

D. The client acknowledged the existence of a substance abuse problem and agreed to follow through with treatment; his/her honesty was acknowledged as a keystone of recovery.

E. The client denied the existence of a substance abuse problem and voiced his/her objection to seeking treatment in this area; he/she was urged to be more realistic.

42. Explore Emotional Pain Related to Substance Abuse (42)

A. Today's therapy session explored the underlying feelings of depression, insecurity, and rejection that have contributed to the client's escape into substance abuse.

B. A psychoanalytic therapy approach was utilized to explore the etiology of the client's escape into substance abuse.

C. Client-centered therapy approaches were employed to help the client discover how his/her escape into substance abuse has arisen out of underlying feelings of depression, insecurity, and rejection.

D. A brief solution-focused therapy approach was used to help the client identify ways to cope with feelings of depression, insecurity, and rejection that are more effective than escaping into substance abuse.

E. The client identified a list of resource people to whom he/she can turn for support when feeling the urge to drink or use drugs, and he/she was urged to use these supports.

43. Develop Agreement to Refrain from Using Substances (43)

A. An agreement was constructed and signed by the client to refrain from using substances.

B. The client was encouraged to post the signed agreement to refrain from using substances in his/her room or on the refrigerator as a reminder.

C. The client agreed to follow through with substance abuse treatment if he/she fails to refrain from using substances.

D. The client refused to sign an agreement that he/she would refrain from using drugs or alcohol, and the focus of treatment was changed to the substance abuse.

EATING DISORDER

CLIENT PRESENTATION

1. Refusal to Consume Necessary Calories (1)*

A. The client has a history of very limited ingestion of food, resulting in weight loss.

B. The client consumes 85% or less of the necessary calories to maintain body weight.

C. Although the client talks of eating three meals per day, a closer analysis indicated that the amount of food consumed was very limited.

D. The client has begun to increase his/her caloric intake as portions of food consumed have gradually increased.

E. The client reported consuming a normal level of calories per day in the recent past.

2. Irrational/Distorted Thoughts (2)

A. The client has developed a number of irrational thoughts about his/her food intake or body image that have contributed to the emergence of the eating disorder.

B. The client verbalized an irrational fear of becoming overweight.

C. The client has acknowledged that his/her fear of becoming overweight is irrational.

D. The client has begun to challenge his/her irrational or distorted thoughts about being too fat.

E. The client has consistently replaced negative thoughts about his/her body image with more positive, reality-based messages.

3. Binge Eating (3)

A. The client described a recurrent pattern of binge eating during times of stress or emotional upset.

B. The client reported experiencing recent episodes of binge eating.

C. The client has not experienced any recent episodes of binge eating.

D. The client has terminated his/her pattern of binge eating.

4. Self-Induced Vomiting (3)

A. The client reported a recurrent pattern of purging to either lose weight or prevent a weight gain.

B. The client reported that he/she has continued to induce vomiting.

C. The client verbally recognized that he/she tends to induce vomiting more often during times of stress or emotional conflict.

D. The client denied any recent episodes of purging.

E. The client has terminated his/her pattern of purging.

---

* The numbers in parentheses correlate to the number of the Behavioral Definition statement in the companion chapter with the same title in *The Adolescent Psychotherapy Treatment Planner,* Fourth Edition (Jongsma, Peterson, McInnis, and Bruce) by John Wiley & Sons, 2006.

5. Use of Laxatives (3)

A. The client reported a history of using laxatives to lose weight or prevent weight gain.

B. The client reported that he/she has recently used laxatives.

C. The client acknowledged that he/she tends to use laxatives more often during times of stress or emotional conflict.

D. The client denied any recent use of laxatives.

E. The client has discontinued his/her pattern of using laxatives to either lose weight or prevent weight gain.

6. Compensatory Behavior to Prevent Weight Gain (4)

A. The client has used inappropriate compensatory behaviors to prevent weight gain.

B. The client has used self-induced vomiting to prevent weight gain.

C. The client has misused laxatives, diuretics, enemas, or other medications to avoid weight gain.

D. The client has used inappropriate fasting to prevent weight gain.

E. The client has used excessive exercise in order to burn calories and prevent weight gain.

F. As treatment has progressed, the client has decreased his/her inappropriate compensatory behavior to prevent weight gain.

7. Extreme Weight Loss (5)

A. The client has lost an extreme amount of weight during the recent past.

B. The client appeared to be in denial and displayed little concern or anxiety about his/her significant weight loss.

C. The client recognized that his/her weight loss is significant and expressed a desire to regain weight.

D. The client has slowly begun to gain weight.

E. The client's weight has returned to the previous normal level.

8. Current Weight (5)

A. The client weighed _____ lbs. at the beginning of treatment.

B. The client has lost _____ lbs. since the last therapy session.

C. The client has gained _____ lbs. since the last therapy session.

D. The client currently weighs _____ lbs.

E. The client weighed _____ lbs. at the end of treatment.

9. Low Food Intake/Loss of Appetite (5)

A. The client's food intake in recent weeks/months has decreased drastically.

B. The client reported that he/she continues to have very little appetite.

C. The client's food intake has continued to be very low.

D. The client reported that his/her appetite is slowly returning to the previous normal level.

E. The client's food intake has returned to the previous normal level.

10. Excessive Strenuous Exercise (5)

A. The client described a history of engaging in very strenuous physical activity or exercise to either lose weight or prevent a weight gain.

B. The client has continued to engage in very strenuous physical activity or exercise.

C. The client has gradually started to decrease the intensity and length of his/her exercise workouts.

D. The client stated that he/she has stopped engaging in any overly strenuous physical exercise.

E. The client has achieved a healthy balance between eating nutritious meals and getting the proper amount of exercise.

11. Self-Evaluation Overly Influenced by Body Characteristics (6)

A. The client has a history of persistent preoccupation with his/her body image, and he/she grossly inaccurately assesses his/her body weight when self-evaluating.

B. The client is beginning to acknowledge that his/her preoccupation with body image is grossly inaccurate and discounts his/her other characteristics.

C. As the client has begun to decrease eating disorder behaviors, his/her anxiety level has increased and the fear of obesity has returned.

D. The client has been able to gain weight up to normal levels without being controlled by a distorted fear of being overweight.

12. Preoccupation with Body Image (7)

A. The client displays a strong preoccupation with his/her body image.

B. The client spoke at length in today's therapy session about his/her body image.

C. The client expressed much dissatisfaction with his/her body image.

D. The client's preoccupation with his/her body image has begun to decrease, and he/she is more willing to discuss his/her painful emotions or conflictual issues.

E. The client expressed satisfaction with his/her body image.

13. Fluid and Electrolyte Imbalance (8)

A. The results from the medical examination revealed a serious fluid and electrolyte imbalance due to the client's eating disorder.

B. The client's fluid and electrolyte levels have gradually started to return to a healthy level.

C. The client's fluid and electrolyte levels have returned to a normal, healthy level.

14. Unrealistic Assessment of Body (9)

A. The client has developed an unrealistic assessment of his/her body image and perceives himself/herself as being overweight.

B. The client has remained in denial about his/her body image and does not see himself/herself as being too thin or emaciated.

C. The client recognized that he/she is too thin or emaciated and needs to regain weight.

D. The client has developed a realistic assessment of his/her body image.

INTERVENTIONS IMPLEMENTED

1. Build Trust (1)*

A. Consistent eye contact, active listening, unconditional positive regard, and warm acceptance were used to help build trust with the client.

B. The client began to express feelings more freely as rapport and trust level were increased.

C. The client has continued to experience difficulty being open and direct in his/her expression of painful feelings; he/she was encouraged to use the safe haven of therapy to express these difficult issues.

2. Gather Eating Disorder History (2)

A. Today's therapy session explored the frequency, type, and chronicity of the client's eating disorder behavior.

B. A complete history of the client's eating disorder behavior was taken in today's therapy session.

C. Today's therapy session explored periods of time when the client lost a significant amount of weight.

D. The frequency and chronicity of the client's bingeing and purging episodes were explored.

E. Today's therapy session explored periods of time when the client used laxatives inappropriately to either lose weight or prevent weight gain.

3. Evaluate Calorie Consumption (3)

A. The client's calorie consumption was compared with an average adult female rate of 1600–2400 calories per day in order to establish the reality of his/her pattern of under- or overeating.

B. The client acknowledged that his/her calorie consumption was not within the normal limits; he/she was supported for this understanding.

C. The client defended his/her calorie consumption for being outside the normal limits and was gently confronted with facts about normal caloric intake.

4. Explore Vomiting Behavior (4)

A. The client was asked to describe any self-induced vomiting to help control caloric intake.

B. The client was supported as he/she acknowledged engaging in vomiting behavior on a regular basis, after eating, in order to reduce caloric intake.

C. The client defended his/her use of vomiting in order to control caloric intake because of his/her distorted belief that he/she would become overweight; he/she was redirected in this area.

D. The client's use of purging techniques was monitored.

---

*The numbers in parentheses correlate to the number of the Therapeutic Intervention statement in the companion chapter with the same title in *The Adolescent Psychotherapy Treatment Planner,* Fourth Edition (Jongsma, Peterson, McInnis, and Bruce) by John Wiley & Sons, 2006.

E. The client was reinforced as he/she reported a decreased use of purging and exercise to control weight.

F. The client denied any recent engagement in vomiting behavior, and this was accepted and reinforced.

5. Explore Dysfunctional Behaviors (5)

A. The client was noted to confirm regular use of laxatives, diuretics, enemas, and other medications for the purpose of reducing body weight.

B. The client was assessed for the use of fasting and excessive exercise.

C. The client minimized his/her use of dysfunctional measures to control body weight; this minimization was pointed out to him/her in a matter-of-fact manner.

D. The client's use of dysfunctional behaviors was monitored.

E. The client reported a decreased use of dysfunctional behaviors to control his/her body weight, and he/she was reinforced for this progress.

F. The client was reinforced as he/she reported no longer using dysfunctional behaviors to control body weight.

6. Assess Eating Disorder with Objective Measures (6)

A. A measure of eating disorders was administered to further assess its depth and breath.

B. The level of self-induced vomiting; misuse of laxatives, diuretics, enemas, or other medications; fasting; or excessive exercise was assessed.

C. *The Eating Disorders Inventory–2* (Garner) was used to assess the client's level of eating disorder symptoms.

D. The results of the eating disorders assessment were reviewed with the client.

E. The eating disorders assessment indicated that the client has significant eating disorder symptoms.

F. The eating disorders assessment indicated that the client has minimal eating disorder symptoms.

7. Refer for Physical Examination (7)

A. The client was referred for a thorough physical examination to assess the effects that the eating disorder has had on his/her health.

B. The client followed through by receiving a thorough physical examination.

C. The client is opposed to receiving a thorough physical examination to assess the effects of his/her eating disorder.

D. The findings from the physical examination revealed that the client's eating disorder has had a detrimental effect on his/her health.

E. The findings from the physical examination do not reveal any serious health problems.

F. The client has not followed through on a physical examination and was redirected to do so.

8. Refer for Dental Examination (8)

A. The client was referred for a complete dental examination.

B. The client followed through by obtaining a complete dental examination.

C. The client has refused to follow through with a dental examination.

D. The findings from the dental examination revealed that the client's eating disorder has negatively affected his/her dental condition.

E. The findings from the dental examination did not reveal the presence of any serious dental problems.

F. The client has not followed through on a dental examination and was redirected to do so.

9. Assess/Refer for Psychotropic Medication (9)

A. The client's need for psychotropic medication was assessed.

B. It was determined that the client would benefit from psychotropic medication, and a referral was made.

C. A need for psychotropic medication was not found, and thus no referral was made.

D. The client cooperated with the physician referral, and psychotropic medication has been prescribed.

E. The client has failed to follow through on the physician referral and was encouraged to do so.

10. Monitor Medication (10)

A. The effectiveness of psychotropic medication and its side effects were monitored.

B. The client reported that the medication has been effective in stabilizing his/her mood; the information is being relayed to the prescribing clinician.

C. The client reported that the psychotropic medication has not been effective or helpful; this information is being relayed to the prescribing clinician.

D. The client has not taken the medication on a consistent basis and was encouraged to do so.

11. Admit to Hospital (11)

A. The recommendation was made that the client be hospitalized in a medical facility because of his/her severe weight loss and seriously compromised health status.

B. The client was admitted into a medical hospital because of his/her severe weight loss and serious health problems.

C. Medical hospitalization was not deemed necessary at this time, although the client's weight and food intake will continue to be closely monitored in the future.

12. Discuss Eating Disorders Model (12)

A. A discussion was held with the client regarding a model of eating disorder development.

B. The client was taught about concepts such as sociocultural pressures to be thin, vulnerability to overvalue body shape and size in determining self-image, maladaptive eating habits, maladaptive compensatory weight management behaviors, and resultant feelings of low self-esteem.

C. The client was taught about concepts related to eating disorders as described in *Overcoming Binge Eating* (Fairburn).

D. The client displayed a clear understanding of the concepts related to eating disorders, and he/she was provided with positive feedback about this insight.

E. The client struggled to understand the information related to eating disorders and was provided with additional feedback in this area.

13. Discuss Rationale for Treatment (13)

A. The rationale for treatment was discussed with the client, including the use of cognitive and behavioral procedures to break the cycle of thinking and behaving that promotes poor self-image, uncontrolled eating, and unhealthy compensatory actions.

B. The rationale for treatment was emphasized, including the building up of physical and mental health–promoting eating practices.

C. The client was reinforced for his/her clear understanding of the rationale for treatment.

D. The client did not have a clear understanding of the rationale for treatment and was provided with remedial information in this area.

14. Assign Reading Materials (14)

A. The client was assigned to read psychoeducational chapters of books or treatment manuals on the development and treatment of eating disorders.

B. The client was directed to read selected portions of *Overcoming Binge Eating* (Fairburn).

C. The client has read the assigned information on the development and treatment of eating disorders, and key concepts were processed.

D. The client has not read the assigned information on eating disorders and was redirected to do so.

15. Assign Self-Monitoring Record (15)

A. The client was assigned to self-monitor and record food intake, thoughts, and feelings.

B. The client was assigned "Reality: Food, Weight, Thoughts, and Feelings" from the *Adolescent Psychotherapy Homework Planner,* 2nd ed. (Jongsma, Peterson, and McInnis).

C. The client was assigned the use of "Daily Record of Dysfunctional Thoughts" from *Cognitive Therapy of Depression* (Beck, Rush, Shaw, and Emery).

D. The client's journal was processed with a focus on challenging maladaptive patterns of thinking and behaving.

E. The client was assisted in replacing maladaptive patterns of thinking and behaving with adapted alternatives.

F. The claimant has not kept a journal record of food intake, thoughts, and feelings, and he/she was redirected to do so.

16. Establish Minimum Daily Caloric Intake (16)

A. The client's minimum daily caloric intake was established.

B. A consultation was held with the client's physician and/or nutritionist about establishing a minimum daily caloric intake.

C. The client verbally agreed to consume enough food to meet the minimum daily caloric intake.

D. The client was to agree to terminate dysfunctional eating behavior.

E. The client was supported for his/her elimination of dysfunctional eating behavior.

F. The client has continued to practice dysfunctional eating behavior and was reminded of the need to discontinue this type of behavior.

17. Set Weight Goals (17)

A. The client was helped to establish healthy weight goals using the Body Mass Index.

B. The client was helped to establish healthy weight goals using the Metropolitan Height and Weight Tables.

18. Provide feedback (18)

A. The client's weight was consistently monitored.

B. Realistic feedback was provided to the client in regard to his/her body thinness.

19. Monitor Fluid Intake and Electrolyte Balance (19)

A. The client's food intake and electrolyte balance were monitored.

B. The client was provided with realistic feedback on his/her progress toward the goal of balance in fluid intake and electrolytes.

C. The client was provided with positive feedback for his/her appropriate electrolyte balance.

D. The client was provided with realistic feedback that his/her electrolytes are out of balance.

20. Refer for Ongoing Fluid/Electrolyte Monitoring (20)

A. The client was noted to have fluid and electrolyte imbalances.

B. The client was referred back to his/her physician for monitoring of fluids and electrolytes.

C. The client has been regularly assessed for his/her fluid and electrolyte balances.

D. It was reflected to the client that his/her improved nutritional habits have discontinued the need for ongoing fluid and electrolyte monitoring.

21. Assess External and Internal Cues (21)

A. The client was assessed for external cues such as persons, objects, or situations that precipitate his/her uncontrolled eating and/or compensatory weight management behaviors.

B. The client was assessed for internal cues such as thoughts, images, and impulses that contribute to his/her uncontrolled eating and/or compensatory weight management behaviors.

C. The client displayed significant insight as he/she identified many external and internal cues for his/her uncontrolled and/or compensatory weight management behaviors.

D. The client struggled to identify many external or internal cues, and he/she was provided with tentative examples of these types of cues.

22. Develop Hierarchy of Triggers (22)

A. The client was directed to develop a hierarchy of high-risk internal and external triggers for uncontrolled eating and/or compensatory weight management behaviors.

B. The client was helped to list many of the high-risk internal and external triggers for uncontrolled eating and/or compensatory weight management behaviors.

C. The client was assisted in developing a hierarchy of high-risk internal and external triggers for uncontrolled eating and/or compensatory weight management behaviors.

D. The client's journaling was used to assist in developing a hierarchy of high-risk internal and external triggers for uncontrolled eating and/or compensatory weight management behaviors.

23. Assist in Developing Insight (23)

A. The client was assisted in developing an awareness of his/her automatic thoughts and underlying assumptions, associated feelings, and actions that lead to maladaptive eating and weight control practices.

B. The client was assisted in developing insight into his/her poor self-image, distorted body image, perfectionism, fear of failure, and/or rejection or fear of sexuality.

C. The client was reinforced for his/her increased awareness of automatic thoughts, underlying associated feelings, and actions that lead to maladaptive eating and weight control practices.

D. The client struggled to develop insight into his/her eating disorder dynamics, and he/she was provided with tentative examples in this area.

24. Identify/Replace Negative Cognitive Messages (24)

A. The client was helped to identify the negative cognitive messages that he/she uses to avoid consuming a normal amount of food.

B. The client was given the homework assignment, "Fears Beneath the Eating Disorder" from the *Adolescent Psychotherapy Homework Planner,* 2nd ed. (Jongsma, Peterson, and McInnis) to help identify the irrational fears that contribute to his/her eating disorder behaviors.

C. The client was given a homework assignment to record in a journal one positive statement each day about himself/herself or his/her body size.

D. The client was trained to establish realistic cognitive messages regarding his/her food intake and body image.

E. The client failed to complete the homework assignment regarding negative cognitions and was redirected to do so.

25. Conduct Exposure and Ritual Prevention (25)

A. Repeated exposures to the client's high-risk situations were conducted, with an emphasis on ritual prevention.

B. Additional exposures to the client's high-risk situations were selected with a bias toward those that would have a high likelihood of being a successful experience for the client.

C. The client was prepared and rehearsed his/her high-risk situations within the session.

D. Cognitive restructuring techniques were used within and after the exposure to high-risk situations.

E. The client's use of exposure and ritual prevention was reviewed and processed within the session.

26. Assign Experiment or Exposure Exercise Homework (26)

A. The client was assisted in identifying a behavioral experiment or exposure exercise that could be repeated as a homework assignment.

B. The client's behavioral experiment or exposure exercise homework was reviewed.

C. Cognitive restructuring techniques, success reinforcement, and corrective feedback were used to help process and reinforce the client's homework exercises.

D. The client has not done homework exercises of repeating the in-session behavioral experiment or exposure exercise, and he/she was redirected to do so.

27. Conduct Interpersonal Therapy (27)

A. Interpersonal therapy techniques were used to help identify themes that may be supporting the eating disorder.

B. The client was assisted in assessing the "interpersonal inventory" of important past and present relationships as themes that may be supporting the client's eating disorder.

C. The client was assisted in listing issues from past or present relationships, such as interpersonal disputes, role transitions, and/or interpersonal deficits.

D. The client's themes that support eating disorder symptoms were identified and processed.

28. Teach Conflict Resolution Skills (28)

A. The client was taught conflict resolution skills such as practicing empathy, active listening, respectful communication, assertiveness, and compromise.

B. Using role-playing, modeling, and behavioral rehearsal, the client was taught implementation of conflict resolution skills.

C. The client reported implementation of conflict resolution skills in his/her daily life and was reinforced for this utilization.

D. The client reported that resolving interpersonal conflicts has contributed to lessening his/her eating disorder concerns.

E. The client has not used conflict resolution skills and was provided with specific feedback about when to implement his/her skills.

29. Help Resolve Interpersonal Problems (29)

A. The client was assisted in resolving interpersonal problems through the use of reassurance and support.

B. The client was helped to clarify cognitive and affective triggers that ignite conflicts.

C. The client was taught active problem-solving techniques to help him/her resolve interpersonal problems.

D. It was reflected to the client that he/she has significantly reduced his/her interpersonal problems.

E. The client continues to have significant interpersonal problems, and he/she was provided with remedial assistance in this area.

30. Address Interpersonal Conflict through Joint Session (30)

A. A conjoint session was held to assist the client in resolving interpersonal conflicts with his/her partner.

B. The client reported that the conjoint sessions have been helpful in resolving interpersonal conflicts with his/her partner and that this has contributed to a lifting of his/her depression.

C. It was reflected that ongoing conflicts with a partner have fostered feelings of depression and hopelessness.

31. Discuss Lapse Versus Relapse (31)

A. The client was assisted in differentiating between a lapse and a relapse.

B. A lapse was associated with the initial and reversible return of eating disorder symptoms.

C. A relapse was associated with decision to return to eating disorder behaviors.

D. The client was reinforced for his/her ability to respond to a lapse without relapsing.

32. Identify and Rehearse Response to Lapse Situations (32)

A. The client was asked to identify the future situations or circumstances in which lapses could occur.

B. The client was asked to rehearse the management of his/her potential lapse situations.

C. The client was reinforced as he/she identified and rehearsed how to cope with potential lapse situations.

D. The client was provided with helpful feedback about how to best manage potential lapse situations.

E. The client declined to identify or rehearse the management of possible lapse situations, and this resistance was redirected.

33. Encourage Use of Therapy Strategies (33)

A. The client was encouraged to routinely use strategies used in therapy.

B. The client was urged to use continued exposure to external and internal cues that arise.

C. The client was reinforced for his/her regular use of therapy techniques when experiencing cues for eating disorder behaviors.

D. The client was unable to identify many situations in which he/she has used therapy techniques, and he/she was redirected to seek these situations out.

34. Schedule Maintenance Sessions (34)

A. Maintenance sessions were proposed to help maintain therapeutic gains and adjust to life without anger outbursts.

B. The client was reinforced for agreeing to the scheduling of maintenance sessions.

C. The client refused to schedule maintenance sessions, and this was processed.

35. Probe Emotional Struggles (35)

A. Today's therapy session explored the client's underlying emotional struggles that may be camouflaged by the existing eating disorder.

B. Today's therapy session was helpful in identifying the underlying emotional struggles or pain that contributed to the emergence of the client's eating disorder.

C. The client was resistant to exploring the possible underlying emotional struggles or conflicts that may have contributed to the emergence of his/her eating disorder.

D. Role-playing and modeling techniques were utilized to teach the client how to express his/her painful emotions to significant others.

36. Family Therapy to Discuss Control (36)

A. A family therapy session was held to provide the client with the opportunity to express his/her genuine thoughts and feelings directly to his/her family members.

B. A family therapy session was held to allow for an open discussion of the control conflicts that exist within the family.

C. A family therapy session was conducted to identify more age-appropriate boundaries within the family system.

D. The family therapy session was helpful in resolving the core conflicts that are related to the issue of control.

E. The parents were challenged to begin to let go and loosen their control to allow the client the opportunity to make age-appropriate decisions for himself/herself.

37. Explore Fear of Sexual Development (37)

A. Today's session focused on the client's fear regarding his/her sexual development and impulses.

B. The relationship between the client's eating disorder and sexual development was explored.

C. The client's eating disorder was explored regarding whether it is related to a past sexual trauma or victimization.

D. Today's therapy session focused on the client's fears about losing control of his/her sexual impulses.

E. Today's therapy session identified how the client's fear of losing control of his/her sexual impulses contributed to his/her being overly thin.

F. Today's therapy session identified how the client's fears or anxieties about his/her sexual impulses are related to significant weight gain or lack of motivation to lose weight.

38. Process Fear of Failure (38)

A. Today's therapy session processed the client's strong fear of failure and how he/she often strives to be perfect to avoid failure and establish a sense of control over his/her life.

B. Today's therapy session explored how the client's fear of failure and striving for perfection are related to his/her body image and attitude about food or dieting.

C. The client acknowledged that his/her perfectionistic strivings and strong need for control contribute to his/her eating disorder behaviors, and he/she was supported for this insight.

D. The client was helped to see that failure is a common experience for all and is a necessary part of learning and growing.

E. The client was assisted in exploring periods of time when he/she was able to learn or grow from failure experiences.

F. The client was helped to identify positive coping strategies that he/she could use to undo or manage failure experiences.

39. Refer to Support Group (39)

A. The client was referred to a support group for people with eating disorders.

B. The client has followed through on the referral to a support group for people with eating disorders and reported having benefited from the meeting.

C. Attendance at the support group for people with eating disorders has helped the client maintain his/her gains in weight and healthy eating; the benefits of this progress were highlighted.

D. The client has not followed through on attendance at a support group for those with eating disorders and was encouraged to do so.

40. Identify Self-Worth Building Blocks (40)

A. The client was helped to identify ways to develop a sense of self-worth apart from his/her body image.

B. Today's therapy session reviewed the client's talents and successes to help him/her develop a basic sense of self-worth apart from his/her body image.

C. Today's therapy session affirmed the client's importance to others to help increase his/her feelings of self-worth.

D. The client's intrinsic spiritual value was reinforced to help increase his/her feelings of self-esteem and self-worth.

E. The client consistently denied any talents, successes, or other ways to increase his/her sense of self-worth apart from his/her body image and was provided with more realistic feedback in this area.

GRIEF/LOSS UNRESOLVED

CLIENT PRESENTATION

1. Parent Death Reaction (1)*

A. The client presented as visibly upset and distressed over the recent loss of his/her parent.

B. Teachers, friends, and others have reported that the client is exhibiting various grief reactions such as anger, depression, and emotional lability around the recent loss of his/her parent.

C. The client indicated he/she cannot think of anything but the death of his/her parent.

D. The client frequently expressed that he/she still cannot accept that this parental death really happened.

E. The client revealed that the feeling of being alone and hopeless has been overwhelming for him/her since the parent's death.

F. The client has started to talk about the loss of his/her parent and has begun to accept consolation, support, and encouragement from others.

2. Termination of Parental Rights (2)

A. The client presented as sad and withdrawn after recently being told that his/her parents' rights are being terminated.

B. The client indicated that he/she refuses to believe that he/she will not see parents again.

C. Foster parents reported that the client is continually angry and upset since receiving the news that his/her parents' rights have been terminated.

D. The client has made progress in coming to terms with his/her parents' loss of their rights and has started to look forward to a new home and family.

3. Parental Incarceration Grief (3)

A. The client expressed feeling a big hole in his/her life since his/her parent went to prison.

B. The client reported being angry most of the time since his/her parent was incarcerated.

C. The client indicated he/she has felt sad and embarrassed about the parent's imprisonment and has socially withdrawn from activities to avoid feeling more uncomfortable.

D. The client has begun to accept and adjust to the parent's imprisonment and return to his/her normal level of functioning.

4. Grief Due to Geographic Move (4)

A. The client presented as depressed and focused on the loss of previous home and friends that were left behind in the move.

B. The client reported feeling angry and upset all the time now at parents for their decision to move him/her away from his/her neighborhood and friends.

---

*The numbers in parentheses correlate to the number of the Behavioral Definition statement in the companion chapter with the same title in *The Adolescent Psychotherapy Treatment Planner*, Fourth Edition (Jongsma, Peterson, McInnis, and Bruce) by John Wiley & Sons, 2006.

C. The parents indicated that the client is always sad and refuses to leave home except to go to school.

D. The client has started to accept the family's new location and is beginning to make new friends and involve himself/herself in other activities.

5. Parent Emotional Abandonment (5)

A. The client verbalized feeling abandoned emotionally since losing nearly all contact with his/her parent.

B. The client reported that he/she has been cut off from nearly all contact with his/her other parent.

C. The client indicated that he/she is devastated by the loss of nearly all meaningful contact with his/her parent.

D. The client has begun to openly grieve the emotional abandonment he/she has experienced from his/her parent.

6. Emotionally Upset (6)

A. The client presented in an upset, tearful, and distraught manner.

B. The client related that he/she is having a difficult time coming to terms with the recent loss he/she has experienced.

C. It appears that the client is stuck in his/her grieving process and is finding it difficult to move beyond being upset and distraught.

D. The client is gradually making progress in coming to terms with and accepting his/her loss, and he/she reports crying less and not being as upset as before.

7. Social Withdrawal (7)

A. The client presents as very withdrawn and nonverbal around his/her past loss(es).

B. "I find it impossible to talk about" is one of the few verbalizations coming from the client.

C. The client, with encouragement and support, has slowly moved from his/her withdrawn state and started to talk about the loss.

8. Angry/Tense (8)

A. Anger and tension dominate the client's affect, mood, and manner.

B. The client reports frequent verbal temper outbursts toward others, breaking things, and incidents of road rage following the loss.

C. Anger is freely vented toward God, doctors, and others who "had a hand" in the loss.

D. There is a decrease in the client's anger as he/she acknowledges and explains that now he/she is feeling more hurt and sadness about the loss.

9. Guilty/Responsible (9)

A. The overall mood and manner of the client reflects a deep sense of guilt and responsibility for the recent loss.

B. To maintain control, the client appears to be stuck in his/her guilt and either unwilling or unable to move beyond this point in the process of grieving.

C. The client reported those things that make him/her feel guilty and responsible for the loss.

D. The client is moving toward letting go of his/her guilt and accepting that he/she is not responsible for the loss.

10. Avoidance of Loss (10)

A. The client presented with a high level of denial and strong resistance to acknowledging and accepting his/her loss.

B. The client's family system has a definite pattern of denial and nonacceptance of losses.

C. The client states, "I don't believe this really happened; I won't accept this," and he/she did not attend any part of the funeral process.

D. Cracks are starting to show in the client's denial, and he/she is now believing the loss is real.

E. The client's denial has broken, and he/she is now being overwhelmed with feelings of anger, hurt, and sadness.

INTERVENTIONS IMPLEMENTED

1. Establish Trust/Express Feelings (1)*

A. Initial trust level was established with the client through the use of unconditional positive regard.

B. Warm acceptance and active listening techniques were utilized to establish the basis for a nurturing relationship with the client.

C. The client has formed a trust-based relationship with therapist and has started to express his/her feelings about the recent loss.

D. Despite the use of active listening, warm acceptance, and unconditional positive regard, the client remains hesitant to trust and begin sharing his/her feelings connected to the recent loss.

2. Tell Story of Loss (2)

A. The client was asked to tell the story of his/her loss using drawings of his/her experience.

B. The client told the story of his/her loss with appropriate affect, and his/her emotions were processed.

C. The client received affirmation and validation for the feelings he/she expressed in telling the story of the loss.

D. The client told the story of the loss with little or no affect, and this was reflected to him/her.

3. Identify/Express Feelings about Loss (3)

A. The client was asked to write a letter to the lost loved one describing his/her feelings, desires, and wishes connected to that person.

---

*The numbers in parentheses correlate to the number of the Therapeutic Intervention statement in the companion chapter with the same title in *The Adolescent Psychotherapy Treatment Planner,* Fourth Edition (Jongsma, Peterson, McInnis, and Bruce) by John Wiley & Sons, 2006.

B. The client read the letter that he/she had written to the lost loved one with appropriate affect and expression of feelings, and it was processed.

C. The client read the letter to the lost loved one with flat affect and showed no outward emotions in his/her voice or facial expression, and this was reflected to him/her.

D. The client has not developed a letter to the lost loved one and was redirected to do so.

4. Assign Grief Journal (4)

A. The client was asked to record his/her thoughts and feelings related to the loss in a journal.

B. The client was assigned an exercise from *Healing Your Grieving Heart Journal for Teens* (Wolfelt) to facilitate his/her working through the grief process.

C. The completed exercise from *Healing Your Grieving Heart Journal for Teens* was processed, giving support for the affirming thoughts and feelings brought out by the exercise.

D. The journaling exercise was not completed by the client and he/she was directed to do so.

5. View Memorabilia (5)

A. The client was asked to collect and bring to a session various photos and other memorabilia related to the lost loved one.

B. The client was asked to complete the "Create a Memory Album" exercise from the *Adolescent Psychotherapy Homework Planner,* 2nd ed. (Jongsma, Peterson, and McInnis) to facilitate expression and sharing of grief.

C. The completed "Create a Memory Album" was reviewed, and important memories were identified and reinforced.

D. The client has not worked on creating a memory album and was encouraged to give effort to this assignment soon.

6. Read Books on Grief (6)

A. Selections from *Common Thread of Teenage Grief* (Tyson) were read and discussed with the client, expanding his/her knowledge of what the grief process is like.

B. The client was asked to read *Straight Talk about Death* (Grollman) and identify five key ideas to discuss in subsequent sessions.

C. It was noted that the client's reading of books on the topic of grief has been helpful in expanding the client's knowledge base and promoting self-understanding.

D. The client has not followed through with the assignment to read material on the topic of grief, and this was interpreted to be due to his/her tendency to avoid this painful topic.

7. Teach Stages of Grieving Process (7)

A. The parents were educated on the stages and process of grief and had their questions answered so they can better understand this process.

B. It was emphasized with the family that grief is not a one-time event ("Just get over it") but an ongoing process.

C. All of the family members were noted to have a better understanding of the grief process and, as a result, seem more capable of showing empathy and support toward one another.

D. Some family members are resistant to any new information about grief and are in denial about the power of its impact on people's lives.

8. View Films Dealing with Grief (8)

A. The client was asked to view one or more of the following films: *Terms of Endearment, Ordinary People,* or *My Girl,* observing how key individuals in each film grieve or avoid grieving.

B. Grief-related films that the client viewed were processed to identify examples of healthy grieving and examples of those who were avoiding the process or became stuck at an early stage.

C. Using the *Five Stages of Grief* (Kubler-Ross), the client was assisted in identifying the various stages of grief of key people in the films.

D. It was reflected to the client that although he/she did view the films related to the grief theme, he/she continues to distance himself/herself from the struggle with grief personally.

E. The client has not followed through with the assignment to view the films and compare his/her experience to that of the films' characters and was reassigned this task.

9. Refer to Support Group (9)

A. The client was referred to and encouraged to attend a grief support group for adolescents.

B. The client's experience in attending a grief support group was processed, and his/her continued attendance was supported and encouraged.

C. The client was resistive to a referral to a support group and has continued to refuse to attend such a group, but was once again encouraged to attend a grief support group.

10. List Ways Grief Was Avoided (10)

A. The client was asked to list all the ways he/she has avoided the pain of grieving.

B. The client's list of his/her grief avoidance tactics was used with the client to help make connections regarding how the avoidance in each instance has had a negative impact on him/her.

C. The client was given the message that he/she is strong enough to work through the grief if he/she will only trust self and those supporting him/her.

D. The client did not identify ways in which he/she has avoided the pain of grieving and was provided with tentative examples in this area.

11. Explore Use of Substances (11)

A. The client's use of substances, past and present, was explored, including the use of mood-altering prescriptions.

B. The client was reminded of the negative long-term impact that substance use can have on the grieving process.

C. The client denied that he/she has been using any mood-altering substances, and this was accepted.

D. The client admitted to the use of mood-altering substances, and this use was interpreted as being due to a desire to escape from the pain of grieving.

12. Contract Abstinence from Substance Use (12)

A. The client contracted to abstain from all substance use.

B. Compliance with the contract to abstain from substance use will be monitored by checking with the client and parents and, if necessary, by drug screens.

C. The client was confronted with the reality of the consequences (e.g., substance abuse evaluation, residential treatment) if he/she is unable to honor the contract to abstain from substance use.

D. The client refused to agree to abstain from substance abuse, and a referral was made to a more intense chemical dependence treatment program.

13. Assign Grief Journal (13)

A. The client was asked to keep a daily grief journal to record his/her thoughts and feelings associated with the loss.

B. The client's grief journal was reviewed, and significant disclosures of thoughts and feelings were supported and reinforced.

C. The client's grief journal was reviewed, but it revealed that the client continues to distance himself/herself from struggling with the pain of grieving.

D. The client has not followed through with recording his/her thoughts and feelings related to grief in a journal and was redirected to do so.

14. Identify Questions about Loss (14)

A. The client was asked to develop a list of any and all questions he/she has that in any way pertain to causes for the loss.

B. The client was assisted in finding resources who could possibly help him/her find the answers to questions about the causes for the loss.

C. The client's questions about the death of the loved one seemed to have been sufficiently resolved, resulting in a loss of guilt and confusion.

D. The client continues to be preoccupied with the cause of the death of the loved one and whether he/she has any responsibility for that death; he/she was urged to look at this in a more in-depth manner.

15. Read *Lifetimes* (15)

A. To help the client understand death more fully, the *Lifetimes* (Mellanie and Ingpen) book was read with him/her.

B. The client's questions that arose from reading *Lifetimes* were answered and supported.

C. The client's lack of questions was gently but firmly confronted as being an avoidance of grieving.

16. Connect Client with Experienced Griever (16)

A. The client was assisted in identifying a peer or adult he/she knows who has successfully worked through the grieving process and might be willing to talk with him/her about the experience.

B. The client was guided in developing a list of questions he/she would like to have answered by the experienced person.

C. The client was encouraged to set a date to talk with the experienced griever, either at a time outside a session or within a conjoint session in the future.

D. The client has followed through with talking with the experienced griever, and this positive experience was processed within today's session.

E. The client has not followed through with contacting an experienced griever, and he/she was redirected to do so.

17. Conduct Conjoint Session with Experienced Peer Griever (17)

A. A conjoint session was held in which the client met with a peer who had experienced and worked through a loss. The client asked him/her a list of questions concerning death, loss, and grieving.

B. The experience of the peer survivor of loss was processed with the client, emphasizing how the survivor had worked through each stage of the grief process.

C. The client's talk with the experienced peer griever was noted to be reassuring and supportive to the client.

18. Assign Interview with Clergy/Adult (18)

A. The client was asked to interview a clergyperson and another adult who has experienced a loss to learn about their experiences and how each has worked through it.

B. The client's interviews with the clergyperson and other adult were reviewed, with key elements of the experience being identified and the message of "You will make it, too" being reinforced.

C. The client failed to follow through with interviewing either a clergyperson or another experienced adult griever, and the assignment was given again.

19. List Positive Things about Deceased (19)

A. The client was asked to list all the positive things about the deceased and how he/she plans to remember each.

B. The list of positive things about the deceased was processed with the client, each positive thing/memory was affirmed, and the importance of remembering each was emphasized.

C. The client enjoyed the experience of listing positive memories about the deceased significant other.

D. The client was overwhelmed with emotion when talking about positive memories about the deceased significant other.

E. The client can now recall positive things about the deceased significant other without becoming overwhelmed with sadness.

20. Explore Thoughts of Guilt and Blame (20)

A. The client's thoughts and feelings of guilt and blame for the loss were explored.

B. The client's irrational thoughts and feelings were identified and replaced with more realistic ones.

C. It was noted that the client's irrational thoughts and feelings of guilt and self-blame are no longer present.

21. **Help Lift Self-Imposed Curse (21)**

A. The client's belief in a self-imposed curse that makes him/her responsible for the death of the significant other was explored.

B. The client was encouraged to ask the person who indicated that the death of the significant other was the client's fault to retract the statement.

C. A role-play phone conversation was done between the client and the deceased in which he/she had the opportunity to apologize for his/her behavior that "caused" the loss.

D. The client's unrealistic belief in a curse that caused the death of the significant other were confronted.

E. It was reflected to the client that he/she no longer believes that he/she was responsible for the death of the significant other through some curse phenomenon.

22. **Implement Absolution Rituals (22)**

A. An absolution ritual was created for the client to assist him/her in resolving guilt and loss.

B. The client was asked for a commitment to implement and follow through with the ritual as created.

C. The ritual was monitored for its effectiveness and adjusted as required.

D. The absolution ritual seems to have been effective in reducing the client's feelings of guilt or blame for the loss.

23. **Encourage and Support Appropriate Anger (23)**

A. The client was encouraged and reminded in sessions to look angry when feeling angry, act angry, and then to put his/her anger into words.

B. The client's fear of looking angry and expressing anger was explored with him/her.

C. The client was supported and given positive verbal feedback when he/she acted angry and expressed it.

D. The client was confronted when he/she appeared to be feeling angry but acted otherwise.

E. It was noted that the client's feelings of anger toward God, self, and others has diminished as he/she was able to express them freely.

24. **Prepare for an Apology/Ask Forgiveness (24)**

A. The client was asked to write either a letter of apology or one asking for forgiveness from the deceased.

B. Role-play was used with the client to practice asking for forgiveness or apologizing to the deceased.

C. Letters and role-play exercises have been successful in reducing the client's feelings of guilt.

D. The client has not participated in writing a letter of apology or forgiveness and was re-directed to do so.

25. **Assign Good-Bye Letter (25)**

A. The client was asked to write a good-bye letter to the deceased loved one.

B. The client was assigned to complete the "Grief Letter" assignment from the *Adolescent Psychotherapy Homework Planner,* 2nd ed. (Jongsma, Peterson, and McInnis).

C. The client has written the good-bye letter to the deceased loved one, and this letter was processed.

D. The client has not written a good-bye letter to the deceased loved one and was redirected to do so.

26. Suggest Grave Visit (26)

A. The client was prompted to make arrangements to visit the loved one's grave site with a friend or relative and to say good-bye to the deceased loved one while at the grave.

B. The client was urged to leave a good-bye letter or drawing at the loved one's grave site.

C. The experience of saying good-bye to the loved one was processed with the client and evaluated in terms of where he/she was in the process of finally letting go.

D. The experience of saying good-bye to the loved one has helped the client take a positive step in the grief process and achieve more closure to his/her feelings.

27. List Grief Resolution Indicators (27)

A. The client was assisted in developing a list of behavioral and emotional indications that would signify that the loss is becoming resolved.

B. The developed list of grief resolution indicators was used to support the fact that the client has made significant progress in accepting the loss.

C. Because many of the grief resolution indicators are not present in the patient's life or experience, it is clear that the patient has yet to attain acceptance of the loss and move on with his/her life; this was reflected to him/her as a normal pattern of grieving.

28. Teach Parents Supportive Methods (28)

A. The parents were taught various specific ways to support and encourage the client in successfully working through the grief process.

B. The parents' efforts to show love, offer consolation, and provide comfort were affirmed and reinforced.

C. The client has responded favorably to the parents' showing more support and empathy for his/her grief, and this was emphasized to the client and parents.

D. The parents have been resistant to increasing their behaviors that show comfort, consolation, and support for the client's grief, and this resistance was processed.

29. Assign Parents to Read Grief Books (29)

A. The parents were assigned to read books to help them become familiar with the grieving process.

B. The client's parents were asked to read *Learning to Say Good-Bye* (LeShan) to give them knowledge of the grieving process.

C. The client's parents were asked to read *The Grieving Teen* (Fitzgerald) to give them knowledge about the grieving process.

D. Accurate information that the parents gathered from their reading on the subject of grief was reinforced, and any questions they had were answered.

E. The parents' unrealistic expectations about the grieving process were confronted and redirected into more healthy or appropriate expectations.

F. The client's parents have not read the material on grief and were redirected to do so.

30. Refer Parents to Grief Group (30)

A. The client's parents were referred to and encouraged to attend a grief/loss support group.

B. The client's parents were open to the suggestion of attending a support group and have committed themselves to attending the next meeting; positive feedback was provided.

C. The client's parents were resistant to the idea of attending a grief/loss support group and refused to follow through with this referral; they were urged to reconsider.

31. Hold Family Session to Express Grief (31)

A. A family session was conducted in which each family member was encouraged to talk about his/her experience related to the loss.

B. Family members who found it impossible to talk about their grief feelings were reminded of the importance of doing so if they were going to work through the loss.

C. Family members were encouraged to talk more about the loss at appropriate times outside sessions.

D. It was reflected to the family that the client felt reassured and understood because family members shared their feelings of grief connected to the loss.

32. Play The Good Mourning Game (32)

A. The Good Mourning Game (Bisenius and Norris) was played by family members in family sessions to encourage sharing their individual grieving processes.

B. The family was encouraged to set aside times to play The Good Mourning Game at home between sessions.

C. The experience of playing the game was processed with the family, and each member identified what he/she had learned about other members' grief processes.

33. Develop New Grieving Rituals (33)

A. The family was assisted in developing new grieving rituals that could help the client heal from the loss.

B. The family was asked to make a commitment to implement these rituals in a timely manner.

C. The new grieving rituals instituted by the family were noted to have provided the client with support in the expression of his/her feelings about the loss.

34. Encourage Involvement in Grieving Rituals (34)

A. The parents were encouraged to allow the client to be a part of all of the grieving rituals he/she requests to participate in.

B. The parents were directed to be sensitive, supportive, and comforting to the client during the grieving rituals he/she attends.

C. The various grieving rituals were explained to the client, and he/she was given the choice of which ones to attend.

D. It was noted that the client's attendance at the funeral and other grieving rituals was beneficial in sharing grief with others and in saying good-bye to the deceased.

35. Educate Family about Anniversary Dates (35)

A. The parents and the client were taught about the effect of anniversary dates and typical feelings associated with these dates.

B. Strategies for effectively dealing with anniversary dates were explored with the client and family.

C. The parents' tendency to assume "Things will be okay after this" was confronted, and the reality of a grief reaction to anniversary dates was reinforced.

36. Prepare Parents to Say Good-Bye (36)

A. The parents were prepared to say good-bye in a healthy, affirming way to their children over whom they have lost custody.

B. The parents' plan to just leave their children without having a final visit to say good-bye was confronted and processed.

C. The parents have made adequate preparations for saying good-bye to their children and have agreed to a final visit to do so.

37. Facilitate Good-Bye Session (37)

A. A good-bye session was facilitated with the parents who were losing custody of their children so the parents could give each child an appropriate message of permission to move on.

B. The parents were given affirmation and positive verbal feedback on their following through in saying good-bye to children in a positive, healthy way.

C. The good-bye session was a conflictual one in that the parents left the child feeling guilty for the parents' grief and sadness.

D. The parents have written a letter of good-bye and affirmation to their children over whom they have lost custody.

38. Develop a Life Book (38)

A. The client was asked to make a record of his/her life in a book format, using pictures and other memorabilia, to help visualize his/her past, present, and future life.

B. The client was assisted in making a life book that reflected his/her past, present, and future by following the exercise "Create a Memory Album" from the *Adolescent Psychotherapy Homework Planner,* 2nd ed. (Jongsma, Peterson, and McInnis).

C. A completed memory album was kept by the client, and one was given to his/her current parents.

D. It was noted that the client's parents affirmed the client's previous life experiences and accepted the memory album with interest.

E. The parents seemed anxious and resistive to the client's talking about his/her previous life experiences outside of the family.

LOW SELF-ESTEEM

CLIENT PRESENTATION

1. Self-Disparaging Remarks (1)*

A. The client's deep sense of inferiority was reflected in frequent self-disparaging remarks about his/her appearance, worth, and abilities.

B. The lack of any eye contact on the client's part and negative remarks about self are evidence of how little the client thinks of himself/herself.

C. The client reported feeling inferior to others and generally believes that he/she is a loser.

D. The client has stopped making self-critical remarks and has even begun to acknowledge some positive traits and successes.

2. Takes Blame Easily (2)

A. The client often explains his/her problems as being due to his/her own negative behavior.

B. The client often takes responsibility for others' problems.

C. The client has begun to make connections between his/her low self-esteem and a tendency to take blame too easily.

D. The client has been able to develop an appropriate level of personal responsibility.

3. Accepting Compliments (3)

A. The client acknowledged his/her difficulty in believing others when they say nice or complimentary things.

B. The parents reported that the client discounts any praise from them or others.

C. The client reported never hearing compliments from parents, so now he/she is unsure how to respond to accolades from anyone.

D. The client has now begun to accept compliments at face value, feeling uncomfortable but good when these instances occur.

4. Refusal to Try New Experiences (4)

A. The client's pervasive failure expectation was reflected in his/her refusal to try new experiences.

B. The client reported being frustrated with his/her pattern of never trying any new experiences.

C. The client listed many experiences in which he/she experienced failure, but his/her perception was often slanted and distorted.

D. The client expressed that failure is his/her greatest fear.

E. The client has begun to take a few risks and try new experiences with encouragement and support.

*The numbers in parentheses correlate to the number of the Behavioral Definition statement in the companion chapter with the same title in *The Adolescent Psychotherapy Treatment Planner*, Fourth Edition (Jongsma, Peterson, McInnis, and Bruce) by John Wiley & Sons, 2006.

5. Avoidant/Quiet (5)

A. The client presented in a quiet, avoidant manner.

B. The client reported that he/she avoids more than brief contact with others and usually has little to say in social situations.

C. The parents reported that the client has always been shy with adults and peers.

D. The client has gradually started to withdraw less and is feeling less tense around others.

6. Cautious/Fearful (5)

A. The client presented with a frightened affect and a very cautious manner.

B. From the earliest times the client can remember, others have always scared him/her and he/she always has been cautious not to upset anyone.

C. The client indicated he/she is cautious and fearful of doing something wrong in social situations.

D. The client has started to be less cautious and now takes some carefully chosen social risks.

7. Pleasing/Friendly (6)

A. The client presented in a friendly, outgoing manner and seems eager to please others.

B. Everything was carefully checked out by the client to make sure what he/she is doing or saying is right or acceptable to others.

C. Past actions done to please others have gotten the client in trouble or left him/her feeling taken advantage of.

D. A noticeable decrease in the client's pleasing behaviors was observed, and he/she is now starting to offer his/her thoughts and opinions more assertively.

8. Inability to Accept/Recognize Positive Traits (7)

A. The client denied having any talents or positive attributes that others would admire.

B. The client struggled to identify any positive traits or talents about himself/herself.

C. The client rejected all the identified positive traits pointed out to him/her by others.

D. The client was able to recognize and accept positive things about himself/herself.

9. Insecure/Anxious (8)

A. There was visible insecurity and anxiousness to the client's affect and manner.

B. The client described several instances in which he/she did not say or do something in front of peers because of fear of ridicule and rejection.

C. The client reported feeling anxious and insecure at home and in all social/peer situations, believing that others may not like him/her.

D. As the session progressed, the client became less anxious and able to open up to the therapist.

E. The client reported feeling more self-confident when in the presence of peers.

10. Acts Out for Acceptance (9)

A. The client has often engaged in self-defeating behavior (e.g., drinking and sexual activity) to gain the acceptance of his/her peers.

B. The client identified that he/she found it easier to feel accepted by peers when he/she was using substances.

C. The client indicated that he/she has done various "bad acts" to gain the attention and acceptance of peers.

D. The client has dropped most of his/her self-defeating behavior and has begun to work on accepting himself/herself.

11. Difficulty Saying No (10)

A. The client indicated he/she rarely says no to others out of fear of not being liked.

B. The client reported believing he/she will not be liked unless he/she says yes.

C. The client identified the paralyzing fear he/she experiences when saying no to others.

D. The client has worked on starting to say no to others and to be more true to his/her real beliefs, values, feelings, or thoughts.

INTERVENTIONS IMPLEMENTED

1. Confront/Reframe Self-Disparaging Remarks (1)*

A. The client's self-disparaging comments were confronted with the strong message that these comments were not an accurate reflection of reality.

B. The client's self-disparaging comments were realistically reframed and given to the client to replace the negative comments.

C. The client reported that he/she is more aware of his/her tendency to make self-disparaging remarks and has been successful at reducing the frequency of this behavior.

2. Explore How Negative Feelings Are Acted Out (2)

A. Client was asked to construct a list of ways he/she sees himself/herself expressing or acting out negative feelings about himself/herself.

B. Client's self-awareness was increased by exploring how he/she expresses or acts out negative feelings about self and how he/she could stop this habit.

C. It was consistently pointed out to the client in a warm, respectful manner whenever he/she was projecting a negative self-image.

3. Refer for Group Therapy (3)

A. The client was referred to group therapy that is focused on building self-esteem.

B. Progress reports reflected that the client is actively taking part in group therapy and is slowly building some self-confidence.

C. The client's fear of social interaction was given as a reason for his/her refusal to attend group therapy; he/she was redirected to attend the group.

4. Assign Reading of *Reviving Ophelia* (4)

A. The client was asked to read selected sections from *Reviving Ophelia* (Pipher) and discuss key points gathered from it.

*The numbers in parentheses correlate to the number of the Therapeutic Intervention statement in the companion chapter with the same title in *The Adolescent Psychotherapy Treatment Planner,* Fourth Edition (Jongsma, Peterson, McInnis, and Bruce) by John Wiley & Sons, 2006.

B. The client has read selected sections from *Reviving Ophelia* and reported an increased awareness of the dynamics of low self-esteem.

C. The client has not read *Reviving Ophelia* and was redirected to do so.

5. Assign Reading of *Why I'm Afraid to Tell You Who I Am* (5)

A. The client was asked to read *Why I'm Afraid to Tell You Who I Am* (Powell) to increase his/her comfort with self-disclosure.

B. The client's hesitancy and fear about self-disclosure were explored and barriers removed.

C. The client has demonstrated increased self-disclosure within therapy sessions and in daily life and was provided with positive feedback.

D. The client has not read *Why I'm Afraid to Tell You Who I Am* and was redirected to complete this assignment.

6. Record Positive Aspects of Self (6)

A. The client was asked to identify one positive thing about himself/herself daily and record it in a journal.

B. The client's journal was reviewed, and positive traits or accomplishments were identified, affirmed, and supported.

C. The client reported that he/she is feeling more positive about self and is more aware of his/her positive traits.

D. The client has not recorded positive aspects of himself/herself and was assisted in identifying and ameliorating barriers to this task.

7. Develop Positive Self-Talk (7)

A. Positive self-talk techniques were taught to the client to assist in boosting his/her confidence and self-image.

B. Role-play was used to practice positive self-talk techniques.

C. A commitment was elicited from the client to employ positive self-talk on a daily basis.

D. The positive self-talk technique has been noted to be effective in increasing the client's self-esteem.

8. Identify Parents' Critical Interactions (8)

A. In family sessions, critical interaction patterns were identified within the family and redirected to supportive, affirming interaction patterns.

B. Videotape of family session was used to illustrate critical family interaction patterns.

C. Negative parenting methods were discussed with the parents, and new, affirming methods were recommended.

D. The parents were supported as they have become more aware of their disparaging parenting methods and reported implementation of more affirming child guidance techniques.

9. Reinforce Positive Statements (9)

A. The client's statements of self-confidence and positive things about self were verbally affirmed and supported.

B. The frequency of the client's positive self-descriptive statements has been noted to be increasing.

10. Develop Affirmations List (10)

A. The client was assisted in developing a list of positive affirmations for himself/herself.

B. A commitment was elicited from the client to read the affirmation list three times each day.

C. The client reported that the regular reading of the self-affirmation list was beneficial in building self-esteem.

D. The client has not regularly used positive affirmations and was redirected to do so.

11. Assign Mirror Exercise (11)

A. The client was asked to examine himself/herself in a mirror for two minutes daily and record his/her responses in order to expand his/her acceptance of his/her physical traits.

B. Positive physical traits that were identified from the mirror exercise were reinforced, and negative ones were downplayed or normalized.

C. The client's predominance of negative responses was discussed and confronted as unrealistic and exaggerated.

12. Assign Self-Esteem Exercise (12)

A. The client was asked to complete exercises designed to help build self-esteem.

B. The client was asked to complete "Self-Esteem—What Is It—How Do I Get It" from *Ten Days to Self-Esteem* (Burns) to provide a road map for attaining self-esteem.

C. Completed self-esteem exercises were processed and discussed, with key points and issues of esteem being emphasized.

D. The client has implemented self-esteem-building thoughts that were learned from the book *Ten Days to Self-Esteem.*

E. The client has not completed or implemented the self-esteem-building exercises and was redirected to do so.

13. Play Therapeutic Games (13)

A. The UnGame (UnGame Company) and The Thinking, Feeling, and Doing Game (Gardner) were played with the client to give opportunities for self-disclosure.

B. Opportunities for identifying feelings during games were seized to affirm the client's self-disclosure.

C. It was reflected to the client that he/she has become more adept at identifying and expressing his/her emotions.

14. Educate about Feelings Identification (14)

A. Education was provided for the client on identifying, labeling, and expressing feelings.

B. The client was given a list of feelings, then given various scenarios and asked to identify what the individual in the scenario might be feeling.

C. The client was asked to keep a daily feelings journal.

D. The client was encouraged for showing that he/she has become more adept at identifying and expressing his/her emotions.

15. Encourage Eye Contact (15)

A. The client's lack of eye contact was discussed with the client.

B. An agreement was obtained from the client to have regular eye contact with the therapist during sessions.

C. The client was confronted by the therapist when he/she was avoiding or failing to make eye contact.

D. The client reported an increase in the frequency of making eye contact with others outside of therapy sessions.

16. Broaden Eye Contact Experience (16)

A. The client was asked to make a commitment to increase eye contact with parents, teachers, and others.

B. The client's experience of making eye contact with all adults was processed, and feelings specific to this experience were identified.

C. The client reported an increase in the frequency of making eye contact with others outside of therapy sessions and was praised for this increase.

17. Assign Reading of *Feed Your Head* (17)

A. The client was asked to read *Feed Your Head: Some Excellent Stuff on Being Yourself* (Hipp and Hanson) to help him/her understand the concept of how to be himself/herself.

B. Risks of being yourself were discussed with the client, and ways to start to do this were explored.

C. The client was assisted in identifying and elaborating on positive recent experiences in expressing honestly his/her thoughts and feelings.

18. Complete Life-Changing Exercise (18)

A. The client was asked to draw representations of the changes he/she desires for himself/herself or his/her life situation.

B. The client was asked to do either the "Three Wishes Game" or "Three Ways to Change Yourself" from the *Adolescent Psychotherapy Homework Planner,* 2nd ed. (Jongsma, Peterson, and McInnis) to help him/her identify desired life changes.

C. The completed life-changing exercise was processed, and a plan of implementation for key desired life changes was developed.

D. The client was asked to make a commitment to implement and follow through on the program.

E. The client reported success at beginning to implement the changes in self that he/she has desired for a long time.

F. The client has not completed the life-changing exercise and was redirected to do so.

19. Utilize Solution-Focused Approach (19)

A. A brief, solution-focused intervention called "Externalizing the Problem" was implemented with the client's approval and commitment to follow through.

B. The client's externalizing of the low-self-esteem problem was monitored for follow-through and effectiveness, and necessary adjustments were made.

C. The client was confronted on his/her lack of consistency in following through on the intervention.

20. Identify Emotional Needs (20)

A. The client was taught basic concepts of how to identify and verbalize his/her emotional needs.

B. Ways to meet more of the client's emotional needs were explored.

C. The client failed to clearly identify and verbalize his/her emotional needs or ways to meet them and was provided with tentative examples in this area.

21. Encourage Sharing of Emotional Needs (21)

A. A family session was conducted in which the parents and the client exchanged and identified their emotional needs.

B. The client and family were educated in ways to be sensitive to each other's needs and to ask for their own emotional needs to be met.

C. The client and family have not focused on sharing their emotional needs and were provided with tentative examples of how they might do this.

22. Explore Incidents of Abuse (22)

A. Possible incidents of physical, sexual, and emotional abuse were explored with the client.

B. Appropriate reporting procedures were followed regarding reports of physical, sexual, and emotional abuse.

C. The client was assisted in exploring how being a victim of abuse has affected his/her feelings about self.

D. The client's denial and resistiveness were explored and resolved so the client could connect past abuse with present negative feelings about self.

23. Identify Distorted Beliefs (23)

A. The client was asked to list his/her beliefs about self and the world.

B. The client's distorted, negative beliefs about self and the world were reframed.

C. The client struggled to identify any positive beliefs about himself/herself and the world and was provided with tentative examples of how others choose to see themselves and the world.

24. Develop Positive Messages (24)

A. The client was helped to identify and develop more positive, realistic messages about self and the world.

B. New positive, realistic life messages were implemented by the client and used on a daily basis.

C. The client was confronted whenever he/she failed to make positive, realistic statements about self or life events.

D. The client reported that he/she has developed a more positive outlook about self and the world, and the benefits of this positive outlook were reviewed.

25. Identify Esteem-Building Tasks (25)

A. The client was helped to identify daily tasks that, when performed, would increase his/her sense of responsibility and esteem.

B. The client's follow-through on daily tasks was monitored for consistency.

C. The client was given positive verbal feedback for his/her follow-through on self-care responsibilities.

D. Positive feedback was provided as the client reported feeling better about himself/herself as he/she has become more active in performing daily responsibilities.

26. Teach Acceptance of Compliments (26)

A. Neurolinguistic and reframing techniques were used to alter the client's self-messages to enable him/her to receive and accept compliments.

B. Role-play techniques were utilized to give the client opportunities to practice accepting compliments.

C. The client reported a positive experience in accepting compliments from others recently.

D. The client has not ceased his/her pattern of refusing to accept compliments from others and was provided with remedial assistance in this area.

27. Assign Letters of Reference (27)

A. The client was asked to provide the names of three nonrelatives from whom letters of reference could be obtained.

B. Letters of reference obtained by the client were read with him/her, and compliments were identified and affirmed.

C. The client was asked to write a thank-you note to each person who wrote a reference letter, confirming each positive characteristic that was identified in the reference letter.

28. Assign Parents to Read *Full Esteem Ahead!* (28)

A. The parents were given the book *Full Esteem Ahead!* (Loomans and Loomans) to read first and then asked to select two or three self-esteem-building ideas they would like to implement with the client.

B. The self-esteem-building ideas chosen by the parents were processed, and a plan for implementation was made.

C. The parents were reminded of the importance of consistent follow-through if the interventions are to be successful.

D. The parents have successfully implemented self-esteem-building ideas from *Full Esteem Ahead!* and the client has reported appreciating their efforts; the benefits of this program were reviewed in session.

29. Assign Increased Peer Group Activities (29)

A. The parents were presented with various options (Scouting, sports, music, etc.) that could help boost the client's self-esteem and were asked to encourage him/her to get involved in at least one of them.

B. The role of extracurricular activities in building the client's self-esteem was explored, with positive aspects being identified.

C. The parents have followed through with enrolling the client in more peer group activities.

D. The client's parents have not followed through with enrolling the client in more peer group activities and were redirected to do so.

30. Explore Parental Expectations (30)

A. Expectations that the parents hold for the client were explored and then affirmed where appropriate and adjusted when they were unrealistic.

B. The parents were educated to understand age-appropriate and realistic developmental expectations for the client given his/her abilities.

C. The parents were challenged in a respectful way when their expectations of the client seemed unrealistically high or age-inappropriate.

D. The parents have been noted to adjust their expectations to a more realistic level given the client's developmental stage.

31. Teach Parents Three R's Discipline Technique (31)

A. The three R's discipline technique was taught to the parents, and they were then encouraged to read *Raising Self-Reliant Children in a Self-Indulgent World* (Glenn and Nelson).

B. The parents were assisted in implementing discipline that is respectful, reasonable, and related (three R's) to the misbehavior and were coached to offer support, guidance, and encouragement as they followed through.

C. The parents have successfully implemented discipline that is respectful, reasonable, and related to the client's behavior.

32. Refer to Positive Parenting Class (32)

A. The parents were asked to attend a parenting class that focuses on the issues of positive parenting.

B. The experiences of positive parenting classes were processed along with key gains received.

C. The parents have not attended the parenting classes to focus on issues of positive parenting and were redirected to do so.

33. Teach Anxiety-Coping (33)

A. The client was taught the "Pretending to Know How" and "The Therapist on the Inside" techniques for facing new and uncomfortable situations.

B. The anxiety-coping techniques were rehearsed using two different situations that the client might face, and the client was asked to commit to using these techniques.

C. The experience of using "Pretending to Know How" and "The Therapist on the Inside" was processed and the client was asked to try these techniques on two additional situations/problems.

D. The client has successfully faced challenging situations using the new coping skills and it was noted that his/her confidence is growing.

E. The client has not used techniques for facing uncomfortable situations and was assisted in brainstorming ways to use these techniques.

34. Read *How to Say No and Keep Your Friends* (34)

A. The client was requested to read *How to Say No and Keep Your Friends* (Scott) to encourage assertiveness.

B. The client was taught that saying no can boost your self-esteem.

C. Role-play was utilized for the client to practice saying no to friends in a variety of social situations.

D. The power of saying no was consistently reinforced with the client.

E. The client reported that he/she has said no to others' requests and that he/she felt justified and affirmed; additional affirmation was provided to the client.

35. Teach Assertiveness and Social Skills (35)

A. The client was asked to list situations in which he/she has had social difficulties or finds it hard to be assertive.

B. Difficult social situations that the client identified were role-played with him/her to teach assertiveness.

C. Behavioral rehearsal was utilized with the client to prepare him/her for facing the identified difficult social situations.

36. Refer to Camp (36)

A. It was recommended to the parents that they schedule an alternative camp weekend experience for the client to build trust and self-confidence.

B. The weekend alternative camp experience was processed with the client, and gains in trust and self-confidence were identified, affirmed, and reinforced.

37. Encourage Parents to Praise Accomplishments (37)

A. The parents were assisted in identifying opportunities they could seize to praise, reinforce, and recognize positive things done by the client.

B. The parents were reminded of the importance of praise, reinforcement, and recognition in building the client's self-esteem.

C. Missed opportunities for praise, reinforcement, or recognition with the client were pointed out to the parents in family session.

D. Both the client and his/her parents report that the frequency of parental praise and recognition for the client's accomplishments has increased.

MANIA/HYPOMANIA

CLIENT PRESENTATION

1. Overly Friendly Social Style (1)*

A. The client becomes overly friendly or gregarious in his/her social interactions with others during his/her manic or hypomanic episodes.

B. The client appeared loud, boisterous, and overly friendly.

C. The client appeared more relaxed, calm, and subdued.

D. The client reported that he/she is more relaxed, calm, and subdued in his/her recent social interactions.

2. Poor Social Judgment (1)

A. The client frequently becomes entangled in interpersonal disputes during his/her manic or hypomanic episodes because of his/her failure to pick up on important social cues or interpersonal nuances.

B. The client has frequently disclosed personal information too readily and makes others feel uncomfortable by demanding that they do the same.

C. The stabilization of the client's mood and reduction in energy level have resulted in improved social relationships and fewer interpersonal conflicts with others.

D. The client has established appropriate boundaries regarding his/her social relationships and has self-disclosed personal information to only his/her close friends.

3. Elated/Euphoric Mood (2)

A. The client's mood often appears extremely euphoric or elated during his/her manic or hypomanic episodes.

B. The client's mood appeared elated, euphoric, and overly enthusiastic.

C. The client's mood has started to stabilize without the extreme amount of euphoria or elation.

D. The client's mood has stabilized and returned to a normal level without the extreme highs or lows.

4. Inflated Sense of Self-Esteem (2)

A. The client has frequently displayed an inflated sense of self-worth and grandiosity during his/her manic or hypomanic episodes.

B. The client expressed grandiose thoughts and made exaggerated claims about his/her abilities during today's therapy session.

C. The client verbalized delusions of grandeur and announced extravagant, unrealistic plans to achieve success.

---

*The numbers in parentheses correlate to the number of the Behavioral Definition statement in the companion chapter with the same title in *The Adolescent Psychotherapy Treatment Planner,* Fourth Edition (Jongsma, Peterson, McInnis, and Bruce) by John Wiley & Sons, 2006.

D. The client has gradually started to decrease the frequency of his/her grandiose statements and is slowly beginning to develop a more realistic picture of his/her capabilities.

E. The client no longer makes grandiose statements and has developed a healthy, realistic understanding of his/her capabilities.

5. Flight of Ideas/Racing Thoughts (3)

A. The client has experienced a flight of ideas or racing thoughts during the manic or hypomanic episodes.

B. The client experienced racing thoughts and a flight of ideas during today's therapy session.

C. The client was able to communicate his/her thoughts in a logical and organized manner.

D. The client reported recently experiencing a significant decrease in his/her flighty or racing thoughts.

6. Pressured Speech (3)

A. The client's speech was pressured, and he/she spoke very rapidly during today's therapy session.

B. The client exhibited a mild decrease in his/her rate of speech during today's therapy session.

C. The client's rate of speech has returned to a normal level.

7. High Energy and Restlessness (4)

A. The client displayed a very high energy level during his/her manic or hypomanic episodes.

B. The client presented with a high energy level and appeared agitated in his/her motor movements.

C. The client appeared calmer and displayed less energy and a mild degree of motor activity.

D. The client was able to sit still without showing an excessive amount of motor activity.

E. The client has recently demonstrated a significant decrease in his/her level of energy and restlessness.

8. Impulsivity (5)

A. The client sought immediate gratification of his/her needs and often failed to stop and consider the consequences of his/her actions during the manic or hypomanic phases.

B. The client has demonstrated good impulse control in the recent past as demonstrated by an improved ability to stop and think about the possible negative consequences of his/her actions.

C. The client has shown an improved ability to delay his/her impulses to receive instant gratification of his/her needs in favor of achieving longer-term goals.

D. The client has consistently demonstrated good impulse control.

9. Reduced Need for Sleep (6)

A. The client has experienced a reduced need for sleep during his/her manic or hypomanic episodes.

B. The client reported feeling little or no need for sleep during his/her most recent manic or hypomanic episodes.

C. The client has continued to stay up at night until early morning without feeling a need to sleep more.

D. The client has started to return to a normal amount of sleep.

E. The client reported that he/she is now sleeping a normal amount on a consistent nightly basis.

10. Family History of Affective Disorder (7)

A. The client and parents reported an extensive history of affective disorders in the family.

B. The client and parents are not aware of any other family member having a serious affective disorder.

C. The parent(s) reported experiencing episodes of a major affective disorder in the past.

11. Angry Outbursts/Aggressive Behaviors (8)

A. The client has a history of losing control of his/her temper and exhibiting frequent angry outbursts or aggressive behavior during the manic or hypomanic episodes.

B. The client appeared angry, irritable, and agitated.

C. The client reported incidents of becoming easily angered over minor or trivial matters.

D. The client has started to control his/her anger and aggressive impulses in a more effective manner.

E. The client has consistently demonstrated good control of his/her anger and has not exhibited any major outbursts or aggressive behaviors.

12. Short Attention Span and Distractibility (9)

A. The parents and teachers reported that the client displays a very short attention span and has difficulty staying focused for any significant length of time during the manic or hypomanic episodes.

B. The client appeared very distractible during today's therapy session and often had to be directed back to the topic of discussion.

C. The client appeared more focused and less distractible during today's therapy session.

D. The parents and teachers reported that the client has consistently demonstrated good attention and concentration at home and school.

13. Failure to Complete Tasks (10)

A. The client frequently switches from one uncompleted activity to another during his/her manic or hypomanic episodes.

B. The client has trouble completing tasks and channeling his/her energy into constructive or sustained, purposeful activities because of his/her high energy level, impulsivity, lack of discipline, and racing thoughts.

C. The client has recently exercised greater self-control and discipline, as evidenced by his/her ability to follow through and complete tasks or projects.

D. The client has been able to complete tasks or projects on a regular, consistent basis.

14. Self-Defeating or Dangerous Behavior (11)

A. The client described a history of engaging in self-defeating, risky, or potentially dangerous behavior during his/her manic or hypomanic episodes.

B. The client's impulsivity and restlessness has contributed to his/her propensity for engaging in self-defeating, risky, or potentially dangerous behavior.

C. The client gained insight into the need to stop and think about the possible consequences of his/her actions for self and others before engaging in self-defeating, risky, or potentially dangerous behaviors.

D. The client has not recently engaged in any self-defeating, risky, or potentially dangerous behaviors.

15. Outlandish Dress/Grooming (12)

A. The client has often dressed or groomed himself/herself in an outlandish manner during the manic/hypomanic phases.

B. The client came to the therapy session dressed and groomed in an unusual and outlandish manner.

C. The client was appropriately groomed and attired.

D. The client has consistently dressed and groomed himself/herself in an appropriate manner since his/her moods have stabilized.

INTERVENTIONS IMPLEMENTED

1. Assess Manic/Hypomanic Episode (1)*

A. A diagnostic interview was conducted to assess whether the client is experiencing symptoms of a manic or hypomanic episode.

B. The client's mood, impulse control, anger control, social judgment, frustration tolerance, rate of speech, thought processes, and self-esteem were all assessed in today's diagnostic interview.

C. The client was noted to be pleasant and cooperative during today's diagnostic interview.

D. The client was noted to be agitated and resistant during today's diagnostic interview.

2. Refer for or Conduct Psychological Testing (2)

A. A psychological evaluation was conducted to determine whether the client is experiencing symptoms of Bipolar Disorder.

B. The client was uncooperative and difficult to engage during the psychological testing.

C. The client approached the psychological testing in an honest, straightforward manner and was cooperative with any request directed toward him/her.

D. The psychological testing results supported the diagnosis of Bipolar Disorder.

E. The psychological testing results did not support the diagnosis of Bipolar Disorder.

F. The results of the psychological testing were discussed with the client and parents.

---

* The numbers in parentheses correlate to the number of the Therapeutic Intervention statement in the companion chapter with the same title in *The Adolescent Psychotherapy Treatment Planner*, Fourth Edition (Jongsma, Peterson, McInnis, and Bruce) by John Wiley & Sons, 2006.

3. Obtain Psychosocial History (3)

A. A complete psychosocial history was gathered from the parents to assess for patterns of mania and the extent of bipolar illness in the client's extended family.

B. A review of the client's background revealed several episodes of mania or hypomania.

C. The psychosocial history information gathered during today's therapy session was helpful in that it revealed a strong history of bipolar illnesses in the client's family.

D. The psychosocial history information did not reveal the presence of any bipolar illnesses in the client's extended family.

4. Identify Stressors That Precipitate Mania (4)

A. The client's background was explored for significant stressors that have precipitated manic/hypomanic episodes.

B. The client was helped to identify how past manic/hypomanic episodes were related to past failure experiences at school and/or threats to self-esteem.

C. The client was helped to realize how the onset of past manic/hypomanic episodes was related to previous rejection experiences by peers or friends.

D. The client was assisted in identifying how the onset of past manic/hypomanic episodes was related to trauma within the family system.

E. The client developed a time line in the therapy session in which he/she identified significant historical events that have occurred near the onset of his/her depressive or manic phases.

5. Refer for a Psychiatric Examination (5)

A. The client was referred for a psychiatric evaluation to help determine the need for medication to stabilize his/her mood.

B. The client and parents agreed to follow through with a psychiatric examination to determine the need for medication.

C. The client's resistance to taking medication was explored and worked through in today's therapy session.

D. The client was strongly opposed to being placed on medication to help stabilize his/her mood.

6. Assess Medication Compliance and Effectiveness (6)

A. The client reported that taking the medication regularly has helped to decrease his/her energy level and stabilize moods without any side effects, and the benefits of this stability were highlighted.

B. The client reported little or no improvement since taking the psychotropic medication and was urged to consult with the prescribing clinician.

C. The client has not complied with taking his/her medication on a regular basis and was redirected to do so.

D. The client and parents were encouraged to report the effectiveness and side effects of the medication to the psychiatrist.

7. Arrange Inpatient Hospitalization (7)

A. Arrangements were made for the client to be hospitalized in a psychiatric facility based on the fact that his/her mania is so intense that he/she could be harmful to himself/herself or others or unable to care for his/her own basic needs.

B. The client acknowledged the need for hospitalization and was cooperative with the admission to the psychiatric facility.

C. The client is resistive to the psychiatric hospitalization, and his/her parents were assisted in admitting him/her to the psychiatric facility.

8. Teach about Mania/Hypomania (8)

A. The client was taught about the biopsychosocial correlates of mania/hypomania.

B. The client's parents were provided with information about the biopsychosocial correlates of mania/hypomania.

C. As the client and parents have gained understanding about the biopsychosocial correlates of mania/hypomania, they have been noted to be able to better cope with these symptoms.

D. The client and parents showed only a partial understanding of the biopsychosocial correlates of mania/hypomania and were provided with remedial information in this area.

9. Recommended Reading Material on Bipolar Disorder (9)

A. The parents were assigned to read information about the symptoms and treatment of Bipolar Disorder.

B. The parents were assigned to read *Bipolar Disorders* (Waltz) to learn more about the symptoms and treatment of Bipolar Disorder.

C. The parents have read material about Bipolar Disorder, and the information was processed.

D. The parents had additional questions regarding Bipolar Disorder symptoms and treatment and were provided with more specific information as it related to their child.

10. Develop Trust Relationship (10)

A. A level of trust was built with the client through consistent eye contact, active listening, unconditional positive regard, and warm acceptance.

B. The client was given support by listening closely to his/her concerns and reflecting his/her feelings.

11. Explore Fears of Abandonment (11)

A. The client's background was explored for a history of abandonment or rejection experiences that may have coincided with the triggering of his/her manic/hypomanic episodes.

B. The client expressed fear that future manic/hypomanic episodes may lead to rejection or abandonment by significant others.

C. The parents expressed their love and pledged their continued support to help alleviate the client's fear of being abandoned or rejected because of his/her manic/hypomanic episodes; the client was directed to how his/her parents are supportive.

D. The client denied any fears of abandonment and was reminded that these are common fears that are difficult to acknowledge.

12. Probe Real or Perceived Losses (12)

A. The client's family background was explored for a history of significant losses or separations that may have coincided with the onset of his/her manic/hypomanic episodes.

B. The client was given the opportunity to express his/her thoughts and feelings about real or perceived losses in the past.

C. The empty-chair technique was employed to facilitate expression of feelings surrounding past losses or separations.

D. The client was instructed to draw pictures that reflect his/her feelings about past separations or losses.

13. Teach Techniques to Resolve Past Losses (13)

A. The client was instructed to use a journal to help him/her express and work through feelings surrounding past losses.

B. The client was assigned a "letting go" exercise (e.g., writing a letter) to help him/her resolve past losses and move ahead in his/her life.

C. The client was assisted in developing an action plan to help him/her cope with past losses and move forward in his/her life.

D. The client was strongly encouraged to participate in positive peer group activities to provide him/her with the opportunity to establish meaningful friendships and replace or cope with past losses.

E. The client was assisted in developing a list of positive peer group activities that will provide him/her the opportunity to establish meaningful friendships.

F. The client has not used techniques to resolve past losses and was redirected to do so.

14. Differentiate Actual and Exaggerated Losses (14)

A. The client was helped to differentiate between real and imagined, actual and exaggerated losses.

B. The client was gently challenged and confronted about his/her fear of abandonment and loss that is based on irrational and faulty thinking.

C. The client was helped to replace irrational thoughts about imagined or exaggerated losses with reality-based thoughts.

D. Client-centered approaches were utilized to help the client work through his/her feelings about real, actual losses.

15. Explore Low Self-Esteem Causes (15)

A. The client's family background was explored for a past history of separation, loss, abandonment, or rejection experiences that may have contributed to his/her feelings of low self-esteem.

B. The client was assisted in developing a time line in which he/she identified significant historical events, both positive and negative, that have occurred in his/her family and have impacted his/her self-esteem.

C. Today's therapy session revealed how the client's feelings of low self-esteem and fear of abandonment are related to significant separations, losses, and abandonment in the past.

16. Conduct Family Therapy to Explore Parental Rejection (16)

A. A family therapy session was held to explore how the onset of the client's manic/hypomanic episodes is related to parental rejection or emotional abandonment.

B. The client was given the opportunity to express his/her thoughts and feelings about past rejection or emotional abandonment.

C. The client was supported as he/she verbalized his/her need to spend greater quality time with parent(s) and receive more frequent praise or positive reinforcement.

D. The disengaged parent(s) were challenged to spend more time with the client in leisure, school, or household activities and increase positive reinforcement.

E. The disengaged parent(s) verbalized a commitment to spend increased time with the client.

17. Confront Grandiosity and Demanding Behaviors (17)

A. The client's grandiose thinking and demanding behaviors were gently confronted.

B. The client's grandiose thoughts and demanding behaviors were firmly confronted.

C. The client was helped to realize how his/her grandiose thoughts are related to underlying feelings of low self-esteem, insecurity, and inadequacy.

D. The client was confronted with how his/her demanding behaviors negatively impact his/her relationship with others.

E. Role-playing techniques were utilized to help the client learn more constructive ways to meet his/her needs instead of placing excessive demands on others.

18. Identify Impact of Impulsivity (18)

A. The client was helped to identify his/her goals of improving impulse control and increasing sensitivity to how his/her impulsive behaviors impact others.

B. The client verbalized a commitment to contact his/her psychiatrist or therapist if he/she demonstrates a significant increase in impulsive behaviors, and this commitment was emphasized as a key to controlling symptoms.

C. The client was assisted in listing the negative consequences of his/her impulsive actions or socially inappropriate actions.

D. The client was firmly and consistently confronted with how his/her impulsive or inappropriate behavior negatively impacts himself/herself and others.

E. Role-reversal techniques were used to help the client realize how his/her impulsive behavior negatively impacts others.

19. List Impulsive Behavior Consequences (19)

A. The client was asked to list the negative consequences of his/her impulsive behavior.

B. Role-reversal techniques were used in the therapy session to help the client realize how his/her impulsive behavior negatively impacts himself/herself and others.

C. The client was encouraged to apologize to individuals who have been negatively impacted by his/her impulsive behavior.

D. The client was taught mediational and self-control strategies (e.g., relaxation techniques, "stop, listen, think, and act") to help delay the need for immediate gratification and inhibit impulses.

20. Confront Thoughtless Impulsivity (20)

A. The client was repeatedly confronted with the consequences of his/her thoughtless, impulsive behavior.

B. The parents were strongly encouraged to set firm, consistent limits for the client's impulsive actions.

C. The client was asked to identify the benefits of delaying his/her need for immediate gratification in favor of longer-term gains.

D. The client was encouraged to use mediational and self-control strategies (e.g., relaxation techniques, "stop, listen, think, and act") to help deter his/her impulsive behaviors during manic/hypomanic episodes.

21. Teach Sensitivity through Role-Playing (21)

A. Role-playing and role-reversal techniques were used to help increase the client's sensitivity to how his/her impulsive behaviors negatively affect others.

B. Through the use of role-playing and role-reversal techniques, the client gained insight into how his/her inappropriate social behavior or impulsive actions negatively impact others.

C. The client had much difficulty staying focused on any one topic in today's session, so the role-playing and role-reversal techniques were not helpful in identifying how his/her impulsive actions affect others.

22. Assign Homework on Negative Consequences of Impulsive Behaviors (22)

A. The client was assigned homework designed to help him/her understand that impulsive behavior has costly negative consequences for himself/herself and others.

B. The client was given the homework assignment "Action Minus Thought Equals Painful Consequences" in the *Adolescent Psychotherapy Homework Planner,* 2nd ed. (Jongsma, Peterson, and McInnis) to help him/her understand how impulsive behaviors have negative consequences for both self and others.

C. The client was given the homework assignment "Action Minus Thought Equals Painful Consequences" to help him/her identify more reasonable, alternative replacement behavior for his/her impulsive behavior.

D. The client reported that the homework assignment helped him/her stop and think about the possible consequences of his/her actions before impulsively embarking on a course of action.

E. The client completed the homework assignment but has continued to act out in an impulsive manner; he/she was redirected to what he/she has learned about impulsivity.

F. The client failed to complete the homework assignment and was again assigned to do it.

23. Encourage Parental Limit Setting and Reinforcing (23)

A. The parents attended today's therapy session and were strongly encouraged to set firm, consistent limits for the client's angry outbursts or rebellious behaviors.

B. The parents were helped to identify appropriate consequences for the client's angry outbursts or rebellious behaviors.

C. The parents were strongly encouraged to reinforce the client's prosocial behaviors.

D. A reward system was designed to reinforce positive social behaviors and deter the client's aggressive or rebellious behaviors.

E. The parents were instructed to observe and record three to five positive behaviors by the client between therapy sessions.

24. Develop Clear Rules and Contingencies (24)

A. The parents were assigned the task of listing rules and contingencies for the home.

B. The parents were given the homework assignment "Clear Rules, Positive Reinforcement, Appropriate Consequences" in the *Adolescent Psychotherapy Homework Planner,* 2nd ed. (Jongsma, Peterson, and McInnis) to help them establish clearly defined rules and expectations for the client.

C. The parents reported that the homework assignment "Clear Rules, Positive Reinforcement, Appropriate Consequences" helped them establish clear rules and identify appropriate consequences for the client's impulsive behaviors.

D. The parents reported that the homework assignment helped them identify natural consequences and follow through with limits in a calm, controlled, and respectful manner.

E. The parents reported that they completed the homework assignment but that the client has continued to test the limits and defy the rules; they were urged to continue to set clear rules.

F. The parents failed to complete the homework assignment and were again asked to do it.

25. Establish Consequences for Acting Out Behavior (25)

A. Today's family therapy session focused on helping the parents to establish clearly defined rules and identifying consequences for the client's manipulative or acting out behavior.

B. The parents were assisted in writing down rules and expectations that the client is expected to follow at home and were encouraged to make sure they will be consistently implemented.

C. The parents were reinforced as they were able to identify appropriate consequences for the client's manipulative and acting out behavior.

D. The parents had difficulty establishing clearly defined rules and identifying appropriate consequences for the client's manipulative or acting out behavior and were encouraged to complete this task.

E. The client was asked to repeat the rules to demonstrate an understanding of the expectations of him/her.

26. Reinforce Parental Limit Setting and Expressions of Love (26)

A. The parents were reinforced for setting reasonable limits on the client's impulsive, manipulative, or acting out behavior.

B. The parents were challenged to follow through in setting reasonable limits for the client's behavior to demonstrate their love and commitment to the client.

C. The parents were encouraged to verbalize their unconditional love and commitment to the client to help reduce his/her feelings of insecurity and fear of rejection.

D. It was noted that the parents' verbalized commitment to love the client unconditionally has helped him/her feel more secure and less afraid of rejection.

27. Provide Structure to Behavior Plans/Conversations (27)

A. The client appeared very flighty and frequently had to be directed back to the focus of the conversation.

B. The therapy session focused on helping the parents increase the structure in the home to help deter the client's impulsivity and help him/her stay focused when performing daily tasks or routines.

C. The client and parents were assisted in designing a schedule of dates and times when the client is expected to perform certain tasks or responsibilities.

D. The parents were encouraged to use effective communication techniques (e.g., maintain good eye contact, request positive behaviors, give one instruction at a time) and clear away as many distractions as possible when talking with the client during his/her manic or hypomanic episodes.

28. Reinforce Slower Speech and Deliberate Thought (28)

A. The client was consistently encouraged to speak more slowly and in a calmer voice.

B. The client was verbally reinforced for speaking more slowly and expressing his/her thoughts in a rational and coherent manner.

C. Client-centered approaches were utilized to help the client stay focused and express his/her thoughts and feelings in a rational, deliberate manner.

D. The client was taught effective communication skills to help slow his/her rate of speech and communicate thoughts and feelings in a constructive manner.

E. The client was often stopped and asked to utilize deep breathing techniques to help slow down his/her rate of speech and communicate thoughts in a more deliberate manner.

29. Reinforce Appropriate Dress and Grooming (29)

A. The client was reinforced for being neatly groomed and appropriately dressed.

B. The client was encouraged to dress more appropriately and improve personal hygiene to enhance his/her chances of establishing meaningful friendships.

C. The client was gently confronted with how his/her outlandish dress and poor grooming interfere with his/her ability to establish friendships.

D. The client was redirected regarding appropriate dress and grooming; this has resulted in more appropriate behavior in this area.

30. Identify Strengths and Interests (30)

A. The client was helped to identify a list of his/her strengths and interests.

B. The client was encouraged to share his/her interests with peers to improve self-esteem and provide opportunities to establish peer friendships.

C. The client reported that his/her self-esteem has increased by sharing his/her interests with others and was urged to continue.

D. The client has continued to have difficulty sharing his/her interests with others because of deep-seated feelings of insecurity and was gently urged to continue.

31. Assign Exercises to Identify Positive Traits (31)

A. The client was assigned exercises to help identify his/her positive character and personality traits.

B. The client was assigned the "I Am a Good Person" exercise from the *Adolescent Psychotherapy Homework Planner,* 2nd ed. (Jongsma, Peterson, and McInnis) to help increase his/her self-esteem by identifying his/her positive character and personality traits.

C. The client successfully completed the exercise and identified several positive character and personality traits.
D. The client did not follow through with completing the exercise and was again asked to work on it.

32. Interpret Underlying Fear and Insecurity (32)

A. The client was helped to recognize how his/her braggadocio and denial of dependency are related to underlying fear and feelings of dependency.
B. The client was supported as he/she verbally recognized how his/her angry outbursts and hostile behaviors are related to underlying fear and insecurity.
C. The client was encouraged to express his/her fears and insecurities more directly to significant others instead of reacting with excessive bragging, boasting, or hostility.
D. The client was helped to identify how his/her braggadocio and excessive boasting are related to the need for acceptance and approval from others.
E. The client was helped to identify more appropriate ways to meet his/her dependency needs.

33. Identify Balance between Dependency and Independence (33)

A. A family therapy session was held to help the client achieve a balance between meeting his/her dependency needs and striving to become more independent.
B. The client and parents were helped to identify specific dates and times when the client could talk one-on-one with the parents or engage in leisure or social activities with them.
C. The client and parents were helped to establish clear-cut rules pertaining to the client's quest for greater independence.
D. The client and parents identified appropriate ways for him/her to achieve greater independence; they were directed to implement the easiest of these techniques.
E. The client was given a homework assignment to engage in three to five responsible and independent behaviors before the next therapy session.

34. Encourage Sharing Deeper Feelings (34)

A. The client was encouraged to share his/her feelings at a deeper level to facilitate openness, intimacy, and greater trust in his/her relationships.
B. The client was helped to identify a list of close, trusted individuals with whom he/she could share his/her more intimate thoughts and feelings.
C. The client was challenged to share his/her more intimate thoughts and feelings with others to counteract his/her pattern of superficiality and fear of intimacy.
D. The client expressed that his/her willingness to share deeper emotions has helped him/her to establish closer, more intimate relationships and was urged to continue.
E. The client's interpersonal relationships have remained at a superficial level because of his/her fear of rejection if he/she shares deeper thoughts and emotions, and he/she was urged to try to increase this in small increments.

35. Identify Negative Cognitive Messages (35)

A. The client was helped to identify the negative cognitive messages that feed his/her fear of rejection and failure.

B. The client was assisted in exploring whether his/her fears of rejection and/or failure are rational or irrational.

C. The client was helped to realize how his/her frequent derogatory remarks about self impede his/her chances of establishing friendships.

36. Identify Positive, Realistic Thoughts (36)

A. The client was helped to identify positive, realistic thoughts that can replace his/her negative self-talk that reinforces low self-esteem and a fear of failure or rejection.

B. The client was encouraged and challenged to replace his/her negative self-talk with positive self-talk.

C. The client's consistent practice of replacing negative self-talk with positive messages has helped to increase his/her self-esteem and confidence.

D. The client was challenged to verbalize positive self-talk when initiating conversations or social contacts to help overcome his/her fear of rejection.

E. The client acknowledged that he/she has not replaced negative self-talk with positive self-talk and, as a result, has continued to be troubled by feelings of low self-esteem.

MEDICAL CONDITION

CLIENT PRESENTATION

1. Diagnosis of a Chronic, Non-Life-Threatening Illness (1)*

A. The client recently received a diagnosis of a chronic, non-life-threatening illness that will have a significant impact on his/her life.

B. The client presented as upset and worried after he/she received confirmation of having a chronic, non-life-threatening medical condition.

C. The client was overwhelmed after he/she received the diagnosis of a chronic illness and the life changes it will require.

D. The client has started to accept his/her medical condition and has begun to make the required life changes.

2. Lifestyle Changes (1)

A. The client reported numerous lifestyle changes that need to be made in order to stabilize his/her medical condition.

B. The client is struggling with letting go of certain things in his/her lifestyle that will assist in treating the medical condition.

C. The client refused to consider making certain life changes that were recommended as part of his/her treatment.

D. Outside pressure from the family has moved the client to make the recommended life changes to improve his/her long-term physical health.

3. Diagnosis of an Acute, Life-Threatening Illness (2)

A. The client presented as very upset after he/she received a diagnosis of having an acute, life-threatening illness.

B. The client reported feeling an overwhelming sadness about having been diagnosed with an acute, life-threatening illness.

C. The client indicated that he/she has not told any of his/her friends about the diagnosis and its seriousness.

D. The client has begun to share his/her diagnosis and what it means with others close to him/her.

4. Diagnosis of a Terminal Illness (3)

A. The client reported with hesitation and difficulty his/her diagnosis of terminal illness.

B. The client failed to disclose his/her diagnosis of a terminal illness until he/she was asked.

C. The client indicated that he/she finds it impossible to talk about his/her diagnosis of terminal illness.

*The numbers in parentheses correlate to the number of the Behavioral Definition statement in the companion chapter with the same title in *The Adolescent Psychotherapy Treatment Planner,* Fourth Edition (Jongsma, Peterson, McInnis, and Bruce) by John Wiley & Sons, 2006.

D. The client has begun to openly acknowledge his/her diagnosis and its terminal nature.

5. Anxious (4)

A. The client presented with anxious feelings related to his/her serious medical condition.

B. The client reported that a discussion of anything related to his/her medical condition makes him/her feel anxious.

C. The client has developed some peace of mind about his/her serious medical condition.

6. Sad/Quiet (4)

A. The client presented in a sad, quiet manner.

B. The client found it very difficult to talk about his/her medical condition.

C. The client reported feeling overwhelming sadness about the loss of his/her health when the condition was diagnosed.

D. The client's sadness has decreased, and he/she has been willing to talk more openly about the medical diagnosis and prognosis.

7. Social Withdrawal (4)

A. Recently, the client has dropped most of his/her friends.

B. The client reported that he/she has been spending all of his/her spare time alone.

C. The client appeared to be avoiding family and friends since learning of his/her medical condition.

D. Due to his/her particular medical condition, the client has seen no reason to interact or have relationships with others.

E. As the client has accepted his/her medical condition, he/she has begun to reconnect with others and has received their support.

8. Suicidal Ideation (5)

A. The client presented in a negative, despondent manner.

B. The client reported feeling very hopeless and helpless regarding the future due to his/her medical condition.

C. Suicidal thoughts and feelings seemed to dominate the client at the present time.

D. The client revealed a plan and a backup plan to take his/her own life.

E. The client has gradually started to feel more hopeful and less despondent about his/her medical condition.

9. Denial (6)

A. The client presented as though there were nothing wrong with him/her despite evidence to the contrary.

B. The client reported that he/she did not agree with the seriousness of the condition diagnosed by the physicians.

C. The client seemed to vacillate between accepting and denying the diagnosed medical condition.

D. The client refused to disclose or acknowledge having any medical condition.

E. The client's denial has started to lessen, and he/she is beginning to talk about his/her condition in a realistic manner.

10. Resistive to Treatment (7)

A. The client presented in a resistive manner.

B. The client reported that he/she is not open to treatment of any kind for his/her medical condition.

C. The client's resistiveness to accepting treatment for his/her medical condition has had a negative effect on his/her general health.

D. The client has refused to cooperate fully with the recommended medical treatments.

E. The client has become more cooperative with medical treatment procedures.

INTERVENTIONS IMPLEMENTED

1. Gather History of Medical Condition (1)*

A. A history of the client's medical condition that included symptoms, treatment, and prognosis was gathered.

B. During the history-gathering process, the client was assisted in connecting feelings to aspects and stages of his/her medical condition.

C. A sketchy, vague history of the client's medical condition was gathered due to his/her unwillingness to provide specific information.

2. Obtain Additional Medical History (2)

A. Informed consent was obtained from the client so family and physician could be contacted for further information on his/her medical condition.

B. Additional information regarding the client's diagnosis, treatment, and prognosis was gathered from his/her physician.

C. Various family members contributed additional information when contacted about the client's medical condition and its progression, and this information was summarized.

D. The client refused to give consent to have either his/her physician or family members contacted about his/her medical condition, and his/her wishes were accepted.

3. Encourage Learning about Medical Condition (3)

A. The client was encouraged to learn about his/her medical condition.

B. The client was asked to learn realistic information about the course of his/her illness.

C. The client was encouraged to learn about pain management and chances of recovery from his/her medical condition.

D. The client was reinforced for his/her knowledge about his/her medical concern.

E. The client has not sought out information about his/her medical condition and was redirected to do so.

4. Monitor/Reinforce Treatment Compliance (4)

A. The client's compliance with the recommended medical treatment regimen was monitored.

---

*The numbers in parentheses correlate to the number of the Therapeutic Intervention statement in the companion chapter with the same title in *The Adolescent Psychotherapy Treatment Planner,* Fourth Edition (Jongsma, Peterson, McInnis, and Bruce) by John Wiley & Sons, 2006.

B. The client's failure to comply with medical treatment recommendations was confronted and addressed.

C. Positive affirmation and encouragement were given to the client for his/her consistent follow-through on all aspects of the medical treatment regimen.

D. Despite gentle confrontation and encouragement, the client still fails to comply with the medical treatment recommendation for his/her medical condition.

5. Explore Factors Interfering with Compliance (5)

A. Misconceptions, fears, and situational factors were explored with the client for their possible interference with medical treatment compliance.

B. The client's misconceptions, fears, and other situational factors were resolved to improve his/her follow-through with recommended medical treatment.

C. Since being helped to make the connection between his/her fears and misconceptions and avoiding medical treatment, the client has started to cooperate fully and responsibly with his/her medical treatment.

D. The client's resistance to compliance with the medical treatment regimen continues to be a problem; brainstorming techniques were used to increase compliance.

6. Confront Defenses That Block Medical Compliance (6)

A. All the client's defense mechanisms that block compliance with the medical regimen were confronted.

B. As defense mechanisms of manipulation and denial have been confronted, the client's compliance with the medical regimen has increased.

C. The client's defense mechanisms continue to block consistent compliance with the medical treatment regimen.

7. Identify Feelings Regarding Medical Condition (7)

A. The client was assisted in identifying and verbalizing feelings connected to his/her medical condition.

B. The client was encouraged to recognize and express feelings related to the medical condition on a daily basis.

C. Instances of the client recognizing, identifying, and expressing his/her feelings were affirmed and reinforced verbally.

D. The client was not open with his/her feelings regarding the current medical condition and was urged to be more open as he/she feels ready to disclose.

8. Explore Family's Feelings Regarding Medical Condition (8)

A. Feelings associated with a family member's medical condition were explored and normalized for the family.

B. Family sessions were conducted to help members clarify and share feelings they have experienced about the client's medical condition.

C. Family members were reminded that having a safe place to express feelings about the client's condition was helpful and healthy for all involved.

D. Family members were assigned "Coping with a Sibling's Health Problems" from the *Adolescent Psychotherapy Homework Planner,* 2nd ed. (Jongsma, Peterson, and McInnis).

E. Strong feelings of helplessness and fear about the client's medical condition deteriorating in the future were expressed.

F. The client's siblings expressed feelings of anger and jealousy regarding the attention focused on the client's medical condition.

9. Assess Social Network Impact (9)

A. An assessment was conducted of the effects of the medical condition on the client's social network.

B. The client was assigned "Effects of Physical Handicap or Illness on Self-Esteem and Peer Relations" from the *Adolescent Psychotherapy Homework Planner*, 2nd ed. (Jongsma, Peterson, and McInnis).

C. The client was helped to realistically review the effects of his/her medical condition on his/her social networks, including both positive and negative effects.

D. Social support was facilitated for the client as available through the client's family and friends.

10. List Limitations Caused by Medical Condition (10)

A. The client was asked to list all changes, losses, and limitations that have resulted from his/her medical condition.

B. The client was assisted in making a list of his/her losses, changes, and limitations that resulted from the medical condition due to his/her difficulty connecting the two things.

C. The changes in the client's life brought on by the medical condition caused feelings of depression, frustration, and hopelessness.

D. The client tended to minimize the limitations caused by his/her medical condition and was provided with more accurate feedback in this area.

11. Teach Stages of Grief (11)

A. The client was educated on the stages and process of grief.

B. The client was asked to identify the stages of the grief process he/she has experienced.

C. Active-listening skills were used as the client reviewed his/her stages of grief.

12. Assign Books on Grief (12)

A. The client was encouraged to expand his/her knowledge of the grieving process by reading recommended books on the subject of grief.

B. The client has followed through with reading some of the recommended material on grief and has developed a deeper understanding of his/her own grief feelings.

C. The client has not followed through with reading the recommended material on grief and was encouraged to do so.

13. Assign a Grief Journal (13)

A. The benefits of keeping a grief journal were explained, identified, and reinforced to the client.

B. The client was asked to commit to keeping a daily grief journal to share in therapy sessions.

C. Daily grief journal material that the client recorded was shared in sessions, and entries were processed.

D. The client has not recorded his/her feelings on a daily basis and was reminded of his/her commitment to keep a grief journal.

14. Assign Daily Mourning Time (14)

A. The client was educated in the value of mourning a loss.

B. Ways for the client to daily mourn loss were explored, and several were selected and developed for implementation.

C. The client was asked to commit to implementing his/her mourning ritual for a specific amount of time daily and then getting on with other daily activities.

D. The daily mourning ritual has been followed by the client, and it has been noted to be effective in focusing grief feelings and increasing productivity during other times of the day.

E. The client has failed to follow through on implementing the daily mourning ritual and has avoided the grieving process; he/she was urged to use the mourning ritual.

F. Instead of limiting the intense grieving to specific times of the day, the client continues to be preoccupied with grief throughout the day and was redirected about the use of the mourning ritual.

15. List Positive Life Aspects (15)

A. The client was assisted in listing all the positive aspects still present in his/her life.

B. The client was challenged to focus on the positive aspects of life that he/she identified rather than the losses associated with the medical condition.

C. The client's focus on positive life aspects within sessions was reinforced.

D. Gentle confrontation was used when the client focused on his/her losses rather than positive life aspects.

16. Confront Denial of Need for Treatment (16)

A. Gentle confrontation was used with the client regarding his/her denial of the seriousness of his/her condition and of the need for compliance with recommended treatment.

B. Denial was normalized as part of the adjustment process, and barriers to acceptance of the need for treatment on the client's part were explored and addressed.

C. Despite gentle confrontation, the client continues to deny the seriousness of his/her condition and refuses to follow through with the recommended treatment.

D. The client was reinforced as his/her denial regarding the reality of the medical condition and the need for treatment has dissipated, resulting in consistent follow-through with medical recommendations.

17. Reinforce Acceptance of Condition (17)

A. The positive aspects of acceptance over denial of the medical condition were reinforced with the client.

B. The client's statements indicating acceptance of the condition were affirmed and reinforced.

C. Ambivalent statements by the client about the medical condition and its treatment were reframed to more positive ones and reinforced.

D. The client's denial regarding the reality of the medical condition and the need for treatment has dissipated, resulting in consistent follow-through with medical recommendations; the benefits of this reality focus were emphasized.

18. Encourage Expression of Fears Regarding Health (18)

A. The client was asked to express his/her fears about failing health, death, and dying.

B. The fear of death and dying expressed by the client were explored and processed.

C. The concept of facing one's fears was presented to and processed with the client.

D. The client was open in expressing his/her fears regarding death and dying; this was reflected to him/her as a resolution of these fears, resulting in peace of mind.

19. Normalize Anxious Feelings (19)

A. The client was assisted and supported in identifying and expressing feelings of anxiety connected to his/her medical condition.

B. The anxious and sad feelings identified by the client were affirmed and normalized.

C. The client was reminded of the value and benefit to his/her health and recovery of identifying and expressing feelings.

20. Assess/Treat Depression and Anxiety (20)

A. The client was assessed for level of depression and anxiety, and treatment was recommended.

B. It was determined that the client's level of depression was significant enough to merit focused treatment.

C. The client's anxiety was explored, and appropriate interventions were implemented to assist the client in coping with these feelings.

D. The client was assisted in recognizing his/her depression and in beginning to express the feelings associated with it.

21. Refer to Support Group (21)

A. The client was educated on the various types of support groups available in the community.

B. The client was referred to a support group of others living with the same medical condition.

C. The benefits of the support group experience were identified and reinforced with the client.

D. The client's experience with attending the support group was processed, and continued attendance was encouraged.

E. The client has failed to follow the recommendation to attend a support group and was redirected to do so.

22. Refer to Family Support Group (22)

A. The purpose and benefits of attending a support group were identified and reinforced with the family.

B. Support group options were provided for the family.

C. The family was referred to a community support group associated with the client's medical condition.

D. The initial support group experience was processed with family, and continued attendance was encouraged and reinforced.

E. The family has not followed through with attending the recommended support group and was redirected to do so.

23. List Pleasurable Activities (23)

A. The client was asked to list all the activities that he/she has enjoyed doing.

B. The client's list of activities was examined for the ones that can still be enjoyed alone and with others.

C. The client was encouraged to again start involving himself/herself in these pleasurable activities on a regular basis.

D. In spite of encouragement, the client continues to resist engagement in pleasurable activities that he/she is capable of participating in.

24. Reinforce Pleasurable Activities (24)

A. The client was asked to make a verbal commitment to increase his/her activity level in pleasurable social and physical activities.

B. The client's involvement in activities was affirmed and reinforced.

C. The client's failure to keep his/her commitment to increase his/her activity level was gently confronted.

D. The client avoided the requested commitment by saying that he/she would give it a try and that was the best he/she could do.

E. In spite of encouragement, the client continues to resist engagement in pleasurable activities that he/she is capable of participating in.

25. Teach Relaxation Techniques (25)

A. Deep muscle relaxation, deep breathing, and positive imagery techniques were taught to the client to enhance the ability to relax.

B. Behavioral rehearsal was utilized to give the client opportunity to practice each relaxation skill.

C. The client was reminded of the benefits of deep muscle relaxation, deep breathing, and positive imagery and encouraged to use each on a regular basis.

D. The client has implemented the relaxation techniques and reports a reduction in stress and anxiety.

E. The client has failed to follow through with implementation of relaxation techniques.

26. Utilize Biofeedback (26)

A. EMG biofeedback was utilized with the client to monitor, increase, and reinforce his/her depth of relaxation.

B. The use of biofeedback with the client has improved his/her overall depth of relaxation.

C. Despite the use of biofeedback, the client has not been able to improve his/her overall depth of relaxation and was provided with additional training in this area.

27. Develop Physical Exercise Routine (27)

A. The client was assisted in developing a plan for a daily physical exercise routine within the limits of his/her medical condition.

B. The benefits of daily physical exercise were identified and reinforced.

C. Positive feedback was provided as the physical exercise plan was implemented by the client along with a commitment to follow the plan on a daily basis.

D. The client's follow-through with daily exercise was monitored and reinforced.

E. The client has not followed through with implementing any regular pattern of physical exercise and was redirected in this area.

28. Identify Distorted, Negative Thoughts (28)

A. The client was assisted in identifying his/her cognitive distortions that contribute to a negative attitude and hopeless feeling regarding the medical condition.

B. The client was assigned to read "Bad Thoughts Lead to Bad Feelings" from the *Adolescent Psychotherapy Homework Planner,* 2nd ed. (Jongsma, Peterson, and McInnis).

C. The connection between cognitive distortions and feelings of helplessness and negativity surrounding the medical condition was established and made clear to the client.

D. The client was resistive to identifying, and in denial of engaging in, cognitive distortion; tentative examples were identified and offered to the client.

29. Teach Positive, Realistic Self-Talk (29)

A. The client was helped to generate a list of positive, realistic self-talk to replace the cognitive distortions and catastrophizing that accompanies his/her medical condition.

B. The techniques of positive self-talk were taught to the client.

C. Role-play situations about the client's medical condition were utilized so that the client could practice using positive self-talk.

D. The benefits of using positive self-talk reported by the client were reinforced.

E. The client has not used positive, realistic self-talk to replace the cognitive distortions and catastrophizing and was assisted in identifying situations in which he/she could use these techniques.

30. Teach Healing Imagery (30)

A. Positive, healing imagery techniques were taught to the client.

B. The client practiced using healing imagery techniques in the session.

C. Plans for implementing positive imagery techniques were developed with the client.

D. The client was asked to make a commitment to use positive imagery techniques as planned.

E. The client reported consistent daily use of the positive, healing imagery techniques and has developed a positive mental attitude regarding the improvement in his/her medical condition.

31. Assess Resources for Support (31)

A. The client's, parents', and siblings' sources of emotional support were probed and assessed.

B. The parents were asked to identify their sources of emotional support.

C. The client was asked to identify his/her source of emotional support.

D. The client's siblings were asked to identify their sources of emotional support.

32. Encourage Acceptance of Support (32)

A. The parents and siblings were assisted in identifying community resources for support.

B. Barriers to accepting support were explored and addressed with the parents and siblings.

C. The parents' and siblings' need for support was identified and reinforced.

D. The parents and siblings were praised as they have accepted their need for support and have followed through in making contact with potential resources for support.

33. Explore Marital Conflict (33)

A. How the parents were dealing with the stress of the client's illness was explored with each individually.

B. The issue of increased conflicts between the parents due to the client's medical condition was addressed.

C. Specific ways that each parent could be supportive and accepting of the other were identified.

34. Assess/Address Family Conflict (34)

A. The conflicts within the client's family were assessed using a conflict resolution approach.

B. Specific conflicts have been identified within the family, and family members have begun addressing their conflicts.

35. Reinforce Family Members' Spirit of Tolerance (35)

A. In family sessions, a spirit of tolerance for individually different responses to stress was facilitated and encouraged between members.

B. Members were reminded of each person's individual differences regarding internal resources and response styles in face of threat.

C. Tolerance was modeled to family members in sessions through active listening and warm acceptance of their feelings and thoughts.

36. Promote the Power of Family Involvement (36)

A. The family was educated in the potential healing power of members' involvement in all aspects of the client's care and recovery.

B. Assistance was provided to the family to help them make their care and home environment as warm, positive, kind, and supportive for the client as possible.

C. The family was provided with ongoing encouragement and reinforcement in providing warm, positive, supportive care to the client.

37. Draw Out Parents' Fears (37)

A. The parents were encouraged to express their underlying fears about the client's possible death.

B. Empathy, affirmation, and normalization were used in responding to the fearful feelings that the parents verbalized.

C. The parents were given the reassurance of God's presence as the giver and supporter of life.

D. The parents were resistant to expressing their underlying fears about the client's possible death and were provided with additional support and empathy.

38. Identify Spiritual Support Resources (38)

A. The client was assisted in identifying sources of spiritual support that could help him/her now.

B. The client was encouraged to actively utilize his/her identified spiritual resources and support on a daily basis.

C. The client has denied any interest in spiritual resources but was urged to remain open to these ideas.

D. The client's spiritual faith was noted to be a deep and significant source of strength and peace during this time of pain and stress.

39. Encourage Reliance on Faith (39)

A. The client was encouraged to rely on the faith-based promises of God's love, presence, caring, and support to bring him/her peace of mind.

B. The client was asked to identify how he/she uses reliance on God to bring peace of mind.

C. The client was reinforced for his/her reliance on faith-based promises of God's love, presence, caring, and support to help bring him/her peace of mind.

D. The client did not identify any significant use of faith-based promises of God's love and was encouraged to seek this out through scriptural study or religious affiliation.

MENTAL RETARDATION

CLIENT PRESENTATION

1. Subaverage Intellectual Functioning (1)*

A. The client has developed significant intellectual or cognitive deficits.

B. The results from the past intelligence testing revealed that the client's overall level of intellectual functioning lies in the Mild Mental Retardation range.

C. The results from the past intelligence testing revealed that the client's overall level of intelligence lies in the Moderate Mental Retardation range.

D. The results from the past intelligence testing revealed that the client's overall level of intelligence lies in the Severe Mental Retardation range.

E. The results from the past intelligence testing revealed that the client's overall level of intelligence lies in the Borderline range of functioning.

2. Impaired Academic Functioning (2)

A. The client has performed significantly below his/her expected grade and age levels in all academic areas.

B. The client's academic performance has been commensurate with his/her overall level of intelligence.

C. The client has performed academically below his/her expected grade and age levels, even when considering the results from the past intellectual testing.

D. Academically, the client has performed above his/her expected levels based on the results from the past intelligence testing.

3. Speech/Language Deficits (2)

A. The results from the past speech/language evaluation demonstrated that the client has developed significant speech/language deficits.

B. The client's vocabulary and expressive language abilities are quite limited.

C. The client often has difficulty understanding what is being said to him/her because of his/her low receptive language skills.

D. The client displayed noticeable speech articulation problems during today's therapy session.

E. The client's speech articulation problems have improved through treatment.

4. Poor Communication Skills (2)

A. The client has much difficulty communicating his/her thoughts and feelings in an effective manner because of his/her speech/language deficits.

B. The client had much difficulty expressing his/her thoughts and feelings in today's therapy session.

*The numbers in parentheses correlate to the number of the Behavioral Definition statement in the companion chapter with the same title in *The Adolescent Psychotherapy Treatment Planner,* Fourth Edition (Jongsma, Peterson, McInnis, and Bruce) by John Wiley & Sons, 2006.

C. The client had difficulty comprehending what was being discussed in today's therapy session because of his/her low receptive language abilities.

D. The client was able to communicate his/her thoughts and feelings in a simplistic but straightforward and effective manner in today's therapy session.

E. The client has demonstrated improvements in his/her ability to identify and express his/her basic thoughts and feelings.

5. Lack of Independent Functioning (2)

A. The parents or caregivers reported that the client's skills for activities of daily living are very low.

B. The client has required a great deal of supervision when performing household chores or simple tasks at school.

C. The client has recently started to perform simple chores at home.

D. The client has recently performed his/her household chores or school responsibilities on a fairly consistent basis with prompting from caregivers.

6. Poor Personal Hygiene (2)

A. The parents or caregivers reported that the client's personal hygiene is often poor.

B. The client appeared unkempt during today's therapy session.

C. The client has a great deal of difficulty dressing himself/herself independently even when clothes have been preselected for him/her.

D. The client appeared neatly groomed and attired during today's therapy session.

E. The client has recently been dressing himself/herself independently.

7. Difficulty Following Instructions (3)

A. The client historically has had much difficulty comprehending and following instructions at home and school.

B. The parents and teachers reported that the client is capable of comprehending and following simple instructions, but has trouble following through with multiple or complex instructions.

C. The teachers reported that the client is best able to follow instructions when they are presented in simple terms and are given one at a time.

D. The parents and teachers reported that the client has shown improvement in following simple instructions on a consistent basis.

8. Memory Impairment (4)

A. The results from past intellectual and cognitive assessments have shown that the client has developed significant short- and long-term memory impairments.

B. The client has often had difficulty retaining or recalling what was said to him/her because of his/her short-term memory deficit.

C. The client has had difficulty recalling significant past events because of his/her long-term memory deficit.

D. The client demonstrated improvements in his/her everyday functioning by following a structured daily routine.

9. Concrete Thinking (5)

A. The client has much difficulty understanding psychological concepts because of his/her intellectual limitations and poor abstract reasoning abilities.

B. The client presented as very concrete in his/her thinking during today's therapy session.

C. The client's concrete thinking and poor abstract reasoning abilities have interfered with his/her problem-solving abilities.

D. The client demonstrated an understanding of basic psychological terms or concepts during today's therapy session.

E. The parents report that the client has demonstrated improvement in his/her ability to resolve or manage everyday, routine problems by following specific, concrete steps that are outlined for him/her.

10. Poor Social Skills (6)

A. The client has developed poor social skills and frequently engaged in immature or socially inappropriate behavior.

B. The client has often failed to pick up on important social cues or interpersonal nuances that are necessary to build and sustain meaningful relationships.

C. The client has started to develop the ability to differentiate between appropriate and inappropriate social behaviors.

D. The client displayed good social skills during today's therapy session.

11. Lack of Insight (7)

A. The client historically has shown very poor insight into the factors contributing to his/her emotional, behavioral, or interpersonal problems.

B. The client demonstrated a lack of insight into the factors contributing to his/her adjustment problems.

C. The client verbalized an awareness of the basic factors contributing to his/her adjustment problems, but had difficulty understanding the more complex factors.

12. Failure to Learn from Experience (7)

A. The client displayed a marked inability to learn from previous experiences or past mistakes because of his/her intellectual limitations.

B. The parents or caregivers reported that the client repeatedly makes many of the same mistakes without appearing to learn from his/her experiences.

C. Parents or caregivers reported that the client has started to show mild improvement in his/her ability to learn from past experiences or mistakes.

D. The client does not repeat as many mistakes when he/she is placed in a highly structured setting with an established routine.

13. Low Self-Esteem (8)

A. The client's intellectual limitations and learning problems have been a significant contributing factor to his/her feelings of low self-esteem, inadequacy, and insecurity.

B. The client's low self-esteem has contributed to his/her hesitancy to try new tasks or apply himself/herself at school.

C. The client verbalized self-derogatory remarks when discussing his/her intellectual limitations or learning problems.

D. The client verbalized positive self-descriptive statements during today's therapy session.

E. The client has developed a healthy acceptance of his/her intellectual and cognitive limitations, as evidenced by his/her ability to consistently verbalize feelings of self-worth.

14. Depression (8)

A. The client's intellectual deficits and academic struggles have contributed substantially to his/her feelings of depression.

B. The client appeared visibly sad when discussing his/her learning problems.

C. The client's feelings of depression have begun to decrease as he/she works toward gaining a greater acceptance of his/her intellectual limitations.

D. The client expressed feelings of happiness about his/her recent accomplishments at home and school.

E. The client's feelings of depression have decreased substantially.

15. Acting Out Behaviors (9)

A. The client has demonstrated a persistent pattern of acting out when he/she becomes frustrated or upset because of his/her intellectual limitations or learning problems.

B. The client began to act in a silly and immature manner in today's therapy session when discussing his/her intellectual limitations or learning problems.

C. The client was helped to realize how he/she frequently begins to act out or engage in disruptive behavior when frustrated or upset about not being able to perform a task.

D. The client has started to seek help when frustrated about not being able to perform a task instead of acting out or engaging in disruptive behavior.

E. The client has demonstrated a significant reduction in the frequency of his/her acting out or disruptive behavior.

INTERVENTIONS IMPLEMENTED

1. Conduct Intellectual and Cognitive Assessment (1)*

A. A comprehensive intellectual and cognitive assessment was conducted to determine the presence of Mental Retardation and help gain greater insight into the client's learning strengths and weaknesses.

B. The findings from the current intellectual and cognitive assessment revealed the presence of Mild Mental Retardation.

C. The findings from the current intellectual and cognitive assessment revealed the presence of Moderate Mental Retardation.

D. The findings from the current intellectual and cognitive assessment revealed the presence of Severe Mental Retardation.

*The numbers in parentheses correlate to the number of the Therapeutic Intervention statement in the companion chapter with the same title in *The Adolescent Psychotherapy Treatment Planner,* Fourth Edition (Jongsma, Peterson, McInnis, and Bruce) by John Wiley & Sons, 2006.

E. The findings from the current intellectual and cognitive assessment demonstrated that the client is currently functioning in the Borderline range of intellectual abilities.

F. The results of the comprehensive intellectual and cognitive assessments were provided to the client and his/her parents.

2. Conduct Psychological Testing for Emotional/ADHD Factors (2)

A. The client received a psychological evaluation to assess whether emotional factors or ADHD are interfering with his/her intellectual functioning.

B. The findings from the psychological testing supported the presence of ADHD, which is interfering with the client's intellectual and academic functioning.

C. The findings from the psychological testing revealed the presence of serious emotional problems that are interfering with the client's intellectual and academic functioning.

D. The findings from the evaluation did not support the presence of ADHD that could be interfering with the client's intellectual and academic functioning.

E. The findings from the psychological testing did not reveal any serious emotional problems that could be interfering with the client's intellectual and academic functioning.

F. The result of the psychological testing was provided for the client and his/her parents.

3. Refer for Neurological Examination/Neuropsychological Testing (3)

A. The client was referred for a neurological examination and neuropsychological testing to rule out possible organic factors that may be contributing to the client's intellectual or cognitive deficits.

B. The findings from the neuropsychological evaluation revealed organic factors that may be contributing to the client's intellectual or cognitive deficits.

C. The findings from the neuropsychological evaluation did not reveal any organic factors that may be contributing to the client's intellectual or cognitive deficits.

D. The results of the neurological examination and neuropsychological testing were interpreted to the client and his/her parents.

4. Refer for Physical/Occupational Therapy (4)

A. The client was referred to physical and occupational therapists to assess for the presence of perceptual or sensory-motor deficits and determine the need for ongoing physical and/or occupational therapy.

B. The evaluation revealed significant perceptual or sensory-motor deficits and the need for ongoing physical and/or occupational therapy.

C. The evaluation did not reveal any significant perceptual or sensory-motor deficits or the need for ongoing physical and/or occupational therapy.

D. The physical/occupational therapy assessment was reviewed with the client and his/her parents.

5. Refer for Speech/Language Evaluation (5)

A. The client was referred for a comprehensive speech/language evaluation to assess possible deficits in this area and to determine the need for speech/language therapy.

B. The comprehensive speech/language evaluation revealed a communication impairment and supported the need for speech/language therapy.

C. The comprehensive speech/language evaluation did not reveal a communication impairment or the need for ongoing speech/language therapy.

D. The results of the speech and language evaluation were interpreted to the client and his/her parents.

6. Attend Individualized Educational Planning Committee (IEPC) Meeting(6)

A. An IEPC meeting was held to determine the client's eligibility for special education services, to design educational interventions, and to establish goals.

B. The decision was made at the IEPC meeting that the client is eligible to receive special education services because of his/her intellectual or academic deficits.

C. The decision was made at the IEPC meeting that the client is not eligible to receive special education services.

D. Consultation was held with the client's parents, teachers, and other appropriate professionals about designing educational interventions to help the client achieve his/her academic goals.

E. The client's academic goals were identified at the IEPC meeting.

7. Design Effective Teaching Programs (7)

A. Consultation was held with the client, his/her parents, teachers, and other appropriate school officials about designing effective teaching programs or interventions that build on the client's strengths and compensate for his/her weaknesses.

B. The client's learning strengths and weaknesses were identified in the consultation meeting with the client, parents, teachers, and other appropriate school officials.

C. Consultation was held with the client, his/her parents, teachers, and other appropriate school officials about the ways to maximize the client's learning strengths.

D. Consultation was held with the client, his/her parents, teachers, and other appropriate school officials about the ways to compensate for the client's learning weaknesses.

8. Consult about Placement Outside the Home (8)

A. Consultation was held with the client's parents, school officials, or mental health professionals about the need for placement in a foster home, group home, or residential program.

B. After consulting with the client's parents, school officials, or mental health professionals, the recommendation was made that the client should be placed in a foster home.

C. The recommendation was made that the client be placed in a group home or residential program to address his/her intellectual, academic, social, and emotional needs.

D. Placement of the client in a foster home, group home, or residential program was not recommended during the consultation meeting with parents, school officials, and mental health professionals.

9. Refer to Sheltered Workshop (9)

A. The client was referred to a sheltered workshop or educational rehabilitation center to help him/her develop basic job skills.

B. The client and parents were supportive of the referral to a sheltered workshop or educational rehabilitation center to develop the client's basic job skills.

C. The client and parents were opposed to the idea of referring him/her to a sheltered work-shop or educational rehabilitation center to develop basic job skills, and the pros and cons of this decision were reviewed.

D. It was reflected to the client and his/her parents that the client's attendance at the sheltered workshop or educational rehabilitation center has helped him/her to develop basic job skills.

E. The client has shown little or no progress in developing basic job skills while attending the sheltered workshop or educational rehabilitation center, and the underlying reasons for this failure were reviewed.

10. Encourage Communication between Home and School (10)

A. The parents, teachers, and school officials were encouraged to maintain regular communication with each other via phone calls or written notes regarding the client's academic, behavioral, emotional, and social progress.

B. Consultation with the teachers and school officials emphasized sending home daily or weekly progress notes informing the parents of the client's academic, behavioral, emotional, and social progress.

C. The client was informed of his/her responsibility to bring home daily or weekly progress notes that allow for regular communication between parents and teachers.

D. The parents were helped to identify the consequences for the client's failure to bring home the daily or weekly progress notes from school.

11. Design Token Economy (11)

A. A token economy was designed for use in the classroom to improve the client's on-task behavior, academic performance, impulse control, and social skills.

B. A token economy was designed for use in the residential program to improve the client's on-task behavior, academic performance, impulse control, and social skills.

C. The client, parents, and teachers agreed to the conditions outlined in the token economy and pledged to follow through with the implementation of the program.

D. The conditions of the token economy were explained to the client in terms that he/she could understand.

12. Praise Positive Behavior (12)

A. The parents were encouraged to provide frequent praise and positive reinforcement for the client's positive social behaviors and academic successes.

B. Positive feedback was provided as the parents praised the client's positive social behaviors and academic performance during today's therapy session.

C. The parents were assisted in identifying opportunities to praise the client's positive social behaviors and academic successes.

D. The client was strongly encouraged to engage in positive social behaviors and work hard to achieve academic goals to receive the parents' approval and affirmation.

E. The client's parents have not used encouragement and praise for the client's positive social behaviors and academic successes and were redirected to do so.

13. Design Reward System/Contingency Contract (13)

A. The client and parents were assisted in identifying a list of rewards to reinforce the client's adaptive or positive social behaviors.

B. A reward system was designed to reinforce the client's adaptive or positive social behaviors.

C. A contingency contract was designed to specify the negative consequences for the client's maladaptive or inappropriate social behaviors and the rewards for specified positive behaviors.

D. The conditions of the contingency contract were explained to the client in terms he/she could understand.

E. The client and parents verbally agreed to the terms outlined in the reward system and/or contingency contract.

F. The client's parents have not used the reward system and contingency contract and were redirected to do so.

14. Educate Parents about Mental Retardation (14)

A. The client's parents were educated about the symptoms of Mental Retardation.

B. The therapy session helped the client's parents gain a greater understanding of the symptoms and characteristics of Mental Retardation.

C. The parents were given the opportunity to express their thoughts and feelings about raising a child with Mental Retardation.

D. The parents were given support in verbalizing their feelings of sadness, hurt, anger, or disappointment about having a child with Mental Retardation.

15. Confront Parents' Denial of Client's Intellectual Deficits (15)

A. A family therapy session was held to assess the parents' denial surrounding the client's intellectual deficits.

B. The parents' denial about the client's intellectual deficits was confronted and challenged so that they will begin to cooperate with the recommendations regarding placement and educational interventions.

C. The therapy session was helpful in working through the parents' denial surrounding the client's intellectual deficits, and they agreed to follow through with recommendations regarding placement and educational interventions.

D. The parents have remained in denial about the client's intellectual deficits and are opposed to following through with the recommendations regarding placement and educational interventions.

16. Assess Excessive Parental Pressure (16)

A. A family therapy session was held to assess whether the parents are placing excessive pressure on the client to function at a level that he/she is not capable of achieving.

B. The parents were asked to verbalize their expectations of the client's level of capabilities.

17. Confront Excessive Parental Pressure (17)

A. The parents were confronted and challenged about placing excessive pressure on the client to function at a level that he/she is not capable of achieving.

B. The parents acknowledged that they have placed unrealistic expectations and/or excessive pressure on the client to function at a level that he/she is not capable of achieving; this insight was reinforced.

C. The parents were reinforced as they agreed to cease placing excessive pressure on the client to perform at unrealistic levels.

D. The parents expressed resistance to the idea that they are placing excessive pressure on the client to function at unrealistic levels and were provided with specific examples of these pressures.

18. Assess Parental Overprotectiveness (18)

A. The parent-child interactions were observed in today's therapy session to assess whether the parents' overprotectiveness or infantilization of the client interferes with his/her intellectual, emotional, or social development.

B. The client and parents were given a task to perform in today's therapy session to assess whether the parents are overprotective of the client.

C. Active-listening skills were used as the parents acknowledged that their pattern of overprotectiveness has interfered with the client's intellectual, emotional, and social development.

D. The therapy session was helpful in identifying various ways that the parents are overprotective of the client and/or interfere with his/her intellectual, emotional, and social development.

E. The parents became defensive in today's therapy session when discussing their pattern of overprotectiveness.

19. Help Parents Develop Realistic Expectations (19)

A. Today's therapy session focused on helping the parents or caregivers develop realistic expectations of the client's intellectual capabilities and level of adaptive functioning.

B. The parents or caregivers were assisted in identifying a number of tasks that the client is capable of performing.

C. The therapy session helped the parents or caregivers identify several tasks that the client is not able to perform because of his/her intellectual capabilities and level of adaptive functioning.

D. The parents or caregivers were instructed to provide supervision initially on tasks that they are not sure that the client is capable of performing.

E. It was noted that the parents or caregivers have developed a good understanding of the client's intellectual capabilities and level of adaptive functioning.

F. The parents or caregivers have continued to have unrealistic expectations for the client and were redirected in this area.

20. Include Client in Family Outings (20)

A. The parents and family members were strongly encouraged to include the client in outings or activities on a regular basis.

B. A family therapy session was held to explore the family members' resistance or objections to including the client in some outings or activities.

C. Positive feedback was provided as the parents and family members pledged to include the client in regular family outings or activities.

D. The client and family members were assisted in identifying a list of outings or activities that they would enjoy doing together.

E. The parents and family members were confronted about their failure to include the client in many outings or activities.

21. Assign Observation of Positive Behavior (21)

A. The parents and family members were instructed to observe and record positive behavior by the client between therapy sessions.

B. The parents were encouraged to praise and reinforce the client for engaging in the positive behavior.

C. The client was praised in today's therapy session for his/her positive behavior.

D. The client was strongly encouraged to continue to engage in the positive behavior to help improve his/her self-esteem, gain parents' approval, and receive affirmation from others.

22. Assign Household Chores (22)

A. The client and family members were assisted in developing a list of tasks or chores that the client is capable of performing at home.

B. The client was assigned a task to perform within the family to provide him/her with a sense of responsibility or belonging.

C. The client was given praise in today's therapy session for the successful completion of his/her assigned task or chore.

D. The client attempted to perform the assigned task or chore, but encountered difficulty when performing it; he/she was encouraged to attempt tasks at his/her own level.

E. The client failed to follow through with completing the assigned chore or task and was redirected in this area.

23. Assign Routine Task (23)

A. The client was placed in charge of a routine or basic task at home to increase his/her self-esteem and increase feelings of self-worth in the family.

B. A reward system was designed to reinforce the client for following through and completing his/her routine or basic task at home.

C. The client was placed in charge of another routine or basic task (appropriate to his/her level of adaptive functioning) after showing he/she could be responsible in performing the earlier assigned task.

D. Today's therapy session explored the reasons the client did not follow through and complete the routine or basic task that was assigned to him/her.

24. Assign Belongingness Exercise (24)

A. The client was assigned homework designed to promote the client's feelings of acceptance and a sense of belonging in the family system, school setting, or community.

B. The client and parents were assigned the "You Belong Here" exercise from the *Adolescent Psychotherapy Homework Planner,* 2nd ed. (Jongsma, Peterson, and McInnis) to promote feelings of acceptance and a sense of belonging in the family system, school setting, or community.

C. The client and parents were given the "You Belong Here" exercise to increase the client's responsibilities or involvement in activities at home, at school, or in the community.

D. The "You Belong Here" exercise was assigned to help the parents develop a greater awareness of the client's intellectual capabilities and level of adaptive functioning.

E. The client and parents successfully completed the exercise and the client was encouraged to continue to engage in the responsible behaviors or social activities to further increase feelings of self-worth.

F. The client and parents failed to follow through and complete the exercise and were challenged to do it again.

25. Assign School/Residential Job (25)

A. Consultation was held with school officials about assigning a job to help build the client's self-esteem and provide him/her with a sense of responsibility.

B. Consultation was held with the staff at the residential program about assigning a job to help build the client's self-esteem and provide him/her with a sense of responsibility.

C. The client was given much praise in today's therapy session for being responsible in performing his/her job at school.

D. The client was given much praise in today's therapy session for being responsible in performing his/her job at the residential program.

E. Today's therapy session explored the reasons for the client's failure to comply with performing his/her job at school or the residential program.

26. Establish Allowance/Finance Management (26)

A. The parents were assisted in establishing an allowance plan to increase the client's responsibilities at home and to help him/her learn simple money management skills.

B. The client and parents were directed to establish a budget whereby a certain percentage of the client's allowance money goes for both savings and spending.

C. The parents were encouraged to consult with school teachers about teaching the client basic money management skills.

D. The parents reported that the allowance plan has been successful in increasing the client's responsibilities around the home and teaching him/her simple money management skills.

E. The parents reported that, unfortunately, the allowance plan has not motivated the client to perform his/her household chores or responsibilities on a consistent basis.

27. Assign "Activities of Daily Living" Program (27)

A. A reward system was designed and implemented to reinforce desired self-care behavior (e.g., combing hair, washing dishes, cleaning bedroom).

B. The parents were directed to use the reward system in the "Activities of Daily Living" program from the *Adolescent Psychotherapy Homework Planner,* 2nd ed. (Jongsma, Peterson, and McInnis) to improve the client's personal hygiene and self-care skills.

C. The parents were strongly encouraged to praise and reinforce the client for improvements in his/her personal hygiene and self-care skills.

D. The parents reported that the "Activities of Daily Living" program has helped to improve the client's personal hygiene and self-care skills.

E. The parents reported that the client has demonstrated little improvement in his/her personal hygiene and self-care skills since utilizing the "Activities of Daily Living" program.

28. Teach Parents Behavior Management (28)

A. The parents were taught effective behavior management techniques to help decrease the frequency and severity of the client's temper outbursts, acting out, and aggressive behaviors.

B. The parents were trained in the use of time out to manage the client's temper outbursts and aggressive behaviors.

C. The parents were instructed to remove privileges if the client engages in specific acting out or aggressive behaviors.

D. The parents were challenged to follow through consistently with limits when the client displays temper outbursts, aggression, or acting out behaviors.

E. The parents reported improvements in the client's behavior since they began consistently using time outs and removal of privileges to deal with the client's temper outbursts, acting out, and aggressive behaviors; they were encouraged to continue this pattern.

F. The parents have not used the behavior management techniques to help decrease the frequency and severity of the client's temper outbursts, acting out, and aggressive behaviors and were redirected to do so.

29. Teach Parents Use of Natural Consequences (29)

A. The parents were instructed to utilize natural, logical consequences for the client's inappropriate social or maladaptive behaviors.

B. The parents were helped to identify natural, logical consequences for a variety of socially inappropriate or maladaptive behaviors.

C. The parents reported improvement in the client's behavior since they began using natural, logical consequences and were encouraged to continue.

D. The therapy session revealed that the parents have not been consistent in following through or using natural, logical consequences to deal with the client's socially inappropriate or maladaptive behavior.

30. Teach Mediational/Self-Control Strategies (30)

A. The client was taught basic mediational and self-control strategies to help delay his/her need for immediate gratification and to inhibit impulses.

B. The parents were encouraged to establish a routine schedule for the client so that he/she postpones recreational or leisure activities until after completing his/her homework or household responsibilities.

C. The client was encouraged to utilize active-listening skills and talk with significant others before making quick, hasty decisions about important matters or acting out without considering the consequences of his/her actions.

D. The client was helped to develop an action plan that outlined specific, concrete steps that he/she could take to achieve his/her identified long-term goals.

E. The client was helped to see the benefits of delaying his/her immediate need for gratification to achieve a longer-term goal.

F. The client has not used the mediational/self-control strategy of delaying his/her immediate gratification and was redirected to do so.

31. Teach Guided Imagery/Relaxation (31)

A. The client was trained in the use of guided imagery or deep muscle relaxation techniques to help calm himself/herself and improve anger control.

B. The client and parents reported that the use of guided imagery and deep muscle relaxation techniques has helped to calm the client and control anger more effectively.

C. The client and parents reported little or no improvement with the use of guided imagery and deep muscle relaxation techniques to help calm the client and control anger.

D. The client failed to utilize the guided imagery and deep muscle relaxation techniques to help him/her control anger and was redirected to do so.

32. Role-Play and Model to Reinforce Social Skills (32)

A. Role-play and modeling techniques were used to teach the client positive social behaviors.

B. A reward system was developed to reinforce specific, positive social behaviors.

C. The parents were strongly encouraged to look for opportunities to praise and reinforce any emerging positive social behaviors.

D. After role-playing in the therapy session, the client expressed a willingness to practice a newly learned social skill in his/her everyday life situations.

E. The client and parents reported that he/she followed through with practicing the positive social skill that was taught through role-playing and modeling.

F. The client did not follow through with practicing the newly acquired social skill that was modeled in the previous therapy session and was encouraged to attempt this skill.

33. Educate Client about Emotions (33)

A. The client was helped to identify and label different emotions in today's therapy session.

B. Client-centered therapy principles were used to help the client identify and express his/her emotions.

C. The parents were encouraged to reflect the client's feelings at home to help him/her express feelings more effectively.

D. The client has demonstrated improvements in his/her ability to identify and express basic emotions since the onset of therapy.

E. The client has continued to have difficulty identifying and labeling his/her basic emotions and was provided with additional assistance in this area.

34. Utilize Art Therapy (34)

A. The client was instructed in today's therapy session to draw faces of basic emotions and then share various times when he/she experienced the different emotions.

B. The art therapy technique helped the client to identify and express different emotions.

C. An art therapy technique was employed, but the client had difficulty sharing times when he/she experienced the different emotions in the past.

35. Teach Communication Skills (35)

A. The client was taught basic communication skills to improve his/her ability to express thoughts, feelings, and needs more clearly.

B. Role-playing, modeling, and behavior rehearsal techniques were used to teach the client effective ways to express his/her thoughts, feelings, and needs.

C. The client was taught the importance of listening well and maintaining good eye contact when communicating his/her thoughts and feelings with others.

D. The client was taught to utilize "I messages" to communicate his/her thoughts, feelings, and needs more clearly.

36. Help Client Accept Intellectual Limits (36)

A. The client was helped to gain greater understanding and acceptance of the limitations surrounding his/her intellectual deficits and adaptive functioning.

B. A client-centered therapy approach was employed to reflect the client's feelings and move toward a greater acceptance of the limitations surrounding his/her intellectual deficits and adaptive functioning.

C. The client was helped to identify his/her unique strengths or interests as well as his/her individual weaknesses.

D. The client's self-worth was affirmed to help him/her come to a greater acceptance of the limitations surrounding his/her intellectual deficits and adaptive functioning.

37. Explore for Depression and Insecurity (37)

A. Today's therapy session explored the underlying feelings of depression, anxiety, and insecurity related to the client's intellectual limitations.

B. The client was provided with support and unconditional positive regard as he/she worked through feelings of depression, anxiety, and insecurity related to his/her cognitive or intellectual limitations.

C. The client was strongly encouraged to utilize his/her unique strengths and engage in activities of interest to help cope with or offset feelings of depression, anxiety, and insecurity related to cognitive or intellectual limitations.

D. Positive feedback was provided to the parents for support and affirmation of the client's self-worth.

38. Encourage Participation in Special Olympics (38)

A. The client was encouraged to participate in the Special Olympics to help build his/her self-esteem.

B. The client and parents followed through with the recommendation to enroll the client in the Special Olympics.

C. The client expressed happiness about his/her participation and experience in the Special Olympics; his/her experience was reviewed.

D. The client and parents failed to follow through with the recommendation to participate in the Special Olympics and were redirected to do so.

39. Identify Components of Goal Accomplishment (39)

A. Today's therapy session identified periods of time when the client achieved success or accomplished a goal.

B. Today's therapy session was helpful in identifying the positive steps that the client took to successfully accomplish goals in the past.

C. The client was strongly encouraged to take steps similar to those he/she successfully took in the past to accomplish present goals.

D. The therapy session revealed that the client achieved past success during periods of time when he/she received strong family support.

40. Identify Times and People to Ask for Help (40)

A. The client was assisted in identifying appropriate and inappropriate times to ask for help.

B. The client was helped to identify several basic or uncomplicated tasks that he/she can perform independently of others.

C. The parents were encouraged to allow the client to independently perform simple or basic tasks that required him/her to follow only one or two simple instructions at a time.

D. The parents were instructed to provide supervision and frequent feedback to the client when he/she performs tasks of moderate or greater difficulty.

E. The client was helped to identify a list of resource people to whom he/she can turn for support, help, and supervision.

F. The client has developed a network of resource people to whom he/she can turn for support, help, and supervision, and the benefits of this were reviewed.

G. The client has often failed to turn to resource people for support when he/she encounters stress or problems and was redirected to do so.

41. Provide Sex Education (41)

A. Sex education was provided to help the client identify appropriate and inappropriate sexual urges and behaviors.

B. The client was assisted in listing several appropriate and inappropriate sexual urges and behaviors.

C. The client had difficulty differentiating between appropriate and inappropriate sexual urges and behaviors and was provided with additional information in this area.

NEGATIVE PEER INFLUENCES

CLIENT PRESENTATION

1. Susceptibility to Negative Peer Influences (1)*

A. The client's parents identified that he/she is easily susceptible to negative peer influences that contribute to problems with authority figures at home, school, and in the community.

B. The client described behaviors that indicate a strong susceptibility to negative peer influences.

C. The client's susceptibility to negative peer influences has contributed to problems with sexual promiscuity and substance abuse.

D. The client has acknowledged his/her easy susceptibility to negative peer influences.

E. The client has shown a decreased susceptibility to negative peer influences.

2. Seek Peers' Reaction to Disruption (2)

A. The client was described as engaging in disruptive, negative, attention-seeking behaviors at school to elicit attention, approval, or support from peers.

B. The client has acted out within the community in order to elicit attention, approval, or support from peers.

C. The client acknowledged that he/she is often disruptive or seeks attention in negative ways in order to get approval or support from his/her peers.

D. As treatment has progressed, the client has decreased his/her pattern of behaviors designed to elicit negative support, attention, or approval from his/her peers.

3. Excessive Willingness to Follow (3)

A. The client has often followed the lead of others in order to attain approval or acceptance from his/her peers.

B. The client's parents describe him/her as being excessively willing to seek approval or acceptance from others through following their lead into negative activity.

C. The client has often been manipulated into taking responsibility for the actions of others and has agreed to do so to obtain approval or acceptance.

D. The client described himself/herself as a follower.

E. The client has begun to think and act on his/her own, rather than simply following the lead of others.

4. Risky Behavior/Thrill-Seeking (4)

A. The client described a propensity for taking ill-advised risks in peer group settings.

B. The client has engaged in thrill-seeking behavior in peer group settings.

C. The client described himself/herself as being caught up in the behavior of the group.

---

* The numbers in parentheses correlate to the number of the Behavioral Definition statement in the companion chapter with the same title in *The Adolescent Psychotherapy Treatment Planner,* Fourth Edition (Jongsma, Peterson, McInnis, and Bruce) by John Wiley & Sons, 2006.

D. The client has gained insight into his/her pattern of ill-advised risks and thrill-seeking behavior.

E. The client used appropriate judgment in peer group settings.

5. Identification for Acceptance (5)

A. The client has identified with the negative peer group as a means of gaining acceptance.

B. The client reports that he/she was often rejected by others and now has gained acceptance with the negative peer group.

C. The client has attempted to elevate his/her status and self-esteem through identification with the negative peer group.

D. The client has no insight into the long-range effects of identification with the negative peer group and is unwilling to give up the acceptance, status, and self-esteem that he/she derives from identifying with that group.

E. The client has disconnected himself/herself from the negative peer group and is attempting to gain acceptance, status, and self-esteem through more positive means.

6. Affiliation for Protection (6)

A. The client has affiliated with a negative peer group in order to protect himself/herself from harm, danger, or perceived threats in the environment.

B. The client has joined a gang in order to feel safer from perceived threats in the environment.

C. The client has experienced increased harm, danger, and threats in the environment due to his/her affiliation with a negative peer group or gang.

D. The client has been assisted in decreasing the harm, danger, or perceived threats in the environment and no longer needs to affiliate with negative peer groups or gangs.

E. The client reports a discontinuation of the affiliation with negative peer groups or gangs.

7. Low Self-Esteem/Insecurity (7)

A. The client's parents described him/her as gravitating toward negative peer groups because of underlying feelings of low self-esteem and insecurity.

B. The client displayed behaviors indicative of low self-esteem within the session (e.g., self-disparaging remarks, difficulty accepting compliments, insecurity, anxiousness, avoidance).

C. The client acknowledged his/her tendency to gravitate toward negative peer groups because of underlying feelings of low self-esteem and insecurity.

D. The client has dropped his/her pattern of affiliating with negative peer groups to increase his/her self-esteem and security feelings and has begun to work on accepting himself/herself.

8. Ostracism/Teasing by Peers (8)

A. The client identified being ostracized, teased, or mocked by peers at school or in the community.

B. The client's parents reported that he/she often comes home upset about being ostracized, teased, or mocked by peers.

C. As the client has gained social skills, his/her pattern of being ostracized, teased, or mocked by peers has decreased.

9. Rejection Experiences (9)

A. The client has experienced a history of rejection experiences.

B. The client identified having been rejected by his/her peer group.

C. The client identified feeling rejected by his/her family members.

D. Rejections from others have contributed to the client's desire to seek out negative peer groups for a sense of belonging.

E. As the client has processed his/her rejection experiences, he/she feels less driven to seek out negative peer groups for belonging.

F. The client has established himself/herself with a more positive peer group and developed healthy experiences of acceptance.

10. Immaturity/Social Skills Deficits (10)

A. The client presented in a socially immature manner.

B. The client has pronounced deficits in his/her social skills.

C. The client has gained an appropriate level of social maturity and social skills proficiency.

D. As the client has matured and gained social skills, he/she has become less susceptible to negative peer influences.

11. Substance Abuse (11)

A. The client has participated in substance abuse in order to gain group acceptance.

B. The client has displayed acting out behaviors in order to gain group acceptance.

C. As the client has affiliated with a more positive peer group, his/her pattern of substance abuse and other acting out behaviors has diminished.

INTERVENTIONS IMPLEMENTED

1. Explore Perceptions, Thoughts, and Feelings (1)*

A. The client's perceptions of how he/she relates to peers were explored.

B. The client was urged to elaborate on his/her areas of conflict within peer relationships.

C. Warm acceptance and active-listening techniques were used to help support the client as he/she expressed thoughts and feelings about peer relationships.

D. The client was reinforced for expressing his/her perceptions, thoughts, and feelings about peer relationships.

E. The client's degree of denial regarding peer relationship conflict was found to be high and he/she was reluctant to express thoughts and feelings in this area.

2. Gather Psychosocial History (2)

A. A detailed psychosocial history was gathered, including information regarding the client's development, family environment, and interpersonal relationships.

B. Insights were drawn and reflected back to the client regarding factors contributing to his/her desire to affiliate with negative peer groups.

---

* The numbers in parentheses correlate to the number of the Therapeutic Intervention statement in the companion chapter with the same title in *The Adolescent Psychotherapy Treatment Planner,* Fourth Edition (Jongsma, Peterson, McInnis, and Bruce) by John Wiley & Sons, 2006.

C. Upon review of the client's detailed psychosocial history, many factors were identified that may contribute to his/her affiliation with negative peer groups.

D. Despite a detailed psychosocial history of the client's development, family environment, and interpersonal relationships, no specific factors were identified that may contribute to his/her affiliation with negative peer groups.

3. Assign Journaling (3)

A. The client was instructed to keep a journal in which he/she records both positive and negative peer experiences that have evoked strong emotions.

B. As the client shared entries from his/her peer association journal, these were processed to uncover factors that contribute to his/her desire to affiliate with negative peer groups.

C. The peer association journal has been helpful in identifying strengths that can allow the client to build positive peer relationships.

D. The client has failed to keep a peer association journal; he/she was redirected to do this journaling.

4. Identify Social-Emotional Needs (4)

A. The client was taught about how social-emotional needs may be met through his/her involvement with negative peer groups.

B. The client was supported as he/she identified his/her social-emotional needs the negative peer group meets (e.g., achieving a sense of belonging and acceptance, elevated status, obtaining material goods, seeking protection).

C. The client failed to identify the social-emotional needs he/she attempts to meet with his/her involvement with negative peer groups and was provided with tentative examples in this area.

5. Establish Parental Rules and Boundaries (5)

A. The parents were assisted in establishing clearly defined rules and boundaries as well as providing greater structure in an effort to deter the client from being highly susceptible to negative peer group influences.

B. A family therapy session was focused on helping establish clearly defined rules and appropriate parent-child boundaries.

C. The parents identified the rules and expectations that the client is expected to follow at home and positive feedback was provided to them for these clear expectations.

D. The parents have had difficulty establishing clearly defined rules and identifying appropriate consequences for the client's misbehavior and were provided with remedial assistance in this area.

6. Promote Communication between Home and School (6)

A. The parents and teachers were encouraged to maintain regular communication with each other via phone calls or written notes regarding the client's relationship with peers.

B. The client's teachers were asked to send home daily or weekly progress notes informing the parents about the client's academic progress.

C. The client was informed of his/her responsibility to bring home daily or weekly progress notes from school, allowing for regular communication between parents and teachers.

D. The parents and teachers were encouraged to follow through with firm, consistent limits if the client engages in acting out, disruptive, or aggressive behavior at school.

E. The increased communication between teachers and parents via phone calls or regular progress notes has been identified as being a significant contributing factor to the client's improved peer relationships.

7. Establish Contingency Contract (7)

A. A contingency contract was designed specifying the consequences for the client if he/she engages in disruptive, acting out, or antisocial behavior with peers.

B. The client and parents signed a contingency contract specifying the consequences of the client acting out with peers.

C. The client was asked to repeat the terms of the contract to demonstrate his/her understanding.

8. Design Reward System (8)

A. The client and parents were assisted in identifying a list of rewards to reinforce the client for engaging in specific positive social behaviors.

B. A reward system was designed to reinforce the client's positive social behaviors and deter the need to affiliate with negative peer groups.

C. Specific behaviors were included in the reward system (e.g., introducing self to others in a positive peer group, displaying kindness, helping another peer with academic or social problems).

9. List Negative Consequences (9)

A. The client was directed to list five to ten negative consequences that his/her participation with negative peer groups has had on himself/herself and others.

B. Positive reinforcement was provided to the client for his/her list of consequences from his/her participation with negative peer groups.

C. The client has not listed negative consequences related to his/her negative peer group affiliation and was redirected to do so.

10. Confront Impact of Negative Peer Group Involvement (10)

A. The client was firmly and consistently confronted with how his/her involvement with negative peer groups impacts himself/herself and others.

B. The client was asked to list the negative consequences of his/her negative peer group interaction for himself/herself and others.

C. Role-reversal techniques were used to help the client realize how his/her negative peer group affiliation has affected others.

D. The client was praised for his/her increased understanding of how his/her negative peer group affiliation has affected himself/herself and others.

E. The client continues to be in denial about the impact of his/her involvement with negative peer groups and the effect on himself/herself and others and was provided with specific, tentative examples of these effects.

11. Challenge Minimization (11)

A. Statements by the client that minimize the impact of his/her involvement with negative peer groups were identified.

B. The client was confronted and challenged when he/she made statements that minimized the impact that his/her involvement with negative peer groups has on his/her behavior.

C. The client accepted the confrontation regarding minimizing the impact that his/her negative peer group involvement has on his/her behavior and was assisted in replacing these minimizations with statements of responsibility for negative social behavior.

D. The client consistently denied any minimization and was provided with examples of such minimization.

12. Confront Blaming (12)

A. Today's therapy session explored the underlying factors contributing to the client's pattern of blaming others for his/her acting out, disruptive, or antisocial behaviors.

B. The client was challenged to accept the consequences of his/her acting out, disruptive, or antisocial behaviors.

C. The client was supported as he/she identified how his/her pattern of blaming others is associated with underlying feelings of low self-esteem, inadequacy, and insecurity.

D. The client was assisted in identifying constructive ways to improve his/her self-esteem to help reduce the pattern of blaming others.

E. The client denied any pattern of blaming others and was provided with specific examples in this area.

13. Challenge Parents to Cease Blaming and Set Limits (13)

A. The client's parents were identified as often blaming the client's misbehavior on his/her peers.

B. The parents were challenged to cease blaming the client's misbehavior on his/her peers.

C. The client's parents were directed to change their focus from blaming the client's peers to setting limits for the client's negative social behaviors that occur while affiliating with peers.

D. Support and encouragement were provided as the parents identified the need to discontinue blaming the client's peers and set firmer limits for him/her.

E. The client's parents have failed to switch from blaming peers to setting limits on the client and were provided with specific examples of how they might make this change.

14. Teach Mediational and Self-Control Techniques (14)

A. The client was taught mediational and self-control techniques to help him/her successfully resist negative peer influences.

B. The client was taught the "stop, listen, think, and act" technique.

C. The client was taught to count to ten or walk away in order to successfully resist negative peer influences.

D. As the client has implemented effective coping strategies to resist negative peer influences, his/her involvement in negative peer groups has decreased.

E. The client has not used mediational and self-control techniques to resist negative peer influences and was redirected to do so.

15. Teach Resistance to Negative Peers and Establishment of Positive Relationships (15)

A. Role-playing, modeling, and behavioral rehearsal techniques were used to teach the client effective ways to resist negative peer influences.

B. Role-playing, modeling, and behavioral rehearsal techniques were used to teach the client more effective ways to meet his/her social needs.

C. The client was assisted in learning techniques to establish lasting, meaningful friendships.

D. The client was taught specific techniques (e.g., walking way from negative peers, changing the subject to a more positive area, just saying "no," initiating positive conversations with positive peers, demonstrating empathy) to resist peer influence.

E. Positive feedback was provided to the client for the use of more effective ways to resist negative peer influences and develop lasting, meaningful friendships.

F. The client has not used new techniques to establish lasting, meaningful friendships and was redirected to do so.

16. Assign Reading on Resisting Negative Peer Influences/Maintaining Friendships (16)

A. The client was provided with reading material about effective ways to resist negative peer influences, yet still maintain friendships.

B. The client was assigned to read *How to Say No and Keep Your Friends* (Scott) to teach him/her effective ways to resist negative peer influences and maintain friendships.

C. The client has read the assigned material on resisting negative peer influences and it was processed within the session.

D. The client has not read the assigned material on resisting negative peer influences and was redirected to do so.

17. Identify Successful Negative Peer Resistance (17)

A. The client was asked to explore periods when he/she has demonstrated successful resistance to negative peer influences and did not engage in acting out, disruptive, or antisocial behaviors.

B. The experiences of resisting negative peer influences were processed and reinforced.

C. The client was encouraged to use similar coping mechanisms that he/she has used successfully in the past in order to control negative peer influences and not engage in acting out, disruptive, or antisocial behaviors.

D. The client shared the realization that use of the successful strategies has helped him/her stay out of trouble.

E. The session revealed that the client was better behaved during periods of time when he/she received strong family support and affiliated with positive peer groups.

18. Teach Assertiveness (18)

A. The client was taught effective communication and assertiveness skills to help him/her successfully resist negative peer pressure.

B. Examples of assertive, effective communication were provided (e.g., "I have to leave now," "I can't afford to get into any more trouble").

C. Positive feedback was provided to the client as he/she displayed a clear understanding of how to use effective communication and assertiveness skills.

D. The client was strongly praised as he/she identified situations in which he/she has effectively used assertive communication skills to resist negative peer pressure.

E. The client has not used effective, assertive communication skills to resist negative peer pressure and was assisted in identifying situations in which he/she might have been more effective in using these skills.

19. Refer for Group Therapy (19)

A. The client was referred to a group therapy program to improve his/her social skills and learn ways to successfully resist negative peer pressure.

B. The client was directed to self-disclose at least two times in each group therapy session about his/her peer relationships.

C. The client has attended the group therapy sessions, and the skills he/she learned there were reviewed and processed.

D. The client has not attended the group therapy sessions and was redirected to do so.

20. Refer to Behavioral Contracting Group (20)

A. The client was referred to a behavioral contracting group.

B. The client has attended the behavioral contracting group, where he/she and other group members developed contracts to increase the frequency of positive peer interactions.

C. The client's review of progress with his/her behavioral contract was processed.

D. The client was praised for achieving goals regarding peer interactions.

21. Teach Positive Social Skills (21)

A. The client was taught positive social skills (e.g., introducing self to others, active listening, verbalizing empathy and concern for others, ignoring teasing).

B. Skillstreaming: The Adolescent Kit (McGinnis and Goldstein) was used to help the client learn how to improve peer relationships and increase chances of developing meaningful friendships.

C. The client was positively reinforced for using social skills that will help improve peer relationships and establish friendships.

D. The client has rarely used positive social skills and was provided with remedial assistance in this area.

22. Assign Social Skills Practice (22)

A. The client was directed to practice newly learned positive social skills at least once each day between therapy sessions.

B. The client's practice of newly learned positive social skills was reviewed.

C. The client was reinforced for his/her successes at implementing newly learned positive social skills.

D. The client was redirected for his/her failures at implementing newly learned positive social skills.

23. Encourage Positive Peer Group/Community Activities (23)

A. The client was encouraged to become involved in positive peer group or community activities where he/she can gain acceptance and status.

B. The client was assisted in identifying positive peer groups and community activities where he/she can gain acceptance and status (e.g., church or synagogue youth groups, YWCA or YMCA functions, school clubs, boys' or girls' clubs).

C. The client was reinforced for becoming involved in positive peer groups and community activities.

D. The client has not become involved in positive peer group and community activities and was redirected to do so.

24. **Consult about Positive Socialization Groups (24)**

A. A consultation was held with school officials about ways to increase the client's socialization with positive peer groups at school.

B. The client was provided with a variety of options of ways to increase socialization with positive peer groups at school (e.g., join school choir or newspaper staff, participate in student government, become involved with school fundraiser).

C. Positive feedback was provided to the client as he/she has become involved with positive peer groups at school.

D. The client has not become involved with positive peer groups at school and was redirected to do so.

25. **Assign Social Contact with Positive Peers (25)**

A. The client was assigned a task of initiating one social contact per day with other peers who are identified as being responsible, dependable, friendly, or well liked.

B. The client has regularly initiated social contact with other peers who are identified as being positive and was provided with positive feedback about this.

C. The client has not regularly initiated social contact with positive peers and was redirected to do so.

26. **Assign Telephone Contacts (26)**

A. The client was assigned to initiate three phone contacts per week to different individuals outside of the identified negative peer group.

B. The client has regularly initiated telephone contact with different individuals outside of the identified negative peer group; his/her experience with these positive interactions was reviewed.

C. The client has not initiated phone contacts outside of the identified negative peer group, and the reasons for his/her failure were reviewed and processed.

27. **Assign Coordination of Overnight Visit (27)**

A. The client was directed to invite a peer or friend (outside the negative peer group) for an overnight visit.

B. The client was directed to set up an overnight visit at a peer or friend's home.

C. The client has completed the overnight visit with a positive peer, and his/her experience was processed and reinforced.

D. The client has not coordinated an overnight visit with a friend (outside the negative peer group) and was redirected to do so.

28. Assign Altruistic Acts (28)

A. The client was given the homework assignment of engaging in three altruistic or benevolent acts with peers before the next therapy session.

B. The client has engaged in altruistic or benevolent acts with peers and was provided with positive feedback.

C. Others' responses to the client's altruistic or benevolent acts were identified and processed.

D. The client has not completed the altruistic or benevolent acts and was redirected to do so.

29. Brainstorm Ways to Meet Needs (29)

A. The client was assisted in brainstorming more adaptive ways for him/her to meet needs for recognition, status, acceptance, material goods, and excitement (other than through his/her involvement with negative peer groups).

B. The client was praised for his/her use of creativity and willingness to identify ways to meet his/her needs other than through negative peer group activities or gang involvement.

C. The client did not identify ways to meet his/her needs outside of the negative peer group and was provided with tentative examples in this area (e.g., attend or participate in sporting events, secure employment, visit amusement park with youth group).

30. Assign *Handling Peer Pressure and Gangs* (30)

A. The client was assigned to view the video *Handling Peer Pressure and Gangs* (Wellness Reproductions and Publishing) to help him/her resist negative peer influences or pressure to join a gang.

B. The client has viewed the video on peer pressure and gangs, and the key ideas were processed.

C. The client has not viewed the video on peer pressure and gangs and was redirected to do so.

31. Identify Resource People (31)

A. The client was assisted in identifying a list of resource people to whom he/she can turn for comfort, support, and guidance when he/she experiences negative peer pressure and/or feels rejected by peers.

B. The client was reinforced for committing to contact a list of resource people, including both peers and adults, available both at school and in the community.

C. The client was given support for his/her use of resource people when he/she experienced negative peer pressure and/or feelings of rejection by peers.

D. The client has not developed a list of resource people to whom he/she can turn for comfort, support, or guidance, and was redirected to do so.

32. Explore Peer Relationship History (32)

A. The client's background of peer relationships was explored in order to assess whether he/she feels rejected, ostracized, or unaccepted by many peers.

B. Active-listening skills were used as the client expressed his/her feelings regarding his/her history of peer relationships.

C. The client was assisted in identifying possible causes of rejection or alienation (e.g., hypersensitivity to teasing, target of scapegoating, poor social skills).

D. The client tended to deny any history of rejection or alienation and was urged to be more open about his/her past experiences.

33. Use Empty-Chair Technique (33)

A. The empty-chair technique was used to help the client express his/her feelings of anger, hurt, and sadness toward individuals who have rejected him/her.

B. The client was supported as he/she used the empty-chair technique to express his/her feelings toward individuals who have rejected him/her.

C. The client was supported as he/she expressed feelings of hurt, anger, and sadness.

D. The client tended to block his/her emotions as he/she used the empty-chair technique and was encouraged to be more open about his/her feelings.

34. Connect Low Self-Esteem and Negative Peer Groups (34)

A. The client was assisted in making a connection between underlying feelings of low self-esteem and insecurity, and his/her gravitation toward negative peer groups to achieve a sense of belonging and acceptance.

B. Active-listening skills were used as the client identified his/her own experience of using negative peer groups to cover up feelings of low self-esteem and insecurity.

C. The client denied any connection between underlying feelings of low self-esteem and gravitation toward negative peer groups and was provided with tentative examples regarding how this may have occurred.

35. Identify Alternative Means to Building Self-Esteem (35)

A. The client was assisted in identifying more constructive ways to build self-esteem and gain approval, other than affiliating with negative peer groups.

B. The client was supported as he/she identified more constructive ways to build self-esteem and win approval and was also encouraged to attempt these techniques.

C. The client did not identify constructive ways to build self-esteem and was provided with tentative examples (e.g., try out for school play, attend a school dance, participate in sporting or recreational activities).

36. List Strengths/Interests (36)

A. The client was directed to identify five to ten strengths or interests.

B. The client was assigned the "Show Your Strengths" exercise from the *Adolescent Psychotherapy Homework Planner,* 2nd ed. (Jongsma, Peterson, and McInnis).

C. The client's list of strengths and interests was reviewed, and he/she was encouraged to utilize his/her strengths to build self-esteem and increase positive peer interactions.

D. The client did not complete the "Show Your Strengths" exercise and was redirected to do so.

37. Identify Healthy Risks (37)

A. The client was asked to identify healthy risks that he/she can take in the near future to improve his/her self-esteem.

B. The client identified several healthy risks that he/she can take in the near future to improve his/her self-esteem and was challenged to take three healthy risks before the next therapy session.

C. The client was provided with tentative examples of healthy risks that he/she can take to improve his/her self-esteem (e.g., try out for sports team, attend new social functions or gatherings, initiate conversations with unfamiliar people outside of the negative peer group); he/she was challenged to attempt three healthy risks before the next therapy session.

D. The client has not engaged in healthy social risks to increase self-esteem and this resistance was processed.

38. Explore Parental Strictness (38)

A. The parent's establishment of rules and boundaries was explored.

B. The parents were provided with feedback about how their rules and boundaries may be so rigid and strict as to constrict the client's opportunity to socialize with peers.

C. It was interpreted that the client rebels from overly rigid or strict rules and boundaries by engaging in acting out behaviors with negative peer groups.

D. Positive feedback was provided as the parents identified their rules and boundaries as overly strict and they were encouraged to loosen these rules and boundaries.

E. The parents rejected the notion that their rules and boundaries are overly strict or rigid and were encouraged to monitor this dynamic.

39. Encourage Loosening of Boundaries (39)

A. The overly rigid parents were challenged to loosen rules and boundaries to allow the client increased opportunities to engage in socially appropriate and positive peer group activities.

B. The parents were encouraged for appropriately loosening rules and boundaries.

C. The parents have not reasonably loosened the rules and boundaries and were redirected to do so.

40. Explore Lack of Supervision (40)

A. A family therapy session was used to explore whether the lack of supervision of the client by the parents and their inability to establish appropriate parent-child boundaries has contributed to the client's gravitation to a negative peer group.

B. It was acknowledged that the lack of supervision of the client has enabled him/her to gravitate toward negative peer group influences.

C. The parents were urged to provide better supervision of the client in order to eliminate gravitation toward negative peer group influences.

41. Conduct/Refer for Substance Abuse Evaluation/Treatment (41)

A. A substance abuse evaluation was conducted.

B. The client was referred for a substance abuse evaluation.

C. The results of the substance abuse evaluation were shared with the client and his/her parents.

D. The focus of treatment was switched to the client's pattern of chemical dependence.

E. The client was referred for treatment of his/her chemical dependence.

F. The client's substance abuse evaluation indicated no significant concerns related to chemical dependence and this was reflected to the client and his/her parents.

OBSESSIVE-COMPULSIVE DISORDER (OCD)

CLIENT PRESENTATION

1. Recurrent/Persistent Thoughts (1)*

A. The client described recurrent and persistent thoughts or impulses that are viewed as senseless, intrusive, and time-consuming and that interfere with his/her daily routine.

B. The intensity of the recurrent and persistent thoughts and impulses is so severe that the client is unable to efficiently perform daily duties or interact in social relationships.

C. The strength of the client's obsessive thoughts has diminished and he/she has become more efficient in his/her daily routine.

D. The client reported that the obsessive thoughts are under significant control and he/she is able to focus attention and effort on the task at hand.

2. Failed Control Attempts (2)

A. The client reported failure at attempts to control or ignore his/her obsessive thoughts or impulses.

B. The client described many different failed attempts at learning to control or ignore his/her obsessions.

C. The client is beginning to experience some success at controlling and ignoring his/her obsessive thoughts and impulses.

3. Recognize Internal Source of Obsessions (3)

A. The client has a poor understanding that his/her obsessive thoughts are a product of his/her own mind.

B. The client reported that he/she recognizes that the obsessive thoughts are a product of his/her own mind and are not coming from some outside source or power.

C. The client acknowledged that the obsessive thoughts are related to anxiety and are not a sign of any psychotic process.

4. Excessive Concern about Dirt and Disease (4)

A. The client displays excessive concern about dirt.

B. The client has many unfounded fears about contracting a dreadful disease or illness.

C. The client has frequently changed his/her behavior due to his/her concerns and fears about germs and illnesses.

D. The strength of the client's fears about dirt, germs, and illnesses has decreased and he/she has become more stable in his/her activities.

E. The client reported that the excessive concerns about dirt and disease are under significant control and he/she is able to focus attention and effort on his/her regular activities.

---

*The numbers in parentheses correlate to the number of the Behavioral Definition statement in the companion chapter with the same title in *The Adolescent Psychotherapy Treatment Planner,* Fourth Edition (Jongsma, Peterson, McInnis, and Bruce) by John Wiley & Sons, 2006.

5. Aggressive/Sexual Obsessions (5)

A. The client described persistent obsessive thoughts about committing aggressive actions.

B. The client has many troubling sexual thoughts and urges.

C. The client described often imagining troubling aggressive or sexual actions.

D. The client described that his/her aggressive, sexual thoughts are not compatible with his/her identifying values and morals.

E. As treatment has progressed, the client reports a decreased pattern of obsessions regarding aggressive or sexual activity.

F. The client reports that his/her aggressive, sexual thoughts, urges, or images are no longer occurring.

6. Religious Obsessions (6)

A. The client described persistent and troubling thoughts about religious issues.

B. The client described excessive concern about whether his/her actions are moral, right, or wrong.

C. When under stress, the client turns the focus away from the stressor and onto religious/moral issues.

D. The client described a decrease in persistent and troubling thoughts about religious issues.

7. Compulsive Compensatory Behavior (7)

A. The client described repetitive and intentional behaviors that are performed in a ritualistic fashion.

B. The client identified that his/her compulsive behaviors are in response to his/her obsessive thoughts and increased feelings of anxiety and fearfulness.

C. The client's compulsive behavior pattern follows rigid rules and has many repetitions to it.

D. The client reported a significant decrease in the frequency and intensity of his/her compulsive behaviors.

E. The client reports very little interference in his/her daily routine from his/her compensatory compulsive behavior rituals.

8. Disconnected Behavioral Compulsions (8)

A. The client reports repetitive and excessive behaviors that are performed to neutralize or prevent discomfort or some dreadful situation.

B. The client has identified that his/her behavior is not connected in any realistic way with what it is designed to neutralize or prevent.

C. The client has identified his/her ritualistic behavior as unconnected to his/her actual fears.

D. As treatment has progressed, the client's repetitive and excessive behaviors have decreased.

9. Compulsions Seen as Unreasonable (9)

A. The client acknowledged that his/her repetitive and compulsive behaviors are excessive and unreasonable.

B. The client's recognition of his/her compulsive behaviors as excessive and unreasonable has provided good motivation for cooperation with treatment and follow through on attempts to change.

10. Cleaning/Washing Compulsions (10)

A. The client has had many cleaning compulsions, including cleaning and re cleaning of many household items.

B. The client has engaged in washing compulsions, including excessive hand washing, bathing, and showering.

C. The client has had such severe hand-washing compulsions that skin breakdown is occurring.

D. As the client has participated in treatment, his/her frequency of cleaning and washing has decreased.

11. Hoarding/Collecting (11)

A. The client regularly engages in hoarding items that are unnecessary.

B. The client described the unnecessary collecting of innocuous items.

C. The client has become quite agitated when others have accidentally or purposefully threatened his/her hoarding or collecting.

D. As the client's functioning has improved, his/her desire to hoard or collect items has decreased.

E. The client's use of hoarding or collecting items has been eliminated.

12. Checking Compulsions (12)

A. The client identified that he/she frequently needs to check and recheck basic tasks.

B. The client frequently checks and rechecks to see whether or not doors or windows are locked.

C. The client frequently checks and rechecks to make sure that his/her homework has been done correctly.

D. The client has severe fears that others have been harmed and frequently checks and rechecks for no direct reason.

E. The client reports that he/she has significantly decreased his/her pattern of checking behaviors.

13. Arrangement Compulsions (13)

A. The client described frequently arranging objects to make certain that they are in "proper order," for no apparent reason (e.g., stacking coins in a certain order).

B. The client described being overly focused on arranging necessary objects (e.g., laying out clothes each evening at the same time, wearing only certain clothes on certain days).

C. As treatment has progressed, the client reports a decrease in his/her compulsion to order or arrange objects.

INTERVENTIONS IMPLEMENTED

1. Assess OCD History (1)*

A. Active listening was used as the client described the nature, history, and severity of his/her obsessive thoughts and compulsive behaviors.

B. Through a clinical interview, the client described a severe degree of interference in his/her daily routine and ability to perform a task efficiently because of the significant problem with obsessive thoughts and compulsive behaviors.

C. The client was noted to have made many attempts to ignore or control the compulsive behaviors and obsessive thoughts, but without any consistent success.

D. It was noted that the client gave evidence of compulsive behaviors within the interview.

2. Conduct Psychological Testing (2)

A. Psychological testing was administered to evaluate the nature and severity of the client's obsessive-compulsive problem.

B. *The Children's Yale-Brown Obsessive-Compulsive Scale* (Scahill et al.) was used to assess the client's frequency, intensity, duration, and history of obsessions and compulsions.

C. The psychological testing results indicate that the client experiences significant interference in his/her daily life from obsessive-compulsive rituals.

D. The psychological testing indicated a rather mild degree of OCD within the client.

E. The results of the psychological testing were interpreted to the client.

3. Refer for Medical Evaluation (3)

A. The client was referred to a physician for an evaluation for a medication prescription to aid in the control of his/her OCD.

B. The client has followed through with the referral for a medication evaluation and has been prescribed psychotropic medication to aid in the control of his/her OCD.

C. The client has failed to comply with the referral to a physician for a medication evaluation and was encouraged to do so.

4. Monitor Medication Compliance (4)

A. The client reported that he/she is taking the psychotropic medication as prescribed; the positive effect on controlling the OCD was emphasized.

B. The client reported complying with the psychotropic medication prescription, but that the effectiveness of the medication has been very limited or nonexistent; this information was relayed to the prescribing clinician.

C. The client has not consistently taken the psychotropic medication as prescribed and was encouraged to do so.

5. Assign Reading Material (5)

A. The client was assigned to read psychoeducational chapters of books or treatment manuals on the rationale for exposure and ritual prevention therapy.

*The numbers in parentheses correlate to the number of the Therapeutic Intervention statement in the companion chapter with the same title in *The Adolescent Psychotherapy Treatment Planner,* Fourth Edition (Jongsma, Peterson, McInnis, and Bruce) by John Wiley & Sons, 2006.

B. The client was assigned to read psychoeducational chapters of books or treatment manuals for the rationale for cognitive restructuring for OCD.

C. The client was assigned to read information from *Up and Down the Worry Hill* (Wagner).

D. The client was assigned to read excerpts from *Brain Lock: Free Yourself from Obsessive-Compulsive Behavior* (Schwartz).

E. The client was assigned to read excerpts from *Obsessive-Compulsive Disorder: Help for Children and Adolescents* (Waltz).

F. The client has read the assigned material on the rationale for OCD treatment; key points were reviewed.

G. The client has not read the assigned material on the rationale for OCD treatment and was redirected to do so.

6. Discuss Usefulness of Treatment (6)

A. A discussion was held about how treatment serves as an arena to desensitize learned fear, reality test obsessional fears and underlying beliefs, and build confidence in managing fears without compulsions.

B. The client was provided with a rationale for treatment as described in *Up and Down the Worry Hill* (Wagner).

C. Positive feedback was provided to the client as he/she displayed a clear understanding of the usefulness of treatment.

D. The client did not display a clear understanding of the usefulness of treatment and was provided with additional feedback in this area.

7. Explore Schema and Self-Talk (7)

A. The client was assisted in exploring how his/her schema and self-talk mediate his/her obsessional fears and compulsive behaviors.

B. The client's schema and self-talk were reviewed as described in *Treatment of OCD in Children and Adolescents* (Wagner).

C. The client's schema and self-talk were reviewed as described in *OCD in Children and Adolescents* (March and Mulle).

D. The client was reinforced for his/her insight into his/her self-talk and schema that support his/her obsessional fears and compulsive behaviors.

E. The client struggled to develop insight into his/her own self-talk and schema and was provided with tentative examples of these concepts.

8. Assess Cues (8)

A. The client was assessed in regard to the nature of any external cues (e.g., persons, objects, situations) that precipitate the client's obsessions and compulsions.

B. The client was assessed in regard to the nature of any internal cues (e.g., thoughts, images, impulses) that precipitate the client's obsessions and compulsions.

C. The client was provided with feedback about his/her identification of cues.

9. Construct a Hierarchy of Fear Cues (9)

A. The client was directed to construct a hierarchy of feared internal and external cues.

B. The client was assisted in developing a hierarchy of internal and external fear cues.

C. The client has developed a useful hierarchy of feared internal and external cues, and positive feedback was provided.

D. The client has struggled to clearly develop a hierarchy of feared internal and external cues and was provided with additional assistance in this area.

10. Select Likely Successful Imaginal Exposure (10)

A. The client was assisted in identifying initial imaginal exposures with a bias toward those that have a likelihood of being successful experiences for the client.

B. Cognitive restructuring techniques were used within and after the imaginal exposure of the OCD cues.

C. Imaginal exposure and cognitive restructuring techniques were used as described in *Treatment of OCD in Children and Adolescents* (Wagner).

D. Imaginal exposure and cognitive restructuring techniques were used as described in *OCD in Children and Adolescents* (March and Mulle).

E. "Gradually Facing a Phobic Fear" from the *Adolescent Psychotherapy Homework Planner,* 2nd ed. (Jongsma, Peterson, and McInnis) was assigned to help the client complete imaginary exposures.

F. The client was provided with feedback about his/her use of imaginal exposures.

11. Assign Cue Exposure Practice (11)

A. The client was assigned a homework exercise in which he/she repeats the exposure to the internal and/or external OCD cues.

B. The client was instructed to use restructured cognitions between sessions and to record his/her responses.

C. The client was assigned to use "Reducing the Strength of Compulsive Behaviors" from the *Adult Psychotherapy Homework Planner,* 2nd ed. (Jongsma).

D. The client's use of the cue exposure homework was reviewed and his/her success was reinforced.

E. Corrective feedback was provided to the client for his/her struggles in using restructured cognitions during exposure to OCD cues.

F. The client was assisted in using restructured cognitions as described in *Up and Down the Worry Hill* (Wagner).

12. Differentiate between Lapse and Relapse (12)

A. A discussion was held with the client regarding the distinction between a lapse and a relapse.

B. A lapse was associated with an initial and reversible return of symptoms, fear, or urges to avoid.

C. A relapse was associated with the decision to return to fearful and avoidant patterns.

D. The client was provided with support and encouragement as he/she displayed an understanding of the difference between a lapse and a relapse.

13. Discuss Management of Lapse Risk Situations (13)

A. The client was assisted in identifying future situations or circumstances in which lapses could occur.

B. The session focused on rehearsing the management of future situations or circumstances in which lapses could occur.

C. The client was reinforced for his/her appropriate use of lapse management skills.

D. The client was redirected in regard to his/her poor use of lapse management skills.

14. Encourage Routine Use of Strategies (14)

A. The client was instructed to routinely use the strategies that he/she has learned in therapy (e.g., cognitive restructuring, exposure).

B. The client was urged to find ways to build his/her new strategies into his/her life as much as possible.

C. The client was reinforced as he/she reported ways in which he/she has incorporated coping strategies into his/her life and routine.

D. The client was redirected about ways to incorporate his/her new strategies into his/her routine and life.

15. Schedule "Maintenance Sessions" (15)

A. "Maintenance sessions" were proposed to help maintain therapeutic gains and adjust to life without anger outbursts.

B. The client was reinforced for agreeing to the scheduling "maintenance sessions."

C. The client refused to schedule "maintenance sessions," and this was processed.

16. Teach Thought-Stopping Techniques (16)

A. The client was taught to interrupt obsessive thoughts by shouting "STOP" to himself/herself silently while picturing a red traffic signal and then thinking about a calming scene.

B. The client was assisted in developing his/her own thought-stopping techniques and images.

C. Positive feedback was provided to the client for his/her helpful use of thought-stopping techniques.

D. The client does not regularly use thought-stopping techniques and was redirected to do so.

17. Assign Thought-Stopping Techniques between Sessions (17)

A. The client was assigned the use of thought-stopping techniques on a daily basis between sessions.

B. The client was assigned "Making Use of the Thought-Stopping Technique" from the *Adult Psychotherapy Homework Planner*, 2nd ed. (Jongsma).

C. The client's implementation of thought-stopping techniques was reviewed and successes were reinforced.

D. The client's use of thought-stopping techniques was reviewed and successes were reinforced. Failures were redirected.

18. Design Award System (18)

A. An award system was designed for the client for his/her successful resistance of the urge to engage in compulsive behaviors.

B. The client was rewarded for openly sharing obsessive thoughts with others.

C. An award system was designed as described in *Treatment of OCD in Children and Adolescents* (Wagner).

D. An award system was developed as described in *OCD in Children and Adolescents* (March and Mulle).

E. "Refocus Attention Away from Obsessions and Compulsion" from the *Adolescent Psychotherapy Homework Planner,* 2nd ed. (Jongsma, Peterson and McInnis) was used to encourage the use of refocusing techniques.

19. Encourage Use of a Coach (19)

A. The client was encouraged to involve a support person or coach who can help him/her to resist the urge to engage in compulsive behavior or to take his/her mind off obsessive thoughts.

B. The client was reinforced as he/she has enlisted the assistance of a coach.

C. The client was urged to regularly use his/her coach.

20. Refer to Support Group (20)

A. The client was referred to a support group to help maintain and support the gains made in therapy.

B. The client's parents were referred to a support group to help support and maintain the gains made in therapy.

C. The client has attended the support group and his/her experience was reviewed.

D. The client's parents have attended the support group and their experience was reviewed.

E. The support group has not been attended and the use of such support groups was reinforced.

21. Explore Unresolved Conflicts (21)

A. As the client's unresolved life conflicts were explored, he/she verbalized and clarified feelings connected to those conflicts.

B. The client was supported as he/she identified key life conflicts that raise his/her anxiety level and intensify the OCD symptoms.

C. As the client was helped to clarify and share his/her feelings regarding current unresolved life conflicts, his/her level of anxiety diminished and the OCD symptoms were reduced.

D. The client has been guarded about his/her feelings regarding current life conflicts and was encouraged to be more open in this area.

22. Develop Parents' Interventions (22)

A. A family therapy session was held to identify specific, positive ways that the parents can help the client manage his/her obsessions or compulsions.

B. The client's parents were reinforced for their identification of specific techniques to help the client manage his/her obsessions or compulsions.

C. The client's parents were provided with tentative examples of ways to help the client manage his/her obsessions or compulsions (e.g., parents refocus attention away from obsessions/compulsions by engaging in recreational activity or talking about other topics; parents encourage the client to participate in feared activity).

D. The family was reinforced for the use of techniques to help the client manage his/her obsessions or compulsions.

E. The family has not regularly prompted the client to use management techniques to control his/her obsessions or compulsions and was redirected to do so.

23. Encourage Calmness and Support (23)

A. The client's parents were encouraged to remain calm, patient, and supportive when faced with the client's obsessions or compulsions.

B. The client's parents were instructed about specific ways in which they can display calmness, patience, and support when faced with the client's obsessions or compulsions.

C. The client's parents were discouraged from reacting strongly with anger or frustration to the client's obsessions or compulsions.

D. The client's parents were reinforced for their calm, patient support for the client.

E. The parents have not consistently displayed calm, patient support of the client and were redirected to do so.

24. Direct Parents Away from Lectures (24)

A. The parents were challenged to cease giving long lectures or becoming locked into long arguments with the client about how his/her OCD symptoms are irrational or unreasonable.

B. The parents were encouraged to provide simple, direct feedback about the client's OCD symptoms.

C. The parents were confronted for their pattern of power struggles over the client's OCD symptoms.

D. The parents were assisted in differentiating oppositional-defiant behavior and obsessive-compulsive behavior.

25. Identify Contributing Factors to OCD Symptoms (25)

A. Family therapy sessions were conducted to help assess the factors contributing to the emergence, maintenance, and exacerbation of the client's OCD symptoms.

B. A variety of possible factors contributing to the emergence, maintenance, and exacerbation of the client's OCD symptoms were identified and processed.

C. The family was provided with tentative examples of factors that may contribute to the emergence, maintenance, and exacerbation of the client's OCD symptoms.

26. Teach about Overprotection (26)

A. The parents were taught about how being overly protective or reassuring can inadvertently reinforce the client's OCD symptoms.

B. The parents were taught about how the client's ability to manage troubling or discouraging thoughts, urges, or images is decreased by overly protective or overly reassuring parental interventions.

C. The parents were encouraged about the appropriate level of support.

27. Encourage Feelings Sharing (27)

A. The client was encouraged, supported, and assisted in identifying and expressing feelings related to key unresolved life issues.

B. As the client shared his/her feelings regarding life issues, he/she reported a decreased level of emotional intensity around these issues; he/she was reinforced for this progress.

C. It was difficult for the client to get in touch with, clarify, and express emotions, as his/her pattern is to detach himself/herself from feelings; this pattern was reflected to the client.

28. Teach Rational Emotive Techniques (28)

A. The client was taught the principles of a rational emotive therapy approach.

B. The client was taught to analyze, attack, and destroy his/her self-defeating beliefs.

C. As the client implemented rational emotive techniques, he/she has decreased ruminations about death and other perplexing life issues; the benefits of this progress were emphasized.

D. The client has not regularly used rational emotive techniques and was provided with remedial training in this area.

29. Assign Ericksonian Task (29)

A. The client was assigned an Ericksonian task of performing a behavior that is centered around the obsession or compulsion instead of trying to avoid it.

B. As the client has faced the issue directly and performed a task, bringing feelings to the surface, the results of this were processed.

C. As the client has processed his/her feelings regarding the anxiety-provoking issue, the intensity of those feelings has been noted to be diminishing.

D. The client has not used the Ericksonian task and was redirected to do so.

30. Create Strategic Ordeal (30)

A. A strategic ordeal (Haley) was created with the client that offered a guarantee of cure for the obsession or compulsion.

B. The client has engaged in the assigned strategic ordeal to help him/her overcome the OCD impulses.

C. It was noted that the strategic ordeal has been quite successful at helping the client reduce OCD symptoms and feelings of anxiety.

D. The client has not been successful at implementing the strategic ordeal consistently and was encouraged to do so.

31. Develop Ritual Interruption (31)

A. The client was helped to develop a ritual of a very unpleasant task that he/she agrees to perform each time he/she experiences obsessive thoughts.

B. The client has begun to implement the distasteful ritual at the times of experiencing obsessive thoughts; his/her experience was reviewed.

C. The client reports that engaging in the distasteful ritual has interrupted the obsessive thoughts and the current pattern of compulsion; his/her progress was reinforced.

D. The client has not used the ritual interruption technique and was reminded to use this helpful technique.

OPPOSITIONAL DEFIANT

CLIENT PRESENTATION

1. Negativistic/Hostile (1)*

A. The client presented in a negative, hostile manner.

B. The client was negative regarding all matters great or small and hostile to all the therapist's responses.

C. The client expressed hostile defiance toward his/her parents.

D. The client has noticeably reduced his/her level of hostility and defiance toward most adults.

2. Acts as if Adults Are the Enemy (2)

A. The client voiced that he/she has seen parents and other adults who have authority as the enemy.

B. The client verbalized a "me versus them" attitude when referring to his/her interactions with most adults, especially those in authority.

C. The client has begun to see some adults, teachers, and even parents as possible allies as he/she has decreased his/her hostile attitude.

3. Temper Tantrums (3)

A. The client described a series of temper tantrums, including screaming, crying, throwing objects, thrashing on the ground, or refusing to move.

B. The parents identified that the client often has temper tantrums and defiance of direction from adult caregivers.

C. The client projected the blame for his/her temper tantrums onto other people.

D. The client has begun to take steps to control his/her temper tantrums.

E. The client has recently demonstrated good self-control and has not engaged in any temper tantrums.

4. Argumentative (4)

A. The client's total mood was argumentative regarding even the most insignificant points.

B. There was an edgy, argumentative manner present in the client.

C. There was a marked decrease in the client taking issue with or arguing most points.

D. The client has reached a point where he/she is able to accept direction without arguing.

5. Unreasonable/Defiant (5)

A. The client presented with a strong sense of defiance toward rules or requests.

B. The client viewed all expectations of him/her as unreasonable and defied them.

C. The client has gradually become more reasonable and less defiant on small issues.

*The numbers in parentheses correlate to the number of the Behavioral Definition statement in the companion chapter with the same title in *The Adolescent Psychotherapy Treatment Planner,* Fourth Edition (Jongsma, Peterson, McInnis, and Bruce) by John Wiley & Sons, 2006).

6. Annoyed/Irritating (6)

A. The client's mood was one of being annoyed with anyone who crosses him/her.

B. Being annoyed with everyone was the predominant mood of the client, who exhibits irritation with those who come in contact with him/her.

C. Overall, the client presented in a manner of being less annoyed with others and being somewhat tolerant of them.

D. The client is slowly coming to the point where he/she does not try to annoy others.

7. Blaming (7)

A. The client displayed an attitude of blaming others for his/her problems.

B. The client refused to take any responsibility for recent decisions and misbehavior, instead projecting it onto the parents and other authority figures.

C. The client carried the air that "I am not responsible or to blame for anything; it's all them."

D. Gradually, the client has started to take some responsibility for his/her decisions and behavior.

E. The client's general mood and manner reflect a noticeable decrease in blaming others for things that happen to him/her.

8. Lying (7)

A. The client continued to lie and to avoid responsibility for his/her actions/decisions without any sign of shame or guilt.

B. The client appeared to be lying regarding how things were going for him/her.

C. There has been a noticeable marked decrease in the client's lying and he/she is beginning to take some responsibility for his/her behavior.

9. Angry/Resentful (8)

A. The client presented in an angry, resentful, and generally uncooperative manner.

B. Anger predominated the client's mood, which was vented freely because "that's what I'm paying for."

C. The client's overall manner was sullen and quiet, which covered a strong mood of anger and resentfulness.

D. The client's general mood and presentation reflected a noticeable decrease in anger and resentfulness.

10. Vindictive/Spiteful (9)

A. The client's mood was vindictive and spiteful toward all whom he/she perceived as "against me."

B. There was a vindictive, spiteful edge toward all key figures in his/her daily life.

C. The client listed and vented acts of vengeance and spite he/she would to do to others.

D. The client has reduced his/her level of vindictiveness and spite toward others and has, at times, showed a little kindness in his/her speech.

11. Significant Impairments in Key Areas of Life (10)

A. The client reported impairments in his/her social, academic, and occupational functioning.

B. The client indicated that, according to most people, he/she was not doing well socially and academically, but it did not concern him/her.

C. The client's social and academic functioning have improved as he/she has taken responsibility for his/her actions and been less defiant.

INTERVENTIONS IMPLEMENTED

1. Build Trust (1)*

A. Initial level of trust was established with the client through use of unconditional positive regard.

B. Warm acceptance and active-listening techniques were utilized to establish the basis for a trusting relationship.

C. The client was noted to have formed a trust-based relationship and has started to share his/her feelings about conflictual relationships.

D. The client was noted to have formed an initial trusting relationship and has started to disclose his/her thoughts and feelings.

2. Identify Oppositional Patterns (2)

A. The client's behavior patterns were explored to establish how he/she responds to rules and authority.

B. Encouragement was provided as the client was willing and able to identify his/her oppositional patterns but did not perceive them as his/her problem.

C. The client's oppositional patterns were reviewed and pointed out with specific behavioral examples from his/her history.

3. Assess Anger Dynamics (3)

A. The client was assessed for various stimuli that have triggered his/her anger.

B. The client was helped to identify situations, people, and thoughts that have triggered his/her anger.

C. The client was assisted in identifying the thoughts, feelings, and actions that have characterized his/her anger responses.

4. Refer for Physical Examination (4)

A. The client was referred to a physician for a complete physical examination to rule out organic contributors (e.g., brain damage, tumor, elevated testosterone levels) to his/her defiant behavior.

B. The client has complied with the physical examination, and the results were shared with him/her.

C. The physical examination has identified organic contributors to poor behavior control, and treatment was suggested.

D. The physical examination has not identified any organic contributors to poor behavior control, and this was reflected to the client.

*The numbers in parentheses correlate to the number of the Therapeutic Intervention statement in the companion chapter with the same title in *The Adolescent Psychotherapy Treatment Planner,* Fourth Edition (Jongsma, Peterson, McInnis, and Bruce) by John Wiley & Sons, 2006).

E. The client has not complied with the physical examination to assess organic contributors and was redirected to do so.

5. Refer/Conduct Psychological Testing (5)

A. A psychological evaluation was conducted to determine whether emotional factors or ADHD are contributing to the client's behavior control problems.

B. The client was reinforced as he/she approached the psychological testing in an honest, straightforward manner and was cooperative with any requests presented to him/her.

C. The client was uncooperative and resistant to engage during the evaluation process and was encouraged to comply with the testing.

D. The client was resistive during the psychological testing and refused to consider the possibility of having ADHD or any serious emotional problems; support and redirection were provided.

E. Feedback was provided to the client and parents regarding the results of the psychological testing.

6. Refer/Conduct Substance Abuse Evaluation (6)

A. The client was referred for a substance abuse evaluation to assess the extent of his/her drug/alcohol usage and determine the need for treatment.

B. The findings from the substance abuse evaluation revealed the presence of a substance abuse problem and the need for treatment.

C. The findings from the substance abuse evaluation revealed the presence of a substance abuse problem that appears to be contributing to the client's behavior control problems.

D. The evaluation findings did not reveal the presence of a substance abuse problem or the need for treatment in this area.

7. Refer for Medication Evaluation (7)

A. The client was referred for a medication evaluation to help stabilize his/her mood and improve anger control.

B. The client and parents were supported as they agreed to follow through with a medication evaluation by a physician.

C. It was noted that the client was strongly opposed to being placed on medication to help stabilize his/her mood and improve anger control.

D. The issues of medication compliance and effectiveness were addressed with the parents and the client.

E. The client reported that the medication has helped to stabilize his/her mood and decrease the frequency and intensity of his/her angry outbursts and was supported for this improvement.

F. Information related to the client's medication compliance and its effectiveness was communicated to his/her physician.

G. The client reported that the medication has not helped to stabilize his/her moods or decrease the frequency or intensity of his/her angry outbursts and he/she was referred back to the prescribing clinician.

8. Reconceptualize Anger (8)

A. The client was assisted in reconceptualizing anger as involving different components that go through predictable phases.

B. The client was taught about the different components of anger, including cognitive, physiological, affective, and behavioral components.

C. The client was taught how to better discriminate between relaxation and tension.

D. The client was taught about the predictable phases of anger, including demanding expectations that are not met, leading to increased arousal and anger, which in turn leads to acting out.

E. The client displayed a clear understanding of the ways to conceptualize anger and was provided with positive reinforcement.

F. The client has struggled to understand the ways to conceptualize anger and was provided with remedial feedback in this area.

9. Identify Positive Consequences of Anger Management (9)

A. The client was asked to identify the positive consequences he/she has experienced in managing his/her anger and behavior.

B. The client was assisted in identifying positive consequences of managing anger and behavior (e.g., respect from others and self, cooperation from others, improved physical health).

C. The client was encouraged to learn new ways to conceptualize and manage anger/behavior.

10. Assign Use of Calming Techniques (10)

A. The client was assigned to implement calming techniques into his/her daily life when facing anger-triggering situations.

B. The client related situations in which he/she has appropriately used calming techniques when facing anger-triggering situations; this progress was reinforced.

C. The client described situations in which he/she has not used calming techniques and these failures were reviewed and redirected.

11. Explore Self-Talk (11)

A. The client's self-talk that mediates his/her angry feelings was explored.

B. The client was assessed for self-talk such as demanding expectations, reflected in "should," "must," or "have to" statements.

C. The client was assisted in identifying and challenging his/her biases and in generating alternative self-talk that correct for the biases.

D. The client was taught about how to use correcting self-talk to facilitate a more flexible and temperate response to frustration.

12. Assign Thought-Stopping Technique (12)

A. The client was directed to implement a "thought-stopping" technique on a daily basis between sessions.

B. The client was assigned "Making Use of the Thought-Stopping Technique" in the *Adult Psychotherapy Homework Planner,* 2nd ed. (Jongsma).

C. The client's use of the thought-stopping technique was reviewed.

D. The client was provided with positive feedback for his/her helpful use of the thought-stopping technique.

E. The client was provided with corrective feedback to help improve his/her use of the though-stopping technique.

13. Teach Assertive Communication (13)

A. The client was taught about assertive communication through instruction, modeling, and role-playing.

B. The client was referred to an assertiveness training class.

C. The client displayed increased assertiveness and was provided with positive feedback in this area.

D. The client has not increased his/her level of assertiveness and was provided with additional feedback in this area.

14. Teach Conflict Resolution Skills (14)

A. The client was taught conflict resolution skills through modeling, role-playing, and behavioral rehearsal.

B. The client was taught about empathy and active listening.

C. The client was taught about "I messages," respectful communication, assertiveness without aggression, and compromise.

D. The client was reinforced for his/her clear understanding of the conflict resolution skills.

E. The client displayed a poor understanding of the conflict resolution skills and was provided with remedial feedback.

15. Construct Strategy for Managing Anger (15)

A. The client was assisted in constructing a strategy for managing his/her anger.

B. The client was encouraged to combine somatic, cognitive, communication, problem-solving, and conflict resolution skills relevant to his/her needs.

C. The client was reinforced for his/her comprehensive anger management strategy.

D. The client was redirected to develop a more comprehensive anger management strategy.

16. Select Challenging Situations for Managing Anger/Behavior (16)

A. Situations were suggested to the client in which he/she may be increasingly challenged to apply his/her new strategies for managing anger and other behaviors.

B. The client was asked to identify his/her likely upcoming challenging situations for managing anger and other behaviors.

C. The client was urged to use his/her strategies for managing anger and other behaviors in successively more difficult situations.

17. Assign Homework to Practice Coping Skills (17)

A. Techniques were used to help the client consolidate his/her new anger management skills.

B. The client was assigned homework exercises to help him/her consolidate new calming, assertion, conflict resolution, or cognitive restructuring skills.

C. The client's use of homework to consolidate his/her coping skills was reviewed.

D. The client has not completed homework to help him/her consolidate his/her coping skills and was redirected to do so.

18. Use Parent Management Training (18)

A. Parent Management Training was used, as developed in *Living with Children* (Patterson).

B. The parents were directed to read *Parenting the Strong-Willed Child* (Forehand and Long).

C. The parents were taught how parent and child behavioral interactions can encourage or discourage positive or negative behavior.

D. The parents were taught about how changing key elements of parent-child interactions can be used to promote positive change.

E. The parents were provided with specific examples of how prompting and reinforcing positive behaviors can be used to promote positive change.

F. The parents were provided with positive feedback for the use of Parent Management Training approaches.

G. The parents have not used the Parent Management Training approach and were redirected to do so.

19. Teach Parents to Define Aspects of Situation (19)

A. The parents were taught how to specifically define and identify their child's problem behaviors.

B. The parents were taught how to identify their reactions to their child's behavior and whether the reaction encourages or discourages the behavior.

C. The parents were taught to generate alternative reactions to their child's problem behavior.

D. Positive feedback was provided to the parents for their skill at specifically defining and identifying problem behaviors, reactions, outcomes, and alternatives.

E. Parents were provided with remedial feedback as they struggled to correctly identify their child's problem behaviors, and their own reactions, responses, and alternatives.

20. Teach Consistent Parenting (20)

A. The parents were taught about how to implement key parenting practices on a consistent basis.

B. The parents were taught about establishing realistic, age-appropriate roles for their child's acceptable and unacceptable behavior.

C. "Switching from Defense to Offense" from the *Adolescent Psychotherapy Homework Planner*, 2nd ed. (Jongsma, Peterson, and McInnis) was assigned to the parents to help teach them key parenting practices.

D. The parents were taught about prompting positive behavior and use of positive reinforcement.

E. The parents were taught about clear direct instruction, time out, and other loss-of-privilege techniques for their child's problem behaviors.

F. The parents were provided with positive feedback, as they have been able to develop consistent parenting practices.

G. The parents have not developed consistent parenting practices and were redirected to do so.

21. Assign Home Exercises to Implement Parenting Techniques (21)

A. The parents were assigned home exercises in which they implement parenting techniques and record results of the implementation exercises.

B. The parents were assigned "Clear Rules, Positive Reinforcement, Appropriate Consequences" in the *Adolescent Psychotherapy Homework Planner*, 2nd ed. (Jongsma, Peterson, and McInnis).

C. The parents' implementation of homework exercises was reviewed within the session.

D. Corrective feedback was used to help develop improved, appropriate, and consistent use of skills.

E. The parents have not completed the assigned homework and were redirected to do so.

22. Assign Parent Training Manuals (22)

A. The parents were directed to read parent training manuals.

B. The parents were directed to read *Parenting Through Change* (Forgatch).

C. The parents were directed to watch videotapes demonstrating the techniques used in parent training sessions.

D. The parents' study of pertinent parent training media was reviewed and processed.

E. The parents have not reviewed the assigned pertinent parent training media and were redirected to do so.

23. Track Hostility and Problem-Solve Solutions (23)

A. The frequency and intensity of the negative, hostile feelings and defiant behaviors were tracked.

B. Problem-solving techniques were developed to help solve the frequency and intensity of the negative, hostile feelings and defiant behaviors.

C. "Stop Yelling" from the *Adolescent Psychotherapy Homework Planner,* 2nd ed. (Jongsma, Peterson, and McInnis) was assigned to the client to help him/her track and problem-solve feelings and behaviors related to anger.

D. "Filing a Complaint" from the *Adolescent Psychotherapy Homework Planner,* 2nd ed. (Jongsma, Peterson, and McInnis) was assigned to the client to help him/her track and problem-solve feelings and behaviors related to anger.

E. A specific plan was developed to help decrease the frequency and intensity of the client's negative, hostile feelings and defiant behaviors.

24. Teach Reciprocity (24)

A. The client was taught about the principle of reciprocity and how this applies to relationships.

B. The client was asked to conduct an experiment in which he/she agrees to treat everyone in a respectful manner for a 1-week period to see if others will reciprocate by treating him/her with more respect.

C. The client was assisted in tracking the results of his/her experiment in respect.

D. The client was assisted in problem-solving issues with respect to help increase the frequency of respectful interactions.

E. It was reflected to the client that he/she has increased his/her pattern of respectful interactions.

F. The client has not increased his/her pattern of respectful interactions and this was reflected to him/her.

25. Play Therapeutic Game (25)

A. The Thinking, Feeling, and Doing Game (Gardner) was played with the client, during which he/she had numerous opportunities to express his/her feelings appropriately.

B. Playing The Thinking, Feeling, and Doing Game with the client has given him/her the opportunity to experiment with recognizing and expressing feelings.

C. It was reflected to the client that he/she has become more free to express his/her feelings in a respectful manner.

26. Videotape Destructive Interaction Patterns (26)

A. Videotaping was utilized in family sessions to help identify destructive patterns of interaction within the family.

B. The family was assisted in identifying destructive interaction patterns from viewing the video of a session and developing new, respectful interactions through role-play, role rehearsal, and modeling.

C. The family members reported an increase in respectful interaction between them and an increase in sensitivity to the pattern of disrespectful interaction that has been so prevalent in the past; they were encouraged for this progress.

27. Teach Respectful Expression of Feelings (27)

A. The client was taught how to recognize and express his/her needs and feelings in a constructive, respectful way.

B. The client was assisted in identifying how his/her needs and wants are connected to his/her behavior.

C. The client was asked to practice expressing his/her needs and feelings to the therapist in a constructive, respectful way.

D. The client was reminded of how his/her disrespectful manner of expressing feelings and wants had a negative impact on self and others.

E. The client and parents reported that the client is expressing his/her feelings and opinions in a more respectful manner; he/she was strongly praised for this success.

28. Reframe Complaints (28)

A. The client was assisted in reframing complaints into requests for positive change.

B. The client was asked to complete the "Filing a Complaint" exercise from the *Adolescent Psychotherapy Homework Planner,* 2nd ed. (Jongsma, Peterson, and McInnis) to assist him/her in reframing complaints into requests.

C. The client was asked to complete the "If I Could Run My Family" exercise from the *Adolescent Psychotherapy Homework Planner,* 2nd ed. (Jongsma, Peterson, and McInnis).

D. The client was asked to identify the pros and cons of complaints versus requests, focusing on which is more respectful.

E. The client's past pattern of disrespectful interactions was reviewed and negative results were reinforced.

F. The client reported several instances of switching from making complaints to making requests of others around him/her and the positive results from this change were highlighted.

G. The client has not completed the "Filing a Complaint" exercise and was redirected to do so.

29. Expose Parental Conflict (29)

A. In family sessions, conflict between the parents was uncovered and the parents made a commitment to work conjointly on resolving the conflict.

B. The parents were confronted in family sessions about the conflicts present between them and shown the role it plays in the client's oppositional behavior.

C. The parents worked in conjoint sessions to resolve the underlying conflicts in their marriage.

30. Utilize Family System Approach (30)

A. A family system approach was utilized to identify family strengths and to use strengths to address areas of family dysfunction.

B. After normalizing dysfunction as a part of all families, the family was able to identify specific dysfunctions in their family and began to address them.

C. Although some dysfunction was normalized as a part of all families, the family was unable to identify specific dysfunctions in their family.

31. Assess Family Interaction Patterns (31)

A. In family sessions, family interaction patterns were analyzed to locate points for a possible intervention.

B. The analysis of interaction patterns was utilized to determine which intervention could be most appropriate for this family.

C. The experiential/strategic/structural intervention was implemented and embraced by the family, with a commitment to follow through with what was prescribed.

32. Sculpt Family (32)

A. A family sculpture was created to depict the family as they are, followed by another sculpture as they would like to be.

B. The family was cooperative in sculpting themselves as they are but were unable to sculpt themselves in terms of how they would like to be.

33. Identify Alternative Interventions for Positive Parenting (33)

A. The parents were assisted in identifying alternative interventions that focus on positive parenting.

B. The parents were asked to complete the "Switching from Defense to Offense" exercise from the *Adolescent Psychotherapy Homework Planner,* 2nd ed. (Jongsma, Peterson, and McInnis) to help explore and establish new ways of intervening with the client.

C. New methods identified by the parents in the switching strategies exercise were refined and plans for implementation made.

D. Role-play was utilized with the parents to increase their confidence and to work out any bugs in the new intervention techniques.

E. The parents are responding positively to their switch of parenting strategies from defensive to offensive, and the client's oppositional behaviors have diminished; positive feedback was provided.

F. The parents have not identified and used alternative interventions for positive parenting and were redirected to do so.

34. Monitor Progress (34)

A. The parents' progress in using new methods of intervention was monitored on a regular basis.

B. The parents were provided with feedback about their changing methods of intervention with the client's behaviors, with a focus on positive parenting.

C. The parents were supported to continue their use of positive parenting.

D. The parents were reinforced for their use of positive parenting.

35. Institute Positive Consequences (35)

A. The client's parents and teachers were worked with to develop positive consequences to administer when the client exhibits negative behavior.

B. The implementation of positive consequences has helped to reduce the client's oppositional behavior.

C. The client's parents and teachers have developed and used positive consequences to help reduce the client's oppositional behavior, but he/she continues to display oppositional behavior; they were encouraged to continue the use of positive consequences.

36. Teach Barkley Method (36)

A. The parents were asked to view Barkley videos or read *Your Defiant Child* (Barkley and Benton) to gain an understanding of the Barkley approach.

B. The parents were asked to make a commitment to pursue this approach or not.

C. The family was assessed for having the strength and commitment to implement and follow through with the Barkley method.

37. Explore Out-of-Home Placement (37)

A. Out-of-home placement options for the client were presented and explored with the parents.

B. The parents were assisted in reaching the decision to pursue out-of-home placement for the client.

C. The parents were confronted about their unrealistic expectations of keeping the teen in their home.

38. Present Legal Emancipation Option (38)

A. The parents were directed to seek legal counsel to explore the option of emancipating the client.

B. Information gathered from their attorney was processed and the parents reached the decision to emancipate the client.

C. The family was asked to identify how postponing this emancipation decision would affect the parents and other siblings.

39. Support Decision to Emancipate Client (39)

A. Past client behaviors and the parents' ineffective interventions were reviewed as a means of supporting the parents' decision to emancipate the client.

B. Feelings of guilt, loss, abandonment, and failure were processed in the wake of parents' emancipation decision.

PANIC/AGORAPHOBIA

CLIENT PRESENTATION

1. Severe Panic Symptoms (1)*

A. The client has experienced sudden and unexpected severe panic symptoms that have occurred repeatedly and have resulted in persistent concerns about additional attacks.

B. The client has significantly modified his/her normal behavior patterns in an effort to avoid panic attacks.

C. The frequency and severity of the panic attacks have diminished significantly.

D. The client reported that he/she has not experienced any recent panic attack symptoms.

2. Fear of Environmental Situations Triggering Anxiety (2)

A. The client described fear of environmental situations that he/she believes may trigger intense anxiety symptoms.

B. The client's fear of environmental situations has resulted in his/her avoidance behavior directed toward those environmental situations.

C. The client has a significant fear of leaving home and being in open or crowded public situations.

D. The client's phobic fear has diminished and he/she has left the home environment without being crippled by anxiety.

E. The client is able to leave home normally and function within public environments.

3. Recognition That Fear Is Unreasonable (3)

A. The client's phobic fear has persisted in spite of the fact that he/she acknowledges that the fear is unreasonable.

B. The client has made many attempts to ignore or overcome his/her unreasonable fear, but has been unsuccessful.

4. Increasing Isolation (4)

A. The client described situations in which he/she has declined involvement with others due to a fear of traveling or leaving a "safe environment" such as his/her home.

B. The client reported that he/she has become increasingly isolated due to his/her fear of traveling or leaving a "safe environment."

C. The client has severely constricted his/her involvement with others.

D. Although the client experiences some symptoms of panic, he/she now feels capable of leaving home.

E. The client has been able to leave his/her "safe zone" on a regular basis.

---

*The numbers in parentheses correlate to the number of the Behavioral Definition statement in the companion chapter with the same title in *The Adolescent Psychotherapy Treatment Planner,* Fourth Edition (Jongsma, Peterson, McInnis, and Bruce) by John Wiley & Sons, 2006.

5. Avoids Public Places and Large Groups (5)

A. The client avoids public places, such as malls or large stores.

B. The client avoids large groups of people.

C. The client has constricted his/her involvement with others in order to avoid social situations.

D. The client has begun to reach out socially and feels more comfortable in public places or with large groups of people.

E. The client reported enjoying involvement with large groups of people and feels comfortable going to public places.

INTERVENTIONS IMPLEMENTED

1. Assess Nature of Panic Symptoms (1)*

A. The client was asked about the frequency, intensity, duration, and history of his/her panic symptoms, fear, and avoidance.

B. *The Anxiety Disorder's Interview Schedule for DSM-IV* (DiNardo, Brown, and Barlow) was used to assess the client's panic symptoms.

C. "Panic Survey" from the *Adolescent Psychotherapy Homework Planner,* 2nd ed. (Jongsma, Peterson, and McInnis) was used to help access the frequency, intensity, duration, and history of the client's panic symptoms, fear, and avoidance.

D. The assessment of the client's panic symptoms indicates that his/her symptoms are extreme and severely interfere with his/her life.

E. The assessment of the client's panic symptoms indicates that these symptoms are moderate and occasionally interfere with his/her daily functioning.

F. The results of the assessment of the client's panic symptoms indicate that these symptoms are mild and rarely interfere with his/her daily functioning.

G. The results of the assessment of the client's panic symptoms were reviewed with the client.

2. Assess Panic Precipitators (2)

A. The nature of stimuli, thoughts, or situations that precipitate the client's panic were assessed.

B. The client was assisted in identifying the particular stimuli, thoughts, or situations that precipitate his/her panic.

C. The client was reinforced for his/her insightful identification of the precipitators for his/her panic.

D. The client struggled to identify the stimuli, thoughts, or situations that precipitate his/her panic and was provided with tentative examples of these precipitators.

3. Administer Assessments for Agoraphobia Symptoms (3)

A. The client was administered psychological instruments designed to objectively assess his/her level of Agoraphobia symptoms.

---

*The numbers in parentheses correlate to the number of the Therapeutic Intervention statement in the companion chapter with the same title in *The Adolescent Psychotherapy Treatment Planner,* Fourth Edition (Jongsma, Peterson, McInnis, and Bruce) by John Wiley & Sons, 2006.

B. The client was administered *The Mobility Inventory for Agoraphobia* (Chambless, Coputo, and Gracely).

C. The client was provided with feedback regarding the results of the assessment of his/her level of Agoraphobia symptoms.

D. The client declined to participate in the objective assessment of his/her level of Agoraphobia symptoms and this resistance was processed.

4. Administer Assessments for Anxiety Symptoms (4)

A. The client was administered psychological instruments designed to objectively assess his/her level of anxiety symptoms.

B. The client was administered *The Anxiety Sensitivity Index* (Reiss, Peterson, and Gursky)

C. The client was provided with feedback regarding the results of the assessment of his/her level of anxiety symptoms.

D. The client declined to participate in the objective assessment of his/her level of anxiety symptoms and this resistance was processed.

5. Refer for Medication Evaluation (5)

A. Arrangements were made for the client to have a physician evaluation for the purpose of considering psychotropic medication to alleviate phobic symptoms.

B. The client has followed through with seeing a physician for an evaluation of any organic causes for the anxiety and the need for psychotropic medication to control the anxiety response.

C. The client has not cooperated with the referral to a physician for a medication evaluation and was encouraged to do so.

6. Monitor Medication Compliance (6)

A. The client reported that he/she has taken the prescribed medication consistently and that it has helped to control the phobic anxiety; this was relayed to the prescribing clinician.

B. The client reported that he/she has not taken the prescribed medication consistently and was encouraged to do so.

C. The client reported taking the prescribed medication and stated that he/she has not noted any beneficial effect from it; this was reflected to the prescribing clinician.

D. The client was evaluated but was not prescribed any psychotropic medication by the physician.

7. Discuss Nature of Panic Symptoms (7)

A. A discussion was held about how panic attacks are "false alarms" of danger and are not medically dangerous.

B. A discussion was held about how panic attacks are not a sign of weakness or craziness.

C. The client's panic attacks were discussed, including how they are a common symptom, but can lead to unnecessary avoidance, thereby reinforcing the panic attack.

8. Assign Information on Panic Disorders and Agoraphobia (8)

A. The client was assigned to read psychoeducational chapters of books or treatment manuals about panic disorders and Agoraphobia.

B. The client was assigned specific chapters from *Mastery of Your Anxiety and Panic* (Barlow and Craske).

C. The client was assigned to read chapters from *Don't Panic: Taking Control of Anxiety Attacks* (Wilson).

D. The client has read the assigned information on panic disorders and Agoraphobia and key points were discussed.

E. The client has not read the assigned information on panic disorders and Agoraphobia and was redirected to do so.

9. Discuss Benefits of Exposure (9)

A. The client was taught about how exposure can serve as an arena to desensitize learned fear, build confidence, and create success experiences.

B. A discussion was held about the use of exposure to decrease fear, build confidence, and feel safer.

C. The client was reinforced as he/she indicated a clear understanding of how exposure can help to conquer panic and Agoraphobia symptoms.

D. The client did not display an understanding about how exposure can help overcome his/her Agoraphobia and panic symptoms and was provided with remedial feedback in this area.

10. Assign Reading on Exposure (10)

A. The client was assigned to read about exposure in books or treatment manuals on social anxiety.

B. The client was assigned to read excerpts from *Mastery of Your Anxiety and Panic* (Barlow and Craske).

C. The client was assigned portions of *Living with Fear* (Marks)

D. The client's information about exposure was reviewed and processed.

E. The client has not read the information on exposure and was redirected to do so.

11. Teach Anxiety Management Skills (11)

A. The client was taught anxiety management skills.

B. The client was taught about staying focused on behavioral goals and riding the wave of anxiety.

C. Techniques for muscular relaxation and paced diaphragmatic breathing were taught to the client.

D. The client was reinforced for his/her clear understanding and use of anxiety management skills.

E. The client has not used his/her new anxiety management skills and was redirected to do so.

12. Urge External Focus (12)

A. The client was urged to keep his/her focus on external stimuli and behavioral responsibilities rather than being preoccupied with internal states and physiological changes.

B. The client was reinforced as he/she has made a commitment to not allow panic symptoms to take control of his/her life and to not avoid and escape normal responsibilities and activities.

C. The client has been successful at turning his/her focus away from internal anxiety states and toward behavioral responsibilities; he/she was reinforced for this progress.

D. The client has not maintained an external focus in order to keep panic symptoms from taking control of his/her life and was reminded about this helpful technique.

13. Assign Information on Breathing and Relaxation (13)

A. The client was assigned to read information about progressive muscle relaxation.

B. The client was assigned information on paced diaphragmatic breathing.

C. The client was directed to read portions of *Mastery of Your Anxiety and Panic* (Barlow and Craske).

D. The client has read the assigned information on progressive muscle relaxation and paced diaphragmatic breathing and his/her key learnings were reviewed.

E. The client has not read the assigned information on progressive muscle relaxation and pace diaphragmatic breathing and was redirected to do so.

14. Counteract Panic Myths (14)

A. The client was consistently reassured of the fact that there is no connection between panic symptoms and heart attack, loss of control over behavior, or serious mental illness.

B. The client was reinforced as he/she verbalized an understanding that panic symptoms do not promote serious physical or mental illness.

15. Utilize Modeling/Behavioral Rehearsal (15)

A. Modeling and behavioral rehearsal were used to train the client in positive self-talk that reassured him/her of the ability to work through and endure anxiety symptoms without serious consequences.

B. The client has implemented positive self-talk to reassure himself/herself of the ability to endure anxiety without serious consequences; he/she was reinforced for this progress.

C. The client has not used positive self-talk to help endure anxiety and was provided with additional direction in this area.

16. Identify Distorted Thoughts (16)

A. The client was assisted in identifying the distorted schemas and related automatic thoughts that mediate anxiety responses.

B. The client was taught the role of distorted thinking in precipitating emotional responses.

C. The client was reinforced as he/she verbalized an understanding of the cognitive beliefs and messages that mediate his/her anxiety responses.

D. The client was assisted in replacing distorted messages with positive, realistic cognitions.

E. The client failed to identify his/her distorted thoughts and cognitions and was provided with tentative examples in this area.

17. Assign Reading Materials (17)

A. The client was assigned to read psychoeducational chapters of books or treatment manuals on the cognitive restructuring.

B. The client was assigned to read psychoeducational chapters of books or treatment manuals for the rationale for cognitive restructuring for panic/Agoraphobia.

C. The client was assigned information from *Mastery of Your Anxiety and Panic* (Barlow and Craske).

D. The client has read the assigned material on cognitive restructuring; key points were reviewed.

E. The client has not read the assigned information on the rationale for panic/Agoraphobia treatment and was redirected to do so.

18. Assign Exercises on Self-Talk (18)

A. The client was assigned homework exercises in which he/she identifies fearful self-talk and creates reality-based alternatives.

B. The client was assigned the homework exercise "Bad Thoughts Lead to Depressed Feelings" from the *Adolescent Psychotherapy Homework Planner*, 2nd ed. (Jongsma, Peterson, and McInnis).

C. The client was directed to do assignments from *10 Simple Solutions to Panic* (Antony and McCabe).

D. The client was directed to complete assignments from *Mastery of Your Anxiety and Panic* (Barlow and Craske).

E. The client was reinforced for his/her successes at replacing fearful self-talk with reality-based alternatives.

F. The client was provided with corrective feedback for his/her failures to replace fearful self-talk with reality-based alternatives.

G. The client has not completed his/her assigned homework regarding fearful self-talk and was redirected to do so.

19. Teach Sensation Exposure Technique (19)

A. The client was taught about sensation exposure techniques.

B. The client was taught about generating feared physical sensations through exercise (e.g., breathing rapidly until slightly light-headed) and the use of coping strategies to keep himself/herself calm.

C. The client was assigned information about sensation exposure techniques in *10 Simple Solutions to Panic* (Antony and McCabe).

D. The client was assigned information about sensation exposure techniques in *Mastery of Your Anxiety and Panic—Therapist's Guide* (Craske, Barlow, and Meadows).

E. The client displayed a clear understanding of the sensation exposure technique and was reinforced for his/her understanding.

F. The client struggled to understand the sensation exposure technique and was provided with remedial feedback.

20. Assign Material on Sensation Exposure

A. The client was assigned to read about sensation (interceptive) exposure in books or treatment manuals on Panic Disorder and Agoraphobia.

B. The client was assigned to read *Mastery of Your Anxiety and Panic* (Barlow and Craske).

C. The client was asked to read *10 Simple Solutions to Panic* (Antony and McCabe).

D. The client has read the assigned information on the sensation exposure technique and was reinforced for his/her understanding of these concepts.

E. The client does not display an understanding of the sensation exposure technique and was provided with remedial feedback in this area.

21. Assign Homework on Sensation Exposure (21)

A. The client was assigned homework exercises to perform sensation exposure and record his/her experience.

B. The client was assigned sensation exposure homework from *Mastery of Your Anxiety and Panic* (Barlow and Craske).

C. The client was assigned sensation exposure homework from *10 Simple Solutions to Panic* (Antony and McCabe).

D. The "Panic Attack Rating Form" from the *Adolescent Psychotherapy Homework Planner*, 2nd ed. (Jongsma, Peterson, and McInnis) was used to help record the client's experiences of anxiety during sensation exposure.

E. The client's use of sensation exposure techniques was reviewed and reinforced.

F. The client has struggled in his/her implementation of sensation exposure techniques and was provided with corrective feedback.

G. The client has not attempted to use the sensation exposure techniques and was redirected to do so.

22. Construct Anxiety Stimuli Hierarchy (22)

A. The client was assisted in constructing a hierarchy of anxiety-producing situations associated with two or three spheres of worry.

B. It was difficult for the client to develop a hierarchy of stimulus situations, as the causes of his/her anxiety remains quite vague; he/she was assisted in completing the hierarchy.

C. The client was successful at creating a focused hierarchy of specific stimulus situations that provoke anxiety in a gradually increasing manner; this hierarchy was reviewed.

23. Select Initial Exposures (23)

A. Initial exposures were selected from the hierarchy of anxiety-producing situations, with a bias toward likelihood of being successful.

B. A plan was developed with the client for managing the symptoms that may occur during the initial exposure.

C. The client was assisted in rehearsing the plan for managing the exposure-related symptoms within his/her imagination.

D. Positive feedback was provided for the client's helpful use of symptom management techniques.

E. The client was redirected for ways to improve his/her symptom management techniques.

24. Assign Information on Situational Exposure (24)

A. The client was assigned to read information about situational (exteroceptive) exposure in books or treatment manuals on Panic Disorder and Agoraphobia.

B. The client was assigned to read *Mastery of Your Anxiety and Panic* (Barlow and Craske).

C. The client was assigned to read *Living with Fear* (Marks).

D. The client has read the assigned information on situational exposure and his/her key learnings were reviewed.

E. The client has not read the assigned information on situational exposure and was redirected to do so.

25. Assign Homework on Situational Exposures (25)

A. The client was assigned homework exercises to perform situational exposures and record his/her experience.

B. The client was assigned "Gradually Facing a Phobic Fear" from the *Adolescent Psychotherapy Homework Planner,* 2nd ed. (Jongsma, Peterson, and McInnis).

C. The client was assigned situational exposures homework from *Mastery of Your Anxiety and Panic* (Barlow and Craske).

D. The client was assigned situational exposures homework from *10 Simple Solutions to Panic* (Antony and McCabe).

E. The client's use of situational exposure techniques was reviewed and reinforced.

F. The client has struggled in his/her implementation of situational exposure techniques and was provided with corrective feedback.

G. The client has not attempted to use the situational exposure techniques and was redirected to do so.

26. Differentiate between Lapse and Relapse (26)

A. A discussion was held with the client regarding the distinction between a lapse and a relapse.

B. A lapse was associated with an initial and reversible return of symptoms, fear, or urges to avoid.

C. A relapse was associated with the decision to return to fearful and avoidant patterns.

D. The client was provided with support and encouragement as he/she displayed an understanding of the difference between a lapse and a relapse.

E. The client struggled to understand the difference between a lapse and a relapse and was provided with remedial feedback in this area.

27. Discuss Management of Lapse Risk Situations (27)

A. The client was assisted in identifying future situations or circumstances in which lapses could occur.

B. The session focused on rehearsing the management of future situations or circumstances in which lapses could occur.

C. The client was reinforced for his/her appropriate use of lapse management skills.

D. The client was redirected in regard to his/her poor use of lapse management skills.

28. Encourage Routine Use of Strategies (28)

A. The client was instructed to routinely use the strategies that he/she has learned in therapy (e.g., cognitive restructuring, exposure).

B. The client was urged to find ways to build his/her new strategies into his/her life as much as possible.

C. The client was reinforced as he/she reported ways in which he/she has incorporated coping strategies into his/her life and routine.

D. The client was redirected about ways to incorporate his/her new strategies into his/her routine and life.

29. Develop a "Coping Card" (29)

A. The client was provided with a "coping card" on which specific coping strategies were listed.

B. The client was assisted in developing his/her "coping card" in order to list his/her helpful coping strategies.

C. The client was encouraged to use his/her "coping card" when struggling with anxiety-producing situations.

30. Explore Secondary Gain (30)

A. Secondary gain was identified for the client's panic symptoms because of his/her tendency to escape or avoid certain situations.

B. The client denied any role for secondary gain that results from his/her modification of life to accommodate panic; he/she was provided with tentative examples.

C. The client was reinforced for accepting the role of secondary gain in promoting and maintaining the panic symptoms and encouraged to overcome this gain through living a more normal life.

31. Differentiate Current Fear from Past Pain (31)

A. The client was taught to verbalize the separate realities of the current fear and the emotionally painful experience from the past that has been evoked by the phobic stimulus.

B. The client was reinforced when he/she expressed insight into the unresolved fear from the past that is linked to his/her current phobic fear.

C. The irrational nature of the client's current phobic fear was emphasized and clarified.

D. The client's unresolved emotional issue from the past was clarified.

32. Encourage Sharing of Feelings (32)

A. The client was encouraged to share the emotionally painful experience from the past that has been evoked by the phobic stimulus.

B. The client was taught to separate the realities of the irrationally feared object or situation and the painful experience from his/her past.

33. Reinforce Responsibility Acceptance (33)

A. The client was supported and reinforced for following through with work, family, and social responsibilities rather than using escape and avoidance to focus on panic symptoms.

B. The client reported performing responsibilities more consistently and being less preoccupied with panic symptoms or fear that panic symptoms might occur; his/her progress was highlighted.

34. Schedule "Maintenance Sessions" (34)

A. "Maintenance sessions" were proposed to help maintain therapeutic gains and adjust to life without panic symptoms or fear.

B. The client was reinforced for agreeing to the scheduling of "maintenance sessions."

C. The client refused to schedule "maintenance sessions" and this was processed.

PARENTING

CLIENT PRESENTATION

1. Poor Communication (1)*

A. The parents complained of a lack of communication with their teenager.

B. Communication with the teenager remains on a superficial level only.

C. The parents cited instances of improved communication with their teenager.

D. The parents reported being pleased with the amount and quality of communication with their teenager.

2. Ineffective Limit Setting (2)

A. The parents described that their attempts to set age-appropriate and effective limits for their teen have been ineffective (i.e., efforts do not result in the desired outcomes).

B. As treatment has progressed, more effective techniques for setting limits were developed and implemented by the parents.

C. The parents described increased efficacy of their attempts to set age-appropriate and effective limits for their teenager.

3. Loss of Connection from Parents Due to Peer Group (3)

A. The parents reported that their teenager's involvement with a peer group has excluded the teen from other family members.

B. The parents reported feeling stressed that their teenager has chosen his/her peer group over involvement with the parents and other family members.

C. The teenager identified his/her preference of his/her peer group to the exclusion of his/her parents and other family members.

D. The parents reported that their teenager has increased involvement with the family and decreased involvement with his/her peer group.

4. Conflict Regarding Parenting Strategies (4)

A. The parents described a lack of agreement regarding strategies for dealing with various types of negative adolescent behaviors.

B. One partner advocates for stricter control, while the other partner endorses a more permissive approach.

C. The adolescent's behavior seems to be unaffected by the parents' variable pattern of disciplinary response.

D. The adolescent's behavior is more out of control due to the parent's lack of agreement regarding limit setting.

E. As communication has increased, the parents have gained an agreement regarding strategies for dealing with various types of negative adolescent behavior.

---

*The numbers in parentheses correlate to the number of the Behavioral Definition statement in the companion chapter with the same title in *The Adolescent Psychotherapy Treatment Planner,* Fourth Edition (Jongsma, Peterson, McInnis, and Bruce) by John Wiley & Sons, 2006.

5. Harsh, Rigid, and Demeaning Behavior (5)

A. The parents often treat the adolescent in a rather harsh manner.

B. The parents are quite rigid in their rules and expectations for the teenager's behavior.

C. The parents act in a demeaning way toward their child.

D. As treatment has progressed, the parents have become more supportive and encouraging toward the child.

6. Physical/Emotional Abuse (6)

A. The teenager has reported that his/her parents have been physically or emotionally abusive.

B. The teenager's report of physical/emotional abuse has been confirmed through independent sources.

C. The parents provided a detailed account of the physical/emotional abuse of the teen.

D. The reports of physical abuse have been referred to Children's Protective Services as required by mandatory reporting statutes.

E. The parents have ceased all physical and emotional abuse.

7. Overindulgent versus Harsh (7)

A. One parent seems to advocate for a more permissive discipline style, while the other partner endorses stricter control.

B. The teenager identified one parent as being overindulgent and the other parent as too harsh.

C. Each parent's more extreme style seems to prompt the opposite extreme style in the other parent (i.e., the overindulgent parent becomes even more extreme due to seeing the other parent as too harsh, and vice versa).

D. As the parents have achieved insight into the effects of their divergent pattern of parenting, they have become more balanced in their approach.

8. Emotional Reactions to Misbehavior (8)

A. The parents often struggle to control their emotional reactions to their child's misbehavior.

B. The parents tend to have extreme emotional reactions to their child's misbehavior.

C. The parents' extreme emotional reactions to their child's misbehavior tend to prompt further misbehavior.

D. As the parents have gained control over their emotional reactions to their child's misbehavior, they have become more effective in their parenting strategies.

E. The parents regularly control their emotional reactions to their child's misbehavior.

9. Outside Requests for Addressing Behavior (9)

A. School officials, court authorities, and/or friends have told the parents that their teenager's behavior needs to be addressed.

B. The parents seem to disregard outside requests for addressing their teenager's behavior.

C. The parents have been motivated by outside requests for addressing their teenager's behavior.

D. Outside sources identify that the teenager's behavior has improved.

10. Opposition Toward Rules/Limit Setting (10)

A. The teenager has become strongly oppositional toward any rule or limit setting.

B. The teenager often disregards rules and limits.

C. As the parents have become more stable in their rules and limit setting, the teenager's oppositional manner has decreased.

D. The teenager is willing to accept the rules and limits.

11. Lack of Knowledge Regarding Developmental Expectations (11)

A. The client reported a lack of knowledge regarding reasonable expectations for a child's behavior at a given developmental level.

B. The client often makes comments reflecting an unreasonable expectation for a child's behavior at a given developmental level.

C. As treatment has progressed, the client has developed more realistic expectations for a child's behavior at a given developmental level.

INTERVENTIONS IMPLEMENTED

1. Engage Parents (1)*

A. Active-listening techniques were used to establish a basis for a trust relationship with the parents.

B. The parents' struggles with parenting were normalized.

C. Information was gathered on the parent's marital relationship, child behavior expectations, and parenting style.

D. The parents appeared to place trust in the therapeutic relationship and were encouraged to provide full information.

2. Assess Marital Conflicts (2)

A. The information received from the parents about their relationship and parenting style was analyzed to assess the presence of marital conflict.

B. It was reflected to the parents that they are experiencing significant marital conflicts, which need to be resolved in order to address the parenting issues.

C. It was reflected to the parents that their marriage appears to be strong and able to cope with the changes that may need to be made in order to become more effective parents.

3. Conduct/Refer for Marital Therapy (3)

A. The parents were referred for marital/relationship therapy in order to resolve the conflicts preventing them from being effective parents.

B. The focus of treatment was shifted to the parents' marital/relationship concerns and the need to resolve the conflicts preventing them from being effective parents.

C. Through the use of marital therapy, the parents have been able to resolve the conflicts preventing them from being more effective parents.

---

*The numbers in parentheses correlate to the number of the Therapeutic Intervention statement in the companion chapter with the same title in *The Adolescent Psychotherapy Treatment Planner,* Fourth Edition (Jongsma, Peterson, McInnis, and Bruce) by John Wiley & Sons, 2006.

D. Despite the use of marital therapy, the parents continue to have conflict and were urged to resolve these in order to become more effective parents.

4. Administer Testing Instruments (4)

A. The parents were directed to complete an objective assessment of their parenting status.

B. The parents were administered the Parenting Stress Index (PSI).

C. The parents were administered the Parent-Child Relationship Inventory (PCRI).

D. The parents have not completed the objective testing instruments and were redirected to do so.

5. Share Assessment Results (5)

A. The results of the objective parenting assessment instruments were shared with the parents.

B. The parents were assisted in identifying issues to begin working on to strengthen the parenting team, based on the results of the assessment instruments.

C. The parents were positively reinforced as they identified issues they need to work on.

D. The parents denied needing to work on any issues to strengthen the parenting team, despite the results of the assessment instruments, and were urged to reconsider this.

6. Identify Parental Strengths (6)

A. The results of the parenting status tests were used to identify parental strengths.

B. The parents were assigned "Evaluating the Strength of Your Parenting Team" from the *Adolescent Psychotherapy Homework Planner,* 2nd ed. (Jongsma, Peterson, and McInnis).

C. The parental strengths were emphasized to the parents in order help build confidence and effectiveness.

D. As a result of the information from the assessments, the parents have increased their confidence and are more effective as a parenting team.

7. Create a Compassionate Environment (7)

A. Empathetic listening, compassion, and support were provided to help the parents become more comfortable in the therapeutic setting.

B. The parents were urged to express the frustrations of parenting.

C. As the parents let their guards down and expressed the frustrations of parenting, they were provided with support and encouragement.

D. Despite a compassionate, empathetic environment, the parents have not been willing to express the frustrations of parenting, and were redirected in this area.

8. Utilize Humor and Normalization (8)

A. Humor was injected into sessions when appropriate to help educate the parents on the full scope of parenting to provide balance and perspective.

B. The parents were encouraged to use humor with each other to help express feelings of frustration, helplessness, and inadequacy that each experiences in the parenting role.

C. The parents' experiences were normalized.

D. Positive feedback was given to the parents as they have used appropriate humor and normalized their own experiences.

E. The parents have had extreme difficulty being humorous toward one another as tension levels are high and were encouraged to help each other use this release to express feelings.

9. Reduce Unrealistic Expectations (9)

A. The parents were assisted in reducing unrealistic expectations of themselves and of their child.

B. The parents were reinforced as they identified some of their unrealistic expectations, both for themselves and for their child.

C. The parents were confronted when they continued to have unrealistic expectations of themselves and their child.

D. The parents were unable to identify their own unrealistic expectations of themselves and their child and were provided with tentative examples in this area.

10. Explore Parents' Unresolved Issues (10)

A. Both parents were asked to describe the stories of their childhoods.

B. Each parent's story of childhood and adolescence was reviewed for unresolved issues that might be present.

C. The parents were assisted in identifying any unresolved issues from their own childhoods.

D. The parents were provided with tentative examples of the unresolved issues they may be experiencing.

E. The parents were assisted in identifying how unresolved adolescent issues from their own pasts are affecting their abilities to effectively parent in the present.

F. Active-listening skills were used as the parents described specific ways in which their unresolved adolescent issues are affecting their abilities to effectively parent.

G. The parents denied any connection between unresolved adolescent issues and their abilities to effectively parent and were provided with specific examples of how these two areas interact.

11. Work Through Parents' Issues (11)

A. The parents were assisted in working through their unresolved childhood issues.

B. The parents were supported as they worked through their childhood issues and the benefits of their healthier functioning were emphasized.

C. The parents have declined to work through childhood issues and were urged to do this when they are able.

12. Evaluate Reactivity (12)

A. The parents' level of reactivity to the client's behavior was evaluated.

B. The parents were assisted in identifying situations in which they have been reactive to the child's misbehavior.

C. The parents were assisted in learning how to respond in a more modulated, thoughtful, planned manner.

D. As treatment has progressed, the parents have become less reactive to the child's behavior and have responded in a more modulated, thoughtful, planned manner; the benefits of these interactions were identified.

E. The parents continue to respond to the child's behavior in a reactive manner and were provided with remedial feedback in this area.

13. Identify Hot Buttons (13)

A. The parents were assisted in becoming aware of the hot buttons they have that the child can push to get a quick negative response.

B. The parents were assisted in identifying how their overreaction to hot button issues reduces their effectiveness as parents.

C. The parents identified several hot buttons and these were processed.

D. As treatment has progressed, the parents have decreased their overreacting pattern of response and these changes were processed.

E. The parents denied any hot buttons and were provided with tentative examples in this area.

14. Role-Play Thoughtful Responses (14)

A. Role-play techniques were used with the parents to practice responding in a thoughtful manner during a reactive situation.

B. The parents were coached on how to replace automatic reactions with thoughtful responses to their child's demands or negative behaviors.

C. Positive feedback was provided as the parents displayed the ability to thoughtfully respond to their child's demands or negative behaviors.

15. Assign Material on Parenting a Challenging Child (15)

A. The parents were directed to read material about parenting methods suggested for the challenging child.

B. The parents were directed to read *The Challenging Child* (Greenspan).

C. The parents were asked to identify what type of difficult behavior pattern their child exhibits.

D. As the parents identified the type of difficult behavior pattern their child exhibits, they were encouraged to implement several of the parenting methods suggested for that type of child.

E. The parents were incorrectly identifying the type of difficult behavior pattern that their child exhibits and were provided with remedial direction in this area.

16. Expand Repertoire of Intervention Options (16)

A. The parents' repertoire of intervention options was expanded by having them read material on parenting difficult children.

B. The parents were directed to read *The Difficult Child* (Turecki and Tonner).

C. The parents were directed to read *The Explosive Child* (Greene).

D. The parents were directed to read *How to Handle a Hard-to-Handle Kid* (Edwards).

E. The parents have failed to follow through on reading material to help expand their repertoire of parenting intervention options and were redirected to complete this reading.

17. Facilitate New Parenting Strategies (17)

A. The parents were supported, encouraged, and empowered in the implementation of new strategies for parenting their adolescent.

B. Feedback and redirection were provided to the parents as they have been implementing new parenting strategies.

C. The parents were supported as they identified strategies that have been implemented and the outcomes of these new strategies were reviewed and processed.

18. Use Parent Management Training (10)

A. Parent Management Training was used, as developed in *Living with Children* (Patterson).

B. Techniques from *Parenting the Strong-Willed Child* (Forehand and Long) were assigned to the parents.

C. The parents were taught how parent and child behavioral interactions can encourage or discourage positive or negative behavior.

D. The parents were taught about how changing key elements of parent-child interactions can be used to promote positive change in the child's behavior.

E. The parents were provided with specific examples as to how prompting and reinforcing positive behaviors can be used to promote positive change in the child's behavior.

F. The parents were provided with positive feedback for the use of Parent Management Training approaches.

G. The parents have not used the Parent Management Training approach and were redirected to do so.

19. Teach Parents to Define Aspects of Situation (19)

A. The parents were taught how to specifically define and identify their child's problem behaviors.

B. The parents were taught how to specifically identify their reactions to their child's behavior and whether each reaction encourages or discourages the behavior.

C. The parents were taught to generate alternative reactions to their child's problem behavior.

D. Positive feedback was provided to the parents for their skill at specifically defining and identifying their child's problem behaviors and their own reactions, outcomes, and alternatives.

E. Parents were provided with remedial feedback as they struggled to correctly identify their child's problem behaviors and their own reactions, responses, and alternatives.

20. Teach Consistent Parenting (20)

A. The parents were taught about how to implement key parenting practices on a consistent basis.

B. The parents were taught about establishing realistic, age-appropriate roles for acceptable and unacceptable behavior.

C. The parents were taught about prompting their child's positive behavior and use of positive reinforcement.

D. The parents were taught about clear direct instruction, time out, and other loss-of-privilege techniques for their child's problem behavior.

E. The parents were taught about negotiation and renegotiation with adolescents.

F. The parents were provided with positive feedback as they have developed consistent parenting practices.

G. The parents have not developed consistent parenting practices and were redirected to do so.

21. **Assign Home Exercises to Implement Parenting Technique (21)**

A. The parents were assigned home exercises in which they implement parenting techniques and record results of the implementation exercises.

B. The parents were assigned "Clear Rules, Positive Reinforcement, Appropriate Consequences" in the *Adolescent Psychotherapy Homework Planner,* 2nd ed. (Jongsma, Peterson, and McInnis).

C. The parents' implementation of homework exercises was reviewed within the session.

D. Corrective feedback was used to help develop improved, appropriate, and consistent use of skills.

E. The parents have not completed the assigned homework and were redirected to do so.

22. **Assign Parent Training Manuals (22)**

A. The parents were directed to read parent training manuals.

B. The parents were directed to read *Parenting Through Change* (Forgatch).

C. The parents were directed to watch videotapes demonstrating the techniques used in parent training sessions.

D. The parents' study of pertinent media was reviewed and processed.

E. The parents have not reviewed the assigned pertinent media and were redirected to do so.

23. **Train in Effective Parenting Methods (23)**

A. The parents were trained in effective parenting methods (e.g., *1-2-3 Magic* by Phelan; *Parenting with Love and Logic* by Cline and Fay).

B. The parents were referred to structured training classes in effective parenting methods (e.g., *1-2-3 Magic* by Phelan; *Parenting with Love and Logic* by Cline and Fay).

C. The parents were reinforced for having completed the structured training in effective parenting methods and having greatly increased their skill, effectiveness, and confidence in parenting.

D. The parents have completed the structured training in effective parenting methods, but were noted to not feel confident in using this program, and therefore were provided with remedial assistance in this area.

E. The parents have not attended the structured training classes in effective parenting methods and were redirected to do so.

24. **Educate about Sex Differences (24)**

A. The parents were educated about the numerous key differences between boys and girls (e.g., rate of development, perspectives, impulse control, anger).

B. The parents were educated about how to handle the sex role differences in the parenting process.

C. The parents reported increased understanding of parenting issues related to a child's sex role; positive feedback was provided.

25. Complete "Parent Report Card" (25)

A. The children were requested to complete the "Parent Report Card" (Berg-Gross).

B. Feedback was provided to the parents based on the "Parent Report Card."

C. The parents were supported for areas of strength.

D. The parents were assisted in identifying parenting weaknesses that need to be bolstered.

26. Identify Weaknesses/Encourage Skills (26)

A. The parental team was assisted in identifying areas of parenting weakness.

B. The parents were assisted in improving their parenting skills and boosting their confidence and follow through.

C. It was reflected to the parents that their increased parenting skills have remediated their areas of weakness.

D. The parental team has not attempted to improve their skills in the identified areas of weakness and was redirected in this area.

27. Identify Support Barriers and Opportunities (27)

A. The parents were assisted in identifying and implementing specific ways that they can support each other as parents.

B. The parents were assigned "Evaluating the Strengths of Your Parenting Team" from the *Adolescent Psychotherapy Homework Planner,* 2nd ed. (Jongsma, Peterson, and McInnis).

C. The parents were assisted in realizing the ways children work to keep the parents from cooperating in order to get their way.

D. The parents were assisted in brainstorming how they can support each other when the children work to keep them from cooperating.

E. The parents failed to identify specific ways they can support each other and were provided with remedial feedback in this area.

28. Give Permission to Decrease Activities (28)

A. The parents were encouraged to decrease outside pressures by choosing not to involve their child and themselves in too numerous activities, organizations, or sports.

B. Feedback was given to the family on how their involvement in activities, organizations, or sports can drain energy and time from the family.

C. The parents were provided with positive feedback as they indicated a need to decrease outside pressures, demands, and distractions (e.g., activities, organizations, sports).

D. The parents were accepted for their decision to maintain the current level of activities, organizations, or support.

29. Evaluate the Family's Level of Activity (29)

A. The parents were asked to provide a weekly schedule of their entire family's activities.

B. The parents were assisted in evaluating their family schedule, looking for which activities are valuable and which can possibly be eliminated to create a more focused and relaxed time to parent.

C. The parents were provided with encouragement as they identified activities that can be eliminated to create a more focused and relaxed time to parent.

D. The parents struggled with identifying activities that are most valuable versus those that can possibly be eliminated and were provided with tentative examples in this area.

30. Teach Listening/Sharing Skills (30)

A. Modeling and role-play techniques were used to teach the parents to listen more than talk to their child.

B. The parents were taught to use open-ended questions that encourage openness, sharing, and ongoing dialogue.

C. The benefits of increased listening and helping the children to share more were reviewed.

31. Use Parent-Child Communication Materials (31)

A. The parents were asked to read material on parent-child communication.

B. The parents were directed to read *How to Talk So Kids Will Listen and Listen So Kids Will Talk* (Faber and Mazlish) or *Parent Effectiveness Training* (Gordon).

C. The parents have read the material on parent-child communication and were assisted in implementing the new communication style in daily dialogue with their children.

D. The parents were assisted in identifying the positive responses that the child has had to the new communication style.

E. The parents have not read the material on parent-child communication and were redirected to do so.

32. Identify Unreasonable Expectations (32)

A. The parents were assisted in identifying any unreasonable and perfectionistic expectations of their child's behavior.

B. The parents were assisted in modifying their unreasonable and perfectionistic expectations of their child's behavior to those that are appropriate and reasonable.

C. The parents have identified their unreasonable and perfectionistic expectations and modified these to more appropriate levels; the benefits of these changes were identified.

D. The parents denied any pattern of unreasonable and perfectionistic expectations and were urged to continue to consider this area.

33. Identify Negative Outcomes of Perfectionism (33)

A. The parents were assisted in identifying the negative consequences/outcomes that perfectionistic expectations have on a child.

B. The parents were assisted in identifying how perfectionistic expectations affect the relationship between the parents and the child.

C. The parents verbalized negative consequences/outcomes of perfectionistic expectations on their child and indicated that they would terminate this pattern; support and encouragement were provided in this area.

D. The parents were reluctant to admit to placing any perfectionistic expectations on their child and were provided with specific examples in this area.

34. Acknowledge Peer Influence (34)

A. The parents were provided with a balanced view about the influence of peers on adolescents.

B. Examples were provided regarding common ways in which peers influence adolescents.

C. Positive feedback was provided as the parents identified an increased awareness and understanding of peer issues regarding parenting adolescents.

D. The parents continued to downplay the importance of peers and their influence on adolescents and were provided with additional feedback in this area.

35. Teach about Turbulence (35)

A. The parents were taught the concept that adolescence is a time of "normal psychosis" (see *Turning Points* by Pittman).

B. The parents were encouraged to adopt the concept of "riding the adolescent rapids" (see *Preparing for Adolescence: How to Survive the Coming Years of Change* by Dobson), until both survive.

C. The parents were provided with encouragement as they displayed a healthy understanding of the turbulence related to the developmental stage of adolescence.

D. It was perceived that the parents continue to deny the experience of turbulence related to adolescence and were provided with additional feedback in this area.

36. Address Fears about Peers (36)

A. The parents were assisted in clarifying their feelings related to negative peer groups, negative peer influence, and fears about losing their influence or their adolescent to these groups.

B. The parents identified their emotional reactions to the influence of negative peer groups and were provided with support and affirmation.

C. The parents have developed a healthy response to their fears regarding negative peer groups, negative peer influences, and losing their influence to these groups.

D. The parents denied any fears regarding loss of their influence or their teen to negative peer groups and were provided with tentative examples of how this occurs.

37. Provide Guidance in Healthy Separation from Adolescent (37)

A. The parents were provided with guidance regarding ways they can allow and support the healthy process of separation from their adolescent.

B. The parents were supported as they identified and implemented constructive, affirming ways to allow the adolescent to gradually separate.

C. The difficulty in allowing the adolescent to separate (even in a healthy manner) was emphasized.

D. Positive feedback was provided to the parents for their use of healthy, constructive, affirming ways of allowing their adolescent to emancipate.

E. The parents have not used healthy techniques to allow the adolescent to separate and were provided with remedial assistance in this area.

38. Resolve Barriers to Connectedness (38)

A. The parents and child identified barriers that prevent or limit connectedness between family members.

B. The parents were directed to complete the "One-on-One" assignment from the *Adolescent Psychotherapy Homework Planner*, 2nd ed. (Jongsma, Peterson, and McInnis).

C. Brainstorming techniques were used to resolve barriers that prevent or limit connectedness between family members.

D. Specific activities that promote connectedness between family members were identified (e.g., games, one-to-one time).

E. Positive feedback was provided to the parents for removing barriers in developing connectedness.

F. The parents have not removed barriers and developed better connectedness with the children and were provided with additional ideas about how to complete this.

39. Teach about Quality Time (39)

A. The thought was planted with the parents that just "hanging out at home" or being around/available is what quality time is about.

B. The parents accepted the idea that quality time is about being accessible and available and were assisted in developing ways in which they can be accessible and available.

C. The parents were provided with specific examples of how "hanging out at home" has been helpful in developing connectedness with their child.

40. Assign Books on Limits (40)

A. The parents were directed to read appropriate books on setting limits for their adolescent.

B. The parents were directed to read *Between Parent and Teenager* (Ginott).

C. The parents were directed to read *Get Out of My Life, but First Could You Drive Me and Cheryl to the Mall?* (Wolf).

D. The parents were directed to read *Grounded for Life* (Tracy).

E. The parents were directed to read *Parents, Teens, and Boundaries* (Bluestein).

F. The parents have read the assigned information on setting limits and key concepts were reviewed.

G. The parents have not read the assigned information on setting boundaries and were redirected to do so.

41. Develop Realistic Expectations (41)

A. The parents were assisted in developing appropriate and realistic expectations on the adolescent's age and level of maturity.

B. The parents were assigned "Transitioning from Parenting a Child to Parenting a Teen" from the *Adolescent Psychotherapy Homework Planner,* 2nd ed. (Jongsma, Peterson, and McInnis).

C. The parents were reinforced for appropriate and realistic expectations of their adolescent's behavior.

D. The parents were redirected for unrealistic and inappropriate expectations about the adolescent's level of maturity.

PEER/SIBLING CONFLICT

CLIENT PRESENTATION

1. Angry/Tense (1)*

A. The client described a pattern of frequent, intense conflict with peers and siblings.

B. The client appeared angry at everything and everybody and was not willing to be very cooperative in the counseling process.

C. The client denied responsibility for the frequent, overt verbal and physical fighting with both peers and siblings.

D. The level of anger and fighting between the client and siblings has decreased as they have actively worked with the therapist in session.

2. Projecting/Blaming (2)

A. The client displayed a propensity for blaming others for his/her problems.

B. The client refused to take any responsibility for the ongoing verbal and physical conflicts he/she has with peers and siblings.

C. All problems or conflicts were viewed by the client as the responsibility of others, not his/hers.

D. Slowly, the client has started to take responsibility for some of the conflicts in which he/she is involved.

3. Parents' Unfairness/Favoritism (3)

A. The client reported that the parents always treat his/her siblings more favorably than they do him/her.

B. The client cited incidences of his/her perception of parents' unfairness toward him/her.

C. The parents acknowledged that they find the other siblings easier to like than the client.

D. The client's complaints about unfairness and favoritism have started to decrease, and the parents are beginning to be seen in a more favorable light.

4. Defiant/Vengeful (4)

A. The client presented in a vengeful, defiant manner.

B. The client reported a long list of people who have wronged or slighted him/her in some way and how he/she has gotten back at them.

C. The client's level of bullying has caused him/her to be constantly at odds with peers and siblings.

D. The client has gradually let go of some of his/her intimidation and vengeance and has started to have less conflict with peers and siblings.

---

*The numbers in parentheses correlate to the number of the Behavioral Definition statement in the companion chapter with the same title in *The* Adolescent *Psychotherapy Treatment Planner,* Fourth Edition (Jongsma, Peterson, McInnis, and Bruce) by John Wiley & Sons, 2006.

5. Isolated/Intense (5)

A. The client presented as a lonely, isolated individual.

B. The client reported a history of aggressive relationships with peers, which he/she resolved by keeping to himself/herself.

C. The client stated that he/she cannot get along with either peers or siblings without trouble, so he/she chooses to keep to himself/herself.

D. Since taking part in the counseling process, the client has gradually started to relate at least superficially with others.

6. Impulsive/Intimidating (6)

A. The client showed a pattern of impulsiveness and intimidation within the session by not considering the consequences of his/her actions and by challenging the therapist.

B. The client described a pattern of relating with peers and siblings in an impulsive, intimidating manner.

C. The client reported a history of impulsive, intimidating actions toward peers that have caused him/her repeated social problems.

D. The client has gradually accepted that he/she is intimidating and that this has been the reason for his/her conflicts with peers and siblings.

7. Aggressive/Mean (7)

A. The client seems to have an aggressive, mean manner of relating to others.

B. The client indicated that he/she has been involved in encounters that resulted in physical injuries to others.

C. No remorse appeared evident on the client's part for the painful way he/she treats others.

D. All his/her aggressive, mean acts are blamed on others or given great justification.

E. As treatment has progressed, the client has displayed less aggressive and mean behavior.

8. Insensitivity (7)

A. The client did not appear to be bothered by the ongoing conflicts he/she has with peers and siblings.

B. The hurtful impact on others of the client's verbally hostile, aggressive behavior does not appear to have an effect on the client.

C. The client has started to understand the effect of his/her conflictual behaviors on others and his/her need to be more sensitive to them.

9. Parents' Hostility (8)

A. The client described instances from his/her childhood in which severe and abusive punishment resulted whenever he/she was blamed for negative behavior.

B. The client described how parents always unfavorably compared him/her with peers and siblings, which led to feelings of anger, inadequacy, and resentment.

C. The parents' style of relating to the client was rude and hostile.

D. The parents' home environment appears to be highly competitive, with one sibling often pitted against the other to outdo him/her in a given area and thus win the parents' praise.

E. The client has begun to understand how his/her attitude and behavior toward others are connected to parents' treatment of him/her in childhood.

F. The parents have begun to treat the client in a more respectful and less hostile manner.

INTERVENTIONS IMPLEMENTED

1. Build Trust (1)*

A. Initial trust level was established with the client through the use of unconditional positive regard.

B. Warm acceptance and active-listening techniques were utilized to establish the basis for a trust relationship with the client.

C. The client seems to have formed a trust relationship with the therapist and has started to share his/her feelings about conflictual relationships.

D. Despite the use of active listening, warm acceptance, and unconditional positive regard, the client appears to be hesitant to trust and to share his/her feelings and conflicts.

2. Explore Relationships and Assess Denial (2)

A. The client's perception of how he/she relates to siblings and peers was explored.

B. The client's degree of denial was found to be high regarding conflict and acceptance of responsibility for any part in it.

C. The client was open in acknowledging the high degree of conflict between the siblings and was supported as he/she accepted responsibility for his/her part in the conflict.

3. Teach Social Learning Techniques (3)

A. The parents and teachers were asked to identify all nonaggressive, cooperative, and peaceful behaviors of the client that they could praise and positively reinforce.

B. Role-play and modeling techniques were used to show the parents and teachers how to ignore the client's nonharmful aggressive behaviors and how to praise prosocial behaviors.

4. Play Anger Control Game (4)

A. The Anger Control Game (Berg) was played with the client to expose him/her to new ways of handling aggressive feelings.

B. The client was asked to make a commitment to handle aggressive feelings by trying one of the new ways learned through playing The Anger Control Game.

C. The client has reported that he/she has successfully implemented new anger control techniques, and his/her successes were reviewed.

D. The client reported that he/she continues to have problems managing anger and was urged to continue to use the techniques to handle these aggressive feelings.

5. Play Helping, Sharing, and Caring Game (5)

A. The Helping, Sharing, and Caring Game (Gardner) was played with the client to expose him/her to feelings of respect for self and others.

*The numbers in parentheses correlate to the number of the Therapeutic Intervention statement in the companion chapter with the same title in *The Adolescent Psychotherapy Treatment Planner,* Fourth Edition (Jongsma, Peterson, McInnis, and Bruce) by John Wiley & Sons, 2006.

B. The client was assisted in identifying how people feel when they show respect to and receive respect from others.

C. The client was reminded of how others feel when they are treated in a rude, disrespectful manner.

D. The client has consistently shown more respect for the feelings of others.

6. Play Social Conflict Game (6)

A. The Social Conflict Game (Berg) was played with the client to introduce prosocial behavioral skills.

B. The client was asked to list all the negative consequences that have resulted from his/her antisocial behaviors.

C. The client was reminded of the emotional and physical pain his/her actions have caused others.

D. The client was assisted in identifying two positive consequences of showing respect and concern for others.

7. Introduce Negotiation (7)

A. The client was urged to stipulate the problems that exist with his/her siblings and suggest concrete solutions.

B. The client and the parents were asked to complete the "Negotiating a Peace Treaty" exercise from the *Adolescent Psychotherapy Homework Planner,* 2nd ed. (Jongsma, Peterson, and McInnis) to introduce the concept of negotiation.

C. The parents were asked to start negotiating key areas of conflict with the client.

D. Role-play sessions involving negotiation were used with the client and the parents to build their negotiating skills.

E. The positive aspects of negotiation versus winning and losing were identified and reinforced with the client.

8. Teach Understanding of Feelings (8)

A. The client was taught to identify basic feelings using a feelings chart.

B. Aggressive actions were focused on to assist the client in identifying how others might feel when they were the object of such actions.

C. The idea of how the client would like to be treated by others was explored, along with what he/she would need to do to make this possible.

9. Refer for Group Therapy (9)

A. The client was referred to a peer therapy group to expand his/her social sensitivity and behavioral flexibility.

B. The client accepted the referral to group therapy and has been attending regularly.

C. The client reported that the group therapy experience has taught him/her to be more sensitive to the feelings of others.

D. The client has been resistive to group therapy and has not attended on a regular basis; he/she was encouraged to attend the group.

10. Play Talking, Feeling, and Doing Game (10)

A. The Talking, Feeling, and Doing Game (Gardner) was played with the client to build and reinforce his/her awareness of self and others.

B. After playing The Talking, Feeling, and Doing Game, the client began sharing more about himself/herself and showing some sensitivity to others.

11. Refer to Behavioral Group (11)

A. The client was asked to attend a behavioral contracting group that works to develop positive peer interactions.

B. The client's group goals for positive peer interaction were set and reviewed each week.

C. The client reported positive verbal feedback from peers within the group on his/her interaction goals.

D. The client's positive gains in peer interaction were verbally reinforced and rewarded.

12. Encourage Involvement in Cooperative Activities (12)

A. The benefits of involving the client in cooperative activities were discussed with the parents.

B. Options for cooperative activities were presented to the parents, and they were asked to make a commitment to get the client involved.

C. The client was assisted in identifying positive gains he/she could make through participating in cooperative activities such as sports, music, scouts.

D. It was noted that the client's involvement in cooperative activities with peers has increased significantly since the parents have encouraged this activity.

13. Refer to Camp (13)

A. The client was referred to a summer camp that focuses on building self-esteem and positive peer relationships.

B. The client was helped to identify a list of specific things he/she could do at camp to increase his/her self-esteem.

C. Gains in self-esteem and in peer relationships reported by the client as having been gained through the camp experience were affirmed and reinforced.

D. The client and his/her parents have not followed through on enrolling the client in a summer camp experience focused on building self-esteem and peer cooperation, and they were encouraged to use this resource.

14. Build Skills in Connecting with Others (14)

A. The parents were assisted in implementing techniques that will help to build the client's skills in connecting with others.

B. The client's parents were asked to read *Helping Your Child Make Friends* (Nevick).

C. The parents have read the assigned material on helping their child build skills in connecting with others, and the key points of this information were reviewed.

D. The parents have implemented specific techniques to help their child build skills in connecting with others, and the usefulness of these techniques was reviewed.

E. The client's parents have not read or implemented the skills assigned and were redirected to do so.

15. Promote Acceptance of Praise and Encouragement (15)

A. The client was assisted in identifying how he/she responds to praise and encouragement from others.

B. The client's barriers to being open to positive feedback were identified.

C. New ways to respond positively to praise and encouragement were taught to the client.

D. Role-play, modeling, and behavioral rehearsal were used to provide the client the opportunity to practice new, accepting responses to praise and encouragement.

16. Teach Parents to Praise (16)

A. The parents were asked to list all the possible ways they might give verbal affection and appropriate praise to the client.

B. The parents' resistance to giving affection and praise to the client for expected behavior was addressed and resolved.

C. The parents were asked to choose three ways to give verbal affection and appropriate praise and to implement each with the client when appropriate.

D. Affirmation and reinforcement was given to the parents for their reported use of verbal affection and praise with the client.

17. Reduce Parental Aggression, Rejection, and Quarreling (17)

A. Parental patterns of aggression and rejection were identified in family sessions.

B. The parents were assisted in removing acts of aggression and messages of rejection from their parenting.

C. Various methods were modeled for the parents to respond to the client in a warm, firm, yet caring way.

D. Parent messages of rejection were blocked and confronted in family sessions.

18. Assign Reading of *Between Parent and Child* (18)

A. The parents were asked to read the chapters "Jealousy" and "Children Who Need Professional Help" in *Between Parent and Child* (Ginott).

B. The parents were assisted in identifying and changing key areas of their family structure to decrease the level of rivalry.

C. The parents were reminded that the level of rivalry within their family system is destructive as they continue to work toward the level of normal family interaction.

19. Assign Reading on Siblings and Rivalry (19)

A. The parents were assigned to read books about siblings and rivalry.

B. The book *Siblings without Rivalry* (Faber and Mazish) was assigned to the parents to read and process with the therapist.

C. Based on their reading of *Siblings without Rivalry,* the parents identified two new ways to reduce rivalry and began implementing them in their family.

D. The parents reported positive results from the new methods that they have implemented to decrease the level of rivalry in the family.

E. The parents gave numerous excuses for their inconsistent use of new parenting methods and for the mixed results they experienced.

F. The parents have not read the material on siblings and rivalry and were redirected to do so.

20. Explore Rejection Experiences (20)

A. The client's rejection experiences with family and friends were probed.

B. Active listening was provided as the client expressed numerous causes for his/her anger, which were based on rejection by family and friends.

C. The client denied any rejection experiences as being the basis for his/her anger, and this was accepted at face value.

21. Reframe Rivalry as Stage (21)

A. Rivalry within the family was reframed as a normal stage and something the siblings will successfully resolve.

B. Reframing of the family's rivalry experiences as normal seems to have relieved concern over this issue and even reduced the rivalry experience itself.

22. Identify Past Success at Decreasing Rivalry (22)

A. Times without sibling conflict problems were identified with the family and probed.

B. A solution was developed for rivalry by analyzing times identified by the family as rivalry free.

C. Encouragement was given to the family to keep implementing the solutions from successful experiences.

D. The family struggled to implement the solutions from the past because they were unclear on the directions and timing; these solutions were fine-tuned.

23. Refer to Parenting Class (23)

A. The parents were referred to and encouraged to attend a support group.

B. The parents reported attending a support group and receiving helpful feedback and encouragement.

C. The parents offered several reasons for not yet attending a support group; they were redirected to do so.

24. Develop Behavior Modification Plan (24)

A. A behavior modification plan targeting cooperative sibling interaction was developed by the parents and the therapist for the client.

B. The parents were taught how to effectively implement and sustain a behavior modification program focused on reinforcing positive sibling interaction.

C. The parents' administration of the behavior modification plan was monitored and encouragement given to the parents to continue their work.

D. The parents were confronted when they failed to immediately reinforce positive interactions by the client.

E. The behavior modification plan to reinforce positive sibling interaction has been successful in increasing such behaviors and reducing the sibling conflicts.

25. Evaluate Behavior Modification Contract (25)

A. The effectiveness of the behavior modification plan was reviewed with the client, and the parents were given positive feedback for implementing the contract.

B. Aspects of the behavior modification contract that focused on reinforcing positive sibling interaction were modified with the client and the parents because expectations were set unrealistically high.

C. The parents and the client were confronted on their lack of follow-through on the behavior modification contract, and resistance issues were addressed and resolved.

26. Teach Use of Positive Consequences (26)

A. The parents were taught to use positive consequences when the client's behavior is unacceptable or disrespectful.

B. The parents were assisted in constructing a list of possible positive consequences to use when the client exhibits unacceptable behavior, along with a plan for implementation of them.

C. The parents reported a reduction in the client's arguments with siblings due to the parents' use of positive consequences, and they were encouraged to continue their use.

D. The parents indicated that they found it difficult to use positive consequences and slipped back into using natural consequences, which were easier.

27. Read Fable Regarding Rivalry (27)

A. "Raising Cain" and "Cinderella" from *Friedman's Fables* (Friedman) were read and processed in family session.

B. The reading and processing of the fables normalized the issue of sibling rivalry and helped family members identify their role in promoting it.

C. Each family member was asked to identify one thing they could do to decrease the rivalry within the family.

28. Confront Disrespect and Teach Conflict Resolution Skills (28)

A. Family members' disrespectful interactions were highlighted and confronted in family session.

B. Conflict resolution skills were taught to the parents and siblings.

C. Role-play, behavioral rehearsal, and modeling were utilized to teach the family effective conflict resolution skills and to give each of them opportunities to practice these new skills.

D. The family has struggled to implement conflict resolution techniques, as they give up easily and fall back on old patterns of arguing and verbal abuse.

29. Identify Environmental Changes (29)

A. The parents were assisted in identifying specific things they could do in their physical environment to reduce conflicts between siblings.

B. The parents implemented the plan to move siblings into separate bedrooms and to stop leaving the older child in charge of the younger; the benefits of this practice were reviewed.

C. Physical changes made by the parents in the home environment were monitored for their effectiveness, and the parents were given support and encouragement for their actions.

30. Assign Reading on Interventions for Sibling Conflict (30)

A. The parents were assigned to read material on interventions for sibling conflict.

B. The parents were asked to read *How to End the Sibling Wars* (Bienick) and select from the reading several interventions to implement with their child.

C. The parents were assisted in implementing chosen techniques from the assigned book, and role-play was utilized to help the parents increase their skills and confidence in the new techniques.

D. The parents' resistance to trying new techniques was addressed, and the advantage of using new approaches was seeded with them.

E. The parents have not read the material on interventions for sibling conflict and were redirected to do so.

31. Assess Dynamics of Underlying Conflicts (31)

A. The dynamics and alliances present in the family were assessed in a family session.

B. A structural intervention was implemented with the family to create new and healthier alliances between the members.

C. Key dynamics that create and promote sibling conflict were confronted.

32. Assign Family to Attend Experiential Camp (32)

A. The family was asked to make a verbal commitment to attend an experiential weekend camp to promote family trust, cooperation, and respect.

B. The experiential weekend camp experience was processed with family, and members identified key things they had gained from the weekend.

33. Develop a Sibling Alliance (33)

A. The siblings were assisted in identifying a common issue to negotiate with the parents.

B. The parents and siblings were taught basic negotiation skills and practiced them in role-play situations.

C. In a family session, siblings negotiated with the parents to expand their freedom and were able to convince the parents to expand their freedom under the condition that the siblings decrease their conflicts.

D. Despite coaching and encouragement, negotiations broke down when siblings started arguing again.

34. Develop Appreciation of Sibling (34)

A. The siblings were asked to list and verbalize an appreciation of each other's unique traits and abilities.

B. The client was asked to complete the "Cloning the Perfect Sibling" exercise from the *Adolescent Psychotherapy Homework Planner,* 2nd ed. (Jongsma, Peterson, and McInnis).

C. The client processed the completed cloning exercise and identified key positive points about differences between siblings.

D. The client processed the completed cloning exercise but refused to see the positive points of individual differences.

35. Refer for Psychiatric/Psychological Evaluation (35)

A. Options for a psychiatric or psychological evaluation were explained to the client and family.

B. The client was referred for a psychiatric evaluation.

C. The client was referred for a psychological evaluation.

D. The parents were asked to make a verbal commitment to follow through with the evaluation and report the results to the therapist.

36. Monitor Implementation of Assessment Recommendations (36)

A. The parents and the client were assisted in implementing the psychological/psychiatric evaluation's recommendations.

B. The importance of follow-through on the assessment recommendations for the client was emphasized with the parents.

C. The parents and the client were confronted for their inconsistent follow-through on the assessment recommendations.

D. The client and the parents reported following through on each of the recommendations of the evaluation and were given positive verbal affirmation for their efforts.

PHYSICAL/EMOTIONAL ABUSE VICTIM

CLIENT PRESENTATION

1. Confirmed Report of Physical Abuse by an Adult (1)*

A. The client's self-report of being assaulted by his/her parent has been confirmed by a children's protective services worker.

B. The client's parent reported that the other parent has physically assaulted the client on more than one occasion.

C. The client provided a detailed account of the assault by his/her parent and the resulting injuries.

D. The physical abuse reported by the client was reported to children's protective services as required by mandatory reporting statutes.

2. Evidence of Victimization (2)

A. Bruises were evident on the client's body.

B. The client worked to explain away the injuries on his/her body, refusing to blame an adult for inflicting the injuries.

C. Past records of bruises and wounds revealed the extent of the client's victimization.

D. Since coming into treatment, the client has not reported receiving any bruises or wounds from his/her caregivers.

3. Fearful/Withdrawn (3)

A. The client appeared very fearful and withdrawn from others and avoids all but necessary interpersonal contacts.

B. Fear seems to dominate the client's contacts with others.

C. The client verbalized fear of further physical abuse by the caregiver.

D. Since establishing trust in counseling, the client has started to be less fearful and withdrawn and a little more open about himself/herself.

4. Closed/Detached (3)

A. The client presented in a closed and detached manner, with little visible interest in others or things.

B. The client showed little interest in the counseling process and was careful not to reveal anything significant about himself/herself.

C. The client seemed very closed and made a conscious effort to keep others at a safe distance and in the dark about himself/herself.

D. Since establishing a relationship with the therapist, the client has started to be more open about himself/herself and less fearful.

---

*The numbers in parentheses correlate to the number of the Behavioral Definition statement in the companion chapter with the same title in *The Adolescent Psychotherapy Treatment Planner,* Fourth Edition (Jongsma, Peterson, McInnis, and Bruce) by John Wiley & Sons, 2006.

5. Mistrustful/Anxious (3)

A. There is a mistrustful, anxious manner to the client when he/she interacts with others.

B. The client's body language and facial expressions seemed to indicate a high level of mistrust of others, especially adults.

C. The client reported a history of not being able to trust adults in his/her family because they rarely did what they said they would and often harmed him/her.

D. The client has begun to verbalize some connections between childhood pain and present attitudes of detachment and fear of others.

6. Low Self-Esteem (3)

A. The client's self-image seemed to be very low, as he/she seldom made eye contact and frequently made self-disparaging remarks.

B. The client reported feeling worthless and unloved for as long as he/she can remember.

C. The client's experience in the accepting environment of counseling has started to boost his/her sense of self-esteem.

7. Angry/Aggressive (4)

A. The client has an angry, aggressive manner that is obvious to nearly everyone.

B. The client reported an increase in the frequency and severity of angry, aggressive behavior toward peers and adults.

C. The blame for aggressive behaviors was projected onto others.

D. The client described having a quick temper that has resulted in his/her destroying many of his/her own possessions.

E. There has been a sharp decrease in the client's anger and aggressiveness since he/she started to disclose about his/her being physically and emotionally abused.

F. The client has begun to realize that his/her anger and aggression are the result of what he/she saw and experienced in the home as a child.

8. Recollections of the Abuse (5)

A. The client indicated he/she felt constantly haunted by the distressing memories of his/her past emotional and physical abuse.

B. The client reported that the memories of the abuse intrude on his/her consciousness under a variety of circumstances.

C. The client described a chaotic childhood in which he/she was the victim of ongoing emotional and physical abuse.

D. The incidence of intrusive thoughts of the abuse has significantly diminished.

E. The client has begun to verbalize some connections between childhood pain and present attitudes of detachment and fear of others.

9. Strong Feelings When around Perpetrator (6)

A. The client indicated that he/she feels intense anger and rage whenever he/she comes into contact with the perpetrator.

B. The caregivers have reported that the client immediately becomes tearful and fearful when the perpetrator is near.

C. The client expressed that he/she experiences mixed feelings of fear, anger, and rage whenever he/she encounters the perpetrator.

D. The client indicated that since talking in therapy, his/her feelings are not as intense or scary when he/she comes into contact with the perpetrator.

10. Depressed/Irritable (7)

A. The client presented with a depressed mood and manner that contained an irritable edge.

B. Between the client's depression and accompanying irritability, he/she was not willing or able to disclose about himself/herself in the counseling session.

C. The client reported a pattern of social withdrawal and detachment from feelings.

D. Since starting on antidepressant medication, the client's depression and irritability have decreased and he/she is beginning to self-disclose in counseling session.

11. Passive/Apathetic (7)

A. There was a strong passive, apathetic quality to the client, he/she reflects little interest in what might happen to self or others.

B. Because of his/her apathetic, passive manner, the client showed little interest in the counseling process.

C. The client reported that as far back as he/she can remember he/she has not been concerned about what happens to him/her.

D. The client has exhibited less apathy and passivity since he/she has become more actively involved in therapy.

12. Sleep Disturbance (8)

A. The client reported having difficulties falling asleep, waking up frequently, and feeling tired and unrested in the morning.

B. The client indicated that he/she has been experiencing frequent night terrors and recurrent nightmares.

C. The client has started to talk about the abuse he/she experienced in childhood and is now reporting fewer night terrors and more restful sleep.

D. The client has begun making connections between his/her sleeping difficulties and the history of being abused.

13. Running Away (9)

A. The client reported running away from home on several occasions to escape from the physical abuse.

B. It seems the client has used running away as an attempt to draw attention to the abusiveness in his/her home.

C. There has not been an incident of running away since the abuse of the client has started to be addressed.

INTERVENTIONS IMPLEMENTED

1. Build Trust (1)*

A. A level of trust was built with the client through use of unconditional positive regard.

B. Warm acceptance and active listening techniques were used to establish trust with the client that would enable him/her to express feelings and facts surrounding the abuse.

C. The client has formed a trust-based relationship, which was noted to increase his/her ability to express facts and feelings about the abuse.

D. Despite the use of unconditional positive regard, warm acceptance, and active listening, the client remains hesitant to share feelings and facts about the abuse.

2. Explore Facts of the Abuse (2)

A. The client was assisted in clarifying and expressing the facts associated with the abuse.

B. Support and encouragement were given to the client to increase his/her level of disclosure of the facts about the abuse.

C. Even with support and encouragement being given to the client, he/she still had difficulty expressing and clarifying the facts about the abuse.

D. The client openly outlined the facts associated with the most recent incident of his/her being a victim of abuse and was praised for his/her bravery.

3. Assign "Take the First Step" Exercise (3)

A. The client was asked to complete the "Take the First Step" exercise from the *Adolescent Psychotherapy Homework Planner,* 2nd ed. (Jongsma, Peterson, and McInnis) to assist him/her in disclosing the story of the abuse.

B. The disclosure exercise that the client completed was processed with the client, and key benefits of disclosing the abuse were identified and reinforced.

C. The client's partially completed disclosure exercise was processed, and he/she was gently confronted about his/her fear of disclosing the abuse.

D. The client showed some relief at being given the opportunity to fully disclose the facts of the abuse that he/she has experienced.

E. The client has failed to complete the disclosure exercise and was again asked to do so.

4. Report Physical Abuse (4)

A. An assessment was conducted on the client to determine the nature and extent of the physical abuse.

B. The client was sent to a physician to confirm and document the physical abuse.

C. The physical abuse of the client was reported to the state child protection agency for further investigation.

D. The parents were notified of the client's revelation of physical abuse and informed that, as required by law, it was reported to the state child protection agency for investigation.

---

*The numbers in parentheses correlate to the number of the Therapeutic Intervention statement in the companion chapter with the same title in *The Adolescent Psychotherapy Treatment Planner,* Fourth Edition (Jongsma, Peterson, McInnis, and Bruce) by John Wiley & Sons, 2006.

5. Assess Veracity of Charges (5)

A. The family, client's physician, and criminal justice officials were consulted to assess the truthfulness of client's allegations of physical abuse.

B. The truthfulness of the client's allegations regarding physical abuse was confirmed by family, physician, and child protective services worker.

C. Consultation with the family, physician, and child protective service worker resulted in divided opinions regarding the veracity of the client's allegations of abuse.

6. Assess for Removal from Home (6)

A. The family environment was assessed to determine if it was safe for the client.

B. The family environment was determined to be unsafe for the client and he/she was moved to a safe, temporary placement outside the home.

C. After the family environment was assessed, a recommendation was made that a temporary restraining order be sought for the perpetrator.

7. Make Home Safe for Children (7)

A. An agreement was made with the perpetrator to move out of the home and not visit until the parents and protective service worker give their approval.

B. It was recommended to the nonabusive parent to seek a restraining order against the perpetrator.

C. The nonabusive parent was assisted in obtaining a restraining order and implementing it on a consistent basis.

D. The nonabusive parent was monitored and supported for consistent implementation of "no contact" agreement between the perpetrator and the victim.

E. The parent was confronted on his/her inconsistent enforcement of the restraining order to keep the perpetrator from the presence of the client.

8. Reassure Client of Protection (8)

A. The client was repeatedly reassured of concern and care of others in keeping him/her safe from further abuse.

B. The client was reassured by the parents and others that they were looking out for his/her safety.

C. The client's anxiety level seems to be diminishing as he/she has been reassured of his/her safety.

9. Explore Feelings about Abuse (9)

A. The client's feelings toward the perpetrator were identified and explored.

B. Encouragement and support were given to the client as he/she was assisted in expressing and clarifying his/her feelings associated with the abuse experiences.

C. The client was asked to complete and process the "My Thoughts and Feelings" exercise from the *Adolescent Psychotherapy Treatment Planner,* 2nd ed. (Jongsma, Peterson, and McInnis) to help him/her practice openness.

D. Even with support and encouragement, the client had difficulty clarifying and expressing any feelings about the abuse experiences.

E. The client expressed pain, anger, and fright as he/she told the story of the abuse.

10. Confront Denial of Family and Perpetrator (10)

A. Family sessions were conducted in which the family's denial of the client's abuse was confronted and challenged.

B. The perpetrator was asked to list all his/her rationalizations for the abuse.

C. Confrontation was used to process the perpetrator's list of rationalizations for the abuse.

D. Confrontation was used with the perpetrator to break through his/her denial of abusing the client.

E. The use of confrontation and challenges has been effective in breaking through the perpetrator's denial, and he/she is now taking ownership of and responsibility for the abuse.

F. The perpetrator remains in denial about abusing the client in spite of confrontation and challenge to his/her rationalizations.

11. Confront Excusing Perpetrator (11)

A. The client was asked to create and process a list of reasons he/she was abused by the perpetrator.

B. Each time the client made an excuse for the perpetrator's abuse, he/she was confronted and reminded that in no way did he/she deserve being abused.

C. The message was given to the client that even though he/she is not perfect, the abuse was not deserved.

D. The client was redirected when he/she continued to excuse the perpetrator for the abuse and engaged in self-blame.

E. Positive feedback was provided, as the client has begun to place clear responsibility for the abuse on the perpetrator and has discontinued self-blame.

12. Reassure That Abuse Not Deserved (12)

A. The client was reassured that the physical abuse he/she received was in no way deserved no matter what he/she had done wrong, if anything.

B. The message of not deserving the abuse no matter what happened was consistently given to the client.

C. The client was educated regarding his/her deserving personal respect and controlled responses in punishment situations.

13. Reinforce Holding Perpetrator Responsible (13)

A. All statements by the client that hold the perpetrator responsible for the abuse were reinforced.

B. The client was asked to list all the reasons the perpetrator was responsible for the abuse.

C. The client was reminded that regardless of any misbehavior on his/her part the abuse was still the perpetrator's fault.

D. Positive feedback was provided, as the client has consistently made statements putting responsibility for the abuse firmly on the perpetrator.

14. Support Confrontation of Perpetrator (14)

A. The client was prepared in order to build his/her confidence for confronting the perpetrator in a family session.

B. Role-play was used with the client to provide him/her with experience in confronting the perpetrator.

C. Family sessions were conducted in which the parents and the client confronted the perpetrator with the abuse.

D. Confrontation of the perpetrator with the abuse was modeled by the parents in family sessions.

E. In the family session, the client read a letter that he/she wrote outlining why the perpetrator was responsible for the abuse.

F. The client declined to confront the perpetrator in a family session, and his/her decision was accepted.

15. Process Perpetrator Apology (15)

A. The client was assessed to determine his/her readiness to hear and accept an apology from the perpetrator.

B. The perpetrator's apology was processed for genuineness and level of honesty.

C. A family session was conducted in which the perpetrator apologized to the client and family for the abuse.

D. The perpetrator's apology was assessed to be disingenuous and dishonest, and it was not accepted as appropriate for a family session.

16. Monitor Perpetrator Group Participation (16)

A. The perpetrator attended and participated in the required effective parenting and anger management groups.

B. The gains made by the perpetrator in group were monitored and reinforced.

C. The perpetrator was confronted on his/her noncompliance with attending required groups.

17. Facilitate Perpetrator Psychological Evaluation/Treatment Referral (17)

A. The perpetrator was referred for a psychological evaluation.

B. The perpetrator cooperated with all aspects of the evaluation.

C. All treatment recommendations of the evaluation were given and explained to the perpetrator.

D. The perpetrator was asked to make a commitment to follow through on each of the treatment recommendations of the evaluation.

18. Evaluate Family for Substance Abuse (18)

A. Family sessions were conducted to assess issues of substance use and abuse within the family.

B. The parents were referred for a substance abuse assessment.

C. The parents cooperated and completed the requested substance abuse assessments.

D. Efforts to assess the issue of substance use and abuse within the family were met with denial and resistance.

E. The perpetrator was referred to a substance abuse program.

F. The perpetrator successfully completed a substance abuse program and is now involved in aftercare.

G. The perpetrator was referred but refused to follow through on completing a substance abuse program.

19. Counsel Parents on Boundaries (19)

A. The parents were counseled on what are and what are not appropriate discipline boundaries.

B. Past inappropriate disciplinary boundaries that allowed for abusive punishment were addressed and new appropriate boundaries established.

C. New appropriate boundaries for nonabusive, reasonable discipline were monitored for parents' honoring and enforcing them.

D. The parents reported that they have successfully implemented disciplinary measures that are nonabusive and reasonable, and they were reinforced for this healthy pattern.

20. List Appropriate Parental Disciplines (20)

A. The parents were asked to list all the acts of appropriate discipline they could envision.

B. The parents' list of appropriate disciplinary behavior was reviewed, with reasonable approaches being encouraged and reinforced.

C. The parents were monitored for their use of discipline techniques that reinforce reasonable, respectful actions and appropriate boundaries.

D. The parents were confronted and redirected when discipline was not reasonable and respectful.

21. Construct Genogram That Identifies Abuse (21)

A. A multigeneration family genogram was constructed with the family members.

B. The family members were assisted in identifying patterns of physical abuse from the multigeneration family genogram.

C. Positive feedback was provided as ways to begin breaking the physically abusive family patterns were identified and implemented by family members.

D. The family members were supported as they acknowledged that the pattern of multigenerational physical abuse is existent and vowed to stop this pattern within their own family.

22. Assess Family Stress Factors (22)

A. Family dynamics were assessed to identify stress factors and events that may have contributed to the abuse.

B. The family members were assisted in identifying effective ways to cope with stress in order to reduce the probability of abuse.

C. The family was directed to key community and professional resources that could assist them in effectively coping with family stressors.

D. The family members were assisted in identifying steps to take to reduce environmental stressors that may contribute to the precipitation of violence.

E. Family members were asked to identify family stress factors and were urged to be more open in this area.

23. Promote Family Support and Nurturing (23)

A. Family members were taught the importance of emotional support and nurturing to the client and how each could provide it for him/her.

B. Positive reinforcement was given to family members for incidents of support and nurturing given to the client.

C. The family position that the client should forget the abuse now and move on was confronted and processed, with members being reminded of the client's need for ongoing support and nurturing in order to fully heal.

24. Assign Letter to Perpetrator (24)

A. The client was asked to write a letter expressing his/her feelings of hurt, fear, and anger to the perpetrator.

B. The completed letter to the perpetrator was processed, providing the client with assistance and support in expressing the feelings connected to the abuse.

C. The client's inability to complete the assigned letter was explored, with blocks being identified and processed.

D. The client was asked to write the letter expressing his/her feelings about the abuse to the perpetrator but refused to do so, saying he/she did not want to feel those feelings again.

25. Interpret Anger Triggered by Perpetrator (25)

A. Expressions of anger and aggression by the client were interpreted as being triggered by feelings toward the perpetrator.

B. Displays of seemingly unrelated anger and aggression were reflected to the client as indications of how angry he/she must be toward the perpetrator.

C. It was reflected to the client that his/her general displays of anger and aggression have diminished as he/she has developed insight into his/her feelings of anger focused on the perpetrator.

D. The client rejected the concept that his/her anger and aggression have been triggered by feelings about the perpetrator and was urged to consider this as he/she is able.

26. Promote Self-Protection (26)

A. Various actions for the client to take to protect himself/herself from future abuse were identified and reinforced.

B. Efforts were made to empower the client to take necessary steps to protect himself/herself if the situation warranted it.

C. The client was bombarded with statements of empowerment regarding protecting himself/herself.

27. Assign "Letter of Empowerment" Exercise (27)

A. The client was asked to complete the "Letter of Empowerment" exercise from the *Adolescent Psychotherapy Homework Planner,* 2nd ed. (Jongsma, Peterson, and McInnis) to assist him/her in expressing thoughts and feelings about abuse.

B. Unconditional positive regard and active listening were used to help the client express thoughts and feelings about the abuse.

C. Barriers and defenses of the client that prevent expression of thoughts and feelings about the abuse were identified, addressed, and removed.

D. Efforts to encourage the client to express thoughts and feelings about the abuse have not been effective, and the client remains closed regarding the abuse.

E. The client completed the "Letter of Empowerment" exercise and reported that it enabled him/her to express thoughts and feelings about the abuse.

F. The client has failed to complete the empowerment exercise and was redirected to do so.

28. Identify a Basis for Self-Esteem (28)

A. The client's talents, importance to others, and spiritual value were reviewed with him/her to assist in identifying a basis for self-worth.

B. The client was asked to verbally affirm each of his/her positive strengths and attributes that were identified.

C. Positive self-talk was developed around the client's strengths and attributes that he/she could use on a daily basis to affirm himself/herself.

29. Reinforce Positive Self-Descriptive Statements (29)

A. Every positive self-descriptive statement made by the client was affirmed and reinforced.

B. The client's negative statements about himself/herself were confronted and reframed.

C. The client's pattern of making more positive than negative self-statements was recognized, reinforced, and encouraged to continue in that direction.

30. Assign Forgiveness Letter (30)

A. The client was educated on the key aspects of forgiveness, with special emphasis being given to the power involved.

B. The client was asked to complete a forgiveness letter to the perpetrator while asserting the right to safety.

C. The client was given a forgiveness exercise to complete and to process in the next session.

D. The assigned letter of forgiveness was processed, and the evident empowerment provided by the experience was reinforced.

E. The client has not completed the forgiveness letter, and the reasons for this were processed.

31. Assign Letting-Go Exercise (31)

A. The potential benefits of the process of letting go of anger and hurt were explored with the client.

B. A letting-go exercise was assigned in which the client would bury an anger list about the perpetrator.

C. The letting-go exercise was processed with the client, and feelings were identified and expressed.

D. The client struggles with letting go of feelings of hurt and anger and is not yet able to reach this objective; he/she was encouraged to do this when he/she is ready.

E. The client reported that he/she has successfully let go of his/her feelings of hurt and anger regarding being an abuse survivor, and this was processed and supported.

32. Formulate Future Plans (32)

A. The client was probed to determine what future plans he/she has developed.

B. The client was asked to complete the following sentences to assist and encourage the idea of future plans: "I imagine that _____," "I will _____," "I dream that someday _____."

C. The client was encouraged to include interaction with peers and family as part of his/her future plans.

D. The client struggled to envision any future plans despite assistance and encouragement to do so.

33. Encourage Participation in Activities (33)

A. The client was encouraged to actively participate in peer group interaction and extracurricular activities.

B. The client's excuses and barriers to increased social involvement were explored and removed.

C. Situations involving peer groups and extracurricular activities were role-played with the client to build his/her social skills and confidence level in social situations.

D. The client was provided with positive feedback for his/her increased involvement in peer groups and extracurricular activity to build his/her social skills and confidence level.

E. Despite encouragement and social skill building, the client remains resistant to peer group and extracurricular activity participation.

34. Refer to Victim Support Group (34)

A. The benefits of the client attending a support group were identified and discussed.

B. The client was referred to a support group for teens who have been abused to decrease his/her feelings of being the only one in this situation.

C. The client's experience of attending a support group with the others who are in the same situation was processed.

D. Active-listening skills were used as the client indicated that he/she felt different from all the others in the support group.

E. The client reported feeling empowered and understood after having attended a support group of fellow survivors of abuse, and this was reinforced.

35. Explore Loss of Trust in Adults (35)

A. The client was encouraged to express his/her loss of trust in adults.

B. The client was assisted in connecting his/her loss of trust to the perpetrator's abuse and the failure of others to protect him/her.

C. The client rejected assistance in identifying and expressing loss of trust and stood firm that he/she still trusts adults.

36. Teach Discriminating Trust Judgments (36)

A. The client was educated in the process of making discriminating judgments about trusting people.

B. The client was assisted in identifying key factors that make some people trustworthy and others untrustworthy.

C. Various scenarios of individuals were presented to the client to practice his/her trust discrimination skills.

37. Teach Share-Check Technique (37)

A. The share-check technique was taught to the client to increase skills in assessing an individual's trustworthiness.

B. Role-play situations were used with the client to build his/her skill and confidence in using the share-check technique.

C. The client was asked to make a commitment to use the share-check technique and report the results of the experience.

D. The client reported success at using the share-check method of gradually building trust in others, and the benefits of this were processed.

38. Assign Drawing Pictures of Self (38)

A. The client was asked to draw pictures that reflect how he/she feels about himself/herself.

B. The client drew detailed pictures of how he/she feels about self, and these were processed.

C. With encouragement, the client drew several vague, undetailed pictures of self.

D. The client willingly talked about each of the pictures he/she drew, identifying specific feelings about himself/herself, and these were processed.

E. The client refused to do such "stupid, childish things" as drawing pictures and was reminded of the benefit of those techniques.

39. Assign Drawing Faces of Self (39)

A. The client was asked to draw pictures of his/her own face before, during, and after the abuse occurred.

B. The client drew three faces in detail and the feelings they represented were processed.

C. The client attempted but could not draw the faces to reflect how he/she felt before, during, and after the abuse occurred and was supported in these efforts.

40. Assess/Educate Regarding Adopting Aggressive Behaviors (40)

A. The client was assessed regarding adopting the aggressive behaviors that he/she had been exposed to in the home.

B. The client was informed that, unless treated, many victims of abuse go on to abuse others, most often those they love.

C. The client's aggressive behaviors were pointed out to him/her and addressed.

D. It was noted that the client's aggressive behaviors have diminished, and he/she has stated a desire to not follow the example or repeat the cycle of aggressive violence.

41. Encourage Empathy for Others' Feelings (41)

A. Role-play and role-reversal techniques were used to sensitize the client to the target of his/her angry feelings.

B. The possible consequences of losing control over angry feelings were identified.

C. The client was reinforced as he/she has verbalized empathy for the pain and fear that his/her aggression causes in others.

42. Assess/Refer for Substance Abuse Treatment (42)

A. The client's pattern of substance abuse was evaluated.

B. The results of the substance abuse evaluation indicated that the client has a chemical dependence problem, and he/she was referred to a substance abuse–specific treatment program.

C. The substance abuse evaluation did not provide evidence of a chemical dependence problem on the part of the client.

D. The substance abuse–specific treatment was started with the client to address his/her chemical dependence issues.

E. The client was unwilling to make a commitment to follow through on the recommended referral for substance abuse treatment.

43. Interpret Substance Use as Maladaptive Coping (43)

A. The client was given the interpretation that substance abuse has been a maladaptive coping behavior to avoid feelings connected to the abuse.

B. The interpretation of substance abuse as a maladaptive coping behavior was processed with the client, and healthier ways to express feelings were explored, identified, and encouraged.

C. The client agreed with the interpretation that he/she was using substance abuse as an escape from feelings of pain and rage.

D. The client denied the interpretation that his/her substance abuse was in any way related to being a victim of abuse.

POSTTRAUMATIC STRESS DISORDER (PTSD)

CLIENT PRESENTATION

1. Traumatic Event (1)*

A. The client described a traumatic experience that exposed him/her to threats of death.

B. The client described a traumatic experience that resulted in serious injury to self and/or others.

C. The client described a history of being physically and/or sexually abused.

D. The client was open and talkative about the traumatic event(s).

E. The client was guarded and reluctant to talk about the traumatic event(s).

2. Intrusive, Distressing Thoughts (2)

A. The client reported that he/she has experienced frequent intrusive, distressing thoughts or images about the traumatic event.

B. The client was visibly upset when describing the distressing images of the traumatic event.

C. The client denied experiencing any intrusive, distressing thoughts or images about the traumatic event.

D. The frequency and intensity of the client's intrusive, distressing thoughts or images have started to decrease as he/she works through his/her thoughts and feelings about the traumatic event.

3. Disturbing Dreams (3)

A. The client reported experiencing frequent nightmares or distressing dreams since the traumatic event first occurred.

B. The client has continued to be troubled by disturbing dreams associated with the trauma.

C. The client has experienced a mild reduction in the frequency of the disturbing dreams.

D. The client has not experienced any disturbing dreams about the traumatic event since the last therapy session.

4. Flashbacks, Hallucinations, Illusions (4)

A. The client reported experiencing numerous flashbacks, hallucinations, or illusions that the traumatic event is recurring.

B. The client experienced a flashback or hallucination during today's therapy session when discussing the traumatic event.

C. The frequency of the client's flashbacks, hallucinations, or illusions has started to decrease as he/she makes productive use of therapy.

D. The client denied experiencing any recent flashbacks, hallucinations, or illusions.

---

*The numbers in parentheses correlate to the number of the Behavioral Definition statement in the companion chapter with the same title in *The Adolescent Psychotherapy Treatment Planner,* Fourth Edition (Jongsma, Peterson, McInnis, and Bruce) by John Wiley & Sons, 2006.

5. Intense Emotional Distress (5)

A. The client has experienced a significant amount of emotional distress and turmoil since the traumatic event first occurred.

B. The client was visibly distressed and upset when discussing the traumatic event.

C. The intensity of the client's emotional distress when discussing the traumatic event has started to diminish.

D. The client has been able to talk about the traumatic event without displaying a significant amount of emotional distress.

6. Strong Physiological Reaction (6)

A. The client reported that he/she often exhibits an intense physiological reaction (e.g., trembling and shaking, palpitations, dizziness, shortness of breath, sweating) when reminded of the traumatic event.

B. The client demonstrated a strong physiological reaction (e.g., trembling and shaking, shortness of breath, sweating) when discussing the traumatic event in today's therapy session.

C. The client's negative physiological reactions have started to decrease in intensity when talking about the traumatic event.

D. The client did not experience any negative physiological reaction when discussing the traumatic event.

7. Avoidance of Talking about Trauma (7)

A. The client has avoided conversations about the trauma and also tries to avoid thinking about it.

B. In an attempt to avoid the feelings associated with the trauma, the client has avoided talking about it.

C. The client's general avoidance of the subject of the trauma has waned, and he/she is willing to discuss it briefly.

D. The client is now able to think about, talk about, and experience feelings about the trauma without fear of being overwhelmed.

8. Avoidance of Activities Associated with Trauma (8)

A. The client has avoided engaging in activities, going places, or interacting with people associated with the traumatic event.

B. The client acknowledged that he/she avoids activities, places, or people that remind him/her of the traumatic event because of the fear of being overwhelmed by powerful emotions.

C. The client has started to tolerate exposure to activities, places, or people that remind him/her of the traumatic event without feeling overwhelmed.

D. The client has returned to a pretrauma level of functioning without avoiding people or places associated with the traumatic event.

9. Limited Recall (9)

A. The client reported that he/she is unable to recall some important aspects of the traumatic event.

B. The client's emotional distress has been so great that he/she is unable to recall many details of the traumatic event.

C. The client has started to recall some of the important details of the traumatic event.

D. The client recalled most of the important aspects of the traumatic event.

10. Lack of Interest (10)

A. The client has displayed little interest in activities that normally brought him/her pleasure before the traumatic event.

B. The client has significantly reduced his/her participation in social or extracurricular activities since the traumatic event.

C. The client verbalized little or no interest in socializing or participating in extracurricular activities.

D. The client has started to participate in more social or extracurricular activities.

E. The client has participated in social or extracurricular activities on a regular, consistent basis.

11. Social Detachment (11)

A. The client has become more withdrawn since the traumatic event first occurred.

B. The client appeared aloof and detached in today's therapy session.

C. The client has started to socialize with a wider circle of peers.

D. The client has become more outgoing and interacts with his/her peers on a regular, consistent basis.

12. Emotionally Constricted (12)

A. The client has generally appeared flat and constricted in his/her emotional presentation since the traumatic event.

B. The client's affect appeared flat and constricted when talking about the traumatic event.

C. The client acknowledged that he/she is reluctant to share his/her deeper emotions pertaining to the traumatic event because of the fear of losing control of his/her emotions.

D. The client has started to show a wider range of emotions about the traumatic event in the therapy sessions.

E. The client has been able to express his/her genuine emotions about the traumatic event without feeling overwhelmed.

13. Pessimistic Outlook (13)

A. The client has developed a pessimistic outlook on the future and often feels overwhelmed by feelings of helplessness and hopelessness.

B. The client verbalized feelings of helplessness and hopelessness during today's therapy session.

C. The client has gradually begun to develop a brighter outlook on the future.

D. The client expressed a renewed sense of hope for the future in today's therapy session.

E. The client's willingness to assert himself/herself and assume healthy risks reflected his/her renewed sense of hope and feelings of empowerment.

14. Sleep Disturbance (14)

A. The client has experienced significant disturbances in his/her sleep patterns since the traumatic event.

B. The client reported having problems falling asleep.

C. The client has experienced frequent early morning awakenings.

D. The client reported recent improvements in his/her sleep.

E. The client reported experiencing a return to his/her normal sleep patterns.

15. Irritability (15)

A. The client has displayed irritability and moodiness since the trauma occurred.

B. The client's irritability has resulted in many incidents of verbal outbursts of anger over small issues.

C. The client is becoming less irritable as the trauma is processed and underlying feelings are resolved.

16. Lack of Concentration (16)

A. The client has not been able to maintain concentration on schoolwork or other tasks.

B. The client states that his/her concentration is interrupted by flashbacks to the traumatic incident.

C. The client's concentration is becoming more focused as the feelings surrounding the trauma are resolved.

17. Hypervigilance/Mistrustfulness (17)

A. The client has developed a deep mistrust of others because of the traumatic event.

B. The client described himself/herself as being overly vigilant when he/she goes out into public places because of fear of possible harm or danger.

C. The client appeared guarded and mistrustful during today's therapy session.

D. The client has slowly begun to develop trust when in the presence of others and relaxed acceptance with several individuals.

E. The client's increased trust in others has helped to stabilize his/her mood and allowed him/her to work through many thoughts and feelings about the traumatic event.

18. Exaggerated Startle Response (18)

A. The client has often displayed an exaggerated startle response when exposed to any sudden, unexpected stimuli.

B. The client displayed an exaggerated startle response in today's therapy session.

C. The client reported that he/she no longer startles as easily or dramatically when exposed to unexpected stimuli.

19. Symptoms for One Month (19)

A. The client has displayed a variety of symptoms associated with posttraumatic stress for over a month.

B. The client's symptom pattern has begun to decrease in intensity.

C. The client reported being free of all symptoms associated with the traumatic incident.

20. Guilt (20)

A. The client has been troubled by strong feelings of guilt since the traumatic event first occurred.

B. The client expressed feelings of guilt about surviving, causing, or not preventing the traumatic event.

C. The client has begun to work through and resolve his/her feelings of guilt about the traumatic event.

D. The client verbally denied experiencing any feelings of guilt about the traumatic event.

E. The client has successfully resolved his/her feelings of guilt about the traumatic event.

21. Depression (20)

A. The client reports experiencing a significant amount of depression and unhappiness since the traumatic event first occurred.

B. The client expressed strong feelings of sadness and hurt about the traumatic event.

C. The client's level of depression has begun to diminish as he/she works through many of his/her thoughts and feelings about the traumatic event.

D. The client did not appear sad or depressed when talking about the traumatic event.

E. The frequency and intensity of the client's depressed moods have decreased significantly.

22. Angry Outbursts/Aggression (21)

A. The client described a persistent pattern of exhibiting intense outbursts of rage or becoming physically aggressive.

B. The client expressed strong feelings of anger and rage about the traumatic event.

C. The client has recently struggled to control his/her hostile/aggressive impulses.

D. The client was able to talk about the traumatic event with much less anger and resentment.

E. The frequency and severity of the client's angry outbursts and aggressive behaviors have decreased significantly.

INTERVENTIONS IMPLEMENTED

1. Build Trust (1)*

A. The focus of today's therapy session was on building the level of trust with the client through consistent eye contact, active listening, unconditional positive regard, and warm acceptance.

B. The client received unconditional positive regard and warm acceptance to help increase his/her ability to identify and express feelings connected to the traumatic event.

C. The therapy session was helpful in building the level of trust with the client.

D. The therapy session did not prove to be helpful in building the level of trust with the client, as he/she remained guarded in talking about the traumatic event.

2. Assess Nature of Anxiety Symptoms (2)

A. The client was asked about the frequency, intensity, duration and history of his/her anxiety symptoms, fear, and avoidance.

*The numbers in parentheses correlate to the number of the Therapeutic Intervention statement in the companion chapter with the same title in *The Adolescent Psychotherapy Treatment Planner,* Fourth Edition (Jongsma, Peterson, McInnis, and Bruce) by John Wiley & Sons, 2006.

B. *The Anxiety Disorder's Interview Schedule for Children—Parent Version* or *Child Version* (Silverman and Albano) was used to assess the client's anxiety symptoms.

C. The assessment of the client's anxiety symptoms indicated that his/her symptoms are extreme and severely interfere with his/her life.

D. The assessment of the client's anxiety symptoms indicates that these symptoms are moderate and occasionally interfere with his/her daily functioning.

E. The results of the assessment of the client's anxiety symptoms indicate that these symptoms are mild and rarely interfere with his/her daily functioning.

F. The results of the assessment of the client's anxiety symptoms were reviewed with the client.

3. Conduct Psychological Testing (3)

A. The client was administered psychological testing to assess for the presence and strength of PTSD symptoms.

B. The client was referred for psychological testing to assess the presence and strength of PTSD symptoms.

C. The client was administered the Clinician-Administered PTSD Scale–Child and Adolescent Version (CAPS-Copy; Nader, Blake, Kriegler, and Pynoos).

D. The psychological testing indicated that the client's PTSD symptoms are extreme and severely interfere with his/her life.

E. The psychological testing indicated that the client's PTSD symptoms are moderate and occasionally interfere with his/her life.

F. The psychological testing indicated that the client's PTSD symptoms are mild and rarely interfere with his/her life.

G. The client declined to complete the psychological testing, and the focus of treatment was changed to this resistance.

4. Explore Facts of Traumatic Event (4)

A. The client was gently encouraged to tell the entire story of the traumatic event.

B. The client was given the opportunity to share what he/she recalls about the traumatic event.

C. The "Impact of Frightening or Dangerous Event" exercise from the *Adolescent Psychotherapy Homework Planner,* 2nd ed. (Jongsma, Peterson, and McInnis) was used to help the client explore the traumatic event.

D. Today's therapy session explored the sequence of events before, during, and after the traumatic event.

E. Despite encouragement, the client struggled to disclose information about the traumatic events.

5. Assess Depression/Suicide Potential (5)

A. The client's depression was assessed.

B. The client's suicide potential was assessed.

C. Appropriate treatment was indicated for the client's level of depression and suicide.

D. Appropriate safety precautions were taken due to the client's high level of depression and suicide potential.

E. The client was judged to have a very low level of depression and no significant suicide potential.

6. Conduct Complete Chemical Dependence Evaluation (6)

A. The client was assessed for his/her chemical dependence concerns, including substance abuse history, the nature of drugs used, peer use, physiological dependence signs, family use, and consequences.

B. An assessment was arranged for the client's chemical dependence concerns, including substance abuse history, the nature of drugs used, peer use, physiological dependence signs, family use, and consequences.

C. The chemical dependence evaluation indicated a high level of substance abuse concerns.

D. The chemical dependence evaluation indicated a moderate level of chemical dependence and substance abuse concerns.

E. The chemical dependence evaluation indicated a low level of chemical dependence and substance abuse concerns.

F. The client declined any involvement in a substance abuse evaluation, and the focus of treatment was changed to this resistance.

7. Explore Substance Use as Coping Mechanism (7)

A. The concept of how substance abuse can be used as a coping mechanism for fear, guilt, and rage associated with the trauma was explained to the client.

B. The client was asked about his/her own use of substance abuse as a coping mechanism.

C. The client was provided with tentative examples of how he/she may have used substance abuse as a coping mechanism.

D. The client denied any use of substances as a coping mechanism for his/her trauma; he/she was encouraged to remain open to this concept.

E. The client endorsed the use of substances as a coping mechanism, and the focus of treatment was shifted to this problem area.

8. Refer for Chemical Dependence Treatment (8)

A. The client was referred for chemical dependence treatment.

B. The client has accepted the referral for chemical dependence treatment, and his/her progress in this area was reviewed.

C. The client has declined any involvement in the chemical dependence treatment, and goals for his/her treatment were reassessed.

9. Refer for Medication Evaluation (9)

A. The client was referred for a medication evaluation to help stabilize his/her moods and decrease the intensity of his/her angry feelings.

B. The client and parent(s) agreed to follow through with the medication evaluation.

C. The client was strongly opposed to being placed on medication to help stabilize his/her moods and reduce emotional distress.

10. Monitor Effects of Medication (10)

A. The client's response to the medication was discussed in today's therapy session.

B. It was noted that the medication has helped the client to stabilize his/her moods and decrease the intensity of his/her angry feelings.

C. It was noted that the client has had little or no improvement in his/her moods or anger control since being placed on the medication.

D. The client was reinforced as he/she has consistently taken the medication as prescribed.

E. The client has failed to comply with taking the medication as prescribed and was redirected to do so.

11. Conduct Multimodality Trauma Treatment (11)

A. The client was treated with multimodality trauma treatment techniques as described in "Cognitive-behavioral psychotherapy for children and adolescents with Posttraumatic Stress Disorder Following a Single-Incident Stressor" (March, Amaya-Jackson, Murray, and Schulte).

B. The client was treated with individual therapy techniques based on the multimodality trauma treatment model.

C. The client was engaged in a group using multimodality treatment techniques.

12. Discuss PTSD Symptoms (12)

A. A discussion was held about how PTSD results from exposure to trauma and results in intrusive recollections, unwarranted fears, anxiety, and a vulnerability to other negative emotions.

B. The client was provided with specific examples of how PTSD symptoms occur and affect individuals.

C. The client displayed a clear understanding of the dynamics of PTSD and was provided with positive feedback.

D. The client has struggled to understand the dynamics of PTSD and was provided with remedial feedback in this area.

13. Assign Reading on Anxiety (13)

A. The client was assigned to read psychoeducational chapters of books or treatment manuals on PTSD.

B. The client was assigned information from *It Happened to Me* (Carter).

C. The client has read the assigned information on PTSD, and key points were reviewed.

D. The client has not read the assigned information on PTSD and was redirected to do so.

14. Discuss Treatment Rationale (14)

A. The client was taught about the overall rational behind treatment of PTSD.

B. The client was assisted in identifying the appropriate goals for PTSD treatment.

C. The client was taught about coping skills, cognitive restructuring, and exposure techniques.

D. The client was taught about techniques that will help to build confidence, desensitize and overcome fears, and see self, others, and the world in a less fearful and/or depressing manner.

E. The client was reinforced for his/her clear understanding of the rational for treatment of PTSD.

F. The client struggled to understand the rationale behind the treatment for PTSD and was provided with additional feedback in this area.

15. Assign Written Information on PTSD (15)

A. The client was assigned to read about stress inoculation, cognitive restructuring, and/or exposure-based therapy in chapters of books or treatment manuals on PTSD.

B. The client was assigned specific chapters from *The PTSD Workbook* (Williams and Poijula).

C. The client has read the assigned information on PTSD; key concepts were reviewed.

D. The client has not read the assigned information on PTSD and was redirected to do so.

16. Teach Stress Inoculation Training (16)

A. The client was taught strategies from stress inoculation training, such as relaxation, breathing, covert modeling, and role-play.

B. The client was taught stress inoculation techniques for managing fears from *A Clinical Handbook for Treating PTSD* (Meichenbaum) until a sense of mastery was evident.

C. The client was taught stress inoculation techniques for managing fears from *Cognitive Behavioral Psychotherapy* (Francis and Beidel) until a sense of mastery was evident.

D. The client was assisted in practicing stress inoculation training techniques.

E. The client displayed a clear understanding of the use of stress inoculation training.

F. The client has not displayed a clear understanding of the stress inoculation training techniques and was provided with additional feedback in this area.

17. Assign Calming and Coping Strategies (17)

A. The client was assigned to read about calming and coping strategies in books or treatment manuals on PTSD.

B. The client was assisted in learning specific calming and coping strategies as described in *I Can't Get Over It* (Matsakis).

C. The client has read the information about calming and coping strategies, and key points were reviewed.

D. The client was assisted in developing specific ways that he/she can implement calming and coping strategies.

E. The client has not read the information about calming and coping strategies and was redirected to do so.

18. Teach Anger Management Techniques (18)

A. The client was taught mediational and self-control strategies to help improve his/her anger control (taking time out, physical exercise).

B. The client was taught guided imagery and relaxation techniques to help improve his/her anger control.

C. Role-playing and modeling techniques were used to demonstrate effective ways to control anger.

D. The client was strongly encouraged to express his/her anger through controlled, respectful verbalizations and healthy physical outlets.

E. A reward system was designed to reinforce the client for demonstrating good anger control.

19. Identify Distorted Thoughts (19)

A. The client was assisted in identifying the distorted schemas and related automatic thoughts that mediate PTSD responses.

B. The client was taught the role of distorted thinking in precipitating emotional responses.

C. The client was reinforced as he/she verbalized an understanding of the cognitive beliefs and messages that mediate his/her PTSD responses.

D. The client was assisted in replacing distorted messages with positive, realistic cognitions.

E. The client failed to identify his/her distorted thoughts and cognitions and was provided with tentative examples in this area.

20. Assign Reading on Cognitive Restructuring (20)

A. The client was assigned to read about cognitive restructuring in relevant books and treatment manuals.

B. The client was directed to read about cognitive restructuring in *The PTSD Workbook* (Williams and Poijula).

C. The client has read the assigned information on cognitive restructuring, and key points were reviewed.

D. The client has not read the assigned information on cognitive restructuring and was redirected to do so.

21. Assign Self-Talk Homework (21)

A. The client was assigned homework exercises in which he/she identifies fearful self-talk and creates reality-based alternatives.

B. The "Bad Thoughts Lead to Depressed Feelings" exercise from the *Adolescent Psychotherapy Homework Planner,* 2nd ed. (Jongsma, Peterson, and McInnis) was used to help the client develop healthy self-talk.

C. The client has completed his/her homework related to self-talk and creating reality-based alternatives; he/she was provided with positive reinforcement for his/her success in this area.

D. The client has completed his/her homework related to self-talk and creating reality-based alternatives; he/she was provided with corrective feedback for his/her failure to identify and replace self-talk with reality-based alternatives.

E. The client has not attempted his/her homework related to fearful self-talk and reality-based alternatives and was redirected to do so.

22. Construct Anxiety Stimuli Hierarchy (22)

A. The client was assisted in constructing a hierarchy of anxiety-producing situations associated with two or three spheres of worry.

B. It was difficult for the client to develop a hierarchy of stimulus situations, as the causes of his/her anxiety remain quite vague; he/she was assisted in completing the hierarchy.

C. The client was successful at creating a focused hierarchy of specific stimulus situations that provoke anxiety in a gradually increasing manner; this hierarchy was reviewed.

D. The client was directed to develop a detailed narrative description of the trauma for imaginal exposure.

23. Use Imaginal Exposure (23)

A. The client was asked to describe a traumatic experience at an increasing but client-chosen level of detail.

B. The client was asked to continue to describe his/her traumatic experience at his/her own chosen level of detail until the associated anxiety reduces and stabilizes.

C. The client was provided with a recording of the session and was asked to listen to it between sessions.

D. The client was directed to do imaginal exposure as described in *Posttraumatic Stress Disorder* (Resick and Calhoun).

E. The client was reinforced for his/her progress in imaginal exposure.

F. The client was assisted in problem-solving obstacles to his/her imaginal exposure.

24. Assign Homework on Exposures (24)

A. The client was assigned homework exercises to perform exposure to feared stimuli and record his/her experience.

B. The client was assigned situational exposures homework from "Gradually Facing a Phobic Fear" from the *Adolescent Psychotherapy Homework Planner,* 2nd ed. (Jongsma, Peterson, and McInnis).

C. The client was assigned situational exposures homework from *Posttraumatic Stress Disorder* (Resick and Calhoun).

D. The client's use of exposure techniques was reviewed and reinforced.

E. The client has struggled in his/her implementation of exposure techniques and was provided with corrective feedback.

F. The client has not attempted to use the exposure techniques and was redirected to do so.

25. Assign Reading Material on Exposure (25)

A. The client was assigned to read about exposure in books or treatment manuals on PTSD.

B. The client was assigned to read information from *Reclaiming Your Life After Rape* (Rothbaum and Foa).

C. The client has read the information on exposure techniques, and key points were reviewed.

D. The client has not read the information on exposure techniques and was redirected to do so.

26. Teach Thought-Stopping (26)

A. The client was taught a thought-stopping technique.

B. The client was taught to internally voice the word "STOP" immediately upon noticing unwanted trauma or other negative unwanted thoughts.

C. The client was taught to imagine something representing the concept of stopping (e.g., a stop sign or stoplight) immediately upon noticing unwanted trauma or other negative unwanted thoughts.

D. "Making Use of the Thought-Stopping Technique" from the *Adult Psychotherapy Homework Planner,* 2nd ed. (Jongsma) was assigned.

E. The client was assisted in reviewing his/her use of thought-stopping techniques and was provided with positive feedback for his/her appropriate use of this technique.

F. Redirection was provided, as the client has not learned to use the thought-stopping technique.

27. Teach Self-Dialogue Procedure (27)

A. The client was taught self-dialogue procedures as described in *Posttraumatic Stress Disorder* (Resick and Calhoun).

B. The client was taught self-dialogue techniques that learn to recognize maladaptive self-talk, challenge its biases, cope with engendered feelings, overcome avoidance, and reinforce accomplishments.

C. The client was reinforced for his/her use of self-dialogue procedures.

D. The client has found significant obstacles to using self-dialogue procedures and was assisted in problem-solving these concerns.

28. Discuss Lapse Versus Relapse (28)

A. The client was assisted in differentiating between a lapse and a relapse.

B. A lapse was associated with the initial and reversible return of symptoms, fear, or urges to avoid.

C. A relapse was associated with the decision to return to fearful and avoidant patterns.

D. The client was reinforced for his/her ability to respond to a lapse without relapsing.

29. Identify and Rehearse Response to Lapse Situations (29)

A. The client was asked to identify the future situations or circumstances in which lapses could occur.

B. The client was asked to rehearse the management of his/her potential lapse situations.

C. The client was reinforced as he/she identified and rehearsed how to cope with potential lapse situations.

D. The client was provided with helpful feedback about how to best manage potential lapse situations.

E. The client declined to identify or rehearse the management of possible lapse situations, and this resistance was redirected.

30. Encourage Use of Therapy Strategies (30)

A. The client was encouraged to routinely use strategies used in therapy.

B. The client was urged to use cognitive restructuring, social skills, and exposure techniques while building social interactions and relationships.

C. The client was reinforced for his/her regular use of therapy techniques within social interactions and relationships.

D. The client was unable to identify many situations in which he/she has used therapy techniques to help build social interactions and social relationships, and he/she was redirected to seek these situations out.

31. Develop a "Coping Card" (31)

A. The client was provided with a coping card on which specific coping strategies were listed.

B. The client was assisted in developing his/her coping card in order to list his/her helpful coping strategies.

C. The client was encouraged to use his/her coping card when struggling with anxiety-producing situations.

32. Utilize Eye Movement Desensitization and Reprocessing (EMDR) (32)

A. The client was trained in the use of EMDR technique to reduce his/her emotional reactivity to the traumatic event.

B. The client reported that the EMDR technique has been helpful in reducing his/her emotional reactivity to the traumatic event; he/she was encouraged to continue this technique.

C. The client reported partial success with the use of the EMDR technique to reduce emotional distress and was provided with further assistance in this area.

D. The client reported little or no improvement with the use of the EMDR technique to decrease his/her emotional reactivity to the traumatic event, and the use of this technique was reevaluated.

33. Encourage Physical Exercise (33)

A. The client was encouraged to consult his/her physician regarding the appropriate routine of physical exercise.

B. The client was referred to a fitness expert for an appropriate physical exercise regimen.

C. The client was encouraged to regularly exercise in order to keep fit.

D. The client was reinforced for his/her regular use of exercise.

E. The client has not regularly exercised and was redirected to do so.

34. Recommend Exercise Program (34)

A. The client was recommended to read appropriate information on implementation of an exercise program.

B. The client was encouraged to read *Exercising Your Way to Better Mental Health* (Leith).

C. The mental health benefits of regular exercise were explained to the client.

35. Monitor Sleep Patterns (35)

A. The client was encouraged to keep a record of how much sleep he/she gets every night.

B. The client was trained in the use of relaxation techniques to help induce sleep.

C. The client was trained in the use of positive imagery to help induce sleep.

D. The client was referred for a medication evaluation to determine whether medication is needed to help him/her sleep.

36. Hold Family Session to Facilitate Offering of Support (36)

A. A family therapy session was held to allow the client to express his/her feelings about the traumatic event in the presence of his/her family members.

B. A family therapy session was held to give family members the opportunity to provide much-needed emotional support to the client.

C. It was noted that the client responded favorably to the show of support from his/her family members.

D. Today's therapy session allowed all the family members to express their feelings about the traumatic event.

E. Today's family therapy session explored the factors that interfere with the family members' ability to provide emotional support and nurturance to the client.

37. Refer to Group Therapy (37)

A. The client was referred for group therapy to help him/her share and work through his/her feelings about the trauma with other individuals who have experienced traumatic incidents.

B. The client was given the directive to self-disclose about his/her traumatic experience at least once during the group therapy session.

C. The client's involvement in group therapy has helped him/her realize that he/she is not alone in experiencing painful emotions surrounding a traumatic event.

D. The client's active participation in group therapy has helped him/her share and work through many of his/her emotions pertaining to the traumatic event.

E. The client has not made productive use of the group therapy sessions and has been reluctant to share his/her feelings about the traumatic event.

38. Replace Distorted, Negative, Self-Defeating Thoughts (38)

A. The client was helped to replace his/her distorted, negative self-defeating thoughts with positive, reality-based self-talk.

B. The client was encouraged to make positive self-statements to improve his/her self-esteem and decrease his/her emotional pain.

C. The client was given the homework assignment to make at least one positive self-statement daily around others.

D. The client's distorted, negative, self-defeating thoughts were challenged to help him/her overcome the pattern of catastrophizing events and/or expecting the worst to occur.

E. The client reported experiencing increased calm by being able to replace his/her distorted, cognitive, self-defeating thoughts with positive, reality-based self-talk; the benefits of this skill were emphasized.

PSYCHOTICISM

CLIENT PRESENTATION

1. Bizarre Thought Content (1)*

A. The client's thought content contains many bizarre elements.

B. Delusions of grandeur, persecution, and reference dominate the client's thought content.

C. The client reported feeling often under the influence and control of others and unable to do anything about it.

D. The client's bizarre thought content has slowly decreased, and he/she is starting to think more clearly and rationally.

2. Illogical Speech (2)

A. The client presented with several speech oddities, which included perseverations, neologisms, and clanging.

B. There is a vague, abstract, and repetitive quality to the client's speech.

C. A looseness of associations dominates the client's speech.

D. The client's speech has begun to be more logical and coherent, free from neologisms and clanging.

3. Perception Disturbances (3)

A. The client's perceptions appeared disturbed by auditory hallucinations.

B. The client revealed a history of having periodic auditory and visual hallucinations.

C. The level or degree of the client's hallucinations has affected all areas of his/her functioning.

D. The client presented in a fearful, preoccupied manner related to his/her persistent auditory hallucinations.

E. Since beginning a medication regime, the client's hallucinations have become manageable and his/her level of daily functioning has markedly improved.

4. Disturbed Affect (4)

A. The client's affect had a blunt, flat quality, with no range being evident.

B. In most situations the client's affect is grossly inappropriate.

C. There is a dull, flat quality to the client's affect.

D. The client has recently started to show some appropriate spontaneity in his/her affect.

E. The client has started to regain his/her range of affect since taking medication regularly.

5. Lost Sense of Self (5)

A. The client presented as being very lost and confused.

B. The client's boundaries and identity seem to be confused and diffused.

*The numbers in parentheses correlate to the number of the Behavioral Definition statement in the companion chapter with the same title in *The Adolescent Psychotherapy Treatment Planner,* Fourth Edition (Jongsma, Peterson, McInnis, and Bruce) by John Wiley & Sons, 2006.

C. Often, the client reported feeling lost and confused as if in a fog.

D. Consistently, the client responds inappropriately to what others do or say to him/her.

E. The client has shown steady improvement in his/her sense of identity and is now able to identify the boundaries between himself/herself and others as well as give an accurate description of person, place, and time.

6. Diminished Volition (6)

A. The client presented exhibiting low energy and little interest in anything.

B. It is evident from talking to the client that he/she has persistent difficulty following a course of action through to its logical conclusion.

C. The client reported having no past or present goals and identified with living mostly for the present moment.

D. Ambivalence dominates the client's talk and actions.

E. The client is showing improved interest initiative and follow-through with activities.

7. Relationship Withdrawal (7)

A. The client presented as withdrawn and fearful.

B. In the recent past, the client has gradually withdrawn more and more from others and become focused on fearful thoughts and feelings.

C. The client gives a clear message of being fearful of others and wanting others at a distance from him/her.

D. The client's fear of social contact has diminished, and he/she is responding appropriately to social overtures from others.

8. Tense/Frightened (7)

A. The client presented in a tense and frightened manner.

B. There is a hypervigilance to the client's reactions and interactions to others that reflects a level of tension and fear.

C. In the counseling session, the client appeared visibly tense and in a state of near fright.

D. Gradually the client has become less tense and frightened and able to relate more openly about himself/herself.

9. Aloof/Distant (8)

A. The manner of the client is aloof and distant.

B. The client's pattern of relationships with others reflects a distance and aloofness, avoiding any closeness.

C. The client reported a history of having no close friends and a preference for a few acquaintances.

D. The client showed no interest in the therapist or the counseling process.

E. Recently, the client is relating with a bit more warmth, spontaneity, and interest in others.

10. Poor Social Skills (8)

A. The client is socially awkward and has an inept manner.

B. In his/her contacts with others, the client makes sure to keep a good degree of emotional distance.

C. The client reported that in most social situations he/she feels awkward and threatened.

D. On a consistent basis the client seems to misinterpret the actions and motives of others.

E. After becoming involved in his/her counseling sessions, the client has started to initiate interactions and does not misinterpret the motives and actions of others to as great a degree.

11. Impulsive Thoughts/Feelings/Actions (9)

A. The client reported a history of sexual and aggressive impulsive acts that have most often been directed at friends and family.

B. The fantasies of the client are consistently sexual and aggressive.

C. The blame for his/her sexual and aggressive impulses and fantasies is often put on others.

D. Since starting on medications, a steady decrease in the client's impulsive and aggressive acts and fantasies has occurred.

12. Psychomotor Abnormalities (10)

A. The client's manner is marked by numerous unusual mannerisms and facial grimaces.

B. The client's interactions with his/her environment are very limited.

C. The client displays catatonic patterns that range from stupor to rigidity to excitement.

D. The client's psychomotor abnormalities have terminated, and no unusual facial or motor reactions to internal stimuli are apparent.

INTERVENTIONS IMPLEMENTED

1. Assess Thought Disorder (1)*

A. A clinical interview was conducted to assess the pervasiveness of the client's thought disorder.

B. The client was guarded yet cooperative throughout the clinical interview.

C. The pervasiveness of the client's thought disorder was established and appropriate interventions developed and implemented to address it.

2. Determine Nature of Psychosis (2)

A. A clinical interview was conducted with the client to determine whether the client's psychosis is brief and reactive or long term in nature.

B. The client was referred for a psychiatric evaluation to confirm the nature of the psychosis.

C. The nature of the psychosis was established and confirmed.

D. The client's psychosis was determined to be brief and reactive in nature.

E. The client's psychosis was determined to be long term in nature.

3. Provide Supportive Therapy (3)

A. Supportive therapy was used with the client to reduce his/her distrust, alleviate fears, and promote openness.

B. An approach of genuine warmth and understanding was used with the client to build trust and a sense of security.

*The numbers in parentheses correlate to the number of the Therapeutic Intervention statement in the companion chapter with the same title in *The Adolescent Psychotherapy Treatment Planner,* Fourth Edition (Jongsma, Peterson, McInnis, and Bruce) by John Wiley & Sons, 2006.

C. The client's fears and mistrust have started to decrease, and he/she was encouraged for beginning to open up.

D. Despite a supportive approach, the client continues to be fearful, mistrustful, and closed.

4. Conduct Psychological Testing (4)

A. A psychological evaluation was conducted to determine the severity and type of the psychosis.

B. The client was referred for psychological evaluation to determine the severity and type of the psychosis.

C. A psychological evaluation could not be completed due to the client's inability to focus.

D. The client was reinforced for approaching the evaluation in a straightforward manner and for being cooperative with the examiner.

E. The results of the psychological testing were provided to the client and his/her parents.

5. Gather Family Mental Illness History (5)

A. The client's family history was explored to identify incidents of mental illness, traumas, or stressors.

B. A positive history of family mental illness was established, and family coping strategies were identified.

C. An exploration of the client's family history revealed no evidence of serious mental illness within known members of the immediate and extended family.

6. Explain Psychotic Process (6)

A. The nature of the psychotic process was explained to the client and his/her family.

B. The biochemical component of psychosis and its confusing effect on rational thought were emphasized to the client and his/her parents.

C. The client's and parents' questions regarding psychotic process were solicited and answered.

D. The importance of family members showing understanding and support of the psychotic member was emphasized and reinforced.

E. Despite attempts to explain the psychotic process, the client and family members were confused by the illness, its causes, and its effects.

7. Refer for Medication Evaluation (7)

A. The client was referred for an evaluation for antipsychotic medications.

B. The client's and family's resistance to psychotropic medication was explored and resolved.

C. The client was asked to make a commitment to take medications as prescribed.

D. The client followed through with the referral to a physician for an evaluation, and antipsychotic medications have been prescribed.

E. The client refused a prescription of psychotropic medication, and he/she was encouraged to reconsider his/her decision about this medical need.

8. Monitor Medication Compliance/Effectiveness (8)

A. The client was monitored for prescription compliance, side effects, and overall effectiveness.

B. The client was redirected, as he/she was inconsistent in taking the prescribed medications.

C. The client was verbally affirmed and reinforced for taking medications as prescribed.

D. The client reported that the prescribed antipsychotic medication is providing relief from the thought disorder symptoms.

9. Arrange for Appropriate Level of Care (9)

A. The client was assessed for his/her needs in terms of level of supervised care.

B. Inpatient treatment was recommended and arranged for the client, as he/she is seriously disabled by the psychotic symptoms.

C. The client does not require inpatient or residential care presently, but he/she will be monitored for his/her need in the future.

D. Family assistance and support were enlisted to secure inpatient treatment for the client.

E. Based on the recommended level of appropriate care, the client has been admitted to a more supervised level of care.

F. Despite the recommendations for a more supervised level of care, the client has not been admitted to any such environment.

10. Probe Stressors (10)

A. Internal and external stressors that may have precipitated the psychotic episode were probed.

B. The client was assisted in identifying recent internal and external stressors in his/her life.

C. An assessment of the client's current life situation revealed significant internal and external stressors in his/her daily life.

D. No significant internal or external stressors could be identified by the client as triggers for the most recent psychotic episode.

11. Explore Feelings Surrounding Stressors (11)

A. The client's feelings surrounding the stressors that triggered the psychotic episode were explored and validated.

B. The client's feelings were processed in a warm, supportive manner.

C. The client was unable to identify and clarify negative feelings associated with the stressors in his/her life and was provided with likely examples of these types of feelings.

12. Identify Threats and Develop Plan (12)

A. The client and family were assisted in identifying the environmental stressors that contributed to the psychotic break.

B. The client and family were helped to develop a plan to cope with or reduce environmental stressors.

C. It was noted that the environmental stressors have been reduced due to the intervention of others on behalf of the client.

D. Despite intervention, the environmental stressors have not been ameliorated, and the client and family were redirected in this area.

13. Explore History of Losses and Traumas (13)

A. The client's history of traumas, losses, and separations was explored.

B. The client was resistive to identifying or talking about losses, traumas, and separations in his/her history, and this resistance was normalized.

C. The client identified several traumatic events in his/her past that have contributed to fear, self-doubt, and emotional fragility.

14. Educate Family Regarding Illness (14)

A. In family sessions, the family members were educated on the client's illness and its causes, symptoms, treatment, and prognosis.

B. Questions raised by the family about the nature, treatment, and prognosis of the client's psychotic illness were answered.

C. Unfounded or unrealistic beliefs or attitudes held by family members were addressed and processed.

15. Encourage Here-and-Now Activities for the Client (15)

A. The value and importance of here-and-now activities in the client's recovery were stressed with the parents and other family members.

B. The parents were asked to identify some here-and-now activities and to encourage the client's involvement.

C. The parents and the client were given affirmation and reinforcement for the client's getting involved in here-and-now activities.

D. The client has been resistant to involving himself/herself in extracurricular social/recreational activities, and he/she was more directly focused onto this area.

16. Encourage Praise for Prosocial Behaviors (16)

A. The parents were encouraged to look for opportunities to praise and reinforce the client for engaging in responsible, adaptive, and prosocial behaviors.

B. Encouragement of the client's healthy behavior was reinforced as a way to model this technique for the parents.

C. It was reflected to the parents that they often praise and reinforce the client for engaging in responsible, adaptive, and prosocial behaviors.

D. The client's parents have not provided praise and reinforcement for the client's responsible, adaptive, and prosocial behaviors and were redirected regarding specific occasions that it would be appropriate for them to do this.

17. Teach Family about Double-Bind Messages (17)

A. The family was taught about double-bind messages that are inconsistent and contradictory and how they negatively impact family members.

B. The family was assisted in recognizing double-bind messages within the family that cause anxiety, confusion, and psychotic symptoms for the client.

C. The family was asked to make a commitment to stop using double-bind messages.

D. Family members were confronted when they used double-bind messages in family sessions.

E. It was reflected to the family that the frequency of the instances of double-bind messages has decreased significantly, as reported by the client and observed within family therapy sessions.

18. Confront Indirect and Disjointed Communications (18)

A. In a family session, the parents were taught to make their communicating consistently clear and direct.

B. Role-play situations were used in a family session to give the parents an opportunity to practice clear and direct communications.

C. The parents were assisted in recognizing the negative impact that indirect and disjointed communication has on the client in terms of confusion and anxiety.

D. Confrontation was utilized with the parents when their communication became indirect and disjointed with the client, and the frequency of this dysfunctional style has diminished.

19. Reduce Family's Level of Criticism and Hostility (19)

A. Family sessions were held in which members were encouraged to express their feelings about the client and his/her illness.

B. Feelings of criticism and hostility toward the client were allowed to be vented by members in family sessions.

C. The family members were supported and affirmed regarding the frustration and difficulty in living with the client and his/her illness.

D. The family members were helped to develop a genuine sense of understanding of the client and his/her illness.

E. The family members were encouraged to practice compassion toward the client and to be understanding of the lack of control the client has over his/her sometimes bizarre symptoms.

20. Assist Parents in Setting Limits on Inappropriate Behavior (20)

A. The parents were encouraged to express their thoughts and feelings about the client's inappropriate aggression and sexual behavior.

B. The parents were assisted in developing and setting firm limits (without hostility toward the client) on his/her inappropriate aggressive and sexual behavior.

C. Consistent support and encouragement were given to the parents for their efforts to set firm limits on the client.

D. The client has responded positively to the parents' setting firm limits, and this was noted to result in a reduction in inappropriate aggressive and sexual behaviors.

21. Encourage Family to Express Feelings Regarding Illness (21)

A. Feelings of frustration, guilt, fear, and depression associated with the client's illness were normalized for family members.

B. Encouragement, support, and understanding were given to family members who shared their feelings about the client's illness and behavior patterns.

C. Family members were confronted and warned about the negative consequences of holding onto negative feelings about the client's illness.

22. Arrange Academic Opportunities (22)

A. Explore with the client and the parents the possibilities for ongoing academic training while the client is in treatment.

B. Arrange for the client to receive ongoing academic training and encourage his/her follow-through and skill development.

C. Although the client has shown a reduction in many of the psychotic symptoms, he/she was noted to be resistant to returning to the academic setting and dealing with the social and cognitive demands inherent in that setting.

23. Educate School Personnel on Client (23)

A. The parents were asked to sign a confidentiality release in order for the therapist and school officials to exchange information.

B. School officials were told what to expect from the client and encouraged to create a supportive, accepting environment for him/her.

C. The client and parents were told that the school personnel have responded favorably to direction and have provided the client with the necessary structure and support in the academic setting.

D. School personnel have not responded favorably to direction and have not provided the client with the necessary structure and support in the academic setting, and further advocacy was provided.

24. Probe Underlying Needs and Feelings (24)

A. The underlying needs and feelings that contribute to the client's internal conflict and irrational beliefs were probed.

B. The client was assisted in connecting his/her feelings and needs with internal conflicts and irrational beliefs.

C. The client was encouraged to let go of unrealistic needs and accompanying feelings.

D. Active listening skills were used as the client described a history of rejection, abandonment, and abuse that has permanently scarred his/her sense of empowerment.

E. The client was unable to identify underlying needs and feelings and was provided with tentative examples in this area.

25. Confront Illogical Speech (25)

A. The client was informed that his/her illogical speech would be gently confronted when they occur in order to refocus his/her thinking.

B. The client was confronted when his/her speech became illogical.

C. To each gentle confrontation the client has responded positively in a cooperative manner and worked to refocus his/her own thoughts.

D. Despite using gentle confrontation, the client still has found it frustrating and not effective in helping him/her refocus.

26. Restructure Irrational Beliefs (26)

A. The client's irrational beliefs were identified and restructured into reality-based phenomena.

B. Each of the client's irrational beliefs was restructured using reality-based evidence.

C. Restructured beliefs were reinforced with the client, and their daily use was encouraged.

D. The client's irrational beliefs have diminished, and his/her thoughts are reality based fairly consistently; he/she was reinforced for this progress.

27. Encourage Focus on External Reality (27)

A. The client was reminded in clear terms of the difference between external reality and distorted fantasy.

B. The client was encouraged and directed to focus on the reality of the external world.

C. The client was directed to check things out with the therapist or others when he/she is confused or unsure of what is reality and what is fantasy.

D. The client has become more adept at differentiating between fantasy and reality and responding appropriately to external circumstances and was reinforced for this progress.

E. Despite encouragement to focus on external reality, the client has continued to struggle with differentiating reality and fantasy and was provided with specific feedback in this area.

28. Help Differentiate Sources of Stimuli (28)

A. The client was assisted in developing skills to differentiate between sources of stimuli from self-generated messages and the reality of the external world.

B. Positive feedback and encouragement were given to the client for successfully differentiating stimuli.

C. The client struggles to differentiate between internal cognitive stimuli and reality-based stimuli and was provided with additional direction.

D. The client was encouraged to consult others when he/she is unsure of the source of the stimuli.

E. It was noted that the client is able to reliably differentiate between internal hallucinatory stimuli and external reality.

29. Interpret Inaccurate Perceptions and Bizarre Associations (29)

A. The client's inaccurate perceptions and bizarre associations were identified.

B. Each bizarre association and inaccurate perception was interpreted to the client as being reflective of unspoken fears of rejection or losing control.

C. The client was asked to use the new interpretations in his/her daily routine when the inaccurate perceptions and bizarre associations occur.

D. The client accepted the interpretations regarding inaccurate perceptions and bizarre associations as being reflective of unspoken fears of rejection or losing control, and he/she was assisted in identifying additional examples in this area.

E. The client denied any connection between his/her inaccurate perceptions or bizarre associations, and unspoken fears of rejection or losing control and was urged to use these interpretations as he/she feels able to do so.

30. Set Limits on Aggressive/Sexual Behavior (30)

A. Firm limits were set for the client on his/her inappropriate aggressive and sexual behavior, along with specific consequences for violating each limit.

B. Appropriate anger and sexual behavior were identified for the client and reinforced.

C. The client was assisted in identifying triggers that precede inappropriate aggressive or sexual acts.

D. The client was taught several techniques to use in controlling his/her impulsiveness.

E. The client's inappropriate sexual and aggressive behavior has ceased as he/she has responded to the setting of firm limits on such behavior.

31. Monitor Daily Level of Functioning (31)

A. The client's daily level of functioning was monitored for reality orientation, personal hygiene, and affect appropriateness.

B. Feedback was given to the client on his/her progress in each area of activities of daily functioning.

C. The client was redirected when he/she was not doing as expected or progressing in each area of his/her daily functioning.

D. Positive progress in areas of daily function was reinforced and further development was encouraged.

E. The client's functioning within the activities of daily living continues to be problematic and shows a lack of progress; remedial assistance was provided.

32. Teach Alternative Social Interactions (32)

A. The client was taught new, positive social skills to be used with family and friends.

B. Role-play and behavioral rehearsal were used to give the client the opportunity to practice each new social skill.

C. The client was asked to make a commitment to try the new social skills he/she has learned with either family or friends.

D. Positive feedback was provided as the client tried new social skills with family and friends; the results of these attempts were reviewed and processed.

E. The client has not attempted to use positive social skills with family and friends and was redirected to do so.

33. Reinforce Appropriate Responses to Others (33)

A. Appropriate social and emotional responses to others were identified with the client.

B. Role-play and behavior rehearsal were used to give the client the opportunity to practice appropriate responses to others and to reinforce the responses.

C. The client's appropriate social and emotional responses to others were verbally encouraged and reinforced.

D. The client was gently confronted and redirected when his/her responses were not socially or emotionally appropriate to others.

34. Refer to a Family Support Group (34)

A. The options for a family support group were explored, and resistance to acknowledging the need for support was addressed.

B. The family was referred to a support group for family members who have a mentally ill loved one.

C. The positives of support groups were identified, and the family was encouraged to attend at least one session.

D. The family members were confronted on their belief that they can "handle it on their own."

E. Despite encouragement, the family is still resistant to trying a support group meeting.

RUNAWAY

CLIENT PRESENTATION

1. Running Away for More Than a Day (1)*

A. The parents reported that the client has run away from home for more than one day on numerous occasions.

B. The client explained that his/her running away was necessary for personal safety until things cooled off at home.

C. The client indicated that his/her running away is nothing to be concerned about.

D. The client has not run away from home since issues within the family have started to be addressed and resolved.

2. Running to Noncustodial Parent (2)

A. The client presented a pattern of running away to the noncustodial parent's home after he/she becomes upset with the custodial parent.

B. The client indicated reluctantly that running to the noncustodial parent's home when he/she is upset has enabled him/her to get his/her way.

C. The parents reported being unhappy with the client's pattern of running to the noncustodial parent but feeling helpless to do anything about it.

D. The client has stopped his/her runaway pattern as he/she has seen the custodial and noncustodial parent begin to work together in their parenting.

3. Running across State Lines (3)

A. The client reported running away from home and traveling to another state.

B. The client indicated that he/she has run away across state lines and has plans to do it again without getting caught.

C. The parents expressed fear that the client would run away again across state lines and never return.

D. The client made an agreement to not run away but to work instead on family issues in therapy sessions.

4. Running Away at Least Twice Overnight (4)

A. The client has run away from home overnight on two or more occasions.

B. The parents indicated that the client has run away overnight on two occasions after he/she was confronted about his/her behavior.

C. The client has agreed to work on conflicts with parents in therapy sessions.

---

* The numbers in parentheses correlate to the number of the Behavioral Definition statement in the companion chapter with the same title in *The Adolescent Psychotherapy Treatment Planner,* Fourth Edition (Jongsma, Peterson, McInnis, and Bruce) by John Wiley & Sons, 2006.

5. Running Away for More Than 48 Hours (5)

A. The client has run away from home for 48 hours or more on at least one occasion.

B. The client has run away for more than 48 hours and had to be returned home by the police.

C. The parents expressed fear that the client has definite plans to run away, as they have discovered him/her making arrangements.

D. The client has offered assurance that he/she does not plan to run away again.

6. Poor Self-Image (6)

A. The client presented with downcast eyes, low voice, and numerous self-disparaging remarks.

B. The client reported that he/she does not like himself/herself and feels ashamed of what he/she is.

C. There is a strong negative, dark, and shame-based quality to all comments the client makes regarding self and life in general.

D. The client has a quick, negative way of responding to any compliments or positive statements.

E. The client's sense of self-worth has increased as issues within the family have started to be addressed.

7. Home Environment (7)

A. The facade of a warm, trusting family has started to crumble as the client has begun telling of parents' neglect and emotional abuse.

B. The client expressed love toward the parents but said that the parents' fighting and drinking upset him/her.

C. The client has begun to express that he/she has never felt wanted or accepted by either parent.

D. The client described his/her home as chaotic, abusive, and sometimes violent.

E. Interviews with the family have brought the abuse and violence to a halt.

8. Conflict with Parents (8)

A. Anger and defiance are very evident in each of the client's responses to the parents' requests.

B. The client reported having numerous angry encounters with parents, teachers, and siblings.

C. The client stated that he/she does not listen to what parents say or follow their "stupid rules."

D. The client's level of conflict with parents has begun to decrease as he/she has taken an active part in the family therapy sessions.

9. Victim of Abuse (9)

A. The client described incidents in which severe abusive punishments were used to address his/her misbehavior.

B. The client's claims of abuse have been reported to the protective services, as mandated by law.

C. The client related a long history of parental emotional abuse that included being blamed for siblings' actions, called negative, hurtful names, and being shamed in front of others.

D. The client identified a pattern of both parents leaving the home for hours or days when conflict occurred.

E. The client has begun to verbalize insight into how his/her history of being abused has played a major role in his/her running away.

10. Trust (9)

A. The client presented in a cautious, mistrustful manner.

B. The client reported that he/she does not trust anyone outside of his/her immediate family and trusts the immediate family on a limited basis.

C. The client sees no one as being worthy of his/her trust, and that is why he/she believes he/she has to watch out for number one.

D. The client stated that he/she has started to trust the therapist a little and that this is an uncomfortable feeling.

INTERVENTIONS IMPLEMENTED

1. Build Trust (1)*

A. Initial level of trust was established with the client through the use of unconditional positive regard.

B. Warm acceptance and active listening techniques were utilized to establish the basis for a trusting relationship with the client.

C. It was noted that the client has formed a trust-based relationship and has started to share his/her feelings with the therapist.

D. Despite the use of active listening, warm acceptance, and unconditional positive regard, the client remains hesitant to trust and share.

2. Explore Causes of Pain (2)

A. The client was educated regarding the many aspects of emotional pain and how it exhibits itself.

B. The client was asked to list the situations that cause him/her to experience emotional and physical pain sufficient to motivate running away.

C. The client was asked to identify his/her pain threshold on a scale of 1 to 10 and indicate at what point he/she begins to express the pain and how he/she does it.

D. Active listening skills were used as the client revealed a history of abuse, neglect, and abandonment that has motivated his/her running away.

E. Emotional support was provided as the client described an ongoing conflict of authority and control that motivated the running away.

F. The client denied any connection between the emotional pain and his/her pattern of running away and was provided with tentative examples of how these may be connected.

---

* The numbers in parentheses correlate to the number of the Therapeutic Intervention statement in the companion chapter with the same title in *The Adolescent Psychotherapy Treatment Planner,* Fourth Edition (Jongsma, Peterson, McInnis, and Bruce) by John Wiley & Sons, 2006.

3. Identify Positive Ways to Resolve Conflict (3)

A. The client was asked to list all the positive, constructive ways he/she could think of to resolve conflictual situations.

B. The client was assisted in choosing from his/her conflict resolution list several constructive ways that conflictual situations could be addressed.

C. In monitoring the client's implementation of new conflict resolution methods, he/she appears to be making an effort to put them into practice when a conflict presents itself.

D. The client is resistive to adopting constructive ways to resolve conflict and continues to project blame for all conflict onto others, and this pattern was reflected to him/her.

4. Teach Conflict Resolution Methods (4)

A. The client was taught various methods of conflict resolution.

B. The client was assisted in selecting two to three resolution techniques to begin implementing into his/her daily life.

C. Positive feedback was provided as the client has successfully implemented effective conflict resolution methods that have led to a more peaceful, respectful interaction within the family.

D. The client is resistive to adopting constructive ways to resolve conflict and continues to project blame for all conflict onto others; he/she was urged to use the conflict resolution technique.

5. Promote Healthy Family Communication (5)

A. Family therapy sessions were conducted to determine the patterns of communication within the family.

B. The parents were instructed in healthy, respectful communication behavior and asked to begin using it immediately.

C. In family sessions, healthy communication styles were modeled for the family, and members were encouraged to implement them.

D. Unhealthy, disrespectful communication patterns were blocked and pointed out in family session, and new, healthy ones were substituted and tried.

E. It was reflected to the family that they have begun to speak to each other with more respect, caring, and understanding instead of the inflammatory, critical, disrespectful style that was used previously.

6. Refer to Problem-Solving Group (6)

A. The client was asked to attend a problem-solving group to improve his/her skills.

B. The client's attendance, participation, and progress were monitored, and verbal affirmation was given the client on progress made.

C. The client has refused to attend the problem-solving group, and his/her reasons for refusal were reviewed and processed.

7. Teach Acceptance of Responsibility (7)

A. The family and client were asked to assign a percentage to their part in causing conflict.

B. The family was assisted in sorting out the question of who is responsible for the problems until a general agreement was reached.

C. The client and parents were asked to use "I statements" to indicate acceptance of their part of the problem(s).

D. It was reflected to the family members that they all have difficulty accepting their role in causing conflict, readily projecting the blame for conflict onto others.

8. Explore Child Abuse Evidence (8)

A. Active-listening skills were used as the client described instances from his/her own childhood of emotional, verbal, and physical abuse.

B. A genogram was constructed with the family that revealed a multigenerational pattern of child abuse that included the client.

C. A strong pattern of maternal physical and emotional neglect during the client's early years was uncovered while completing the biopsychosocial assessment with family.

D. It was noted that the family has a multiyear history of involvement with protective services.

E. Past incidents of physical abuse were minimized by family members, and the pattern was reflected to them.

F. Family members would not directly answer questions related to physical or sexual abuse and were urged to provide information in this area.

9. Procure Respite Care for Client (9)

A. Options for respite placement were presented to the client and family for their consideration and reaction.

B. Conditions for the placement of the client outside of the home were worked out with the family (i.e., visitation, criteria for returning home).

C. A schedule for individual and family sessions was established with the goal of working on the specific issues that need to be resolved before the client can return safely to the home.

D. The client has been removed from the home and placed in an alternative, protective setting while resolution of family issues is sought.

10. Assess Parental Substance Abuse (10)

A. The parents were referred to a local substance abuse agency for a full substance abuse assessment.

B. A substance abuse assessment was conducted on both parents.

C. It was recommended that the parents submit to a substance abuse assessment, which they declined as they saw no need for it.

D. It is evident that the parents have serious substance abuse problems, and a referral for treatment has been made.

E. No substance abuse concerns were identified for the client's parents.

11. Create Genogram (11)

A. The family was assisted in developing a multigeneration genogram that had a special focus on relationships between members and continuing unresolved conflicts.

B. The family was assisted in identifying relationship patterns and family conflicts that are still unresolved.

C. The parents were resistive to acknowledging long-standing conflict between extended family members and themselves and also resisted taking any responsibility for these conflicts; these patterns were reflected to them.

D. The parents were supported as they acknowledged long-standing conflicts with extended family members and indicated sincere interest in attempting to resolve these conflicts.

12. Resolve Extended Family Conflicts (12)

A. The parents were assisted in focusing on unresolved conflicts between themselves and their parents, and they were encouraged to take the necessary steps now to begin resolving those long-standing conflicts.

B. The parents were given several options, rituals, and acts of restoration that could resolve issues with their now-deceased parents.

C. Encouragement was provided as the parents have taken constructive steps toward beginning a healing of broken relationships between themselves and other extended family members.

D. The parents have continued their feuding attitude toward extended family members, refusing to take steps toward conflict resolution, and they were redirected in this area.

13. Identify Parental Rejection (13)

A. The parents were helped to look closely at their parenting style and techniques to identify any interaction, techniques, or messages that convey rejection to the client.

B. New approaches, techniques, and messages were explored to replace the negative ones that were identified as conveying rejection to the client.

C. The parents were supported as they acknowledged that they are conveying messages of rejection and have begun to attempt to convey affirmation and acceptance to the client.

D. The parents are resistive to any suggestion that they have harmed the client by messages of rejection and were provided with examples of this dynamic.

14. Refer for Parenting Class (14)

A. The parents were strongly encouraged to attend a parenting class, and resistance to the idea was resolved.

B. The parents' gains from attending parenting classes were affirmed and supported.

C. The parents have rejected the idea of attending classes to learn more effective parenting skills.

15. Assign Books on Parenting (15)

A. The parents were assigned books on parenting.

B. The parents were encouraged to read *Between Parent and Teenager* (Ginott) or *P.E.T.* (Gordon) or *Raising Self-Reliant Children in a Self-Indulgent World* (Glenn and Neilsen) to further their knowledge and understanding of adolescents.

C. The parents have followed through on reading about parenting techniques, and key ideas that they have learned from the reading were processed.

D. The parents have begun to implement some of the new ideas learned from reading about effective parenting, and the benefits of these changes were reviewed.

E. The parents have not followed through on reading about effective parenting and were redirected to do so.

16. Help Parents Affirm and Value Client (16)

A. The parents were guided in looking at the things parents can do to make children feel affirmed, valued, and part of the family.

B. The parents were asked to list five affirming things they could begin to do as part of relating to and parenting the client.

C. A commitment was requested from the parents to implement and use consistently these affirming techniques.

D. The parents were reinforced as they have made significant progress in implementing actions that affirm the client's value.

17. Identify and Communicate Unmet Needs (17)

A. The client was asked to make a complete list of all of his/her needs that he/she feels are not being met within the family system.

B. The client had difficulty identifying significant social, emotional, or physical needs and was assisted in identifying those needs.

C. The client listed many serious physical and emotional needs that have not been met within the family system, and these were processed.

D. The client read his/her list of unmet needs to the parents in family session, with the parents being instructed to just listen and affirm what they heard.

18. Teach Meeting Own Needs (18)

A. The client was assisted in looking at his/her unmet needs and deciding which of them the client could meet himself/herself.

B. The client was taught the value of meeting one's own needs whenever possible.

C. Positive feedback was provided, as the client has taken healthy, constructive steps toward meeting some of his/her own emotional needs.

D. The client remains focused on blaming the parents for not meeting his/her needs and refuses to take constructive steps to meet his/her own needs; he/she was redirected in this area.

19. Assign a Feelings about Home Exercise (19)

A. The client was assigned to write a description of how he/she perceives his/her family dynamics, and to keep a daily journal of incidents that support or refute his/her perception.

B. The client was asked to complete the "Home by Another Name" or "Undercover Assignment" exercise from the *Adolescent Psychotherapy Homework Planner,* 2nd ed. (Jongsma, Peterson, and McInnis) to assist in externalizing issues that have been kept covert.

C. Verbal support and encouragement were given to the client to aid him/her in taking the risks to look at long-hidden, difficult family conflict issues.

D. The client was firmly but respectfully confronted on his/her pattern of keeping secrets and shown how doing this has a negative impact on him/her and the family.

E. The client was supported as he/she revealed family conflict issues that have been denied and covered for a long time.

F. The client has not completed the assignment to journal his/her issues and feelings connected to the family and was redirected to do so.

20. Assign Grievance Exercise (20)

A. The client was assisted in identifying specific issues of conflict that he/she has with the family.

B. The client was asked to complete the "Airing Your Grievances" exercise from the *Adolescent Psychotherapy Homework Planner,* 2nd ed. (Jongsma, Peterson, and McInnis) to help him/her verbalize and address important personal issues.

C. The parents were confronted about unrealistic developmental expectations or unrealistic solutions to adolescent issues.

D. Completing the "Airing Your Grievances" exercise has helped the client to clarify and verbalize important personal issues.

E. The client has not completed the "Airing Your Grievances" exercise and was redirected to do so.

21. Encourage Respectful Verbalization of Feelings (21)

A. The client's angry and negative feelings were normalized as part of the education about feelings.

B. The client's expression of negative feelings and anger was encouraged, with an emphasis on being respectful and using "I statements."

C. Fears and barriers to the client taking risks and sharing negative feelings were explored, and solutions that would allow him/her to express these angry feelings were suggested.

D. Support was provided as the client has begun to express feelings of anger and hurt that had been previously suppressed.

E. The client has found it very difficult to express his/her negative emotions and continues to suppress feelings like anger, hurt, frustration, and disappointment; he/she was urged to do this in small steps.

22. Teach Communication with Parents (22)

A. Ways to increase constructive, respectful communication between the client and the parents were identified, and a commitment from him/her was elicited to implement and consistently follow through on this style of communicating.

B. The client's implementation and follow-through were monitored, and the client was confronted regarding his/her inconsistent use of the new communication techniques.

C. The client has developed ways to increase constructive, respectful communication between himself/herself and the parents, and the benefits of this improved communication were reviewed.

23. Explore Fears of Independence (23)

A. The client's fears of independence were explored and challenged.

B. A list was created with the client to put in black and white the advantages and disadvantages of independence and dependence.

C. The client acknowledged having a lack of confidence in his/her ability to live independent of parents and was supported for this realism.

D. The client now seems to want to emancipate from the home responsibly, and the ramifications of this decision were reviewed.

24. Help Parents Promote Independence and Maturity (24)

A. The parents were asked to list all the specific ways they could help the client toward becoming more mature and independent.

B. The parents were assisted in selecting and implementing the best ways to foster independence and maturity with the client.

C. It was noted that the parents are supporting, encouraging, and reinforcing the client in becoming more independent and mature.

D. The parents were confronted for their failure to develop and implement ways to increase the client's independence and maturity.

25. Assist in Feelings Identification (25)

A. A printed list of feeling adjectives was used to increase the client's ability to identify and label his/her own feelings and those of others.

B. Various situations were created and presented to the client for him/her to identify how the individuals in those situations might be feeling.

C. The client was asked to keep a daily feelings journal and share it weekly with the therapist.

D. Although it is difficult for the client, he/she has begun to identify and express his/her feelings with some clarity and openness; he/she was encouraged to continue.

26. Develop/Promote Role Awareness (26)

A. The client was asked to describe his/her role in the family and how that role impacts his/her parents.

B. The client's awareness of how his/her role affects the parents was expanded by the therapist's perception and feedback.

C. The client was confronted with specific ways his/her role has a negative impact on the parents and their relationship.

D. The client was requested to take a leave of absence from his/her role of "assistant parent."

27. Identify Covert Family Conflicts (27)

A. In family sessions, the family was supported and assisted in identifying unresolved conflicts within the family that have not yet been addressed.

B. The family members were asked what were they willing to do to change things within the family and then asked if they were ready to free the client from being the symptom bearer of the family problem.

C. The client was prepared for letting go of the role of symptom bearer and coached about how that role could be replaced with a responsible, adjusted teenager.

28. Make Structural Changes within Family (28)

A. During a family session, the structure of the family was assessed to determine whether structural changes could increase healthy family interaction.

B. A structured intervention was developed from the assessment and implemented by the family.

C. The structured intervention that was implemented was reported to be working well.

D. The structured intervention that was implemented to increase healthy family interaction was reported to be working poorly, and brainstorming techniques were used to fine-tune this intervention.

29. Develop/Implement Strategic Change (29)

A. The family was assessed during family session to determine the strategic intervention that would best address family issues and increase their degree of healthy functioning.

B. A strategic intervention was developed with the family, who agreed to fully and consistently implement the intervention.

C. The strategic intervention was monitored and adjusted to maximize positive results.

D. It was noted that all family members reported a positive impact from the newly implemented strategic intervention.

E. The strategic intervention has not had a positive impact, and it was modified.

30. Arrange or Conduct Psychological Evaluation (30)

A. The client was referred for a complete psychological evaluation to establish or rule out affective disorder, psychotic process, ADHD, or substance abuse.

B. The parents were asked to sign a release for exchange of information and recommendations with the evaluation partner.

C. Significant emotional and behavioral problems were revealed through the psychological/psychiatric evaluation of the client.

D. It was confirmed that the client has serious substance abuse problems that need to be addressed in chemical dependence treatment.

E. The client was diagnosed with a serious mental illness that needs to be addressed through treatment.

F. The client was diagnosed with an attention-deficit disorder that contributes to his/her current behavioral problems.

31. Monitor Evaluation Follow-Through (31)

A. Positive feedback was provided as the family reported following through on each of the evaluation's recommendations.

B. The parents' failure to follow through on the psychological evaluation recommendations was addressed.

C. The parents' resistance and concerns about the client taking psychotropic medication were addressed, and the issue was resolved when the parents committed to a medication trial.

32. Contract for a Neutral Placement (32)

A. The parents and the client were assisted in developing a contract for the client's placement in a neutral setting as a temporary living arrangement.

B. Basic guidelines were established regarding the client living outside of the family, which included specification of the frequency of contact with parents and the nature of this contact.

C. A schedule for regular, consistent family sessions was established to continue to actively work on family conflicts while the client is living outside the family.

SCHOOL VIOLENCE

CLIENT PRESENTATION

1. Threats of Violence (1)*

A. The client described a pattern of making threats of violence against students, teachers, and/or administrators.

B. The client projected the blame for his/her threats of violence onto other people.

C. The client has shown increasing control over his/her threatening manner.

D. The client has recently demonstrated good self-control and not engaged in any threatening behavior.

2. Feelings of Alienation (2)

A. The client described feelings of alienation from most peers within the school.

B. The client reports a pattern of failure to connect with his/her peers within the school setting.

C. The client identified a desire to be more involved with his/her peers.

D. The client has developed an increased sense of connection with his/her peers within the school setting.

3. Bullied/Intimidated (3)

A. The client described a history of often being intimidated by his peers.

B. The client identified several incidences of being bullied by his/her peers.

C. The client has felt unable to stop the bullying or intimidation from his/her peers.

D. The client reported a decrease in the bullying and intimidation from his/her peers.

E. The bullying and intimidation toward the client have stopped.

4. Ridicule, Teasing, and Rejection (4)

A. The client has been subjected to ridicule, teasing, and rejection from his/her peers.

B. The client has had strong emotional responses to his/her experience of ridicule, teasing, or rejection from his/her peers.

C. The client has learned healthy responses to his peers' ridicule, teasing, and rejection.

D. The client reported a decrease in ridiculing and teasing.

E. The client feels more accepted by his/her peers.

5. Loss of Temper (5)

A. The client described situations in which he/she has lost his/her temper, which have led to violent or aggressive behavior.

B. The client described a series of incidents in which he/she has become aggressive when upset or frustrated.

*The numbers in parentheses correlate to the number of the Behavioral Definition statement in the companion chapter with the same title in *The Adolescent Psychotherapy Treatment Planner,* Fourth Edition (Jongsma, Peterson, McInnis, and Bruce) by John Wiley & Sons, 2006

C. The client did not take responsibility for his/her aggressive behavior.

D. The client has begun to take steps to control his/her violent and aggressive behavior.

E. The client has recently demonstrated good self-control and not engaged in any violent or aggressive behaviors, even when upset or frustrated.

6. Substance Abuse (6)

A. The client has engaged in a significant amount of substance abuse.

B. The client's substance abuse has contributed substantially to his/her violent and aggressive behavior.

C. The client has verbally denied any recent use of drugs or alcohol.

D. The client's discontinuation of the use of drugs and alcohol has been confirmed by independent sources (parents, school administrators, drug testing).

E. The client has ceased his/her substance abuse.

7. Weapons Fascination (7)

A. The client has a fascination with weapons of all kinds.

B. The client has easy access to weapons.

C. The client often comments about ways in which he/she would like to use weapons.

D. As treatment has progressed, the client's fascination with weapons has decreased.

E. The client's access to weapons has been eliminated.

8. Hurting Animals (8)

A. The client identified a history of hurting animals.

B. The client's parents identified concerns that the client often hurts animals.

C. The client reported that he/she no longer has the desire to hurt animals.

D. The client has demonstrated an attitude of kindness toward animals.

9. Authority Conflicts (9)

A. The client described a negativistic attitude and was highly argumentative during today's therapy session.

B. The client has often tested the limits and challenged authority figures at home, at school, and in the community.

C. The client has often talked back to authority figures in a disrespectful manner when reprimanded.

D. The client has recently been more cooperative with authority figures.

E. The client has been cooperative and respectful toward authority figures on a consistent basis.

10. Poor Academic Performance (10)

A. The client's teachers and parents reported a history of poor academic performance that is below the expected level given the client's measured intelligence or performance on standardized achievement tests.

B. The client verbally admitted that his/her current academic performance is below his/her expected level of functioning.

C. The client has started to assume more responsibility for completing his/her school and homework assignments.

D. The client has taken active steps (e.g., study at routine times, seek outside student tutor, consult with teachers before and after class) to improve his/her academic performance.

E. The client's academic performance has improved to his/her level of capability.

11. Feels Disrespected (11)

A. The client described that he often feels as though his/her peers do not respect him/her.

B. The client described situations in which he/she has felt disrespected by adults.

C. The client blamed his/her temper outbursts on his/her peers and adults for not respecting him.

D. As treatment has progressed, the client has identified ways in which peers and adults are more respectful of him/her.

12. Lacks Close Attachment (12)

A. The client does not have close attachment with other family members.

B. Due to the client's family dynamics, it has been difficult for him/her to attach to other family members.

C. The client has begun to build attachment with other family members.

D. The client reports close attachment with family members.

INTERVENTIONS IMPLEMENTED

1. Explore Attitudes/Feelings Regarding School Experience (1)*

A. The client's attitude and feelings regarding his/her school experience were explored.

B. The client was asked his/her opinion regarding his/her academic performance, peer relationships, and staff relationships.

C. The client was supported as he/she freely expressed his/her feelings regarding his/her school experience.

D. The client was guarded and defensive when asked about his/her school experience and gave very little information.

2. Refer for Psychological Testing (2)

A. The client was referred for a psychological evaluation to assess his/her emotional adjustment, with a focus on possible depression symptoms.

B. The client was administered psychological testing (e.g., MMPI-A, MACI, Beck Depression Inventory).

C. The client was uncooperative and resistant during the psychological testing and was urged to be more open for this evaluation.

*The numbers in parentheses correlate to the number of the Therapeutic Intervention statement in the companion chapter with the same title in *The Adolescent Psychotherapy Treatment Planner*, Fourth Edition (Jongsma, Peterson, McInnis, and Bruce) by John Wiley & Sons, 2006.

D. The client was supported, as he/she has approached the psychological testing in an honest, straightforward manner, and was cooperative with any requests presented to him/her.

E. The psychological evaluation results were reviewed with the client and his/her parents.

3. Assess Current Violence Potential (3)

A. The client's violence potential was assessed by evaluating his/her depth of anger, degree of alienation from peers and family, substance abuse, and fascination with and/or access to weapons.

B. The client's violence risk was assessed by exploring for the presence of threats made directly or indirectly, or the articulation of a violence plan.

C. The client's past was explored for any previous violence.

D. Proper authorities were notified of the client's pointed threat of violence, according to agency/clinic guidelines and state and local legal requirements.

E. Steps were taken to remove the client's access to weapons.

F. The client was assessed to be at low risk of committing violence at this time.

4. Develop a Sociogram (4)

A. The client was directed to develop a sociogram that depicts friends and other peers in concentric circles, with the client in the center and the closest friends on the closest circle.

B. The client was assisted in developing a sociogram, identifying the client's closest friends and other peers.

C. The client was asked to disclose his/her impression of each person in his/her sociogram.

D. The client has completed the sociogram, and the results were processed.

E. The client has refused to develop a sociogram, and this resistance was processed.

5. Explore Social Rejection (5)

A. Painful experiences of social rejection of the client by his/her peers were explored.

B. Active listening and unconditional positive regard were used to encourage the sharing of feelings about social rejection and lost relationships.

C. The client was given the opportunity to share his/her feelings of grief about broken close relationships.

D. The client was supported as he/she expressed his/her feelings of hurt and anger related to social rejection by peers.

E. The client was guarded and defensive when asked to identify painful experiences of social rejection by peers, and then was asked to share these experiences as he/she feels comfortable doing so.

6. Identify Issues That Precipitate Peer Conflict (6)

A. The client was asked to identify issues that precipitate his/her conflict with peers.

B. The client was assisted in identifying issues that precipitate his/her conflict with peers.

C. Support and encouragement were provided as the client identified the issues that have precipitated his/her conflict with peers.

D. The client struggled to identify issues that precipitate his/her conflict with peers and was provided with tentative examples in this area.

7. Teach Problem-Solving Skills (7)

A. The client was taught basic problem-solving skills.

B. The client was taught how to use the following problem-solving system: identify the problem, brainstorm solutions, evaluate the pros and cons of each solution, select an option, implement a course of action, and evaluate the outcome.

C. The client was asked to apply his/her problem-solving skills to peer conflict issues.

D. The client displayed an adequate understanding of problem-solving skills and was assisted in applying these to peer conflict issues.

E. The client has used problem-solving skills to resolve some of his/her peer conflict issues and was provided with positive feedback about his/her use of these skills.

F. The client has not developed healthy solutions to peer conflict issues and was provided with remedial information in this area.

8. Teach Peer Relationship Skills (8)

A. The client was taught about ways of coping with and improving conflicted peer relationships.

B. The client was taught about many ways to improve conflicted peer relationships, including social skills training, use of outside intervention with bullies, conflict resolution training, reaching out to build new friendships, and identifying empathetic resource peers or adults in school to whom the client can turn when hurt or angry.

C. The client has implemented coping skills for conflicted peer relationships, and the results were processed.

D. The client has not developed or implemented coping skills for conflicted peer relationships, and the reasons for this failure were reviewed and processed.

9. Teach Application of Social Problem-Solving Skills (9)

A. Role-playing techniques were used to assist the client in learning the application of social problem-solving skills.

B. Modeling and behavioral rehearsal techniques were used to assist the client in learning the application of social problem-solving skills.

C. The client was praised for his/her clear understanding of the social problem-solving skills.

D. The client has implemented the social problem-solving skills, and the results were reviewed.

E. The client has not implemented the social problem-solving skills and was redirected to do so.

10. Brainstorm about Extracurricular Activities (10)

A. The client was assisted in brainstorming possible extracurricular activities he/she might enjoy.

B. The client was asked to commit to pursue involvement in one or two of new extracurricular activities in order to build a positive attitude toward school and peers.

C. Positive reinforcement was provided as the client agreed to pursue a specific extracurricular activity.

D. The client declined to commit to pursue involvement in an extracurricular activity, and the reasons for his/her resistance were processed.

11. Process Increased Social Involvement (11)

A. The client's experience with increased social involvement within the school environment was reviewed.

B. The client was reinforced for successes in his attempts to increase social activities within the school environment.

C. The client was redirected in areas in which he/she felt negatively about the increase in social activities within the school environment.

12. Explore Emotional Effects of Family Relationships (12)

A. Today's therapy session explored the client's feelings related to his/her family relationships.

B. Today's therapy session revealed that the client is experiencing a significant amount of distress in regard to his/her family relationships.

C. Feelings of alienation, isolation, emotional detachment, resentment, distrust, and anger were identified regarding the client's family relationships.

D. The client agreed to meet with his/her family members in an upcoming therapy session to share his/her feelings of anger, hurt, and sadness about family relationships.

E. The client denied any emotional despair related to his/her fractured family relationships, and this denial was reflected back to him/her.

F. The client indicated that he/she is not ready to meet with family members to share his/her feelings regarding the family issues and was encouraged to prepare himself for doing so at a later date.

13. Promote Communication in Family Therapy (13)

A. A family therapy session was held to promote communication of the client's feelings regarding family issues.

B. The family members were reinforced as they demonstrated empathy, support, and understanding for the client's feelings of sadness, hurt, and anger.

C. Family members appeared to become defensive when the client began to share his/her feelings of sadness, hurt, and anger and were redirected to provide support.

D. The client and parents were given a homework assignment to meet for 10 to 15 minutes each day to allow the client an opportunity to share his/her thoughts and feelings about important family issues.

14. Train Client to Identify Early Warning Signs (14)

A. The client was assisted in recognizing early signs that he/she is becoming frustrated, angry, or agitated.

B. The client identified early signs of frustration and agitation and was directed to take specific steps to remain calm and cope with frustration when these occur.

C. The client was uncertain about the early signs of frustration and anger and was provided with tentative examples (e.g., muscular tension, hot face, hostile remarks).

D. The client was reinforced as he/she has regularly identified early signs of anger and taken specific steps to remain calm and cope with the frustration.

E. The client continues to become quite angry and does not intervene during his/her early warning signs; he/she was redirected to use this technique.

15. Identify and Defuse Trigger Situations (15)

A. The caregivers and school officials were assisted in identifying specific situations or events that routinely lead to explosive outbursts or aggressive behavior by the client.

B. The caregivers and school officials were taught effective strategies to defuse the client's anger and to deter his/her aggressive behavior.

C. Positive feedback was provided as the caregivers and school officials have identified and defused situations that routinely lead to the client's explosive outbursts or aggressive behavior.

16. Assign Anger Management Reading (16)

A. The client was assigned to read material regarding learning to manage anger more effectively.

B. The client was assigned to read *Everything You Need to Know about Anger* (Licata).

C. The client has read the information about how to handle anger more effectively, and this information was processed with him/her.

D. The client has not read the information about managing anger and was redirected to do so.

17. Explore Family Dynamics (17)

A. A family therapy session was conducted to explore the family dynamics that may contribute to the emergence of the client's violent behavior.

B. Specific patterns were looked for within the family therapy sessions, including parental modeling of aggressive behavior; sexual, verbal, or physical abuse of family members; substance abuse in the home; and neglect.

C. Family dynamics were connected to the emergence of the client's violent behavior.

D. As family dynamics have improved, the client's violent behavior has been noted to decrease.

18. Assign Time for Communicating Concerns (18)

A. The caregivers were instructed to set aside between 5 and 10 minutes each day to listen to the client's concerns and to provide him/her with the opportunity to express his/her anger in an adaptive manner.

B. The caregivers were reinforced for setting aside between 5 and 10 minutes each day to listen to the client's concerns and to provide him/her with the opportunity to express his/her anger in an adaptive manner.

C. Although the caregivers have set aside time to listen to the client's concerns, they have generally reacted to these concerns in a rejecting or punitive manner; they were directed to simply allow the client to express his/her concerns during this period without endorsing or trying to change these thoughts and feelings.

D. The caregivers have not set aside time each day to allow the client to express his/her anger in an adaptive manner and were redirected to do so.

19. Assign Disengaged Parent to Increase Time with Client (19)

A. The disengaged parent was given a directive to spend more quality time with the client.

B. The disengaged parent was given a homework assignment of performing a specific task with the client.

C. Positive feedback was provided as the client and the disengaged parent have developed a list of tasks or activities that they would like to do together.

D. The client reported that the time spent with the previously disengaged parent has helped the two of them to establish a closer relationship; the benefits of this closer relationship were reviewed.

E. The client reported that his/her relationship with the disengaged parent remains distant because the two have spent little time together; the disengaged parent was redirected to increase time with the client in leisure, school, or work activities.

20. Identify Family Activities (20)

A. The family was assisted in identifying several activities the family could engage in together.

B. The family was assigned to engage in at least one structured activity together every week.

C. The family has engaged in structured activities together, and this experience was processed.

D. The client and family have not engaged in structured activities together and were redirected to do so.

21. Assign Reward System for Anger Control (21)

A. A reward system was developed in which the parent is to reinforce the client's expression of his/her anger in a controlled manner.

B. The client and his/her parents were assigned the "Anger Control" exercise from the *Adolescent Psychotherapy Homework Planner,* 2nd ed. (Jongsma, Peterson, and McInnis) to increase reinforcement of the client for demonstrating good control of his/her anger.

C. The anger control exercise was utilized to help the client identify the core issues that contribute to his/her angry outbursts and aggressive or destructive behavior.

D. The parents were encouraged to use the positive incident reports of the "Anger Control" exercise to reinforce the client for showing good control of his/her anger.

E. The parents have not implemented the reward system to reinforce the client's expression of his/her anger in a controlled manner and were redirected to do so.

22. Teach Anger Management Techniques (22)

A. The client was taught mediational and self-control strategies to manage his/her anger more effectively (e.g., taking a time out, journaling feelings, talking to a trusted adult, engaging in physical exercise).

B. The client's implementation of anger management techniques was processed.

C. The client was reinforced for successes in anger management.

D. The client's failures in anger management were redirected.

E. The client has not regularly used the anger management techniques; these techniques were reviewed with him/her, and he/she was directed to use them on a regular basis.

23. Refer to Anger Management Group (23)

A. The client was referred to an anger management group to improve his/her anger control and interpersonal skills.

B. The client was given the directive to self-disclose at least one time during the group therapy session.

C. The client was encouraged to demonstrate empathy and concern for the thoughts, feelings, and needs of others during the group therapy sessions.

D. Positive feedback was provided for the client's regular involvement in the anger management group.

E. The client has not attended the anger management group and was redirected to do so.

24. Assign Letter of Forgiveness (24)

A. The client was assigned to write a letter of forgiveness to a target of anger as a step toward letting go of his/her anger.

B. The client's letter of forgiveness was processed, and options for what to do with the letter were identified.

C. The client has decided not to do anything else with the letter and was accepted for this decision.

D. The client has decided to present the letter of forgiveness to his/her target of anger, and the effects of this decision were processed.

E. The client has presented his/her letter of forgiveness to the target of his/her anger, and this experience was processed.

F. The client has not completed the letter of forgiveness to a target of anger and was redirected to do so.

25. Identify Irrational Thoughts (25)

A. The client was helped to identify how irrational, distorted thoughts have contributed to the emergence of his/her anger problems and violent behavior.

B. The client was helped to replace irrational thoughts with more adaptive ways of thinking to help control anger.

C. The client was unable to identify irrational thoughts that contribute to the emergence of violent behavior and was provided with the following examples: believing that aggression is an acceptable way to deal with teasing or name-calling; justifying acts of violence or aggression as a means to meet his/her needs or to avoid restrictions.

26. Arrange Substance Abuse Evaluation (26)

A. The client was referred for a substance abuse evaluation to access the extent of his/her drug/alcohol usage and determine the need for treatment.

B. The findings from the substance abuse evaluation revealed the presence of a substance abuse problem, and the need for treatment was presented to the client.

C. The findings from the substance abuse evaluation were presented revealing the presence of a substance abuse problem that appears to be contributing to the client's anger control problems.

D. The evaluation findings were presented revealing the absence of a substance abuse problem or the need for treatment in this area.

E. The client has not complied with the substance abuse evaluation recommendation and was redirected to do so.

27. Identify Positive Attributes (27)

A. The client was given a homework assignment of identifying between 5 and 10 unique strengths, interests, or positive attributes.

B. The client's list of positive attributes, strengths, and interests was reviewed, and he/she was encouraged to use these to build a positive self-image.

C. The client has used his/her positive attributes, strengths, and interests to build a more positive self-image, and the benefits of this were reviewed.

D. The client has not developed a list of his/her unique strengths, interests, or positive attributes and was redirected to do so.

28. Inventory and Externalize Strengths, Interests, and Accomplishments (28)

A. The client was assisted in taking an inventory of his/her strengths, interests, or accomplishments.

B. The client was asked to bring to the therapy session objects or symbols that represent his/her strengths or interests.

C. The client was encouraged to use his/her interests to build self-esteem.

D. The client was assigned the "Symbols of Self-Worth" exercise from the *Adolescent Psychotherapy Homework Planner*, 2nd ed. (Jongsma, Peterson, and McInnis).

E. The client has not developed symbols of his/her strengths or interests and was redirected to do so.

29. Assign Self-Esteem Video (29)

A. The client was assigned to view the video entitled *10 Ways to Boost Low Self-Esteem* (The Guidance Channel).

B. The client was asked to identify effective strategies to elevate self-esteem and increase confidence in himself/herself as identified in the video.

C. The client has viewed the *10 Ways to Boost Low Self-Esteem,* and the techniques from this video were reviewed.

D. The client has not viewed the self-esteem video and was redirected to do so.

30. Assign Self-Esteem Exercise (30)

A. The client was asked to complete an exercise to help increase his/her self-esteem.

B. The client was asked to complete the chapter "Self-Esteem—What Is It—How Do I Get It?" from *Ten Days to Self-Esteem* (Burns) to provide a road map for attaining self-esteem.

C. The client has completed self-esteem exercises, and these were processed and discussed, with key points and issues being emphasized.

D. The client has implemented self-esteem-building thoughts that were learned from the book *Ten Days to Self-Esteem,* and the benefits of these techniques were reviewed.

E. The client has not completed the self-esteem exercise and was redirected to do so.

31. Develop Positive Self-Talk (31)

A. Positive self-talk techniques were taught to the client to assist in boosting his/her confidence and self-image.

B. Role play was used to practice positive self-talk techniques.

C. A commitment was elicited from the client to employ positive self-talk on a daily basis.

D. The client was reinforced for using the self-talk technique that has had a positive effect on increasing his/her self-esteem.

E. The client was provided with specific examples of positive self-talk (e.g., "I am capable," "I can do this," "I am kind," "I can dance well") as a means of increasing his/her confidence and developing a positive self-image.

32. Assign Positive Statements (32)

A. The client was assigned the task of making three positive statements about himself/herself daily.

B. The client was assigned to record his/her positive self-statements in a journal.

C. The client's statements of self-confidence and positive things about himself/herself were verbally affirmed and supported.

D. It was noted and reflected that the frequency of the client's positive self-descriptive statements has increased.

33. Encourage Parents/Caregivers and Teachers to Praise Accomplishments (33)

A. The parents/caregivers and teachers were assisted in identifying opportunities they could seize to praise, reinforce, and recognize positive things done by the client.

B. The parents/caregivers and teachers were reminded of the importance of praise, reinforcement, and recognition in building the client's self-esteem.

C. Missed opportunities for praise, reinforcement, or recognition with the client were pointed out to the parents in a family session.

D. The client, his/her parents/caregivers, and his/her teachers report that the frequency of praise and recognition for the client's accomplishments has increased.

34. Assign Parents/Caregivers to Record Positive Behaviors (34)

A. The parents/caregivers were instructed to observe and record between three and five positive responsible behaviors by the client before the next therapy session.

B. The parents/caregiver's list of the client's positive behaviors was reviewed, and the client was encouraged to continue to engage in these behaviors to boost his/her self-esteem.

C. The parents/caregivers have not recorded the client's positive, responsible behaviors and were redirected to do so.

35. Confront/Challenge Hostile or Critical Remarks (35)

A. The client's parents were confronted and challenged to cease making overly hostile or critical remarks about the client and his/her behavior that only reinforce his/her feelings of low self-esteem.

B. The parents were encouraged to verbalize the positive, specific behaviors or changes that they would like to see the client make.

C. The parents/caregivers were provided with positive feedback for changing critical remarks into positive specific behaviors they would like to see from the client.

D. The parents have continued to make overly hostile and critical remarks and were provided with additional information and feedback in this area.

36. Teach Effective Communication (36)

A. The client and his/her parents were taught the importance of using effective communication skills.

B. The client and his/her parents were taught to practice active listening, use "I messages," avoid blaming statements, identify specific positive changes that other family members can make, and other techniques to improve the lines of communication, facilitate closer family ties, and resolve conflict more constructively.

C. Positive feedback was provided to the family members for the use of better communication skills.

D. The family has not used better communication skills and was provided with remedial assistance in this area.

37. Sensitize about Lack of Empathy (37)

A. The client was focused on his/her need to learn to be empathic toward others.

B. The client was taught the negative consequences of his/her aggression on others (e.g., loss of trust, increased fear, distancing, physical pain).

C. The client was provided with positive feedback as he/she identified the negative consequences of his/her aggression on others and seemed to be displaying empathy for them.

D. The client revealed little feeling about the negative consequences of his/her behavior on others and was provided with additional feedback and confrontation in this area.

38. Teach Impact of Aggression (38)

A. Role-reversal techniques were used to get the client to verbalize the impact of his/her aggression on others.

B. Through the use of the role-reversal technique, the client was able to increase his/her understanding of the impact of his/her aggression on others.

C. Despite the use of role-reversal techniques, the client has not accurately verbalized the impact of his/her aggression on others.

39. Use Empty-Chair Technique (39)

A. The client was assigned to address an empty chair in giving an apology for pain that he/she has caused the victim.

B. The client has successfully used the empty-chair technique to be able to verbalize an apology for the pain that he/she has caused the victim.

C. Despite the use of the empty-chair technique, the client has not been able to appropriately apologize for the pain that he/she has caused the victim and was provided with remedial assistance in this area.

SEXUAL ABUSE PERPETRATOR

CLIENT PRESENTATION

1. Arrest and Conviction for a Sexual Offense (1)*

A. The client has been charged with and convicted of a sexual offense and ordered into treatment.

B. The client is currently on probation for a sexually related offense.

C. The client reported a history of repeated sexually related offenses.

D. The client has not been charged with or investigated for any sexual offense since he/she began treatment.

2. Sexual Abuse of Younger Victim (2)

A. The client has been arrested and convicted for sexually abusing a younger sibling.

B. The client has been charged with sexually abusing a younger child in his/her community.

C. The client is suspected of sexually abusing his/her younger siblings and other younger children in the community.

D. There have been no further accusations or charges of abuse brought against the client since he/she started treatment.

3. Language with Sexual Content (3)

A. The client presented as being unusually open with talk that was very sexually explicit.

B. It is reported by teachers and other adults that the client's talk frequently contains sexual innuendos and references.

C. The client confirmed that he/she likes to talk about sexual things.

D. The client's sexual references have diminished significantly.

4. Sexualized Relationships (4)

A. The client's relationships have a definite and consistent sexual context to them.

B. The client seemed to quickly sexualize most if not all relationships.

C. The client acknowledged having sexual feelings toward most people with whom he/she relates.

D. The client has started to consciously work at forming genuine, respectful relationships.

5. Sexually Preoccupied (5)

A. The client seemed to be sexually preoccupied a majority of his/her free time.

B. The client reported having frequent thoughts, dreams, and fantasies about sexual things.

C. The client indicated that whenever his/her mind wanders it always goes to sexual things.

D. The client has engaged in the use of pornographic magazines, videos, and Internet sites.

---

*The numbers in parentheses correlate to the number of the Behavioral Definition statement in the companion chapter with the same title in *The Adolescent Psychotherapy Treatment Planner,* Fourth Edition (Jongsma, Peterson, McInnis, and Bruce) by John Wiley & Sons, 2006.

E. The client has recently reported a decrease in his/her sexual preoccupation and now will think of other things.

6. Sexual Self-Interest (5)

A. The client reported a history of numerous sexual encounters with partners with whom he/she had little or no emotional attachment.

B. The described sexual behaviors are focused on self-gratification only and with no interest in the needs or concerns of the other partner.

C. The client indicated he/she sees sexual satisfaction as his/her right.

D. The client has begun working at changing his/her thinking regarding the issue of sexual self-interest.

7. Family History of Incest (6)

A. The client and parents reported a multigenerational pattern of sexual abuse within the family.

B. The parents indicated that several family members have been convicted of sexually related offenses that include incest.

C. The parents denied any history of incest, despite legal documents that indicate otherwise.

D. The client revealed several family secrets that involved incestuous relationships between family members.

8. Childhood Sex Abuse (7)

A. The client is very guarded and closed about his/her childhood sex abuse.

B. The client provided specific examples from his/her childhood of instances in which he/she was sexually abused.

C. The client has begun to verbalize some insight and understanding into how previous instances of childhood pain are connected to his/her acts of sexual perpetration and a sense of detachment from others.

9. Use of Pornographic Materials (8)

A. The client admitted having in his/her possession a significant amount of sexually explicit videos and magazines.

B. The client acknowledged being caught by parents visiting adult Internet sites and calling 900 numbers.

C. The client admitted spending a large portion of his/her free time with a variety of pornographic materials.

D. The client reported he/she has disposed of all his/her pornographic materials but experienced some difficulty in doing so.

INTERVENTIONS IMPLEMENTED

1. Build Trust (1)*

A. Initial trust level was established with the client through the use of unconditional positive regard.

B. Warm acceptance and active-listening techniques were utilized to establish the basis for a trusting relationship in which thoughts and feelings could be openly shared.

C. The client has been engaged in a trust-based relationship and has started to share openly his/her thoughts and feelings.

D. Despite the use of active listening, warm acceptance, and unconditional positive regard, the client remains guarded, mistrustful, and willing to disclose only on a superficial level.

2. Initiate Self-Disclosure (2)

A. A celebrity interview format was utilized to start the client talking about nonthreatening topics.

B. The client's self-disclosures were affirmed, encouraged, and reinforced.

C. Despite the use of nonthreatening approaches, the client remained guarded and willing to disclose only superficial information.

3. Develop a No-Sexual-Contact Agreement (3)

A. The client and family were assisted in developing a no-sexual-contact agreement between the client and any others.

B. The parents agreed to implement and enforce the no-sexual-contact contract.

C. The client was asked to and did sign the no-sexual-contact agreement.

4. Monitor No-Sexual-Contact Agreement (4)

A. The no-sexual-contact agreement was monitored for the parents' and the client's follow-through.

B. The parents were confronted on their inconsistency of follow-through on enforcing the no-sexual-contact agreement.

C. The parents were given positive feedback on enforcing and monitoring the no-sexual-contact agreement.

D. The client was given positive verbal feedback on his/her compliance in abiding by the no-sexual-contact agreement.

E. The client was confronted on his/her pushing the limits of the no-sexual-contact agreement.

F. Since the client failed to keep the no-sexual-contact agreement, a more restrictive, supervised treatment setting was sought for him/her.

G. The client was referred to a 24-hour residential treatment program specifically designed for adolescent sexual offenders.

---

* The numbers in parentheses correlate to the number of the Therapeutic Intervention statement in the companion chapter with the same title in *The Adolescent Psychotherapy Treatment Planner,* Fourth Edition (Jongsma, Peterson, McInnis, and Bruce) by John Wiley & Sons, 2006.

5. Explore Incidents of Sexual Misconduct (5)

A. The client was asked to describe in detail each incident of sexual misconduct he/she committed.

B. The client's history of incidents of sexual misconduct was processed and examined for incompleteness and lack of honesty.

C. Positive feedback was provided as the client expressed ownership for his/her sexual misconduct.

D. Denial and rationalizations were offered by the client for his/her sexual misconduct, and he/she was confronted about this pattern.

6. Introduce Key Treatment Concepts (6)

A. The client was asked to complete an exercise on sexual boundaries to begin his/her education and treatment of his/her offense cycle.

B. The client was assigned a sexual boundary exercise from the Safer Society Press Series (Freeman-Longo and Bays).

C. The client was asked to complete and process the "Getting Started" exercise from the *Adolescent Psychotherapy Homework Planner,* 2nd ed. (Jongsma, Peterson, and McInnis) to familiarize him/her with treatment-specific terminology.

D. The client was assisted in gaining a working knowledge of key treatment concepts.

E. The client was encouraged to ask questions about any aspects of or concepts related to his/her treatment.

F. The client has not completed the assignments to begin the process of education and treatment of his/her offense cycle and was redirected to do so.

7. Increase Awareness and Respect of Boundaries (7)

A. The client was assisted in building his/her awareness of and respect for personal boundaries.

B. The client's barriers to being aware of personal boundaries were identified and addressed.

C. The client was encouraged to ask questions when he/she was in doubt about personal boundaries.

D. Key points of the necessity of maintaining appropriate boundaries were clarified and reinforced with the client.

E. Role plays were used with the client to practice maintaining appropriate boundaries in social situations.

F. The client was given feedback regarding his/her actions in the role plays, and appropriate behaviors were modeled for him/her.

G. The client was given positive feedback for honoring and respecting appropriate personal boundaries.

8. Confront Sexual References in Speech/Behavior (8)

A. Sexual references in the client's speech and behavior were pointed out to him/her.

B. The client was assisted in increasing his/her awareness of sexual references in his/her speech and behaviors.

C. The client's feelings and thoughts that underlie the sexual references were explored and processed.

D. The client was resistive to sexual references being pointed out in his/her speech and behavior.

9. Assign Gathering of Feedback about Sexualized Speech (9)

A. The client was asked to gather feedback from others regarding sexual references they note in the client's speech and behavior.

B. Feedback that was gathered by the client from others was processed and language options were explored.

C. The client was encouraged to identify and implement alternative behavior and language patterns.

10. Gather Sexual History (10)

A. A thorough sexual history was collected from the client and the parents.

B. The client and family were confronted on the vagueness of the information given regarding their sexual histories.

C. The client and family were supported for providing complete and honest information regarding the client's sexual history.

11. Explore for Sexual Abuse (11)

A. The client's childhood history was gently explored for sexual, physical, or emotional abuse.

B. The client was asked specifically how others respected or violated his/her physical boundaries as a child.

C. The client was presented with data on the percent of perpetrators who are themselves abused, and the data was processed for his/her response.

D. The possibility of the client being a victim of sexual, physical, or emotional abuse was explored with his/her parents.

E. The client and the parents were supported as they acknowledged that the client has been a victim of sexual, physical, or emotional abuse.

F. The client and parents denied any history of sexual abuse, and this was accepted.

12. Identify Connection between Sexual Abuse and Offense (12)

A. The client was asked to list the consequences of being a victim of sexual abuse.

B. The list of consequences resulting from being a victim of sexual abuse was processed with the client.

C. The client was assisted in making the connection between his/her own victimization and the development of his/her current attitudes and patterns of sexual abuse perpetration.

D. The client was unable to identify any concrete consequences of being a victim of sexual abuse and stated that the abuse had no impact on his/her current behavior; he/she was provided with tentative examples in this area.

13. Play Games to Initiate Disclosure (13)

A. Various therapeutic tools were used to assist the client in becoming capable of identifying, labeling, and expressing his/her feelings.

B. The UnGame (UnGame Company) and The Talking, Feeling, and Doing Game (Creative Therapeutics) were played with the client to give him/her opportunities to share things about himself/herself and to increase self-awareness.

C. The client was assisted in identifying his/her likes and dislikes to help expand self-awareness.

D. Positive affirmation and reinforcement were given to the client's self-disclosures while playing The UnGame.

E. The client was reinforced for his/her use of new skills to label and express his/her emotions.

F. Despite the use of therapeutic tools, the client was unwilling to identify, label, or express his/her feelings, and he/she was provided with tentative interpretations in this area.

14. Reinforce Feeling Recognition (14)

A. The client was reminded of the positive benefits of identifying, labeling, and expressing his/her own feelings and of being sensitive to the feelings of others.

B. The client was given feedback on each occasion where he/she failed to show an awareness of the feelings of others.

C. Positive reinforcement was given to the client on each occasion where he/she showed recognition of the feelings of others without outside direction.

15. Support Client in Describing Sexual, Emotional, or Physical Victimization (15)

A. Barriers and defenses that prevented the client's openness regarding being sexually, physically, or emotionally abused were addressed and removed.

B. The client's fears about disclosing the details of his/her own abuse were processed and resolved.

C. The client was encouraged and supported in telling the story of his/her own sexual, emotional, or physical victimization.

D. Even with support and encouragement, the client was unable to tell any of the details related to his/her own abuse.

16. Support Client Telling Parents of Victimization (16)

A. The client's fears about revealing his/her victimization to his/her parents were identified, processed, and resolved.

B. The worst-case-scenario approach was used in preparing the client to tell parents about his/her victimization.

C. The client was assisted and supported in telling the story of his/her own abuse to the parents.

D. The client's experience of telling the story of abuse to the parents was processed.

E. Even with preparation, assistance, and support, the client refused to tell parents the story of his/her abuse experience and again started denying any such experience.

17. Refer to Perpetrator Group Treatment (17)

A. The need for group treatment for sexual perpetrators was explained to the client.

B. The client was referred to a group treatment program specifically developed for sex offenders.

C. The client's acceptance of group treatment was affirmed and reinforced.

D. The client was very resistive to the referral to a group therapy treatment program for sex offenders.

18. Identify Exploitive Beliefs (18)

A. The client was assisted in identifying and processing his/her thoughts and beliefs that gave him/her justification for being sexually abusive.

B. The client was assisted in identifying socially acceptable thoughts that are respectful and not exploitive of others.

C. New respectful, nonexploitive thoughts were affirmed and reinforced with the client as he/she used them in daily interactions.

D. The client's justification for holding to old beliefs and resistance to new respectful, non-exploitive ones were confronted and addressed.

19. Connect Thinking Errors to Offending Behaviors (19)

A. The client was educated on how thinking errors can have a significant impact on sexual offending behavior.

B. The client was assisted in identifying his/her own thinking errors and connecting them with his/her sexual offending behaviors.

C. Various ways to correct thinking errors were explored with the client.

D. The client struggled to make connections between his/her thinking errors and offending behaviors, and only with assistance did he/she make a weak connection.

20. Conduct Psychological Testing (20)

A. Psychological testing was arranged for the client to confirm or rule out severe emotional issues or psychopathology.

B. The psychological testing results indicated that the client has severe emotional issues that underlie his/her perpetration of sexual abuse.

C. No significant or severe emotional issues were discovered by the psychological testing.

D. The results of the psychological testing were presented and interpreted to the client, and his/her questions were answered.

E. The recommendations of the testing for ongoing treatment were emphasized with the client.

F. The client was asked to make a commitment to follow through in completing all the recommendations of the psychological testing.

G. The client was disinterested in the psychological evaluation recommendations and would not make a commitment to follow through on them.

21. Refer for Medication Evaluation (21)

A. The client was referred for a physician evaluation for psychotropic medications.

B. The client followed the recommendations and completed the physician evaluation for possible medications.

C. Psychotropic medications have been ordered for the client, and he/she has agreed to take them consistently.

22. Monitor Medication (22)

A. The client's psychotropic medication was monitored for effectiveness and for the client's compliance in taking as prescribed.

B. The client and parents were directed and encouraged to report any side effects of the psychotropic medication to the prescribing physician.

C. The client was confronted on his/her failure to take the medication as prescribed.

D. The client's compliance and the overall effectiveness of the psychotropic medication were reported to the prescribing physician.

23. "Anger Control" Exercise (23)

A. The client was asked to complete the "Anger Control" exercise from the *Adolescent Psychotherapy Homework Planner,* 2nd ed. (Jongsma, Peterson, and McInnis) to increase anger recognition and ways to effectively control it.

B. The client was asked to complete an exercise from the *Anger Workbook* (Blodeau) to increase anger recognition and ways to effectively control it.

C. The "Anger Control" exercise was processed, and gains in ways to control anger were identified and affirmed.

D. The client has learned new strategies to control his/her anger and has reported that these have been effective in helping him/her manage anger more effectively.

E. The client has not completed the assigned exercises regarding anger control and was redirected to do so.

24. Refer to Anger Management Group (24)

A. The client was referred to an anger management group to build skills in effectively controlling angry feelings.

B. The benefits and gains from attending an anger management group were explored and identified.

C. The client followed through on referral to the anger management group and reported positive gains.

D. The client has not followed through on the referral to the anger management group and was redirected to do so.

25. Encourage Increased Peer Involvement (25)

A. The client was helped to identify specific ways he/she could increase positive social involvement with peers.

B. Barriers that have held the client back from involvement with peers were explored, processed, and removed.

C. The client was asked to identify two ways to increase socialization that he/she would like to try and then to plan how he/she would go about implementing them.

D. Role plays of peer social situations were used to give the client the opportunity to build confidence and comfort with peer interactions.

E. The experience of the social situation role plays was processed to reinforce gains.

F. The client reported that he/she is feeling more confident and comfortable with peer interactions and was encouraged to continue.

26. Promote New Social Activity (26)

A. A list of possible new social activities was developed with the client, and he/she was asked to choose one to implement each week.

B. The client was monitored for his/her compliance of trying one new social activity each week.

C. The client was asked to engage a peer in conversation once daily.

D. The client processed the experience of the new social activity/conversation and identified the specific gains he/she obtained from the experience.

E. The client's failure to attempt a new social activity/conversation was explored and addressed.

27. Assign Books on Dating (27)

A. The client was assigned books to help build his/her awareness of what is appropriate or inappropriate behavior when interacting with the opposite sex.

B. The client was asked to read *Dating for Dummies* (Browne) or *The Complete Idiot's Guide to Dating* (Kuriansky) to increase his/her awareness of appropriate and inappropriate behaviors with the opposite sex.

C. All questions raised by the client's reading of dating books were answered and processed.

D. Role play was used to further build the client's relationship skills and awareness of appropriate behavior with the opposite sex.

E. The client politely declined to read dating books that were recommended.

28. Teach SAFE Formula for Relationships (28)

A. The SAFE formula for relationships (avoid relationships that are Secret, Abusive, used to avoid Feelings, or Empty of caring and commitment) was taught to the client.

B. All the client's questions about the SAFE formula were addressed and answered.

C. The client was given various scenarios of relationships and asked how they did or did not fit the SAFE formula.

D. The client was assisted in identifying how to implement the SAFE formula into his/her daily life.

E. The client was monitored and redirected in his/her use of the SAFE formula.

F. Positive feedback and reinforcement were given to the client for consistently putting the SAFE formula into daily practice.

29. Explore Family Patterns of Sexual Abuse (29)

A. A genogram was developed with the family that depicted the extended family's boundary-breaking patterns of interaction and identified members' inappropriate sexual behavior.

B. Boundary-breaking patterns of interaction and sexual abuse behavior identified by the genogram were processed and addressed with the family.

C. Ways to begin breaking unhealthy patterns of interaction and sexual behavior were explored with the family.

30. Explore Family Sexual Patterns, Beliefs, Behaviors (30)

A. Family sessions were conducted in which the family members' sexual patterns, beliefs, and behaviors were explored and identified.

B. The family was assisted in identifying which sexual patterns, beliefs, and behaviors need to be changed and coached on how they might begin to go about doing it.

C. The family was encouraged to implement their planned changes of identified inappropriate sexual patterns, beliefs, and behaviors.

D. The family members were confronted on their resistance to moving beyond identification and changing the identified unhealthy sexual patterns, beliefs, and behaviors.

31. Develop/Implement Structural Intervention (31)

A. Family sessions were conducted in which structural interventions were developed, specific plans for implementation made, and a verbal commitment elicited for follow-through.

B. Structural interventions were monitored for their effectiveness and adjusted as needed.

C. The family was monitored and encouraged regarding their follow-through on the structural interventions that they developed.

D. The family's lack of follow-through on structural interventions was confronted, addressed, and resolved.

32. Refer to Parenting Education Group (32)

A. The parents strengths and weaknesses in parenting were explored.

B. Concerns of the parents about parenting teens were explored and processed.

C. The parents were referred to an education group on parenting teenagers.

D. The parents accepted the referral to an education group on parenting techniques and have begun to attend the meetings.

E. The parents have refused to accept a referral to a parenting education group.

33. Assign Books on Parenting (33)

A. The parents were assigned books to help expand their understanding of adolescence and to build their parenting skills.

B. It was suggested that the parents read books such as *Between Parent and Teenager* (Ginott) to expand their understanding of teens and to build their parenting skills.

C. Knowledge gained by the parents from reading books on parenting techniques was processed, and key concepts were reinforced.

D. The parents read small portions of the books that were suggested and processed what information they had gained.

E. The parents have not followed through on the recommendation to read any of the material recommended on effective parenting techniques and were reminded to do so.

34. Develop New Family Rituals (34)

A. The members were educated on the meaning, use, and benefits of establishing rituals for the family.

B. The family was assisted in identifying and developing family rituals of transition, healing, belonging, and identity that would increase family structure, connection, and meaning.

C. Ways to implement the new family rituals were explored and agreed to.

D. Continued work to establish the family rituals was encouraged and reinforced.

35. Assign Feelings Awareness Exercises (35)

A. The client was taught the importance of expanding his/her awareness of his/her feelings and those of others.

B. The client was asked to complete the exercise "Your Feelings and Beyond" or "Surface Behavior/Inner Feelings" from the *Adolescent Psychotherapy Homework Planner,* 2nd ed. (Jongsma, Peterson, and McInnis) to expand his/her awareness of feelings.

C. A variety of scenarios were given to the client to help him/her identify how he/she would feel and how he/she thought others might feel in a given situation.

D. The client was gently confronted and helped to recognize situations where he/she was showing a lack of awareness of others' feelings.

E. It was noted that the client has demonstrated an increased ability to recognize and express his/her own feelings as well as to recognize the feelings of others.

36. Assign Fantasy Journal (36)

A. The client was asked to keep a daily journal of his/her sexual fantasies.

B. The client's sexual fantasy journal was reviewed for patterns of appropriate and inappropriate fantasies in order to provide feedback, redirection, and reinforcement.

C. The client was worked with to make his/her journal entries less vague and more specific.

D. The client was confronted on his/her journal entries that lacked openness and honesty.

E. A review of the client's sexual fantasy journal material shows evidence of a preoccupation with inappropriate sexual urges.

F. A review of the client's sexual fantasy journal material shows evidence of only appropriate and expected sexual thoughts.

37. Define Appropriate/Inappropriate Sexual Fantasies (37)

A. The client was asked to a make a list of the major themes of each of his/her sexual fantasies.

B. Education and guidance were given to the client concerning what constitutes an appropriate and inappropriate sexual fantasy.

C. The client was assisted in creating appropriate sexual fantasies.

D. Feelings of other parties that were a part of the client's sexual fantasies were reflected to the client to increase his/her sensitivity to others.

E. The client was given feedback that rejected fantasies involving pain and exploitation as inappropriate.

38. Assign "Opening the Door to Forgiveness" Exercise (38)

A. The client's attitudes regarding apologizing to his/her victim and forgiving himself/herself were explored and assessed.

B. The client was asked to complete the "Opening the Door to Forgiveness" exercise from the *Adolescent Psychotherapy Homework Planner,* 2nd ed. (Jongsma, Peterson, and McInnis) to prepare him/her to apologize to the victim and to forgive himself/herself.

C. The sincerity of the client's remorse was assessed to determine his/her ability to make a genuine apology for the abuse.

D. The sincerity of the client's remorse for his/her sexual abuse was questionable.

E. The client seemed sincere in his/her remorse and regret for his/her acts of sexual abuse.

F. The client's barriers to making a genuine apology were addressed and processed to their resolution.

39. Letter of Apology (39)

A. The purpose and benefit of writing a letter of apology to the victims of his/her sexual abuse were explored and processed with the client.

B. The client was asked to write a letter of apology to his/her victim that is genuine.

C. The client's written letter of apology was presented and processed, and feedback was given on his/her letter of apology regarding its sincerity and genuineness.

D. The client was given direct feedback on the lack of sincerity and genuineness in his/her letter of apology.

40. Role-Play Verbal Apology (40)

A. Role-play was used with the client to assess his/her readiness to verbally apologize to the victim and to evaluate what further work needs to be done.

B. Role-playing revealed that the client is ready to make an apology to the victim, and that process was set in motion.

C. Role-playing clearly identified the issues that the client still needs to work on in order for him/her to be at the point of making an apology.

D. Role reversal was used with the client to further his/her sensitivity to the feelings and reactions of the victim.

41. Support Apology to Victim and Family (41)

A. A family session was conducted in which the client, in the presence of his/her family, apologized to the victim and victim's family.

B. The apology session was processed with the client, and his/her feelings were identified and expressed.

C. The client's follow-through on giving a sincere, genuine apology was affirmed and reinforced.

42. Identify Relapse Triggers/Coping Strategies (42)

A. Education was provided to the client regarding identifying, recognizing, and handling triggers that could cause a relapse into perpetrating sexual abuse.

B. The client was assisted in specifically identifying his/her sexual abuse relapse triggers.

C. The importance of maintaining awareness of sexual abuse relapse triggers was emphasized with the client.

D. The need for behavioral and cognitive coping strategies for sexual abuse relapse triggers was presented and explained to the client.

E. Specific behavioral and cognitive strategies were developed for each of the client's identified sexual abuse relapse triggers.

F. Role-play and behavioral rehearsal were used for the client to practice implementing the behavioral and cognitive coping strategies developed for his/her relapse triggers.

G. The client was reminded of the importance of maintaining an awareness of relapse triggers and timely use of the cognitive and behavioral strategies.

43. Develop and Process an Aftercare Plan (43)

A. The client was educated on the components of an effective aftercare plan to prevent future sexual abuse perpetration.

B. The client was asked to develop a written aftercare plan.

C. The aftercare plan developed by the client was processed in a family session, and family input and feedback was incorporated into a revised aftercare plan.

D. A copy of the finalized aftercare plan was given to each family member.

E. The client was assisted in implementing his/her aftercare plan.

F. The client was monitored and redirected for implementation and follow-through on his/her aftercare plan.

44. Hold Checkups and Give Feedback (44)

A. Regular checkup sessions were held in which the client's aftercare plan was reviewed for its effectiveness and his/her follow-through with its components.

B. After review, the client was given feedback on the aftercare plan and necessary adjustments were suggested.

C. The client's failure to follow through with the aftercare plan was identified, addressed, and resolved.

45. Refer for Sex Offender Risk Assessment (45)

A. The client was referred to complete a sex offender risk assessment.

B. The client followed through on the referral and completed a specific sex offender assessment.

C. Despite encouragement, the client refused to follow through with the recommended sexual offender risk assessment referral.

46. Report Revealed Sexual Offenses/Process Outcomes (46)

A. The client was informed of the therapist's legal requirement to report any sexual offenses that are revealed to him/her.

B. Sexual offenses revealed by the client were reported to the appropriate authorities.

C. The client reported the outcome of the investigation and the results were processed.

D. Issues of responsibility for behavior and respecting personal boundaries were processed in regard to the incident of sexual abuse perpetration.

E. The client was firmly confronted on his/her failure to take responsibility for the incidents of sexual abuse perpetration.

SEXUAL ABUSE VICTIM

CLIENT PRESENTATION

1. Self-Report of Sexual Abuse (1)*

A. The client reported that he/she has been sexually abused.

B. The client was guarded and evasive when being questioned about whether he/she has ever been sexually abused.

C. The client has previously reported being sexually abused but has since recanted these earlier statements.

D. The client has verbally denied being sexually abused, although there is other evidence to suggest that he/she has been abused.

2. Physical Signs of Sexual Abuse (2)

A. The medical examination revealed physical signs of sexual abuse.

B. The medical examination did not reveal any physical signs of sexual abuse.

3. Vague Memories of Sexual Abuse (3)

A. The client reported that he/she has vague memories of inappropriate childhood sexual contact.

B. The client's vague memories of inappropriate childhood sexual contact have been corroborated by significant others.

C. The client's vague memories of inappropriate childhood sexual contact have not been corroborated by significant others.

4. Strong Interest in Sexuality Issues (4)

A. The client has displayed a strong interest in or curiosity about issues related to sexuality since his/her sexual victimization.

B. The client exhibited a strong interest in or curiosity about issues related to sexuality in the therapy session.

C. The client's strong interest in or curiosity about issues related to sexuality has masked deeper feelings of sadness, hurt, and helplessness about his/her own sexual victimization.

D. The client has demonstrated less preoccupation with issues related to sexuality since addressing his/her own sexual abuse issues.

5. Sexual Promiscuity/Sexualization of Relationships (5)

A. The client has become sexually promiscuous since being sexually abused.

B. The client has demonstrated a pattern of sexualizing many of his/her interactions with others.

C. The client's sexual promiscuity and sexualization of relationships have arisen out of his/her underlying feelings of sadness, anger, hurt, and vulnerability about the past sexual abuse.

---

*The numbers in parentheses correlate to the number of the Behavioral Definition statement in the companion chapter with the same title in *The Adolescent Psychotherapy Treatment Planner,* Fourth Edition (Jongsma, Peterson, McInnis, and Bruce) by John Wiley & Sons, 2006.

D. The client acknowledged that he/she engages in frequent seductive or sexually promiscuous behavior to meet his/her unmet dependency needs.

E. The client has successfully worked through his/her thoughts and feelings about the past sexual abuse and eliminated his/her pattern of engaging in overly seductive or sexually promiscuous behavior.

6. Recurrent and Intrusive Recollections of Sexual Abuse (6)

A. The client has experienced recurrent, intrusive, and distressing recollections of the past sexual abuse.

B. The client has reexperienced intrusive and distressing recollections of the past sexual abuse after coming into contact with the perpetrator and/or having exposure to sexual topics.

C. The client denied being troubled any longer by intrusive recollections of the sexual abuse.

7. Recurrent Nightmares (6)

A. The client has experienced recurrent nightmares of the past sexual abuse.

B. The client reported that he/she continues to be troubled by recurrent nightmares of the past sexual abuse.

C. The client has reexperienced nightmares of the sexual abuse since coming into contact with the perpetrator and/or being exposed to sexual topics.

D. The client stated that he/she is no longer troubled by nightmares of the past sexual abuse.

8. Dissociative Flashbacks, Delusions, or Hallucinations (7)

A. The client reported experiencing dissociative flashbacks of the past sexual abuse.

B. The client reported experiencing delusions and hallucinations related to the past sexual abuse.

C. The client reported reexperiencing dissociative flashbacks, delusions, or hallucinations since coming into contact with the perpetrator and/or being exposed to sexual topics.

D. The client stated that dissociative flashbacks, delusions, or hallucinations have ceased.

9. Anger and Rage (8)

A. The client expressed strong feelings of anger and rage about the past sexual abuse.

B. The client has exhibited frequent angry outbursts and episodes of rage since the onset of the sexual abuse.

C. The frequency and intensity of the client's angry outbursts have decreased since he/she has felt more secure and started to work through his/her feelings about the sexual abuse.

D. The intensity of the client's anger has decreased whenever he/she talks about the past sexual abuse.

E. The client has demonstrated a reduction in the frequency and intensity of his/her angry outbursts and episodes of rage.

10. Disturbance of Mood and Affect (9)

A. The client has experienced frequent and prolonged periods of depression, anxiety, and irritability since the sexual abuse occurred.

B. The client appeared visibly depressed when talking about the sexual abuse.

C. The client appeared anxious when talking about the sexual abuse.

D. The client's moods have gradually started to stabilize as he/she works through his/her feelings of sadness, anxiety, insecurity, and anger about the past sexual abuse.

E. The client's moods have stabilized and he/she reports no longer being troubled by frequent or prolonged periods of depression, anxiety, or irritability.

11. Fearfulness/Distrust (10)

A. The client stated that he/she has felt strong feelings of fearfulness and a marked distrust of others since being sexually abused.

B. The client's fearfulness has slowly started to diminish and he/she is beginning to establish trust with significant others.

C. The strong support from family and individuals outside the family has helped to decrease the client's fearfulness and distrust.

D. The client has successfully worked through many of his/her feelings surrounding the sexual abuse and has established close, trusting relationships with significant others.

12. Social Withdrawal (10)

A. The client has become significantly more withdrawn from others since the onset of the sexual abuse.

B. The client appeared detached and withdrawn in today's therapy session when the topic of the sexual abuse was being discussed.

C. The client acknowledged that he/she has become more withdrawn because of his/her feelings of low self-esteem and distrust of others.

D. The client has started to become more assertive and outgoing in interactions with family members, significant adults, and peers.

13. Feelings of Guilt and Shame (11)

A. The client expressed strong feelings of guilt and shame about the past sexual abuse.

B. The client has continued to experience strong feelings of guilt and shame about the past sexual abuse, despite being given reassurance that he/she is not responsible for the sexual abuse.

C. The client's feelings of guilt and shame have started to decrease as he/she now recognizes that the perpetrator is responsible for the sexual abuse.

D. The client has successfully worked through and resolved his/her feelings of guilt and shame about the past sexual abuse.

14. Low Self-Esteem (11)

A. The client expressed strong feelings of low self-esteem and insecurity about the past sexual abuse.

B. The client's self-esteem has started to improve as he/she works through his/her feelings about the past sexual abuse.

C. Strong family support has helped to increase the client's self-esteem.

D. The client verbalized several positive self-descriptive statements during today's therapy session.

15. Substance Abuse (12)

A. The client reported engaging in a significant amount of substance abuse since the sexual abuse began.

B. The client has often used alcohol or drugs as a maladaptive coping mechanism to ward off painful emotions associated with the sexual abuse.

C. The client has begun to use positive coping mechanisms to deal with his/her painful emotions surrounding the sexual abuse instead of turning to drug or alcohol abuse.

D. The client has ceased using alcohol or drug abuse as a way to ward off painful emotions associated with the sexual abuse.

16. Inappropriate Sexual Behavior (13)

A. The client has a history of engaging in inappropriate sexual behavior with younger children.

B. The client acknowledged that his/her sexual behavior with younger children is inappropriate.

C. The client's unresolved feelings about his/her past sexual victimization have contributed to the emergence of his/her inappropriate sexual behavior with younger children.

D. The client reported that he/she has not recently engaged in any inappropriate sexual behavior.

E. The client's risk for engaging in inappropriate sexual behavior toward younger children appears to be greatly reduced because of the successful resolution of issues related to his/her past sexual victimization.

INTERVENTIONS IMPLEMENTED

1. Build Trust (1)*

A. Today's therapy session focused on building the level of trust with the client through consistent eye contact, active listening, unconditional positive regard, and warm acceptance.

B. The therapy session was helpful in building the level of trust with the client.

C. The therapy session did not prove to be helpful in building the level of trust with the client, as he/she remained guarded in talking about the sexual abuse.

2. Encourage Expression of Feelings (2)

A. The client was given encouragement and support to tell the entire story of the sexual abuse and to express feelings that he/she experienced during and after the abuse.

B. The client was assigned the exercise "My Story" in the *Adolescent Psychotherapy Homework Planner,* 2nd ed. (Jongsma, Peterson, and McInnis).

C. Support was provided as the client described the sequence of events before, during, and after the sexual abuse incidents, but did not show or talk of any feelings.

D. Client-centered principals were used to encourage and support the client in expressing his/her feelings about the past sexual abuse.

---

*The numbers in parentheses correlate to the number of the Therapeutic Intervention statement in the companion chapter with the same title in *The Adolescent Psychotherapy Treatment Planner,* Fourth Edition (Jongsma, Peterson, McInnis, and Bruce) by John Wiley & Sons, 2006.

E. The parent(s) were encouraged to allow the client opportunities at home to express his/her thoughts and feelings about the sexual abuse.

F. The client has not been able to tell the entire story of the sexual abuse and express feelings that he/she experienced during and after the abuse, and he/she was redirected to do so.

3. Report Sexual Abuse (3)

A. The sexual abuse was reported to the appropriate child protection agency.

B. Criminal justice officials have been informed of the sexual abuse.

C. The client has been referred for a medical examination to determine whether there are any physical signs of the sexual abuse and/or to evaluate any health problems that may have resulted from the sexual abuse.

D. The client and family members were supportive of the sexual abuse being reported to the appropriate child protection agency or criminal justice officials.

E. The client and family members objected to the sexual abuse being reported to the appropriate child protection agency or criminal justice officials.

4. Assess Veracity of Sexual Abuse Charges (4)

A. A consultation was held with the child protection case manager and criminal justice officials to assess the veracity of the client's sexual abuse charges.

B. A consultation was held with the physician who examined the client to assess the veracity of the sexual abuse charges.

C. A consultation held with the child protection case managers, criminal justice officials, and physician has provided strong support for the client's reports that he/she has been sexually abused.

D. A consultation held with the child protection case managers, criminal justice officials, and physician has provided inconclusive evidence about whether the client has been sexually abused.

E. A consultation held with the child protection case managers, criminal justice officials, and physician has provided little or no support for the client's reports that he/she has been sexually abused.

5. Develop Appropriate Treatment Interventions (5)

A. A consultation was held with the criminal justice officials and child protection case managers about developing appropriate treatment interventions.

B. A consultation was held with the client's physicians about developing appropriate treatment interventions.

C. After consulting with the child protection case managers, criminal justice officials, and physician, the recommendation was made that the client should receive individual therapy to address sexual abuse issues.

D. The consultation meeting with the child protection and criminal justice officials produced the recommendation that family therapy be mandatory.

E. After consulting with the child protection case managers and criminal justice officials, it was determined that the perpetrator should be required to participate in his/her own therapy.

6. Reveal Sexual Abuse to Family (6)

A. A conjoint therapy session was held to reveal the sexual abuse to key family member(s) or caregiver(s).

B. A family therapy session was held to eliminate the secrecy about the client's sexual abuse.

C. A conjoint therapy session was held to reveal the nature, frequency, and duration of the sexual abuse to key family member(s) and/or caregiver(s).

7. Confront Denial within Family System (7)

A. The family members' denial about the impact of the sexual abuse was confronted and challenged so that they can begin to provide the support the client needs in order to make a healthy adjustment.

B. The family members' denial of the sexual abuse was strongly challenged, and responsibility for the sexual abuse was placed on the perpetrator.

C. The therapy session was helpful in working through the family members' denial surrounding the sexual abuse, and they agreed to follow through with the necessary treatment and support.

D. The therapy session was not successful in working through the family members' denial about the sexual abuse.

8. Remove Perpetrator from Home (8)

A. A consultation was held with criminal justice officials and child protection case managers to determine whether the perpetrator should be removed from the home.

B. A recommendation was made that the perpetrator be removed from the home in order to protect the client and siblings from future occurrences of sexual abuse.

C. The perpetrator was court-ordered to leave the home and was forbidden to have any contact with the client and/or family member(s).

D. The perpetrator was required to leave the home but will be allowed supervised visitation with the client and/or family member(s).

E. A recommendation was made that the perpetrator be allowed to remain in the home under the condition that he/she agrees to and follows through with treatment.

9. Protect Client and Other Children (9)

A. A consultation was held with criminal justice officials and child protection case managers about implementing the necessary steps to protect the client and other children in the home from future sexual abuse.

B. A family therapy session was held to discuss and identify the appropriate steps that need to be taken to protect the client and other children in the home from future sexual abuse.

C. An individual therapy session was held to provide the client with the opportunity to identify what steps he/she feels need to occur in order to feel safe.

10. Consult about Placement of Client (10)

A. A consultation was held with criminal justice officials and child protection case managers to assess whether the client is safe to remain in the home or should be removed.

B. The decision was made that the client be allowed to remain in the home, and the perpetrator was required to leave.

C. The decision was made to allow the client to continue living in the home because it was felt that the nonabusive parent would take the necessary steps to protect him/her from further sexual abuse.

D. A recommendation was made that the client be placed in a foster home to ensure his/her protection from further sexual abuse.

E. A recommendation was made that the client be placed in a residential treatment program to ensure his/her protection from further sexual abuse and provide treatment for his/her emotional/behavioral problems.

11. Empower Client Self-Protection (11)

A. Today's therapy session sought to empower the client by reinforcing the steps necessary to protect himself/herself.

B. Today's therapy session sought to empower the client by praising and reinforcing his/her decision to report the sexual abuse to the appropriate individuals or agencies.

C. The client was strongly encouraged to contact a child protection hot line, police, or the therapist if he/she is ever sexually abused in the future.

D. The client was helped to identify a list of safe places to go when he/she feels at risk of sexual abuse.

E. The client was taught effective assertiveness and communication skills to help him/her stand up for himself/herself and feel safe.

12. Establish Boundaries within Family System (12)

A. The family members were counseled about establishing appropriate parent-child boundaries to ensure the protection of the client and other children in the home from further sexual abuse.

B. The family members were counseled about establishing appropriate adult-child boundaries regarding privacy, physical contact, and verbal content.

C. An assessment of the family system revealed weak and blurred parent-child boundaries.

D. Today's therapy session sought to strengthen the roles and responsibilities of the nonabusive parent in enforcing appropriate privacy, physical contact, verbal content, and adult-child boundaries.

E. It was noted that appropriate boundaries have not been established within the family system, and the nonabusive parent was directed to enforce appropriate privacy, physical contact, verbal contact, and adult-child boundaries.

13. Identify Stress Factors or Precipitating Events (13)

A. Today's therapy session explored the stress factors or precipitating events that contributed to the emergence of the sexual abuse.

B. Today's therapy session explored the family dynamics that have contributed to the emergence of the sexual abuse.

C. Today's therapy session was helpful in identifying the stress factors or precipitating events that contributed to the emergence of the sexual abuse.

D. Today's therapy session identified several family dynamics that have contributed to the emergence of the sexual abuse.

E. The family members were taught positive coping strategies and effective problem-solving approaches to help them manage stress and overcome the identified problems.

14. Gather Details about Where Abuse Occurred in Home (14)

A. The client was given an assignment to draw a diagram of the house where the sexual abuse occurred, indicating where everyone slept, to help gain greater insight into the factors or precipitating events that led up to the sexual abuse.

B. Active listening skills were used as the client recounted the story of the sexual abuse as he/she shared the diagram of the house where the sexual abuse occurred.

C. The client's drawing of where the sexual abuse occurred was reviewed and found to be helpful in identifying the precipitating events leading up to the sexual abuse.

D. The client shared a diagram of the house where the sexual abuse occurred but was guarded in talking about the details or the precipitating events that led up to the sexual abuse; he/she was supported and encouraged.

E. The client refused to complete the assignment of drawing a diagram showing where the sexual abuse occurred, and the reasons for this were reviewed.

15. Construct Family Sex Abuse Genogram (15)

A. The client and family members were assisted in constructing a multigeneration family genogram that identified the history of sexual abuse within the family.

B. The construction of the multigeneration family genogram helped the client to realize that other family members have been sexually abused and that he/she is not alone.

C. The construction of the multigeneration family genogram helped the perpetrator recognize the cycle of repeated boundary violations within the extended family.

D. The construction of a multigeneration family genogram helped the family members voice their commitment to taking the necessary steps to end the cycle of sexual abuse within their family.

E. The client and family tended to downplay any issues of multigenerational family sexual abuse issues and were directed to provide more complete information in this area.

16. Assign Letter to Perpetrator (16)

A. The client was given a homework assignment to write a letter to the perpetrator and bring it to the following therapy session for processing.

B. It was reflected that the client expressed strong feelings of sadness, hurt, and disappointment in his/her letter to the perpetrator.

C. It was reflected that the client expressed strong feelings of anger about the sexual abuse in his/her letter to the perpetrator.

D. The client was supported as he/she expressed a willingness to share the letter directly with the perpetrator.

E. After processing the letter, the client reported that he/she is not ready to share his/her thoughts and feelings about the sexual abuse directly with the perpetrator.

17. Utilize Empty-Chair Technique (17)

A. The empty-chair technique was utilized to help the client express his/her feelings about the sexual abuse to the perpetrator.

B. The empty-chair technique was utilized to help the client express and work through his/her feelings toward the nonabusive parent.

C. The client made productive use of the empty-chair technique to express strong feelings of sadness, hurt, and anger about the sexual abuse to the perpetrator.

D. The client made productive use of the empty-chair technique to express strong feelings of sadness, hurt, and anger toward the nonabusive parent for failing to protect him/her from the sexual abuse.

E. The client appeared uncomfortable with the empty-chair technique and had difficulty expressing his/her thoughts and feelings about the sexual abuse.

18. Assign Feelings Journal (18)

A. The client was instructed to keep a journal in which he/she records experiences or situations that evoke strong emotions pertaining to the sexual abuse.

B. The client shared several entries from his/her journal; it was noted that the journal reflected his/her strong emotions about the sexual abuse.

C. The client reported that the journal has helped him/her work through many of his/her thoughts and feelings about past sexual abuse, and he/she was encouraged to continue to use the journal.

D. Today's therapy session explored why the client has failed to keep a journal.

19. Utilize Art Therapy to Express Feelings toward Perpetrator (19)

A. Art therapy techniques (e.g., drawing, painting, sculpting) were employed to help the client identify and express his/her feelings toward the perpetrator.

B. The client made productive use of the therapy session and was able to express strong feelings of anger toward the perpetrator in his/her artwork.

C. It was noted that the client's artwork reflected feelings of sadness, anger, hurt, and disappointment that he/she experiences in regard to his/her relationship with the perpetrator.

D. The client appeared uncomfortable and had difficulty expressing his/her feelings toward the perpetrator through art, and these feelings were noted and accepted.

20. Teach Guided Fantasy and Imagery Techniques (20)

A. Guided fantasy and imagery techniques were used to help the client identify and express his/her thoughts and feelings associated with the sexual abuse.

B. The client reported a positive response to the use of guided fantasy and imagery techniques to help him/her identify his/her thoughts, feelings, and unmet needs associated with the sexual abuse.

C. Guided fantasy and imagery techniques were used, but the client still had difficulty identifying and expressing his/her thoughts, feelings, and unmet needs associated with the sexual abuse.

21. Assign Emotion Exercise (21)

A. The client's feelings of guilt and shame connected to the sexual abuse were explored and resolved.

B. The client was given the "You Are Not Alone" exercise from the *Adolescent Psychotherapy Homework Planner,* 2nd ed. (Jongsma, Peterson, and McInnis) to help him/her express feelings connected to the sexual abuse and decrease feelings of guilt and shame.

C. The client reported that he/she found the "You Are Not Alone" exercise helpful in reducing his/her feelings of guilt, shame, anger, and fear, and these were further processed in the session.

D. The client did not follow through with completing the "You Are Not Alone" exercise, and the assignment was given again.

22. Employ Art Therapy to Express Impact on Life (22)

A. The client was instructed to create a drawing or sculpture that reflected how the sexual abuse has impacted his/her life and feelings about himself/herself.

B. The client made productive use of the art therapy session and was able to vividly express how the sexual abuse has impacted his/her life and feelings about self.

C. It was noted that the client's artwork reflected how the sexual abuse has caused the client to feel small, helpless, and vulnerable.

D. It was noted that the client's artwork reflected feelings of guilt and shame about the sexual abuse.

E. It was reflected to the client that he/she appeared uncomfortable and had difficulty expressing through his/her artwork how the sexual abuse has impacted his/her life or feelings about self.

23. Elicit Support from Family Members (23)

A. The family members were encouraged to provide emotional support and nurturance for the client to help him/her cope with the sexual abuse.

B. Today's therapy session was successful in eliciting support and nurturance for the client from the other family members.

C. An individual therapy session was held with the nonabusive parent to explore the factors contributing to his/her resistance to providing emotional support and nurturance for the client.

D. A family therapy session was held with the siblings to explore their reluctance to provide emotional support and nurturance for the client.

E. The parent(s) were instructed to provide frequent praise and positive reinforcement to the client to help him/her build self-esteem and feel accepted in the family system.

F. The parents have not provided frequent praise and positive reinforcement to the client to help him/her build self-esteem and feel accepted in the family system, and they were redirected to do so.

24. Assign Reading Material Regarding Sexual Addiction and Recovery from Sexual Abuse (24)

A. The client was assigned reading material to increase his/her knowledge of sexually addictive behavior and to learn ways to help him/her recover from sexual abuse.

B. The client's parents and significant others were assigned to read *Allies in Healing* (Davis) to assist them in understanding how they can help the client recover from the sexual abuse.

C. The client's family was assigned to read *Out of the Shadows* (Carnes) to expand their knowledge of sexually addictive behaviors.

D. The client's parents and family members have read the assigned material and found it to be helpful in identifying ways they can help the client recover from the sexual abuse and in expanding their knowledge of sexually addictive behaviors.

E. The parents have failed to read the assigned material and were redirected to do so.

25. Assign Increased Time Spent between Nonabusive Parent and Client (25)

A. The disengaged, nonabusive parent was directed to spend more time with the client in leisure, school, or household activities.

B. The client and the disengaged, nonabusive parent were assisted in identifying a list of activities that they would like to do together.

C. The client verbalized his/her need to spend greater time with the disengaged, nonabusive parent in leisure, school, or household activities, and this was normalized.

D. The disengaged, nonabusive parent verbalized a commitment to spend increased time with the client and was encouraged to do so.

E. Today's therapy session explored the factors contributing to the distant relationship between the client and the nonabusive parent.

F. The nonabusive parent has not increased his/her time spent with the client and was redirected to do so.

26. Confront Perpetrator (26)

A. The perpetrator's denial of the sexual abuse was confronted.

B. The client was helped to prepare to confront the perpetrator about the sexual abuse.

C. The client confronted the perpetrator about how the sexual abuse has negatively impacted his/her life and feelings about self.

D. The perpetrator was confronted about minimizing the significance of the sexual abuse.

E. The perpetrator was confronted with the facts of the sexual abuse but continued to deny sexually abusing the client.

27. Facilitate Perpetrator Apology (27)

A. The perpetrator was helped to prepare to apologize to the client and other family members about the sexual abuse.

B. Positive feedback was provided as the perpetrator apologized to the client and family members for the sexual abuse, taking full responsibility for the abuse.

C. The perpetrator listened appropriately to the client and family members' expression of anger, hurt, and disappointment about the sexual abuse and then offered a sincere apology; the client, the family, and the perpetrator were supported through this task.

D. A decision was made to postpone the apology session because the perpetrator does not appear ready to offer a sincere or genuine apology to the client and family members.

28. Refer to Sexual Offenders Group (28)

A. The perpetrator was referred to a sexual offender group to address his/her inappropriate sexual behaviors.

B. The perpetrator was required by the legal system to attend a sexual offenders group.

C. The perpetrator has consistently attended the sexual offenders group, and his/her learning in this area was reviewed.

D. The perpetrator has been an active participant in the sexual offenders group and stated that it has helped him/her identify the factors contributing to his/her inappropriate sexual behaviors.

E. The perpetrator has failed to consistently attend the sexual offenders group and was redirected to do so.

29. Assign Forgiveness Letter (29)

A. The client was given a homework assignment to write a forgiveness letter to the perpetrator and bring it to the following session for processing.

B. The client was assigned the "Letter of Forgiveness" exercise in the *Adolescent Psychotherapy Homework Planner,* 2nd ed. (Jongsma, Peterson, and McInnis).

C. It was noted that the client's letter reflected his/her readiness to offer forgiveness to the perpetrator and/or significant family member(s).

D. The client verbalized his/her forgiveness to the perpetrator and/or significant family member(s) in today's therapy session; he/she was supported for this growth.

E. After processing the client's letter, it was evident that the client is not ready to offer forgiveness to the perpetrator and/or significant family member(s).

30. Facilitate Symbolically Letting Go (30)

A. The client was directed to bring an object to the next therapy session that symbolizes the significance of the sexual abuse in his/her life.

B. The client brought in an object to today's therapy session that has been identified as a symbol of the significance of the sexual abuse in his/her life.

C. The client was assisted in identifying what he/she would like to do with the symbol of the sexual abuse.

D. The client identified ways to dispose of the symbol of the sexual abuse to signify his/her readiness to move on with his/her life; positive feedback and assistance were provided.

E. The client was unable to identify a symbol for the significance of the sexual abuse in his/her life and was provided with tentative examples in this area.

31. Differentiate between Victim and Survivor (31)

A. The client was helped to differentiate between being a victim and being a survivor.

B. The client was assisted in identifying both the positive and negative consequences of being a victim and being a survivor.

C. The client was assisted in verbalizing that his/her increased confidence and positive feelings about himself/herself have allowed him/her to feel more like a survivor of sexual abuse than a victim.

D. The client reported that he/she continues to harbor unresolved feelings about the sexual abuse, and it was noted that he/she is not ready to label himself/herself a survivor of sexual abuse.

32. Reinforce Ability to Survive Sexual Abuse (32)

A. The idea that the client can survive sexual abuse was introduced by asking, "What will you be doing in the future that shows you are happy and have moved on with your life?"

B. The client was assisted in identifying several positive behaviors or tasks that he/she would be performing in the future that would show he/she is happy and has moved on with his/her life.

C. The client was reinforced for taking positive steps to work through the issues related to his/her sexual victimization.

D. The client was reinforced for taking active steps to achieve personal happiness and move on with his/her life.

E. The factors contributing to the client's reluctance or resistance to taking positive steps to move on with his/her life were explored.

33. Refer to Survivor Group (33)

A. The client was referred to a survivor group with other adolescents to assist him/her in realizing that he/she is not alone in having experienced sexual abuse.

B. The client was given the directive to self-disclose at least once during the group therapy session.

C. The client's participation in the survivor group with other adolescents has helped him/her realize that he/she is not alone in experiencing sexual abuse.

D. The client has actively participated in the survivor group therapy sessions and verbalized many of his/her feelings about the past sexual abuse.

E. The client has offered support to other members of the survivor group when they have shared their thoughts and feelings about their own sexual abuse experiences.

F. The client has not attended the sexual abuse survivor group, and his/her reasons for not attending this group were processed.

34. Encourage Participation in Peer Group Activities (34)

A. The client was encouraged to participate in positive peer group or extracurricular activities to improve his/her self-esteem and gain a sense of acceptance.

B. The client was assisted in developing a list of positive peer group or extracurricular activities that will provide him/her with the opportunity to establish friendships and improve self-esteem.

C. The client reported that his/her participation in positive peer group or extracurricular activities has helped him/her improve self-esteem and gain a sense of acceptance.

D. The client acknowledged that his/her feelings of low self-esteem and shame have contributed to his/her reluctance to become involved in positive peer group or extracurricular activities in the past; he/she was encouraged to do this as a way to increase self-esteem.

35. Teach Share-Check Method of Building Trust (35)

A. The client was taught the share-check method of building trust to help him/her realize that the amount of information he/she shares with others is related to a proven level of trustworthiness.

B. The client reported that learning the share-check method has helped him/her decide how much information he/she can share with certain individuals.

C. The client identified a list of individuals whom he/she feels are trustworthy, and this was reviewed.

D. The client has continued to struggle with issues of trust and has difficulty sharing his/her thoughts and feelings with even trustworthy individuals and was encouraged to increase this trust as possible.

36. Teach Appropriate/Inappropriate Touching (36)

A. The client was helped to identify both appropriate and inappropriate forms of touching and affection.

B. The client was encouraged to accept and initiate appropriate forms of touching with trusted individuals.

C. The client reported that allowing himself/herself to give and receive affection has helped him/her cope with the pain of the sexual abuse; the benefits of this progress were reviewed.

D. It was noted that the client's mistrust of others has remained high, and as a result, he/she has much difficulty accepting and initiating appropriate forms of touching, even with trusted individuals.

37. List Supportive People (37)

A. The client was asked to develop a list of resource people outside of the family to whom he/she can turn for support, guidance, and affirmation.

B. The client was given a homework assignment to seek support or guidance from at least one individual outside of his/her family before the next therapy session.

C. Active-listening skills were used as the client reported that he/she has benefited from receiving support, guidance, and affirmation from individuals outside of his/her family.

D. It was noted that the support that the client has received from resource people outside of the family has helped him/her cope with the trauma of the sexual abuse.

E. The client has been hesitant to turn to the resource people outside of the family for support, guidance, or affirmation because of his/her mistrust and was urged to do this in small steps.

38. Connect Painful Emotions to Promiscuous Behavior (38)

A. The therapy session was helpful in identifying how underlying painful emotions (e.g., fear, hurt, sadness, anxiety) are related to the emergence of the client's sexually promiscuous or seductive behavior.

B. The client was supported as he/she acknowledged that his/her sexually promiscuous or seductive behavior has been associated with underlying painful emotions arising from the sexual abuse.

C. A client-centered therapy approach was utilized to help the client make a connection between his/her underlying painful emotions and his/her sexually promiscuous or seductive behavior.

D. Role-playing and modeling techniques were used to demonstrate appropriate ways for the client to express his/her underlying painful emotions.

E. The client was helped to identify more appropriate ways to express his/her painful emotions and meet his/her needs instead of through sexually promiscuous or seductive behavior.

F. The client has not used more appropriate ways to express his/her underlying painful emotions and was provided with remedial assistance in this area.

39. Provide Sex Education (39)

A. The client was provided with sex education in an attempt to eliminate his/her pattern of engaging in sexually promiscuous or seductive behavior.

B. The client was helped to identify the risks involved with his/her sexually promiscuous or seductive behavior.

C. The client was assisted in exploring the factors contributing to his/her sexually promiscuous or seductive behavior.

40. Arrange for Substance Abuse Evaluation (40)

A. The client was referred for a substance abuse evaluation to assess the extent of his/her drug or alcohol usage and to determine the need for treatment.

B. The findings from the substance abuse evaluation revealed the presence of a substance abuse problem and the need for treatment.

C. The evaluation findings did not reveal the presence of a substance abuse problem or the need for treatment in this area.

D. The client was supportive of the recommendation to receive substance abuse treatment.

E. The client voiced his/her objection to receiving substance abuse treatment.

41. Arrange for Psychological Testing (41)

A. The client was referred for psychological testing to rule out the presence of a severe psychological disorder.

B. The findings from the psychological testing reveal the presence of serious emotional problems and the need for a medication evaluation.

C. The findings from the psychological testing do not support the presence of any severe psychological disorder.

D. The client approached the psychological testing in an honest, straightforward manner and was cooperative with any request directed toward him/her.

E. The client was uncooperative and resistant to engage during the evaluation process and was redirected to be more involved in the evaluation.

42. Assign Self-Portrait (42)

A. The client was instructed to draw a self-portrait to assess his/her self-esteem.

B. The client's self-portrait during the beginning stage of treatment was noted to reflect his/her feelings of low self-esteem, helplessness, and worthlessness.

C. The client's self-portrait during the middle stage of therapy was noted to reflect increased feelings of self-worth and esteem.

D. The client's self-portrait during the end stage of therapy was noted to reflect significant improvements in his/her self-esteem.

43. Assess Parents' Psychiatric and/or Substance Abuse Problem (43)

A. The client's parent(s) were assessed for the possibility of having a psychiatric disorder and/or a substance abuse problem.

B. Positive feedback was provided as the client's parent(s) agreed to seek substance abuse treatment.

C. Because of denial, the client's parent(s) have refused to seek substance abuse treatment and were redirected in this area.

D. A referral for a psychiatric evaluation and therapy was made to address the psychiatric disorder of the parent(s).

E. The parent(s) refused to comply with the recommendation to seek a psychiatric evaluation and/or therapy.

SEXUAL ACTING OUT

CLIENT PRESENTATION

1. Sexual Self-Interest (1)*

A. The client reported a history of multiple sexual encounters with casual partners where there was little if any emotional attachment.

B. The lone interest in any encounter for the client is his/her own sexual self-gratification.

C. The client talks readily and freely about his/her sexual adventures in graphic detail.

D. Since becoming engaged in the counseling process, there has been a decrease in the client's sexual behaviors and sexualized talk.

2. Sexually Active without Birth Control (2)

A. The client reported being sexually active for more than a year without using any birth control.

B. The client has had an abortion in the past year.

C. The client showed little if any concern about becoming pregnant, despite being very sexually active.

D. Recently the client has expressed concern over becoming pregnant and made an appointment at a family planning agency.

3. Sexually Active with No Commitment (3)

A. The client indicated that he/she is involved in a sexual relationship but does not see it lasting.

B. The client reported being sexually active with one partner but said that both are free to "date others."

C. The client verbalized being sexually active with one partner but did not want this to tie him/her down.

D. The client has expressed a desire to have a relationship in which there is mutual commitment.

4. Ignores Safe Sex (4)

A. The client verbalized that safe sex is not an important concern for him/her.

B. The client reported he/she does not bother with safe sex practices, as they spoil being "free and spontaneous."

C. The client presents in a manner that reflects little regard for himself/herself.

D. The client expressed an increasing commitment to practicing safer sex.

---

*The numbers in parentheses correlate to the number of the Behavioral Definition statement in the companion chapter with the same title in *The Adolescent Psychotherapy Treatment Planner,* Fourth Edition (Jongsma, Peterson, McInnis, and Bruce) by John Wiley & Sons, 2006.

5. Sexually Provocative Dress and Behavior (5)

A. The client's dress and behavior are sexually provocative.

B. The client indicated that his/her dress and behavior have been labeled by others as highly sexual.

C. The client denied being aware that his/her behavior and dress are sexually provocative.

D. The client has begun to dress and act in a less sexually provocative manner.

6. Talks Freely of Sexual Activity (6)

A. If not stopped, the client would have filled the session with his/her sexual exploits.

B. The client talked freely and without any sense of shame about his/her sexual experiences.

C. The client indicated that talking about his/her sexual experiences has turned off others.

D. The amount of bragging about his/her sexual exploits has decreased as the client has become engaged in therapy and started to share more about his/her personal self.

7. Substance Abuse (7)

A. The client reported a pattern of using alcohol and drugs previous to and during his/her sexual activity.

B. The client does not see any connection between his/her substance abuse and his/her sexual activity.

C. The client refuses to see anything wrong with his/her substance use.

D. The client showed an attitude of liking to party because that's what everyone is doing.

E. The client acknowledged that his/her substance abuse is an escape and has terminated it.

8. Low Self-Esteem (8)

A. A sense of low self-esteem predominates the client's manner, and he/she rarely makes eye contact or has a positive thing to say about himself/herself.

B. The client frequently makes self-disparaging remarks and is negative about the future.

C. The client indicated that he/she has always felt inferior to and less than others.

D. The client expressed that his/her feelings are not worth the therapist's time.

E. As the client has begun to talk in counseling, there has been a decrease in self-disparaging remarks and a more positive view of the future.

F. The client made a connection between his/her low self-esteem and his/her sexual promiscuity.

9. Depressed/Irritable (9)

A. The client presented in a manner that is both depressed and irritable.

B. The client's touchiness and irritability seem to be a shield and mask for his/her underlying depression.

C. The client's irritability makes it difficult for him/her to invest in the counseling process.

D. As the client's irritability has lessened, he/she has started to talk about the termination of sexual acting out.

10. Sad/Quiet (9)

A. The client presented in a sad, quiet manner.

B. The client prefers doing to talking and seems to view talking as a waste of time.

C. There is a deep sense of sadness to the client that he/she finds difficult to identify or put into words.

D. The client has started to emerge from his/her quietness and start talking more about himself/herself.

11. Hypomania (10)

A. The client presented as very impulsive and energetic, with an inability to focus and pressured speech.

B. The client's impulsiveness and energy has caused him/her difficulties in school, at home, and in the community.

C. The client's inability to focus has made it difficult to establish a relationship in therapy with him/her.

D. The client has started to become engaged in therapy and is able to focus and disclose some about himself/herself.

12. Friendly/Outgoing (10)

A. The client presents a friendly and outgoing manner to nearly everyone.

B. There seems to be little shame or social anxiety present with this client.

C. The client quickly became overfamiliar with the therapist.

D. The client seems to use his/her friendly, outgoing manner to keep others from getting too close or knowing him/her more than superficially.

E. As treatment has progressed, the client has become more socially appropriate in his/her manner.

13. Oppositional (11)

A. The client displayed an attitude of opposition to all authority figures.

B. The client described a pattern of not following social mores, ignoring parental rules, and not respecting authorities.

C. There is present within the client the belief that "I don't have to" or "I am not going to listen to anyone."

D. The client reported openly about his/her sexual activity without regard for social mores.

E. As treatment has progressed, the client has become less oppositional in his/her manner.

14. Angry/Rebellious (11)

A. The client's manner is dominated by anger and rebellion.

B. The client's anger and rebellion have made it difficult for him/her to form positive, supportive relationships with others.

C. The client's anger and rebellion have diminished, and he/she is now starting to talk more openly and honestly about self.

15. Conflict within the Family (12)

A. The client described his/her childhood as being very unstable, with constant family conflict.

B. The client provided numerous examples from his/her childhood of parents blaming him/her for their problems and misbehavior.

C. The client was aware of the details of parental history of sexual relationships with numerous partners.

D. The client has begun to verbalize some insight into how childhood experiences are connected to his/her present sexual behaviors.

INTERVENTIONS IMPLEMENTED

1. Build Trust (1)*

A. An initial trust level was established with the client through use of unconditional positive regard to facilitate the expression of intimate facts and feelings.

B. Warm acceptance and active listening techniques were used to establish the basis for a trusting relationship.

C. The client has formed a trust-based relationship and has started to identify and express some intimate facts and feelings.

D. Despite the use of active listening, warm acceptance, and unconditional positive regard, the client remains closed to sharing and identifying intimate facts and feelings.

2. Gather Sexual History (2)

A. The client's history of sexual activity, education, and practices was gathered.

B. The client's history of sexual partners was explored to assess the degree of emotional attachment he/she had with each.

C. Only a partial history was gathered due to client's refusal to provide information in some areas.

3. Explore Feelings about Sexual Activity (3)

A. Client thoughts and feelings about his/her sexual history and current practices were explored.

B. Positive verbal reinforcement was given to the client for identifying thoughts and feelings.

C. The client's lack of feelings connected to sexual behavior was pointed out.

4. List Reasons for Sexual Activity (4)

A. The client was asked to list the reasons for his/her sexual activity.

B. The client was confronted with the negative consequences of engaging in sexual activity at such an early age.

C. The client's reasons for his/her sexual activity were probed, and faulty logic was addressed and restructured.

---

*The numbers in parentheses correlate to the number of the Therapeutic Intervention statement in the companion chapter with the same title in *The Adolescent Psychotherapy Treatment Planner,* Fourth Edition (Jongsma, Peterson, McInnis, and Bruce) by John Wiley & Sons, 2006.

5. Process the Reasons for Sexual Activity (5)

A. The client's completed list of reasons for sexual activity was processed, with the pros and cons of each being identified.

B. After considering the pros and cons of the reasons for sexual activity, the client was asked to identify any changes he/she would now make in his/her sexual activity.

6. Explore History for Sexual Abuse (6)

A. The client's history was explored to determine whether he/she had been a victim of sexual abuse.

B. The parents were asked whether the client had been a victim of sexual abuse.

C. It was confirmed that the client has been a victim of sexual abuse and that this experience has had a significant impact on his/her sexual attitudes and behavior.

D. It was noted that neither the parents nor the client provided any evidence that the client has been a victim of sexual abuse.

7. Connect Sexual Abuse and Current Sexual Activity (7)

A. The client was assisted in looking at the connection between being treated as a sexual object and treating others as such.

B. Verbal support and encouragement was given to the client as he/she shared how sexual abuse has affected him/her.

C. The client was assisted in developing insight into the impact of his/her being a sexual abuse victim on his/her current sexual acting out.

D. The client denied any connection between his/her sexual abuse experience and his/her current sexual activity and was provided with tentative examples in this area.

8. Explore Feelings of Low Self-Esteem (8)

A. The client was asked to make a list of his/her positive and negative characteristics.

B. Client's feelings of low self-esteem were explored in terms of awareness, depth of feeling, and means of expression.

C. Positive characteristics identified by the client about himself/herself were affirmed and reinforced.

D. Despite a warm, supportive approach, the client still talked negatively about himself/herself.

E. It was noted that the client's low self-esteem was evident in his/her lack of ability to identify positive characteristics about himself/herself and in frequent self-disparaging remarks.

9. Identify Sources of Low Self-Esteem (9)

A. The client was assisted in identifying the negative messages he/she received and where each came from.

B. The client was shown the connection between the negative messages he/she has received and his/her low self-esteem.

C. With support, the client was able to identify and express his/her feelings of hurt and shame about his/her rejection and abuse experiences.

D. With assistance, the client identified negative messages he/she has received, but he/she insisted these messages had no effect on him/her.

10. Connect Past Rejection with Current Fear (10)

A. The client was helped to become aware of his/her fear of rejection and its connection to his/her past life experiences of abuse, abandonment, and rejection.

B. Past experiences of rejection and abandonment were explored with the client to build his/her awareness of their current impact on sexual acting out in search of acceptance and affirmation.

C. The client was supported as he/she acknowledged the connection between his/her history of rejection and abuse and his/her current sexual promiscuity.

D. The client remains in denial about the impact of past experiences of rejection and abandonment; this denial was reflected to the client.

11. Connect Underlying Feelings with Current Sexual Activity (11)

A. The client was assisted in making connections between his/her low self-esteem, fear of rejection, and current sexual promiscuity.

B. The idea of building self-esteem by saying no to sexual activity was seeded with the client.

C. The client has acknowledged the connection between his/her history of rejection and abuse and his/her current sexual promiscuity; he/she was supported for this insight.

D. Despite assistance, the client still found it difficult to connect his/her low self-esteem, fear of rejection, and current sexual promiscuity.

12. Identify Constructive Ways to Build Self-Esteem (12)

A. The client's use of sexual activity as a vehicle to build his/her self-esteem was confronted as self-defeating behavior.

B. The negative consequences of using sex to build self-esteem were reviewed with the client.

C. Positive ways to build self-esteem were explored with the client.

D. A plan was developed with the client to build his/her self-esteem in positive ways, and he/she was asked to make a commitment to implement the plan.

E. The client's plan to build self-esteem was monitored for implementation, with gains being recognized and reinforced.

F. The client was unable to identify constructive ways to build self-esteem and was provided with specific examples in this area.

13. Assign Changes Exercise (13)

A. The client was assigned a homework exercise in which he/she was asked to draw pictures of the desired changes to himself/herself.

B. Using the "Three Ways to Change Yourself" exercise from the *Adolescent Psychotherapy Homework Planner,* 2nd ed. (Jongsma, Peterson, and McInnis), the client was asked to draw three pictures of changes he/she desires.

C. The completed exercise on changes for self was processed, and the details of the desired changes were affirmed and reinforced with the client.

D. The client completed the exercise, but upon review details were very sketchy and the client would not be pinned down.

E. A plan for implementation to achieve the changes desired by the client was made and a commitment solicited about when and how this plan would begin.

F. The client has not completed the homework assignment to describe his/her desired changes to himself/herself and was redirected to do so.

14. Explore Family Rejection Affirmation (14)

A. The family-of-origin dynamics of rejection versus affirmation were explored with the client.

B. The family messages of rejection that were identified were challenged and alternative interpretations were offered to the client.

C. Support and acceptance were provided as the client is beginning to connect negative/rejecting family messages with his/her current sexual behavior.

D. Even with assistance, the client struggled to identify affirming or rejecting messages in his/her family of origin.

15. Assist Family in Expressing Their Feelings (15)

A. Family sessions were held that focused on members' feelings toward each other and the ways in which they interact.

B. Family members revealing feelings toward each other cleared the air and allowed new ways of interaction to be implemented.

C. In family sessions, the family members remained superficial in their expression of feelings and socially polite in their interactions, thus keeping and ensuring the status quo of distance; this pattern was reflected to the family.

16. Interpret Sexual Activity (16)

A. The client's sexual activity was interpreted to him/her as a maladaptive way of seeking attention and affirmation that was missing in the family.

B. On a scale of 1 to 10 (10 being absolute truth), the client rated the truth of the interpretation that he/she was searching for affirmation as a ____, and this rating was processed.

C. The interpretation of the client's sexual activity as a search for affirmation was presented to the family in a session for each member's reaction and feedback.

D. The client rejected the interpretation that his/her sexual activity is a search for affirmation on the grounds that no one controls his/her behavior.

17. Teach Value of True Sexual Intimacy (17)

A. The client was taught the value of reserving sexual intimacy for a committed, mutually respectful relationship with longevity.

B. The client was assisted in developing a list of relationship characteristics that would indicate the potential for true sexual intimacy.

C. The client denied the benefit of preserving sexual intimacy for a committed, mutually respectful relationship with longevity and was provided with remedial information in this area.

18. Teach the Rewards of Respectful Sexual Activity (18)

A. The client was taught the benefits of sexual activities that are respectful and mutual versus the negatives of using sex as a way of getting someone to love you or merely obtaining pleasure.

B. The client was assisted in identifying the pros and cons of sexual activity based on mature love versus self-centered motivations.

C. The client indicates that he/she has a hard time understanding any reason for sex other than self-based pleasure and was provided with remedial assistance in this area.

19. Assess Depression (19)

A. The client was assessed for level of depression and the possibility of a referral for medication.

B. The client was cooperative in his/her assessment for depression.

C. The concept and feeling of depression were explored with the client to find out his/her perception of what depression is and what it is like when he/she is depressed.

20. Arrange for Psychological Testing (20)

A. A psychological evaluation was conducted with the client to assess for emotional or personality factors that may contribute to sexual acting out.

B. With encouragement, the client followed through in a cooperative way with the psychological evaluation.

C. A psychological evaluation could not be completed due to the client's uncooperative, oppositional behavior.

D. The psychological assessment found evidence of emotional and personality factors that contribute to the client's sexual acting out.

E. No underlying emotional or personality factors were identified through the psychological assessment.

21. Interpret Sexual Activity as Coping Strategy for Depression (21)

A. The interpretation of sexual activity as a coping strategy for depression was given to the client.

B. On a scale of 1 to 10 (with 10 being absolute truth), the client rated the truth of the interpretation that his/her sexual activity was an antidote for depression as a _____, and the rating was processed.

C. The client rejected the interpretation of sex as the only sure good feeling he/she knows.

22. Teach Birth Control/Safe Sex (22)

A. The value of using birth control and practicing safe sex, as well as the risks associated with promiscuity, was taught to the client.

B. The client was referred to Planned Parenthood for its birth control resources and educational programs regarding the risks attached to sexual promiscuity.

C. The issue of birth control and safer sex was the focus of a family session.

D. Although the client has indicated he/she will continue to be active sexually, he/she did give a commitment to obtaining birth control and practicing safer sex; this commitment was encouraged.

23. Explore Underlying Causes for Reckless Sexual Practices (23)

A. The possible underlying wishes of the client for pregnancy or death as a motivation for reckless sexual practices were explored.

B. In the exploration, the client acknowledged that he/she did not care what happened as a result of the sexual activity.

C. The client remained in denial and oblivious to any underlying wishes that have been attached to reckless sexual behavior.

24. Explore Substance Abuse (24)

A. The client's pattern and extent of substance abuse was explored and evaluated.

B. The client was not open when asked to talk about his/her substance use.

C. When asked, the client denied any use of experimentation with substances.

D. In exploring the client's substance use, he/she revealed a pattern of substance use before, during, or after sexual activity.

25. Identify Role of Substance Abuse (25)

A. The client was assisted in identifying the role substance abuse played in numbing, escaping, or avoiding feelings of fear, guilt, and shame associated with sexual promiscuity.

B. It was difficult for the client to connect his/her substance use with escaping or numbing feelings; he/she was encouraged to review this concept.

C. The client was supported as he/she acknowledged that feelings of guilt and shame surround his/her sexual promiscuity and agreed that he/she used substance abuse to cope with these feelings.

26. Solicit a Commitment to Terminate Substance Abuse (26)

A. The client was asked to make a commitment to terminate all substance use immediately.

B. The client's verbal commitment to terminate substance use was monitored for follow-through and to give encouragement, reinforcement, and guidance.

C. The client refused to commit to terminate all substance abuse; the focus of treatment was changed to the substance abuse issue.

27. Assess Impulsiveness (27)

A. The level of the client's impulsiveness was assessed to rule out or confirm ADHD or mania as contributing factors to his/her sexual activity.

B. The client was cooperative and helpful in the assessment process.

C. A referral was made for a psychiatric evaluation to confirm a diagnosis of Bipolar Disorder.

D. The client refused to cooperate with the assessment, saying that everything is fine with him/her.

28. Assess Need for Medications (28)

A. The client was assessed for his/her need for or possible benefit from psychotropic medication.

B. The parents and the client were consulted about their feelings regarding psychotropic medication.

C. The parents' and the client's resistance to psychotropic medication was addressed and resolved.

D. Despite being provided additional information, the parents and client were still resistive to a prescription for psychotropic medication for the client.

29. Refer for Psychotropic Medication Evaluation (29)

A. The client was referred for a medication evaluation by a physician.

B. The client followed through and completed a medication evaluation.

C. The parents and the client filled the prescription, and the client has started to take the prescribed medication.

D. The client was not prescribed psychiatric medication.

30. Monitor/Assess Medication Effectiveness (30)

A. The client was monitored for medication compliance.

B. The effectiveness of the client's medication was assessed, and possible side effects were monitored.

C. The effectiveness of the client's medication was communicated to the prescribing physician.

D. The client was confronted with his/her own inconsistency in taking prescribed medications.

E. The client was asked to report all side effects to either parents, therapist, or physician.

F. The client reported that the medication has had a positive impact in reducing the targeted symptoms; the benefits of this progress were reviewed.

SEXUAL IDENTITY CONFUSION

CLIENT PRESENTATION

1. Confused/Uncertain (1)*

A. The client showed a good deal of uncertainty about his/her basic sexual orientation.

B. The client exhibited a high level of anxiety regarding the issue of his/her sexual orientation.

C. The client has gradually begun to be more comfortable and less anxious about his/her sexual orientation.

2. Sexual Fantasies/Desires Surrounding Same-Sex Partners (2)

A. The client expressed distress about his/her fantasies and desires for a same-sex partner.

B. The client tried hard to convince himself/herself that the desire for a same-sex partner did not upset him/her.

C. The client reported a long history of fantasies and desires for same-sex partners that went back to late childhood.

D. The client reported feelings of conflict and distress around sexual fantasies and desires with same-sex partners.

E. The client has begun to process his/her desires and fantasies involving same-sex partners and is no longer feeling overwhelmed.

3. Guilt/Shame (3)

A. A strong sense of guilt and shame dominates the client's mood and manner.

B. The client reported a pattern of guilt and shame surrounding the homosexual feelings, desires, and fantasies he/she was experiencing.

C. The client described being unable to feel comfortable with others due to guilt and shame he/she constantly feels.

D. The client's feelings of guilt and shame have decreased since he/she has started to accept his/her sexual orientation.

4. Feelings of Worthlessness (3)

A. The client's presentation reflected a low sense of self-esteem, and he/she avoided any eye contact and made consistent self-disparaging remarks.

B. The client described himself/herself as being totally worthless.

C. Due to his/her homosexual feelings, the client did not see any way for him/her to feel okay about self.

D. As the client has acknowledged his/her homosexual orientation, he/she has started to entertain the possibility of feeling okay about self.

---

*The numbers in parentheses correlate to the number of the Behavioral Definition statement in the companion chapter with the same title in *The Adolescent Psychotherapy Treatment Planner,* Fourth Edition (Jongsma, Peterson, McInnis, and Bruce) by John Wiley & Sons, 2006.

5. Depressed/Withdrawn (4)

A. The client presented in a depressed, withdrawn manner with low energy and a lack of interest in things.

B. The client reported a pattern of depression that has led him/her to withdraw from others and from life's activities.

C. The client described a history of being depressed that he/she can trace back to early teens and his/her questions about his/her homosexual orientation.

D. Since stating his/her sexual orientation, the client appeared less depressed and has started to interact with others.

6. Concealing Sexual Identity from Parents (5)

A. The client admitted that he/she has always worked hard to keep his/her homosexual urges hidden from parents.

B. The client reported avoiding any sexual questions parents have raised concerning him/her.

C. The client has started to be more open with his/her parents regarding his/her struggle with sexual identity.

7. Sexual Experimentation (6)

A. The client reported recent homosexual experimentation that has raised questions about his/her sexual orientation.

B. The client has involved himself/herself in impulsive, reckless sexual experimentation.

C. The client's homosexual experimentation has strengthened his/her conviction that he/she is not heterosexual.

D. The client indicated curtailing most of his/her sexual experimentation because he/she feels more certain of his/her sexual orientation.

8. Parents' Concern over Client's Possible Homosexuality (7)

A. The parents showed distress and concern about the possibility of their child being homosexual.

B. The parents raised numerous questions about the issue of their child's possible homosexuality.

C. The parents verbalized feelings of anger and rejection toward the client as the client talked of his/her homosexual orientation.

D. The level of the parents' distress and concern has decreased since openly discussing the issue of the client's homosexuality.

9. Disclosure of Homosexuality to Parents (8)

A. The client reported that he/she recently disclosed his/her homosexuality to parents.

B. The client indicated that his/her parents are struggling with his/her disclosure of homosexuality.

C. The client was crushed by the parental rejection he/she received on disclosing his/her homosexuality.

D. The client was surprised and shocked by the acceptance he/she received from parents after disclosing his/her homosexuality.

10. Parents' Feelings of Failure (9)

A. The client reported that his/her parents are feeling responsible and to blame for his/her homosexuality.

B. The parents expressed feelings of failure in regard to their child's homosexuality.

C. The parents denied any feeling of responsibility or failure due to the client's homosexuality.

D. The parents have begun to work through their feelings of failure in regard to the client's homosexuality.

INTERVENTIONS IMPLEMENTED

1. Build Trust (1)*

A. Trust was actively built with the client through the use of unconditional positive regard and active listening.

B. Warm acceptance and active listening techniques were utilized to build trust with the client.

C. An initial level of trust was established with the client, and he/she is now being encouraged to express his/her feelings concerning own sexual identity.

D. The client is now being encouraged to express the fear, anxiety, and distress he/she is feeling about his/her sexual identity confusion.

E. Despite trust and encouragement, the client struggled to express even a few feelings around his/her identity confusion.

2. Conduct Suicide Assessment (2)

A. A suicide assessment was conducted with the client, who was open and honest about his/her feelings.

B. Inpatient care was recommended and arranged for the client since a serious suicide risk was assessed.

C. The client was uncooperative throughout the suicide assessment.

D. The results and recommendations of the suicide assessment, which did not find serious risk to exist, were communicated to the client and the parents.

E. Although the client denied any suicide plan or ideation, his/her level of anxiety and depression related to the sexual identity struggle suggests that ongoing monitoring of suicide potential is necessary.

3. Sign No-Self-Harm Contract (3)

A. A no-self-harm contract was developed, and the client was encouraged to sign it.

B. The client was encouraged to verbalize a commitment to and to sign a no-self-harm contract.

C. The no-self-harm contract was monitored for follow-through, and a more supervised level of care was determined to be necessary.

*The numbers in parentheses correlate to the number of the Therapeutic Intervention statement in the companion chapter with the same title in *The Adolescent Psychotherapy Treatment Planner,* Fourth Edition (Jongsma, Peterson, McInnis, and Bruce) by John Wiley & Sons, 2006.

4. Gather Sexual History (4)

A. A history of sexual desires, experiences, and fantasies was gathered.

B. The client's current level of sexual functioning could not be fully assessed due to his/her resistance to revealing information on sexual experiences, desires, and fantasies.

5. Explore Questions about Sexual Identity (5)

A. The reasons the client began to question his/her sexuality were explored.

B. The client identified the questions he/she has about his/her sexuality and the experiences that have triggered the questions.

C. The client was reluctant to identify the questions that he/she has about his/her sexuality and was provided with acceptance and encouragement to help him/her explore these questions.

6. Teach Commonality of Same-Sex Experiences (6)

A. The client was taught the commonality of same-sex experiences in youth and informed that these do not necessarily indicate homosexuality.

B. Questions and concerns regarding same-sex experiences were processed and answered.

C. The client was reminded that same-sex experiences in youth do not necessarily indicate homosexuality but are a common part of sexual exploration.

7. Assign Rating of Sexual Attraction (7)

A. The client was asked to rate on a scale of 1 to 10 his/her sexual attraction to both males and females.

B. The ratings of the client were processed and assessed.

C. It was noted that the client gave a high rating to his/her sexual attraction to same-sex peers and a low rating to opposite-sex peers.

D. It was noted that the client gave a high rating to attraction to opposite-sex peers and a relatively low rating to same-sex peers.

E. It was noted that the client gave sexual attraction ratings of approximate equal value to both same-sex and opposite-sex peers.

8. Assign Writing of Future Autobiography (8)

A. The client was asked to write two autobiographies, projected 20 years into the future, one of life as a homosexual and the other of life as a heterosexual.

B. The client's two future autobiographies were read and processed.

C. The question "Which life was more satisfying, and which had more regret?" was asked and processed.

D. The client's projected future was noted to show a strong identification of self as a homosexual.

E. The client's projected future was noted to show a clear identification of self as a heterosexual.

9. Allow Self-Evaluation of Identity Evidence (9)

A. A nonjudgmental atmosphere was created to allow the client to evaluate the evidence and to resolve his/her confusion regarding sexual identity.

B. After a review of his/her sexual experiences, thoughts, and feelings, the client has identified himself/herself as homosexual.

C. After a review of his/her sexual experiences, thoughts, and feelings, the client has identified himself/herself as heterosexual.

D. Despite an accepting, nonjudgmental atmosphere, the client has not been able to identify his/her sexual orientation and was provided with additional support and encouragement in this area.

10. List Deciding Factors (10)

A. The client was asked to make a list of all the factors that influenced his/her decision on sexual identity.

B. The completed list was processed, and key factors were confirmed.

C. The client's list could be processed only in a limited way due to its being incomplete and vague.

D. The client's list was noted to have a preponderance of factors that supported the homosexual identity.

E. The client's list was noted to have a preponderance of factors that supported a heterosexual identity.

F. The client has not completed a list of factors to help him/her decide on his/her sexual identity and was reassigned this task.

11. Explore Feelings about Self as Homosexual (11)

A. The client's feelings regarding seeing self as homosexual were explored.

B. The client was assisted in identifying and expressing feelings about accepting self as a homosexual.

C. Feelings that were identified by the client as egosyntonic were affirmed and reinforced.

D. The client was noted to be relieved to finally accept himself/herself as homosexual.

E. Active-listening skills were used as the client expressed strong feelings of anxiety and fear of the future regarding accepting self as a homosexual.

12. Explore Negative Emotions about Hiding Sexual Identity (12)

A. The client's negative emotions related to hiding and denying his/her sexuality were explored.

B. Specific reasons for the client hiding or denying his/her sexuality were identified.

C. Specific reasons for the client hiding or denying his/her sexual identity were probed and challenged.

D. A warm, accepting, nonjudgmental approach was used to encourage the client to take risks and be more open about his/her sexual identity.

13. Explore Religious Conflicts with Sexual Identity (13)

A. The client's religious convictions were explored for ways they may cause conflict with his/her sexual identity.

B. The shame and guilt surrounding religious convictions and sexual identity were assessed and processed.

C. The client was assessed for the presence of religious conflicts with his/her sexual identity, but none were noted.

14. Refer to Compassionate Clergy (14)

A. The client was referred to a compassionate clergy member who will listen to his/her struggles on sexual identity.

B. The client's experience with clergy was processed, and positive aspects of the experience were affirmed and reinforced.

15. Teach Safer Sex (15)

A. Guidelines for safer sex were taught to the client.

B. The client's questions related to the details of safer sex practices were answered.

C. The client was asked to make a commitment to consistently follow safer sex guidelines.

D. The client's adherence to a safer sex commitment was monitored, and he/she was confronted when not following that commitment.

16. Identify Myths and Replace with Positive Beliefs (16)

A. The client was assigned to identify 10 myths about homosexuals and, on a scale of 1 to 5, rate how firmly he/she believes in each.

B. The identified myths and their ratings were processed; then the client was assisted in replacing each with more realistic positive beliefs.

C. The client was reminded of the positive beliefs about homosexuality to reinforce his/her sexual identity.

D. Myths and negative statements about homosexuality by the client were confronted.

17. List Advantages/Disadvantages of Disclosing Sexual Identity (17)

A. The client was asked to make a list of advantages and disadvantages of disclosing sexual orientation to family and significant others.

B. The client was assisted in processing his/her list of advantages and disadvantages of disclosing sexual orientation to the family and significant others.

C. The client's inability to list advantages of disclosing sexual identity was explored and addressed.

18. Explore Homophobic Peer Experiences (18)

A. The client's peer relationships were explored.

B. Assistance was provided to the client in describing homophobic experiences in peer relationships.

C. Ways to respond to homophobic and rejection experiences in peer relationships were identified.

D. The client's peer relationships were explored for homophobic experiences, but none were identified.

19. Identify Gay/Lesbian Peers (19)

A. The client was encouraged to identify other lesbian and gay adolescents from school and support groups as possible companions in social activities.

B. The client's fears regarding initiating social contact were addressed and resolved.

C. The client was asked to commit to making one attempt each week to initiate a social activity with a gay or lesbian peer(s).

D. The client has not followed through on initiating social contacts with gay/lesbian peers and was redirected to do so.

20. Support Group Referral (20)

A. The client was assisted in identifying the benefits of attending a support group for lesbian and gay adolescents.

B. The client was referred to a lesbian/gay adolescent support group.

C. The client's experience in attending the support group was processed, and positive aspects were affirmed and reinforced.

D. The client's resistance to attending a support group was explored and resolved.

E. The client was provided with positive feedback as he/she made a commitment to attend a support group for gay and lesbian adolescents.

F. The client has not attended a support group for gay and lesbian adolescents and was redirected to do so.

21. Develop Plan of Sexual Identity Disclosure (21)

A. The client was asked to develop a detailed plan for disclosing his/her sexual orientation.

B. The client's plan for disclosing his/her sexual identity was probed, and possible questions and reactions from others were identified and addressed.

C. The client's inability to develop a plan for disclosing his/her sexual identity was explored.

D. The client was assessed to be ready to go forward with the plan for disclosing his/her sexual identity.

22. Role-Play Sexual Orientation Disclosure (22)

A. Role-play was utilized to prepare the client for disclosing sexual orientation to significant others.

B. Issues that were identified from role-plays were addressed and resolved.

C. Feelings that emerged from role-plays were recognized, expressed, and processed.

23. Support and Guide Sexual Identity Disclosure Plan (23)

A. The plan developed by the client for disclosure of sexual identity was reviewed, and he/she was encouraged to enact the plan.

B. The client was given support, encouragement, and guidance as he/she implemented his/her sexual orientation disclosure plan.

C. The client's hesitancy and fear to go forward with his/her plan were explored and addressed.

24. Process Reactions to Sexual Orientation Disclosure (24)

A. The client was probed about the reactions of significant others to his/her disclosure.

B. Significant others' reactions were role-played to provide opportunities to process their reactions.

C. Encouragement and positive feedback were given to the client for disclosing his/her sexual orientation.

D. Active-listening skills were used as the client reported that family members were shocked, angry, disappointed, and worried when he/she announced his/her sexual orientation.

E. Support and encouragement were provided as the client reported that family members were accepting and supportive when he/she disclosed his/her sexual orientation.

25. Solicit Parents' Cooperation with Family Sessions (25)

A. Conjoint sessions were arranged with the parents to process the client's disclosure of his/her homosexual orientation.

B. The parents were encouraged to attend and participate in family therapy sessions.

C. The parents' resistance to attending family sessions about their child's sexual orientation was addressed.

26. Process Parents' Reactions to Client's Identity Disclosure (26)

A. The parents' reactions to the client's disclosure of homosexual identity were explored.

B. Emotional support and understanding were provided to the parents in regard to their reaction to the client's disclosure.

C. The parents were encouraged to express their thoughts and feelings about the disclosure.

D. The client's parents were noted to be very resistive to supporting the client's sexual identity.

E. The client's parents were noted to be supportive of the client's homosexual identity, but they expressed fears regarding future adjustment.

27. Educate Parents about Homosexuality (27)

A. The parents were educated about homosexuality, its possible causes, reversibility, lifestyle choices, and so forth.

B. The parents' questions regarding aspects of homosexuality were elicited and answered.

C. The parents were specifically reminded that homosexuality is not caused by faulty parenting or mental illness.

D. The benefits to the parents and the client of accepting the client's sexual orientation were explored and identified.

28. Assign Parents Books on Homosexuality (28)

A. The parents were directed to books and other resources on homosexuality and the homosexual individual.

B. Questions from the parents' readings were answered.

C. The parents were encouraged to seek opportunities to increase their knowledge and understanding of homosexuality.

D. The parents have refused to follow through on reading information regarding homosexuality and were reminded to do this reading.

29. Refer to Parent Support Group (29)

A. Options for the parents to attend a support group for parents and friends of lesbians and gays (PFLAG) were explored and barriers identified.

B. The possible benefits of attending a support group were identified and processed.

C. The parents were referred to and encouraged to attend a support group for parents and friends of lesbians and gays.

D. Barriers to attending a support group were resolved, and the parents were encouraged to attend.

E. The parents' support group experience was processed, and positive benefits were identified and reinforced.

F. The parents have not attended a support group for the parents and friends of lesbians and gays and were redirected to do so.

30. Process Parents' Religious Beliefs about Homosexuality (30)

A. The parents were asked to list their religious beliefs regarding homosexuality.

B. The parents' religious beliefs were processed, and beliefs that were problematic to acceptance of homosexuality were identified.

C. Empathy was conveyed to the parents in regard to coming to some peace with their religious beliefs and the client's homosexuality.

D. It was noted that the parents' religious beliefs were firmly opposed to acceptance of homosexual relationships and behavior.

E. Although the parents have held religious beliefs that are contrary to homosexual practice, they are open to reexamining these beliefs.

31. Refer Parents to Clergy (31)

A. The parents were referred to a gay/lesbian-positive member of the clergy to assist them in coming to terms with their beliefs regarding the Bible's condemnation of the client's homosexuality.

B. Gay- and lesbian-positive books were suggested for the client and parents to read and discuss.

C. The parents have not followed up with the referral to a clergy member, and their resistance to this contact was reviewed.

32. Assign Parents Books on Religion and Homosexuality (32)

A. The parents were asked to read Chapter 4 in *Beyond Acceptance* (Griffen, Wirth, and Wirth) and to process key ideas with the client.

B. The parents were asked to read the chapter entitled "The Bible and Homosexuality: The Last Prejudice" from *The Good Book* (Gomes) and to process key concepts and reactions with the client.

C. Assigned readings were processed with the parents, and opportunities to increase their level of acceptance were explored and encouraged.

D. The parents have not done the assigned reading and were redirected to do so.

SOCIAL PHOBIA/SHYNESS

CLIENT PRESENTATION

1. Shyness/Social Anxiety (1)*

A. The client described himself/herself as being shy and anxious in many social situations.

B. The client appeared anxious (e.g., hand tremors, lack of eye contact, fidgeting, restless, stammering) and inhibited during today's therapy session.

C. The client's social anxiety has gradually started to diminish, and he/she reported feeling more at ease in his/her conversations with others.

D. The client reported feeling confident and relaxed in the majority of his/her recent social interactions.

E. The client has interacted socially with his/her peers on a regular, consistent basis without excessive fear or anxiety.

2. Avoidance of Unfamiliar People (1)

A. The client has consistently avoided contact with unfamiliar people.

B. The client expressed feelings of anxiety about interacting with unfamiliar people.

C. The client has started to initiate more conversations with unfamiliar people.

D. The client has initiated social contacts with unfamiliar people on a consistent basis.

3. Social Isolation/Withdrawal (2)

A. The client described a persistent pattern of withdrawing or isolating himself/herself from most social situations.

B. The client acknowledged that his/her social withdrawal interferes with his/her ability to establish and maintain friendships.

C. The client has gradually started to socialize with a wider circle of peers.

D. The client has become more outgoing and interacts with his/her peers on a regular, consistent basis.

4. Excessive Isolated Activities (2)

A. The client has spent an excessive or inordinate amount of time involved in isolated activities instead of socializing with peers.

B. The client verbalized an understanding of how his/her excessive involvement in isolated activities interferes with his/her chances of establishing friendships.

C. The client reported spending less time in isolated activities and has started to seek out interactions with his/her peers.

D. The client has achieved a healthy balance between time spent in isolated activities and social interactions with others.

---

*The numbers in parentheses correlate to the number of the Behavioral Definition statement in the companion chapter with the same title in *The Adolescent Psychotherapy Treatment Planner,* Fourth Edition (Jongsma, Peterson, McInnis, and Bruce) by John Wiley & Sons, 2006.

5. Hypersensitivity to Criticism/Rejection (3)

A. The client has been very hesitant to become involved with others for fear of being met by criticism, disapproval, or perceived signs of rejection.

B. The client described a history of experiencing excessive or undue criticism, disapproval, and rejection from parental figures.

C. The client acknowledged that he/she tends to overreact to the slightest sign of criticism, rebuff, or rejection and subsequently withdraws from other people.

D. The client has begun to tolerate criticism or rebuff from others more effectively.

E. The client has continued to interact with others even in the face of criticism, disapproval, or perceived slights from others.

6. No Close Friendships (4)

A. The client described a history of having few or no close friendships.

B. The client does not have any close friends at the present time.

C. The client expressed feelings of sadness and loneliness about not having any close friends.

D. The client has begun to take steps (e.g., greeting others, complimenting others, making positive self-statements) to try to establish close friendships.

E. The client has now established close friendships at school and/or in the community.

7. Enmeshed Family Relationships (4)

A. The client has established an enmeshed relationship with his/her parents that interferes with his/her opportunities to socialize with peers.

B. The parents verbally recognized that they reinforce the client's excessive dependency at the expense of his/her peer friendships.

C. The parents have encouraged the client to become more independent.

D. The parents have reinforced the client's positive social behavior and set limits on overly dependent behavior.

E. The client has achieved a healthy balance between socializing with his/her peers and spending time with family members.

8. Avoidance of Interpersonal Contact (5)

A. The client displays a persistent pattern of avoidance of situations that require a degree of interpersonal contact.

B. The client consistently chooses options that decrease his/her level of interpersonal contact.

C. As treatment has progressed, the client has increased his/her amount of interpersonal contact.

D. The client is regularly involved with others in social activities.

9. Reluctance to Take Risks (6)

A. The client has been reluctant to engage in new activities or take personal risks because of the potential for embarrassment or humiliation.

B. The client verbalized a desire to engage in new activities or take healthy risks to help improve his/her self-esteem and develop friendships.

C. The client has started to take healthy risks in order to find enjoyment, build self-esteem, and establish friendships.

D. The client has engaged in new activities and assumed healthy risks without excessive fear of embarrassment or humiliation.

10. Performance Anxiety (7)

A. The client described a debilitating pattern of performance anxiety.

B. The client consistently avoids required social performance situations.

C. The client has become quite anxious when the social focus has been placed on him/her.

D. As treatment has progressed, the client has increased his/her ability to perform in social situations.

11. Physiological Distress (8)

A. The client's social anxiety has been manifested in his/her heightened physiological distress (e.g., increased heart rate, profuse sweating, dry mouth, muscular tension, trembling).

B. The client was visibly anxious (e.g., trembling, shaking, sweating, appearing tense and rigid) when talking about his/her social relationships.

C. The client reported that he/she has recently experienced less physiological distress when interacting with others.

D. The client has been able to consistently interact with other people in a variety of social settings without experiencing physiological distress.

INTERVENTIONS IMPLEMENTED

1. Build Trust (1)*

A. Today's therapy session focused on building the level of trust with the client through consistent eye contact, active listening, unconditional positive regard, and warm acceptance.

B. Unconditional positive regard and warm acceptance helped the client increase his/her ability to identify and express feelings.

C. The therapy session was helpful in building the level of trust with the client, and he/she became more open and relaxed.

D. The session was not helpful in building the level of trust with the client, who remained quiet and reserved in his/her interactions.

2. Assess Nature of Social Discomfort Symptoms (2)

A. The client was asked about the frequency, intensity, duration, and history of his/her social discomfort symptoms, fear, and avoidance.

B. *The Anxiety Disorders Interview Schedule for DSM-IV* (DiNardo, Brown, and Barlow) was used to assess the client's social discomfort symptoms.

C. The assessment of the client's social discomfort symptoms indicated that his/her symptoms are extreme and severely interfere with his/her life.

*The numbers in parentheses correlate to the number of the Therapeutic Intervention statement in the companion chapter with the same title in *The Adolescent Psychotherapy Treatment Planner*, Fourth Edition (Jongsma, Peterson, McInnis, and Bruce) by John Wiley & Sons, 2006.

D. The assessment of the client's social discomfort symptoms indicates that these symptoms are moderate and occasionally interfere with his/her daily functioning.

E. The results of the assessment of the client's social discomfort symptoms indicate that these symptoms are mild and rarely interfere with his/her daily functioning.

F. The results of the assessment of the client's social discomfort symptoms were reviewed with the client.

3. Explore Social Discomfort Stimulus Situations (3)

A. The client was assisted in identifying specific stimulus situations that precipitate social discomfort symptoms.

B. The client could not identify any specific stimulus situations that produce social discomfort; he/she was helped to identify that they occur unexpectedly and without any pattern.

C. The client was helped to identify that his/her social discomfort symptoms occur when he/she is expected to perform basic social interaction expectations.

4. Administer Social Anxiety Assessment (4)

A. The client was administered a measure of social anxiety to further assess the depth and breadth of his/her social fears and avoidance.

B. The client was administered *The Social Interaction Anxiety Scale and/or Social Phobia Scale* (Mattick and Clarke).

C. The result of the assessment of social anxiety indicated a high level of social fears and avoidance; this was reflected to the client.

D. The result of the assessment of social anxiety indicated a medium level of social fears and avoidance; this was reflected to the client.

E. The result of the assessment of social anxiety indicated a low level of social fears and avoidance; this was reflected to the client.

F. The client declined to participate in an assessment of social anxiety; the focus of treatment was turned to this resistance.

5. Refer for Medication Evaluation (5)

A. Arrangements were made for the client to have a physician's evaluation for the purpose of considering psychotropic medication to alleviate social discomfort symptoms.

B. The client has followed through with seeing a physician for an evaluation of any organic causes for the anxiety and the need for psychotropic medication to control the anxiety response.

C. The client has not cooperated with the referral to a physician for a medication evaluation and was encouraged to do so.

6. Monitor Medication Compliance (6)

A. The client reported that he/she has taken the prescribed medication consistently and that it has helped to control the anxiety; this was relayed to the prescribing clinician.

B. The client reported that he/she has not taken the prescribed medication consistently and was encouraged to do so.

C. The client reported taking the prescribed medication and stated that he/she has not noted any beneficial effect from it; this was reflected to the prescribing clinician.

D. The client was evaluated but was not prescribed any psychotropic medication by the physician.

7. Refer to Group Therapy (7)

A. The client was referred to a small (closed-enrollment) group for social anxiety.

B. The client was enrolled in a social anxiety group as defined in *The Group Therapy Treatment Planner,* 2nd ed. (Paleg and Jongsma).

C. The client was enrolled in a social anxiety group as defined in "Social Anxiety Disorder" (Turk, Heimberg, and Hope) from the *Clinical Handbook of Psychological Disorders* (Barlow).

D. The client has participated in group therapy for social anxiety; his/her experience was reviewed and processed.

E. The client has not been involved in group therapy for social anxiety concerns, and he/she was redirected to do so.

8. Discuss Cognitive Biases (8)

A. A discussion was held regarding how social anxiety derives from cognitive biases that overestimate negative evaluation by others, undervalue the self, increase distress, and often lead to unnecessary avoidance.

B. The client was provided with examples of cognitive biases that support social anxiety symptoms.

C. The client was reinforced as he/she identified his/her own cognitive biases.

D. The client was unable to identify any cognitive biases that support his/her anxiety symptoms, and he/she was provided with tentative examples in this area.

9. Assign Information on Social Anxiety, Avoidance, and Treatment (9)

A. The client was assigned to read information on social anxiety that explains the cycle of social anxiety and avoidance, and provides a rationale for treatment.

B. The client was assigned information about social anxiety, avoidance, and treatment from *Overcoming Shyness and Social Phobia* (Rapee).

C. The client was assigned information about social anxiety, avoidance, and treatment from *Overcoming Social Anxiety and Shyness* (Butler).

D. The client has read the information on social anxiety, avoidance, and treatment, and key concepts were reviewed.

E. The client has not read the assigned material on social anxiety, avoidance, and treatment, and he/she was redirected to do so.

10. Discuss Cognitive Restructuring (10)

A. A discussion was held about how cognitive restructuring and exposure serve as an arena to desensitize learned fear, build social skills and confidence, and reality-test biased thoughts.

B. The client was reinforced as he/she displayed a clear understanding of the use of cognitive restructuring and exposure to desensitize learned fear, build social skills and confidence, and reality-test biased thoughts.

C. The client did not display a clear understanding of the use of cognitive restructuring and exposure, and he/she was provided with remedial feedback in this area.

11 Assign Information on Cognitive Restructuring and Exposure (11)

A. The client was assigned to read about how cognitive restructuring and exposure–based therapy could be beneficial.

B. The client was assigned to read excerpts from *Managing Social Anxiety* (Hope, Heimberg, Juster, and Turk).

C. The client was assigned to read portions of *Dying of Embarrassment* (Markaway, Carmin, Pollard, and Flynn).

D. The client has read the assigned information on cognitive restructuring and exposure–based therapy techniques, and key points were reviewed.

E. The client has not read the assigned information on cognitive restructuring and exposure–based therapy techniques, and he/she was redirected to do so.

12. Teach Anxiety Management Skills (12)

A. The client was taught anxiety management skills.

B. The client was taught about staying focused on behavioral goals and riding the wave of anxiety.

C. Techniques for muscular relaxation and paced diaphragmatic breathing were taught to the client.

D. The client was reinforced for his/her clear understanding and use of anxiety management skills.

E. The client has not used his/her new anxiety management skills and was redirected to do so.

13. Assign Calming and Coping Strategy Information (13)

A. The client was assigned to read about calming and coping strategies in books or treatment manuals on social anxiety.

B. The client was assigned to read portions of *Overcoming Shyness and Social Phobia* (Rapee).

C. The client has read the assigned information on calming and coping strategies, and key points were reviewed.

D. The client has not read the information on calming and coping strategies, and he/she was redirected to do so.

14. Identify Distorted Thoughts (14)

A. The client was assisted in identifying the distorted schemas and related automatic thoughts that mediate social anxiety responses.

B. The client was taught the role of distorted thinking in precipitating emotional responses.

C. The client was reinforced as he/she verbalized an understanding of the cognitive beliefs and messages that mediate his/her anxiety responses.

D. The client was assisted in replacing distorted messages with positive, realistic cognitions.

E. The client failed to identify his/her distorted thoughts and cognitions and was provided with tentative examples in this area.

15. Assign Reading on Cognitive Restructuring (15)

A. The client was assigned to read information about cognitive restructuring in books or treatment manuals on social anxiety.

B. The client was assigned to read excerpts from *The Shyness and Social Anxiety Workbook* (Antony and Swinson).

C. The client has read the assigned information on cognitive restructuring, and key points were reviewed.

D. The client has not read the assigned information on cognitive restructuring and was redirected to do so.

16. Assign Exercises on Self-Talk (16)

A. The client was assigned homework exercises in which he/she identifies fearful self-talk and creates reality-based alternatives.

B. The client was assigned "Bad Thoughts Lead to Depressed Feelings" from the *Adolescent Psychotherapy Homework Planner,* 2nd ed. (Jongsma, Peterson, and McInnis).

C. The client was directed to do assignments from *The Shyness and Social Anxiety Workbook* (Antony and Swinson).

D. The client was directed to complete assignments from *Overcoming Shyness and Social Phobia* (Rapee).

E. The client's replacement of fearful self-talk with reality-based alternatives was critiqued.

F. The client was reinforced for his/her successes at replacing fearful self-talk with reality-based alternatives.

G. The client was provided with corrective feedback for his/her failures to replace fearful self-talk with reality-based alternatives.

H. The client has not completed his/her assigned homework regarding fearful self-talk and was redirected to do so.

17. Construct Anxiety Stimuli Hierarchy (17)

A. The client was assisted in constructing a hierarchy of anxiety-producing situations associated with his/her phobic fear.

B. It was difficult for the client to develop a hierarchy of stimulus situations, as the causes of his/her fear remain quite vague; he/she was assisted in completing the hierarchy.

C. The client was successful at completing a focused hierarchy of specific stimulus situations that provoke anxiety in a gradually increasing manner; this hierarchy was reviewed.

18. Select Exposures That Are Likely to Succeed (18)

A. Initial in vivo or role-played exposures were selected, with a bias toward those that have a high likelihood of being a successful experience for the client.

B. Cognitive restructuring was done within and after the exposure using behavioral strategies (e.g., modeling, rehearsal, social reinforcement).

C. In vivo or role-played exposures were patterned after those in "Social Anxiety Disorder" by Turk, Heimberg, and Hope in the *Clinical Handbook of Psychological Disorders* (Barlow).

D. A review was conducted with the client about his/her use of *in vivo* or role-played exposure.

E. The client was provided with positive feedback regarding his/her use of exposures.

F. The client has not used in vivo or role-played exposures and was redirected to do so.

19. Assign Reading on Exposure (19)

A. The client was assigned to read about exposure in books or treatment manuals on social anxiety.

B. The client was assigned to read excerpts from *The Shyness and Social Anxiety Workbook* (Antony and Swinson).

C. The client was assigned portions of *Overcoming Shyness and Social Phobia* (Rapee).

D. The client's information about exposure was reviewed and processed.

E. The client has not read the information on exposure and was redirected to do so.

20. Assign Homework on Exposure (20)

A. The client was assigned homework exercises to perform sensation exposure and record his/her experience.

B. The client was assigned "Gradually Facing a Phobic Fear" from the *Adolescent Psychotherapy Homework Planner,* 2nd ed. (Jongsma, Peterson, and McInnis).

C. The client was assigned sensation exposure homework from *The Shyness and Social Anxiety Workbook* (Antony and Swinson).

D. The client was directed to complete assignments from *Overcoming Shyness and Social Phobia* (Rapee).

E. The client's use of sensation exposure techniques was reviewed and reinforced.

F. The client has struggled in his/her implementation of sensation exposure techniques and was provided with corrective feedback.

G. The client has not attempted to use the sensation exposure techniques and was redirected to do so.

21. Build Social and Communication Skills (21)

A. Instruction, modeling, and role-playing were used to build the client's general social and communication skills.

B. Techniques from *Social Effectiveness Therapy* (Turner, Beidel, and Cooley) were used to teach social and communication skills.

C. The client was assigned the "Greeting Peers" exercise from the *Adolescent Psychotherapy Homework Planner,* 2nd ed. (Jongsma, Peterson, and McInnis).

D. The client was assigned the "Reach Out and Call" exercise from the *Adolescent Psychotherapy Homework Planner,* 2nd ed. (Jongsma, Peterson, and McInnis).

E. Positive feedback was provided to the client for his/her use of increased use of social and communication skills.

F. Despite the instruction, modeling, and role-playing about social and communication skills, the client continues to struggle with these techniques and was provided with additional feedback in this area.

22. Assign Information on Social and Communication Skills (22)

A. The client was assigned to read about general social and/or communication skills in books or treatment manuals on building social skills.

B. The client was assigned to read *Your Perfect Right* (Alberti and Emmons).

C. The client was assigned to read *Conversationally Speaking* (Garner).

D. The client has read the assigned information on social and communication skills, and key points were reviewed.

E. The client has not read the information on social and communication skills and was redirected to do so.

23. Differentiate between Lapse and Relapse (23)

A. A discussion was held with the client regarding the distinction between a lapse and a relapse.

B. A lapse was associated with an initial and reversible return of symptoms, fear, or urges to avoid.

C. A relapse was associated with the decision to return to fearful and avoidant patterns.

D. The client was provided with support and encouragement as he/she displayed an understanding of the difference between a lapse and a relapse.

E. The client struggled to understand the difference between a lapse and a relapse, and he/she was provided with remedial feedback in this area.

24. Discuss Management of Lapse Risk Situations (24)

A. The client was assisted in identifying future situations or circumstances in which lapses could occur.

B. The session focused on rehearsing the management of future situations or circumstances in which lapses could occur.

C. The client was reinforced for his/her appropriate use of lapse management skills.

D. The client was redirected in regard to his/her poor use of lapse management skills.

25. Encourage Routine Use of Strategies (25)

A. The client was instructed to routinely use the strategies that he/she has learned in therapy (e.g., cognitive restructuring, exposure).

B. The client was urged to find ways to build his/her new strategies into his/her life as much as possible.

C. The client was reinforced as he/she reported ways in which he/she has incorporated coping strategies into his/her life and routine.

D. The client was redirected about ways to incorporate his/her new strategies into his/her routine and life.

26. Develop a "Coping Card" (26)

A. The client was provided with a coping card on which specific coping strategies were listed.

B. The client was assisted in developing his/her coping card in order to list his/her helpful coping strategies.

C. The client was encouraged to use his/her coping card when struggling with anxiety-producing situations.

27. Teach Family about Treatment Goals and Support (27)

A. A family session was held in which the family was taught the treatment goals for the subject's social phobia/shyness problems.

B. The family was taught how to provide support to the client as he/she faces his/her fears.

C. A discussion was held about how to prevent reinforcing the client's fear and avoidance.

D. The family was provided with encouragement, support, and redirection.

E. Positive feedback was provided, as the family has been able to provide support to the client.

F. The family continues to interact with the client in a manner that reinforces the client's fear and avoidance; redirection was provided to the family about this pattern.

28. Teach Family Problem-Solving (28)

A. The family was taught problem-solving skills.

B. Conflict resolution skills were taught to the family.

C. The family was urged to use problem-solving and conflict resolution skills to manage problems within the family unit.

D. The family was reinforced for their successful negotiation of problem areas.

E. The family continues to have a great deal of turmoil and was redirected to the problem-solving and conflict resolution skills.

29. Encourage Family Modeling of Constructive Skills (29)

A. The family was urged to model constructive skills that they have learned for dealing with social shyness.

B. The family was encouraged to model the therapeutic skills that the client is learning (e.g., calming, cognitive restructuring, nonavoidance of unrealistic fears).

C. The client reported that he/she has received constructive examples of how to use therapeutic skills.

30. Explore History of Traumas (30)

A. The client's background was explored for a history of rejection experiences, harsh criticism, abandonment, or trauma that may have contributed to the client's low self-esteem and social anxiety.

B. The client was assisted in developing a time line in which he/she identified significant historical events, both positive and negative, that have occurred in his/her background.

C. The client identified a history of abandonment and/or traumatic experiences that coincided with the onset of his/her feelings of low self-esteem and social anxiety, and this connection was highlighted.

D. Exploration of the client's background did not reveal any significant rejection or traumatic experiences that contributed to the onset of his/her social anxiety.

31. Assign Shame Books (31)

A. The client was assigned to read books about shame.

B. The client was assigned to read *Healing the Shame That Binds You* (Bradshaw).

C. The client was directed to read excerpts from *Facing Shame* (Fossum and Mason).

D. The client has read books on shame, and key ideas were processed.

E. The client has not read books about shame and was redirected to do so.

32. Identify Defense Mechanisms (32)

A. The client was assisted in identifying the defense mechanisms that he/she uses to avoid close relationships.

B. The client was assisted in reducing his/her defensiveness so as to be able to build social relationships and not alienate himself/herself from others.

33. Utilize Transactional Analysis (TA) Approach (33)

A. A TA approach was used to uncover and identify the client's beliefs and fears that contribute to social anxiety.

B. The TA approach was used to alter the client's beliefs and actions in a more adaptive and positive mode.

C. The client reported successful social interactions after utilization of the TA approach.

34. Assign TA Reading (34)

A. The client was assigned to read a book on improving social relationships using TA.

B. The client was assigned to read excerpts from *Achieving Emotional Literacy* (Steiner).

C. The client has read the assigned information on TA, and key points about how to improve social relationships were reviewed.

D. The client has not read the assigned information on TA and was redirected to do so.

35. Schedule a "Booster Session" (35)

A. The client was scheduled for a booster session between 1 and 3 months after therapy ends.

B. The client was advised to contact the therapist if he/she needs to be seen prior to the booster session.

C. The client's booster session was held, and he/she was reinforced for his/her successful implementation of therapy techniques.

D. The client's booster session was held, and he/she was coordinated for further treatment, as his/her progress has not been sustained.

SPECIFIC PHOBIA

CLIENT PRESENTATION

1. Persistent and Unreasonable Fear (1)*

A. An immediate anxiety response has been exhibited by the client each time he/she encounters the phobic stimulus.

B. The client reported that the strength of his/her phobic response has been increasing in the past several months.

C. The client described the level of fear he/she experiences in response to the phobic stimulus as paralyzing.

D. The client indicated that although the phobia is of recent origin, it has quickly become very persistent and unreasonable.

E. As the client has become engaged in therapy, there has been a decrease in the intensity and frequency of the phobic response.

2. Avoidance and Endurance of Phobia (2)

A. The client reported that his/her avoidance of the phobic stimulus has caused major interference in his/her normal daily routines.

B. The client indicated that the intensity of his/her anxiety in response to the phobic stimulus has resulted in marked personal distress.

C. The client questioned whether he/she would ever be able to resolve the phobia.

D. The client has progressed to the point that the phobic stimulus does not create interference in his/her normal daily routines or cause him/her marked distress.

3. Fear Seen as Unreasonable (3)

A. The client acknowledged that his/her persistent fear is excessive and unreasonable.

B. The client's recognition of his/her persistent fear as excessive and unreasonable has provided good motivation for cooperation with treatment and follow-through on attempts to change.

4. Sleep Disturbance (4)

A. The client reported that his/her sleep has been disturbed by frequent dreams of the feared stimulus.

B. The client indicated his/her disturbed sleep pattern has started to affect his/her daily functioning.

C. The client's sleep has improved as he/she has worked toward resolving the feared stimulus.

---

*The numbers in parentheses correlate to the number of the Behavioral Definition statement in the companion chapter with the same title in *The Adolescent Psychotherapy Treatment Planner*, Fourth Edition (Jongsma, Peterson, McInnis, and Bruce) by John Wiley & Sons, 2006.

5. Dramatic Fear Reaction (5)

A. At the slightest mention of the phobic stimulus, the client indicated he/she has a dramatic fear reaction.

B. The client's reaction to the phobic stimulus is so dramatic and overpowering that it is difficult to calm him/her down.

C. The client reported that his/her reaction to the phobic stimulus is rapidly becoming more and more dramatic.

D. There has been a marked decrease in the client's dramatic fear reaction to the phobic stimulus since he/she has started to work in therapy sessions.

6. Parental Reinforcement (6)

A. The parents have catered to the client's fear and have thus reinforced and increased it.

B. The parents' own fears seemed to be projected onto and acted out by the client.

C. The parents have worked to curb their reaction to the client's fears, which has resulted in a marked decrease in the client's level of fear.

INTERVENTIONS IMPLEMENTED

1. Build Trust (1)*

A. An initial trust level was established with the client through the use of unconditional positive regard.

B. Warm acceptance and active-listening techniques were utilized to establish the basis for a trusting relationship.

C. The client has formed a trust-based relationship and was urged to begin to express his/her fearful thoughts and feelings.

D. Despite the use of active listening, warm acceptance, and unconditional positive regard, the client remains hesitant to trust and to share his/her thoughts and feelings.

2. Assess Fear and Avoidance/Administer Fear Survey (2)

A. An objective fear survey was administered to the client to assess the depth and breadth of his/her phobic fear.

B. The *Anxiety Disorders Interview Schedule for Children—Parent Version* or *Child Version* (Silverman and Albano) was used to assess the level of phobia symptoms.

C. The fear survey results indicated that the client's phobic fear is extreme and severely interferes with his/her life.

D. The fear survey results indicate that the client's phobic fear is moderate and occasionally interferes with his/her daily functioning.

E. The fear survey results indicate that the client's phobic fear is mild and rarely interferes with his/her daily functioning.

F. The results of the fear survey were reviewed with the client.

---

*The numbers in parentheses correlate to the number of the Therapeutic Intervention statement in the companion chapter with the same title in *The Adolescent Psychotherapy Treatment Planner,* Fourth Edition (Jongsma, Peterson, McInnis, and Bruce) by John Wiley & Sons, 2006.

3. Administer Client-Report Measure (3)

A. A client-report measure was used to further assess the depth and breadth of the client's phobic responses.

B. *Measures for Specific Phobias* (Antony) was used to assess the depth and breadth of the client's phobic responses.

C. The client-report measure indicated that the client's phobic fear is extreme and severely interferes with his/her life.

D. The client-report measure indicated that the client's phobic fear is moderate and occasionally interferes with his/her life.

E. The client-report measure indicated that the client's phobic fear is mild and rarely interferes with his/her life.

F. The client declined to complete the client-report measure, and the focus of treatment was changed to this resistance.

4. Refer for Medication Evaluation (4)

A. The client was referred for a physician evaluation for possible psychotropic medications.

B. The client was asked to commit to following through on all recommendations of the physician evaluation.

C. Communication was established with the physician pre- and postevaluation.

D. The client was prescribed psychotropic medication.

E. The client was assessed but not prescribed psychotropic medication.

5. Monitor Medication Compliance and Effectiveness (5)

A. The client was informed about major side effects of the medication and asked to report any that he/she experiences.

B. The client was monitored for compliance with the prescription, and the effectiveness was also noted.

C. The client was confronted when he/she reported not taking the medication consistently, and positive aspects of medication were reinforced with the client.

6. Normalize Phobias (6)

A. A discussion was held about how phobias are very common.

B. The client was shown that phobias are a natural but irrational expression of our fight or flight response.

C. It was emphasized to the client that phobias are not a sign of weakness but cause unnecessary distress and disability.

D. The client was reinforced as he/she displayed a better understanding of the natural facets of phobias.

E. The client struggled to understand the natural aspects of phobias and was provided with remedial feedback in this area.

7. Discuss Phobic Cycle (7)

A. The client was taught how phobic fears are maintained by a cycle of unwarranted fear and avoidance that precludes positive, corrective experiences with the feared object or situation.

B. The client was taught how treatment breaks the phobic cycle by encouraging positive, corrective experiences.

C. The client was taught information from *Mastery of Your Specific Phobia—Therapist Guide* (Craske, Antony, and Barlow) regarding the phobic cycle.

D. The client was taught about the phobic cycle from information in *Specific Phobias* (Bruce and Sanderson).

E. The client was reinforced as he/she displayed a better understanding of the phobic cycle of unwarranted fear and avoidance, and how treatment breaks the cycle.

F. The client displayed a poor understanding of the phobic cycle and was provided with remedial feedback in this area.

8. Assign Reading on Specific Phobias (8)

A. The client was assigned to read psychoeducational chapters of books or treatment manuals on specific phobias.

B. The client was assigned information from *Mastery of Your Specific Phobia—Client Manual* (Antony, Craske, and Barlow).

C. The client was directed to read information about specific phobias from *The Anxiety and Phobia Workbook* (Bourne).

D. The client has read the assigned information on phobias, and key points were reviewed.

E. The client has not read the assigned information on phobias and was redirected to do so.

9. Discuss Unrealistic Threats, Physical Fear, and Avoidance (9)

A. A discussion was held about how phobias involve perceiving unrealistic threats, bodily expressions of fear, and avoidance of what is threatening that interact to maintain the problem.

B. The client was taught about factors that interact to maintain the problem phobia from information in *Mastery of Your Specific Phobia—Therapist Guide* (Craske, Antony, and Barlow).

C. The client was taught about factors that interact to maintain the problem phobia from information in *Specific Phobias* (Bruce and Sanderson).

D. The client displayed a clear understanding of how unrealistic threats, bodily expression of fear, and avoidance combine to maintain the phobic problem; his/her insight was reinforced.

E. Despite specific information about factors that interact to maintain the problem, the client displayed a poor understanding of these issues; he/she was provided with remedial information in this area.

10. Discuss Benefits of Exposure (10)

A. A discussion was held about how exposure serves as an arena to desensitize learned fear, build confidence, and make one feel safer by building a new history of success experiences.

B. The client was taught about the benefits of exposure as described in *Mastery of Your Specific Phobia—Therapist Guide* (Craske, Antony, and Barlow).

C. The client was taught about the benefits of exposure as described in *Specific Phobias* (Bruce and Sanderson).

D. The client displayed a clear understanding of how exposure serves to desensitize learned fear, build confidence, and make one feel safer by building a new history of success experiences; his/her insight was reinforced.

E. Despite specific information about how exposure serves to desensitize learned fear, build confidence, and make one feel safer by building a new history of success experiences, the client displayed a poor understanding of these issues; he/she was provided with remedial information in this area.

11. Teach Anxiety Management Skills (11)

A. The client was taught anxiety management skills.

B. The client was taught about staying focused on behavioral goals and positive self-talk.

C. Techniques for muscular relaxation and paced diaphragmatic breathing were taught to the client.

D. The client was reinforced for his/her clear understanding and use of anxiety management skills.

E. The client has not used new anxiety management skills and was redirected to do so.

12. Assign Reading about Calming Strategies (12)

A. The client was assigned to read psychoeducational chapters of books or treatment manuals describing calming strategies.

B. The client was assigned portions of *Mastery of Your Specific Phobia—Client Manual* (Antony, Craske, and Barlow).

C. The client has read the assigned information on calming strategies, and his/her favorite strategies were reviewed.

D. The client has not read the assigned information on calming strategies, and he/she was redirected to do so.

13. Assign Calming Skills Exercises (13)

A. The client was assigned a homework exercise in which he/she practices daily calming skills.

B. The client's use of the exercises for practicing daily calming skills was closely monitored.

C. The client's success at using daily calming skills was reinforced.

D. The client was provided with corrective feedback for his/her failures at practicing daily calming skills.

14. Use EMG Biofeedback (14)

A. EMG biofeedback techniques were utilized to facilitate the client's relaxation skills.

B. The client achieved deeper levels of relaxation from the EMG biofeedback experience.

C. The client did not develop deep relaxation as a result of EMG biofeedback.

15. Teach Applied Tension Technique (15)

A. The client was taught the applied tension technique to help prevent fainting during encounters with phobic objects or situations.

B. The client was taught to tense his/her neck and upper torso muscles to curtail blood flow out of the brain to help prevent fainting during encounters with phobic objects or situations involving blood, injection, or injury.

C. The client was taught specific applied tension techniques as indicated in "Applied Tension, Exposure In Vivo, and Tension-Only in the Treatment of Blood Phobia" in *Behaviour Research and Therapy* (Ost, Fellenius, and Sterner).

D. The client was provided with positive feedback for his/her use of the applied tension technique.

E. The client has struggled to appropriately use the applied tension technique and was provided with remedial feedback in this area.

16. Assign Daily Applied Tension Practice (16)

A. The client was assigned a homework exercise in which he/she practices daily use of the applied tension skills.

B. The client's daily use of the applied tension technique was reviewed.

C. The client was reinforced for his/her success at using daily applied tension skills.

D. The client was provided with corrective feedback for his/her failure to appropriately use daily applied tension skills.

17. Identify Distorted Thoughts (17)

A. The client was assisted in identifying the distorted schemas and related automatic thoughts that mediate anxiety responses.

B. The client was taught the role of distorted thinking in precipitating emotional responses.

C. The client was reinforced as he/she verbalized an understanding of the cognitive beliefs and messages that mediate his/her anxiety responses.

D. The client was assisted in replacing distorted messages with positive, realistic cognitions.

E. The client failed to identify his/her distorted thoughts and cognitions and was provided with tentative examples in this area.

18. Assign Reading about Cognitive Restructuring (18)

A. The client was assigned to read about cognitive restructuring in books or treatment manuals on Panic Disorder and Agoraphobia.

B. The client was assigned to read *Mastery of Your Specific Phobia—Client Manual* (Antony, Craske, and Barlow).

C. The client was assigned to read excerpts from *The Anxiety and Phobia Workbook* (Bourne).

D. The client has read the assigned material on cognitive restructuring, and important concepts were reviewed within the session.

E. The client has not read the assigned material on cognitive restructuring and was redirected to do so.

19. Assign Homework on Self-Talk (19)

A. The client was assigned homework exercises to identify fearful self-talk, create reality-based alternatives, and record his/her experience.

B. The client was assigned "Bad Thoughts Lead to Depressed Feelings" from the *Adolescent Psychotherapy Homework Planner,* 2nd ed. (Jongsma, Peterson, and McInnis).

C. The client's use of self-talk techniques was reviewed and reinforced.

D. The client has struggled in his/her implementation of self-talk techniques and was provided with corrective feedback.

E. The client has not attempted to use the self-talk techniques and was redirected to do so.

20. Model/Rehearse Self-Talk (20)

A. Modeling and behavioral rehearsal were used to train the client in positive self-talk that reassured him/her of the ability to work through and endure anxiety symptoms without serious consequences.

B. The client has implemented positive self-talk to reassure himself/herself of the ability to endure anxiety without serious consequences; he/she was reinforced for this progress.

C. The client has not used positive self-talk to help endure anxiety and was provided with additional direction in this area.

21. Construct Anxiety Hierarchy (21)

A. The client was directed and assisted in constructing a hierarchy of anxiety-producing situations.

B. The client was successful in identifying a range of stimulus situations that produced increasingly greater amounts of anxiety, and this hierarchy was reviewed.

C. The client found it difficult to identify a range of stimulus situations that produce increasingly greater amounts of anxiety and was provided with assistance in this area.

22. Select Initial Exposures (22)

A. Initial exposures were selected from the hierarchy of anxiety-producing situations, with a bias toward likelihood of being successful.

B. A plan was developed with the client for managing the symptoms that may occur during the initial exposure.

C. The client was assisted in rehearsing the plan for managing the exposure-related symptoms within his/her imagination.

D. Positive feedback was provided for the client's helpful use of symptom management techniques.

E. The client was redirected for ways to improve his/her symptom management techniques.

23. Assign Reading about Situational Exposure (23)

A. The client was assigned to read about situational exposure.

B. The client was assigned to read excerpts from *Mastery of Your Specific Phobia—Client Manual* (Antony, Craske, and Barlow).

C. The client was assigned to read portions of *Living with Fear* (Marks).

D. The information that the client has read regarding situational exposures was reviewed and processed within the session.

E. The client has not read information about situational exposure and was redirected to do so.

24. Conduct Graduated Exposure (24)

A. The client was assisted in conducting exposures to his/her feared stimuli.

B. Modeling was used to help the client cope within the exposure situation.

C. The client was reinforced for his/her success in the exposure situation.

D. The client's level of exposure was gradually increased.

E. The client was congratulated on his/her ability to function within the exposure situation without any assistance.

25. Assign Homework on Situational Exposures (25)

A. The client was assigned homework exercises to perform situational exposures and record his/her experience.

B. The client was assigned "Gradually Facing a Phobic Fear" from the *Adolescent Psychotherapy Homework Planner,* 2nd ed. (Jongsma, Peterson, and McInnis).

C. The client was assigned situational exposure homework from *Mastery of Your Specific Phobia—Client Manual* (Antony, Craske, and Barlow).

D. The client was assigned situational exposure homework from *Living with Fear* (Marks).

E. The client's use of situational exposure techniques was reviewed and reinforced.

F. The client has struggled in his/her implementation of situational exposure techniques and was provided with corrective feedback.

G. The client has not attempted to use the situational exposure techniques and was redirected to do so.

26. Differentiate between Lapse and Relapse (26)

A. A discussion was held with the client regarding the distinction between a lapse and a relapse.

B. A lapse was associated with a temporary and reversible return of symptoms, fear, or urges to avoid.

C. A relapse was associated with the decision to return to fearful and avoidant patterns.

D. The client was provided with support and encouragement as he/she displayed an understanding of the difference between a lapse and a relapse.

E. The client struggled to understand the difference between a lapse and a relapse, and he/she was provided with remedial feedback in this area.

27. Discuss Management of Lapse Risk Situations (27)

A. The client was assisted in identifying future situations or circumstances in which lapses could occur.

B. The session focused on rehearsing the management of future situations or circumstances in which lapses could occur.

C. The client was reinforced for his/her appropriate use of lapse management skills.

D. The client was redirected in regard to his/her poor use of lapse management skills.

28. Encourage Routine Use of Strategies (28)

A. The client was instructed to routinely use the strategies that he/she has learned in therapy (e.g., cognitive restructuring, exposure).

B. The client was urged to find ways to build his/her new strategies into his/her life as much as possible.

C. The client was reinforced as he/she reported ways in which he/she has incorporated coping strategies into his/her life and routine.

29. Develop a "Coping Card" (29)

A. The client was provided with a coping card on which specific coping strategies were listed.

B. The client was assisted in developing his/her coping card in order to list his/her helpful coping strategies.

C. The client was encouraged to use his/her coping card when struggling with anxiety-producing situations.

30. Employ Stimulus Desensitization Interventions (30)

A. A session was conducted with the client in which he/she was surrounded with pleasant pictures, readings, and storytelling related to the phobic stimulus situation.

B. The client remained calm and relaxed while the phobic stimulus situation was depicted in pictures, informational material, and storytelling.

C. The client's ability to face the phobic fear was affirmed, and his/her ability to cope was reinforced.

D. The client had an extreme reaction to the pictures, reading, and storytelling related to the phobic situation and was provided with support for his/her use of coping techniques during this anxiety.

31. Interject Use of Humor (31)

A. Situational humor, jokes, riddles, and stories about the phobic stimulus were used to decrease the client's tension and seriousness regarding the fear.

B. The client was asked to start each day by telling the parents a joke, riddle, or silly story about the phobic stimulus.

C. A humorous side was pointed out for each issue/fear the client raised.

32. Enlist Family Support (32)

A. In family session, the parents were taught various ways to give support to the client when he/she experienced his/her phobic fear and were coached not to give support when the client panicked or failed to face fear.

B. The parents' implementation of the support intervention strategy was monitored, and they received support, encouragement, and, as necessary, redirection.

C. It was noted the client has been more successful in overcoming the phobic stimulus situation since the parents have reinforced the client's encounters.

D. The client's parents have not reinforced the client's successes in overcoming the phobic stimulus situation and were redirected to do so.

33. Identify Parental Reinforcement of Phobia (33)

A. The parents were assisted in identifying the ways in which they reinforce the client's phobia.

B. The family was assisted in identifying ways each member could reinforce the client's success in overcoming the phobia.

C. The parents were confronted when they were observed reinforcing the client's fear.

D. The parents denied any reinforcement of the phobia and were encouraged to monitor this dynamic.

34. Assess Family Members Modeling Fear (34)

A. Family members were assessed for their own phobic fear responses that teach the client to be afraid.

B. Family members were confronted on their own phobic fear responses that reinforce the client's phobic fear.

C. Family members were taught new ways of responding to their phobic stimulus situations that would not reinforce the phobic fear.

D. The family members who continue to experience phobic fear of their own were referred for individual counseling to treat this condition.

35. Explore Symbolic Meanings of Phobic Situation (35)

A. The possible symbolic meaning of the client's phobic stimulus was probed and discussed.

B. Selected interpretations of the phobic stimulus were offered to the client, and each was processed with him/her.

36. Clarify and Differentiate Present Fears from Past Pains (36)

A. The client was asked to list his/her present fears and also past emotionally painful experiences that may be related to the current fear.

B. The client was assisted in clarifying and separating his/her present irrational fears from past emotionally painful experiences.

C. It was noted that since the client was successful in separating past emotionally painful experiences from the present, he/she has reduced his/her level of phobic fear.

37. Encourage the Expression of Feelings (37)

A. The positive value of expressing feelings was emphasized with the client.

B. Using active-listening and unconditional positive regard techniques, the client was encouraged to express his/her feelings regarding the past painful experiences.

C. Gentle questioning was used with the client to help him/her start sharing feelings from the past.

D. Feelings that were shared regarding past painful experiences were affirmed and supported.

38. Link Past Pain with Present Anxiety (38)

A. The connection the client was making between his/her past emotional pain and present anxiety was pointed out.

B. When talking about his/her present fear the client was reminded of how he/she connected it to his/her past emotional pain.

C. It was noted that since the client was successful in separating past emotionally painful experiences from the present, he/she has reduced his/her level of phobic fear.

SUICIDAL IDEATION/ATTEMPT

CLIENT PRESENTATION

1. Recurrent Thoughts of or Preoccupation with Death (1)*

A. The parents reported that the client exhibits a strong preoccupation with the subject of death and talks about this topic frequently.

B. The client spoke about death at length in today's therapy session.

C. The client's music preferences, artwork, poetry, written notes, and/or letters have often reflected themes of death.

D. The client did not talk about death in today's therapy session.

E. The client denied experiencing any recent thoughts of death.

2. Suicidal Ideation without a Plan (2)

A. The client reported experiencing suicidal thoughts, but has not developed a specific plan to carry out those thoughts.

B. The client acknowledged expressing suicidal thoughts as a "cry for help" but denied having a specific plan to harm himself/herself.

C. The client denied experiencing any recent suicidal thoughts.

D. The client has taken positive steps to overcome his/her depression or manage stress and has not experienced any further suicidal thoughts.

3. Passive Death Wishes (2)

A. The parents reported that the client has expressed wishes that he/she were dead.

B. The client reported a passive wish to die but has not developed any specific suicidal thoughts or plans.

C. The client denied experiencing any recent passive death wishes.

D. The client has developed a renewed interest in life and has not experienced any further passive death wishes.

4. Suicidal Ideation with a Plan (3)

A. The client expressed suicidal thoughts in today's therapy session and admitted that he/she has developed a specific plan to take his/her life.

B. The client's suicide risk is high because of his/her recurrent suicidal thoughts, development of a specific plan, and the means to carry out the plan.

C. The client acknowledged that he/she has recently contemplated suicide briefly but has not experienced a desire or urge to follow through on a specific plan.

D. The client verbally denied experiencing any recent suicidal thoughts or having a plan to harm himself/herself.

*The numbers in parentheses correlate to the number of the Behavioral Definition statement in the companion chapter with the same title in *The Adolescent Psychotherapy Treatment Planner,* Fourth Edition (Jongsma, Peterson, McInnis, and Bruce) by John Wiley & Sons, 2006.

E. The client's suicide risk has decreased substantially since the onset of therapy, and he/she no longer experiences suicidal thoughts.

5. Recent Suicide Attempt (4)

A. The client and parents reported that the client has made a recent suicide attempt.

B. Received a phone call that the client has made a serious suicide attempt.

C. The client reported that he/she has recently made a slight or superficial suicidal gesture.

D. The client denied making any recent suicide attempts.

E. The client's suicide risk has decreased significantly since the onset of therapy, and he/she has not made any further suicide attempts.

6. History of Suicide Attempt (5)

A. The client's current suicidal risk needs to be closely monitored because he/she has made suicide attempts in the past.

B. The client reported making a serious suicide attempt in the past.

C. The client denied ever making any suicide attempts.

7. Family History of Depression (6)

A. The client and parents reported a strong history of depression in the family background.

B. The client and parents reported a history of suicide in the family background.

C. The client expressed strong feelings of sadness about the death of a family member who committed suicide.

D. The client has experienced recurrent suicidal thoughts and compared himself/herself to another family member who has committed suicide.

8. Depression (6)

A. The client reported a history of depression that has been present for several months.

B. The client reported a history of mood swings from elation to depression that occur within a day.

C. The client appeared visibly depressed during today's therapy session and expressed a desire to die.

D. The client reported feeling somewhat less depressed recently.

E. The client's depression has lifted, and he/she is showing renewed interest in life and the future.

9. Helplessness/Hopelessness (7)

A. The client is troubled by strong feelings of helplessness and hopelessness and questions whether life is worthwhile.

B. The client has developed a bleak, pessimistic outlook on life and doubts that his/her life will ever improve.

C. The client sees little hope that he/she will be able to overcome his/her current life stressors or problems.

D. The client's feelings of helplessness and hopelessness have decreased, and he/she is beginning to develop a new sense of hope for the future.

E. The client has experienced a renewed sense of hope and empowerment and no longer questions his/her ability to cope with life's stressors.

10. **Painful Life Events (8)**

A. The client has experienced suicidal thoughts since his/her parents separated or obtained a divorce.

B. The client has experienced suicidal thoughts since experiencing the death of a family member or close friend.

C. The client experienced suicidal thoughts after experiencing a traumatic event.

D. The client experienced suicidal thoughts after a recent failure experience.

E. The client experienced suicidal thoughts after feeling humiliated around his/her peers or family members.

11. **Rejection Experiences/Broken Relationships (8)**

A. The client reported feeling rejected by his/her family members.

B. The client reported experiencing suicidal thoughts after feeling rejected by his/her peers.

C. The client contemplated suicide after experiencing a broken relationship.

D. The client experienced suicidal thoughts after having a serious falling out with a close friend.

12. **Social Withdrawal (9)**

A. The emergence of the client's suicidal thoughts have coincided with his/her social withdrawal from others.

B. The client has become more withdrawn and questions whether other people truly care about him/her.

C. The client has begun to seek out support, affirmation, or acceptance from others.

D. The client has taken active steps to socialize with others.

13. **Lethargy and Apathy (9)**

A. The client appeared lethargic, listless, and apathetic during today's therapy session.

B. The client expressed apathy about his/her life and finds little joy or reward in living.

C. The client reported recently experiencing some pleasure or reward in his/her life.

D. The client reports regaining a sense of direction in life and feeling motivated to achieve personal goals.

14. **Potentially Dangerous Behavior (10)**

A. The client described a pattern of engaging in reckless or potentially dangerous behavior and showing little regard for his/her personal safety.

B. The client acknowledged that he/she has engaged in reckless or potentially dangerous behavior as a way to seek thrills and excitement and also escape from his/her emotional pain.

C. The client reported that he/she has recently engaged in reckless, potentially dangerous behavior.

D. The client denied engaging in any recent reckless, potentially dangerous behavior.

E. The client's behavior and moods have stabilized since the onset of therapy, and he/she has not engaged in any reckless or potentially dangerous behavior.

15. Dangerous Drug or Alcohol Abuse (10)

A. The client reported a history of engaging in dangerous drug or alcohol abuse as a way to escape from his/her emotional distress.

B. The client reported a history of engaging in dangerous drug or alcohol abuse that demonstrated little regard for his/her personal safety.

C. The client has continued to abuse drugs and alcohol as a maladaptive coping mechanism for emotional distress.

D. The client has not engaged in any recent drug or alcohol abuse.

E. The client has ceased his/her pattern of engaging in dangerous drug or alcohol abuse and has found more adaptive ways to deal with his/her emotional pain.

INTERVENTIONS IMPLEMENTED

1. Assess Suicidal Risk (1)*

A. The client's suicide risk was assessed by evaluating the extent and/or severity of his/her suicidal thoughts.

B. The client's suicide risk was assessed by exploring for the presence of primary and backup suicide plans.

C. The client's past was explored for any previous suicide attempts.

D. The client's family history was assessed for previous suicide attempts.

2. Monitor Suicide Potential (2)

A. The client's suicide potential has continued to be closely monitored in the therapy sessions.

B. Consultation was held with the client's parents and significant others to assess the client's suicide potential.

3. Notify Family/Significant Others (3)

A. The client's family and significant others were notified after the client expressed suicidal ideation.

B. The client's family and significant others were instructed to form a 24-hour suicide watch until the crisis subsides.

4. Arrange for Psychological Assessment (4)

A. The client was referred for a psychological evaluation to assess the severity of his/her depression and risk for suicide.

B. The results from the psychological assessment showed that the client is experiencing strong feelings of depression and is at high risk for suicide.

C. The results from the psychological testing indicated that the client is experiencing a moderate amount of depression and is at risk for suicide.

---

*The numbers in parentheses correlate to the number of the Therapeutic Intervention statement in the companion chapter with the same title in *The Adolescent Psychotherapy Treatment Planner,* Fourth Edition (Jongsma, Peterson, McInnis, and Bruce) by John Wiley & Sons, 2006

D. The results from the psychological testing indicated that the client is experiencing a mild amount of depression and is at low risk for suicide.

E. The results from the psychological testing did not reveal the presence of a depressive disorder, even though the client has expressed suicidal thoughts in the past.

F. The client has not completed the psychological assessment and was redirected to do so.

5. Refer for Antidepressant Medication (5)

A. The client was referred for a psychiatric evaluation to help determine whether an antidepressant would help to reduce his/her feelings of depression and risk for suicide.

B. The client and parents agreed to follow through with a psychiatric evaluation.

C. The client verbalized his/her strong opposition to being placed on medication to help reduce his/her feelings of depression.

6. Monitor Medication Effectiveness (6)

A. The client reported that the antidepressant medication has helped to decrease his/her feelings of depression.

B. The client reported little or no improvement in his/her moods since being placed on the antidepressant medication but was encouraged to continue.

C. The client was reinforced as he/she reported that he/she has consistently taken the antidepressant medication as prescribed.

D. The client has failed to consistently take the antidepressant medication as prescribed and was encouraged to do so.

7. Evaluate Need for Hospitalization (7)

A. The client was assessed for the need for inpatient hospitalization after expressing suicidal thoughts.

B. The client was admitted to an inpatient psychiatric unit because of his/her suicide risk.

C. The decision was made to place the client in a partial hospitalization program because of his/her suicide risk and depth of depression.

D. The evaluation did not reveal the need for inpatient hospitalization, but the client's suicide potential will continue to be closely monitored on an outpatient basis.

E. The client was involuntarily placed in an inpatient psychiatric unit after expressing suicidal thoughts and refusing to be evaluated for admission into a hospital setting.

8. Solicit Promise to Contact Therapist or Help Line (8)

A. The client was reinforced as he/she agreed to contact an emergency help line, parents, significant others, or therapist if he/she experiences a strong urge to harm himself/herself in the future.

B. The client refused to promise to contact an emergency help line, parents, significant others, or therapist if he/she experiences a strong urge to harm himself/herself in the future; therefore, arrangements were made to admit the client to an inpatient psychiatric unit.

C. The client's parents agreed to contact an emergency help line, significant others, or therapist if they perceive the client as being at risk for suicide in the future.

D. The client's parents were instructed to bring the client to the emergency room in the future if he/she makes a serious suicide threat or attempt.

9. Provide Emergency Help Line (9)

A. The client was given the telephone number of a 24-hour-a-day emergency help line in the event that he/she experiences a strong wish to die in the future.

B. The client refused to agree to contact an emergency help line in the future if he/she becomes suicidal; therefore, arrangements were made to admit the client to an inpatient psychiatric unit.

C. The client reported that he/she recently contacted an emergency help line after experiencing suicidal thoughts and found the consultation helpful in lifting his/her mood and ceasing his/her suicidal thoughts.

D. The client has not used the emergency help line after experiencing suicidal thoughts and was redirected to do so.

10. Establish Suicide Contract (10)

A. A suicide contract was formulated, with the client identifying what he/she will and won't do when experiencing suicidal thoughts or impulses in the future.

B. The client was supported as he/she signed a suicide contract agreeing to contact an emergency help line, family members, significant others, or therapist if he/she experiences strong suicidal thoughts or impulses in the future.

C. The client refused to sign a suicide contract; therefore, arrangements were made to admit the client to an inpatient psychiatric unit.

D. The client signed the "No-Self-Harm Contract" from the *Adolescent Psychotherapy Homework Planner,* 2nd ed. (Jongsma, Peterson, and McInnis) that stipulated his/her promise not to harm himself/herself.

E. By signing the "No-Self-Harm Contract," the client was refocused on the fact that there is a supportive network of individuals or agencies to whom he/she can turn when experiencing suicidal thoughts or urges.

F. The client was instructed to place the "No-Self-Harm Contract" in a private but easily accessible place where important telephone numbers could be quickly obtained if needed.

G. After experiencing suicidal thoughts between therapy sessions, the client complied with the terms of the "No-Self-Harm Contract" and contacted one of the individuals or agencies listed; his/her use of this resource was supported.

11. Inform about Telephone Availability of Therapist (11)

A. The client was informed of the therapist's availability through telephone contact if a life-threatening urge develops.

B. The client was encouraged to contact the emergency service or the answering service if he/she develops a life-threatening urge after normal work hours.

C. The client was supported for his/her contact with the therapist/emergency service when experiencing life-threatening urges.

D. The client has not accessed the therapist/emergency service when experiencing life-threatening urges and was redirected to do so.

12. Remove Lethal Weapons (12)

A. The parents were instructed to remove any firearms or other potentially lethal weapons from the client's easy access in the event that he/she experiences suicidal thoughts in the future.

B. The parents complied with the recommendation to remove firearms or other lethal weapons from the client's easy access.

C. The parents were confronted about their failure to remove firearms or other lethal weapons from the client's easy access.

13. Assess Parents' Understanding of Client's Distress (13)

A. A therapy session was held with the parents to assess their understanding of the causes for the client's emotional distress and suicidal thoughts.

B. The therapy session with the parents proved to be helpful in identifying the significant contributing factors or causes of the client's emotional distress or suicidal urges.

C. Active listening was used as the parents expressed confusion and uncertainty about the causes of the client's emotional distress and suicidal urges.

D. The client's perspective of the causes for his/her emotional distress was shared with the parents.

E. The parents were encouraged to provide support and empathy for the client's perspective of what is contributing to his/her emotional distress.

14. Explore Despair Related to Family Relationships (14)

A. Today's therapy session explored the client's feelings of despair related to his/her family relationships.

B. Today's therapy session revealed that the client is experiencing a significant amount of distress in regard to his/her family relationships.

C. The client denied that his/her emotional despair is related to his/her family relationships, and this was accepted.

D. The client agreed to meet with his/her family members in an upcoming therapy session to share his/her feelings of anger, hurt, and sadness about family relationships and was provided with assurance of support.

E. The client reported that he/she does not feel ready to meet with family members to share his/her feelings of anger, hurt, and sadness about family issues; he/she was encouraged to do this when he/she is ready.

15. Promote Communication in Family Therapy (15)

A. A family therapy session was held to promote the communication of the client's feelings of hurt, sadness, and anger.

B. The family members were reinforced as they demonstrated empathy, support, and understanding for the client's feelings of sadness, hurt, and anger.

C. Family members appeared to become defensive when the client began to share his/her feelings of sadness, hurt, and anger and were encouraged to provide support.

D. The client and parents were given the homework assignment to meet for 10 to 15 minutes each day to allow the client the opportunity to share his/her significant thoughts and feelings about any important issues.

16. Explore Sources of Emotional Pain (16)

A. Today's therapy session explored the sources of the client's emotional pain that underlie his/her suicidal ideation and feelings of hopelessness.

B. The exploration of the client's emotional pain revealed that he/she is experiencing a lot of unresolved feelings about a past traumatic incident.

C. The exploration of the client's emotional pain revealed that the client is experiencing a lot of unresolved feelings about a past broken relationship.

D. Today's therapy session explored periods of time when the client felt empowered in order to identify positive coping mechanisms that he/she used in the past to resolve conflict or deal with stress.

E. The client failed to connect his/her emotional pain and suicidal ideation and was provided with tentative examples in this area.

17. Identify Hopelessness and Helplessness (17)

A. The client's sadness and depression were interpreted as an expression of his/her feelings of hopelessness and helplessness.

B. The client's suicidal thoughts or wishes for death were interpreted as a cry for help.

C. The client's dangerous acts of rebellion were interpreted as reflecting underlying feelings of hopelessness and a cry for help.

D. The client was helped to identify more effective ways to meet his/her needs so that he/she will not remain depressed or suicidal.

E. The client was helped to identify more effective ways to meet his/her needs instead of acting out in a dangerous or rebellious manner.

18. Explore Causes for Suicidal Behavior (18)

A. The client was encouraged to express his/her feelings related to suicidal behavior to gain insight into the causes and motives for this behavior.

B. The client was noted to gain insight into the causes and motives for his/her suicidal actions after he/she identified the feelings he/she was experiencing before the suicidal behavior.

C. The client appeared guarded and was reluctant to share his/her feelings pertaining to the recent suicidal behavior and was encouraged to do so.

D. A client-centered therapy approach was utilized to help the client get in touch with his/her feelings related to the recent suicidal behavior.

E. A psychoanalytic therapy approach was utilized to explore the etiology of the client's suicidal behavior.

19. Assign "Renewed Hope" Exercise (19)

A. The client was taught about the benefit of sharing emotional pain instead of internalizing it and brooding over it.

B. The client was instructed to read the short story "Renewed Hope" from the *Adolescent Psychotherapy Homework Planner,* 2nd ed. (Jongsma, Peterson, and McInnis) to show him/her the benefit of sharing emotional pain instead of internalizing it.

C. The client shared that "Renewed Hope" helped him/her identify the causes and/or sources of his/her emotional pain and suicidal thoughts.

D. The client reported that he/she was able to share his/her painful emotions with significant others after reading "Renewed Hope."

E. The client reported that he/she read "Renewed Hope" but did not gain insight into the factors contributing to his/her emotional pain.

F. The client failed to read "Renewed Hope" and was again asked to read it.

20. Identify Positive Things in Life (20)

A. The client was helped to identify positive things in his/her present life situation to help reduce his/her feelings of depression and provide a sense of hope.

B. In today's therapy session, the client was first asked to identify his/her strengths and interests, then was encouraged to share these strengths or interests with his/her family members and peers in the upcoming week.

C. The client was instructed to record one positive self-descriptive statement in a journal each day.

D. The client was given the homework assignment to verbally share three positive things about his/her day with family members at dinner or before going to bed.

E. The client was encouraged to look for or verbally recognize the positives in other people to help him/her relate to others and gain acceptance.

F. The client did not identify positive aspects to his/her life and was provided with tentative examples in this area.

21. Reinforce Statements of Hope (21)

A. The client was reinforced for expressing statements that reflected hope and a desire to live.

B. The parents were encouraged to reinforce any positive statements by the client that reflect hope and an interest in living.

C. The client was helped to identify the positive steps that he/she took to overcome feelings of helplessness and cease having suicidal urges.

D. The client was encouraged to continue to engage in healthy or adaptive behavior that has provided him/her with a renewed sense of hope and contributed to resolution of suicidal urges.

E. The client identified the support from significant others as being helpful in providing him/her with a renewed sense of hope and eliminating suicidal urges; he/she was reinforced for this progress.

22. Assign "Symbols of Self-Worth" (22)

A. The client was asked to bring symbols of achievement and personal meaning to the session to reinforce their importance.

B. The client was given the "Symbols of Self-Worth" assignment from the *Adolescent Psychotherapy Homework Planner,* 2nd ed. (Jongsma, Peterson, and McInnis) to increase his/her feelings of self-worth and provide a renewed sense of hope.

C. The client completed the "Symbols of Self-Worth" assignment and brought in several objects reflecting past achievements and personal meaning.

D. The client brought in several objects symbolizing his/her strengths or interests and was encouraged to share these strengths or interests with peers in the upcoming week.

E. The client reported that after completing the "Symbols of Self-Worth" assignment, he/she regained an interest in and enthusiasm for previously enjoyed social or extracurricular activities.

F. The client failed to complete the "Symbols of Self-Worth" assignment but was again asked to read it and bring in his/her symbols of self-worth to the next therapy session.

23. Teach Coping Strategies (23)

A. The client was helped to identify various coping strategies that he/she can use to minimize the risk of him/her becoming suicidal in the future.

B. The client was strongly encouraged to express his/her thoughts and feelings directly to others instead of internalizing them and becoming suicidal.

C. The client was given the homework assignment to initiate three social contacts each day to help him/her become less internally focused.

D. The client was encouraged to engage in regular physical exercise or activity to help reduce stress and eliminate a pattern of brooding about life's problems.

24. Identify Negative Cognitive Messages (24)

A. Today's therapy session helped the client develop an awareness of how his/her negative self-talk reinforces feelings of hopelessness and helplessness.

B. The client was encouraged to replace his/her negative cognitive messages with more positive ways of thinking to overcome feelings of hopelessness and helplessness.

C. The client was given the homework assignment to verbalize three positive statements each day in the presence of others to overcome feelings of helplessness and hopelessness.

D. The client reported that the use of positive self-talk between therapy sessions helped to reduce his/her feelings of helplessness and hopelessness; he/she was urged to continue this technique.

E. The client failed to follow through with utilizing self-talk and, as a result, has continued to be troubled by feelings of helplessness and hopelessness; he/she was urged to use this technique.

25. Replace Catastrophizing, Fortune-Telling, and Mind Reading (25)

A. The therapy session identified how the client's tendency to overcatastrophize painful life events proves to be self-defeating, as it reinforces his/her feelings of hopelessness and helplessness.

B. The client was taught how to use realistic self-talk to learn more effective ways to cope with painful life events.

C. The client was taught effective communication and assertiveness skills to help him/her resolve conflict and communicate feelings more directly, instead of falling back on previous patterns of catastrophizing, fortune-telling, and mind reading.

D. The therapy session helped the client become aware of how catastrophizing, fortune-telling, and mind reading only reinforce his/her sense of hopelessness and helplessness.

E. The client has continued to catastrophize, fortune-tell, and mind read and was provided with more specific redirection in this area.

26. Utilize Past Successful Problem-Solving Approaches (26)

A. The client was first asked to review problem-solving approaches that were successful in the past, then encouraged to utilize these approaches to solve the problems in his/her current life situation.

B. The client was helped to realize how his/her reliance on previous problem-solving techniques no longer seems to be helpful, and he/she was encouraged to find new, alternative ways to solve current life problems.

C. The client was taught effective assertiveness skills to help him/her manage stress and overcome current life problems.

D. The client was encouraged to seek compromises as a way to resolve or end conflict with significant others.

E. The client was encouraged to brainstorm with a friend or consult with a mentor to identify ways to overcome current life problems.

27. Employ Penitence Ritual (27)

A. The client was given empathy and support in expressing his/her feelings of grief, guilt, and helplessness about surviving an incident fatal to others.

B. The client was helped to develop a penitence ritual to help overcome his/her feelings of guilt about the fatal incident.

C. Today's session focused on processing when, where, and how to implement the penitence ritual.

D. In today's follow-up therapy session, the client shared his/her thoughts and feelings about implementing the penitence ritual.

E. The client reported that the penitence ritual was helpful in decreasing his/her feelings of guilt about the fatal incident, and this was processed.

F. The client has not used a penitence ritual and was encouraged to do so.

28. Encourage Participation in Social Activities (28)

A. The client was strongly encouraged to reach out to friends and participate in enriching social or school activities.

B. The client was given the homework assignment to engage in at least one social activity per week with his/her peers.

C. The client reported that he/she has complied with the therapeutic recommendation to initiate at least one social contact per week and that this has helped to renew his/her interest and enthusiasm for life; the benefits of this compliance were reviewed.

D. Today's therapy session processed the client's experiences in various social activities and reinforced his/her socialization initiatives.

E. The client was instructed to perform acts of altruism or kindness with friends and peers to help improve his/her self-esteem and gain acceptance.

F. The client has not increased participation in social activities and was redirected to increase his/her use of this technique.

29. Role-Play Social Skills (29)

A. Behavior rehearsal, modeling, and role-play techniques were used to teach the client positive social skills and how to relate to peers more efficiently.

B. The client was supported, as he/she was able to identify several positive social skills after engaging in the behavior rehearsal and role-playing exercises.

C. After role-playing, the client expressed a willingness to practice the newly learned social skills in his/her everyday situations.

D. The client reported that the newly learned social skills have helped him/her relate to peers and gain acceptance; the benefits of these skills were emphasized.

E. The client reported that he/she did not follow through with practicing many of the social skills that were modeled in the previous therapy sessions and was redirected to do so.

30. Encourage Broadening Social Network (30)

A. The client was encouraged to broaden his/her social network by initiating one new social contact per week instead of excessively clinging to one or two friends.

B. The client complied with the directive to initiate one social contact per week and reported that it has helped to increase his/her confidence in conversing with others.

C. Role-playing techniques were utilized to model effective ways to initiate conversations with social contacts.

D. The client was given the homework assignment to initiate three phone calls per week to different individuals.

E. The client failed to follow through with the directive to initiate one social contact per week because of his/her feelings of insecurity and inadequacy and was redirected to do this task.

31. Monitor Appetite and Sleep Patterns (31)

A. The client was encouraged to return to his/her normal patterns of eating and sleeping to help reduce his/her depression.

B. The client was instructed to monitor his/her patterns of eating and sleeping between therapy sessions.

C. The client reported that the monitoring of his/her food intake helped him/her realize the need to return to normal eating patterns; he/she was reinforced for this insight.

D. The client was referred for a medication evaluation to determine whether medication would help reduce feelings of depression and help induce sleep.

E. The client was taught relaxation techniques to use at night to help induce calm and readiness for sleep.

Printed in the United States of America
ED-12-17-10